Our Halcyon Dayes

Our Halcyon Dayes

*English
Prerevolutionary Texts
and Postmodern
Culture*

Lawrence Venuti

The University of Wisconsin Press

The University of Wisconsin Press
114 North Murray Street
Madison, Wisconsin 53715

The University of Wisconsin Press, Ltd.
1 Gower Street
London WC1E 6HA, England

Printed in the United States of America

Cover illustrations. *Left:* Inigo Jones, "Sketch for the King's Costume." The Trustees of the Chatsworth Settlement. In *The King's Arcadia: Inigo Jones and the Stuart Court,* compiled by John Harris, Stephen Orgel, and Roy Strong (London: Arts Council of Great Britain, 1973). *Right:* Robert Longo, "Untitled (Men in the Cities)," 1981–88. 96″ × 60″. Courtesy of Metro Pictures. Photo by Kevin Noble.

Library of Congress Cataloging-in-Publication Data
Venuti, Lawrence.
Our halcyon dayes:English prerevolutionary texts and postmodern
culture/Lawrence Venuti.
332 pp.   cm.
Includes bibliography and index.
1. English literature—Early modern, 1500–1700—History and
criticism—Theory, etc. 2. Literature and society—Great Britain—
History—17th century. 3. Great Britain—History—Charles I,
1625–1649—Historiography. 4. Postmodernism (Literature)
5. Marxist criticism.   I. Title.
PR438.S63V46   1989
820'.9'003—dc19   88-34625
ISBN 0-299-12250-6
ISBN 0-299-12254-9 (pbk.)

For Lindsay

But for the time being we are free
And meanwhile the songs
Protect us, in a way, and the special climate.

Men make their own history, but they do not make it just as they please; they do not make it under circumstances chosen by themselves, but under circumstances directly found, given and transmitted from the past. The tradition of all the dead generations weighs like a nightmare on the brain of the living. And just when they seem engaged in revolutionising themselves and things, in creating something entirely new, precisely in such epochs of revolutionary crisis they anxiously conjure up the spirits of the past to their service and borrow from them names, battle slogans and costumes in order to present the new scene of world history in this time-honoured disguise and this borrowed language. Thus Luther donned the mask of the Apostle Paul, the Revolution of 1789 to 1814 draped itself alternately as the Roman Republic and the Roman Empire, and the Revolution of 1848 knew nothing better to do than to parody, in turn, 1789 and the revolutionary tradition of 1793 to 1795. In like manner the beginner who has learnt a new language always translates it back into his mother tongue, but he has assimilated the spirit of the new language and can produce freely in it only when he moves in it without remembering the old and forgets in it his ancestral tongue.

Karl Marx, *The Eighteenth Brumaire of Louis Bonaparte*

Contents

Our Halcyon Dayes

Introduction

The Symptomatic Reading

> Tourneyes, Masques, Theatres, better become
> Our *Halcyon* dayes; what though the German Drum
> Bellow for freedome and revenge, the noyse
> Concernes not us, nor should divert our joyes.
>
> > Thomas Carew, "In answer of an Elegiacall Letter,
> > upon the death of the King of Sweden, from
> > Aurelian Townshend, Inviting me to write
> > on that subject"

O UR HALCYON DAYES is a Marxist intervention into English Renaissance studies which takes as its primary object texts produced during the reign of Charles I (1625–49). Drawing on recent developments in Marxist social and literary theory initiated by the French philosopher Louis Althusser and elaborated for literary criticism by British and American critics from Fredric Jameson and Terry Eagleton to Catherine Belsey and Jonathan Dollimore, this study seeks to elucidate the ideology of two bodies of writing: selected literary forms during the Caroline period and the critical discourses which have processed those forms from the seventeenth century to the present. This is an ideological critique which historicizes both literary and critical texts, demonstrating how they reflect and intervene into specific social conjunctures—Caroline literature into the conflicts that erupted in the bourgeois revolution against the royal government, romantic and modern criticism into the conflicts that accompanied the development of capitalism. The Marxist discourse which processes this writing is itself situated in a specific social conjuncture, the contemporary phase of consumer capitalism which has increasingly been seen as the ground of a distinctively postmodern culture. Accordingly, this study includes an autocritique which examines its relationship to its own social conditions. The overriding assumption in all of what follows is that cultural practices are both the ideological resolution of real social problems and the expression of utopian aspirations for social life.[1]

The methodological instrument deployed to perform the ideological critique is Althusser's notion of symptomatic reading (*lecture symptomale*).[2] This reading assumes that textual production is a social practice, although not immediately reducible to such other social practices as economic exchange and political action, that it has its own cultural materials (tropes, genres, conventions, themes) and its own modes of transforming them. These materials come to the text always already social in their significance and functioning, always shared by specific social groups, always allied to social representations, values, and beliefs which serve the competing interests of those groups, always acting, in other words, as an *ideological* resolution of contradictory social conditions, the relations of domination and exploitation in any social formation. This ideological function becomes apparent through discontinuities which exist among the varied cultural materials assimilated by the text and which the text introduces into those materials as it assimilates them. The text is always discontinuous because the textual work is a differential process of signification which foregrounds the differences among its constitutive materials even as it tries to organize and absorb them, and which thereby exhibits its contradictory social conditions even as it provides an ideological resolution for them. Formal discontinuities reveal the relationship between the text and the conflicting ideologies of its social conjuncture. The discontinuities may take such forms as narrative inconsistencies and improbabilities, transformations of genres and conventions, logical contradictions. They may be described generally as presenting an interpretive crux that hinders the articulation of a coherent meaning in the text. Their elucidation requires a close textual analysis in which they are read symptomatically, as the sign of the text's ideological operation on conflicting social forces, of its imperfect attempt to resolve a political struggle in imaginary terms. The symptomatic reading is thus designed to respect the linguistic and literary specificity of the text, the discontinuous textual work, while inserting it into the social formation where it is produced and circulated by exposing its ideological determinations.

The symptomatic reading rests on a materialist social theory in which human subjectivity is seen as socially determinate. As Marx puts it in *A Contribution to the Critique of Political Economy*, "It is not the consciousness of men that determines their being, but, on the contrary, their social being that determines their consciousness."[3] Althusser has enabled a more rigorous development of the determinate subject by theorizing the social formation as a set of productive practices—economic, political, ideological—which are determined by and determine one another in complicated, uneven ways, and which undergo a relatively autonomous development, each with its own internal coherence, its own constitutive materials, its own operations to transform them. Social formations persist because these practices construct subjectivity: they act as the "definers and distributors" of "places and functions" for social agents, the "agents of production," who are "the occupants of these places, insofar as they are the 'supports' (*Träger*) of these functions."[4] Institutions like the family, school, and church assist in social reproduction because they operate as "ideological state apparatuses," consensual rather than coercive or "repressive" means to reproduce social relations. These institutions house ideological practices which constitute agents as subjects in metaphysical or social hierarchies and thereby represent hierarchical social relations as natural or right.[5] In this process of ideological subjection which Althusser calls "interpellation," agents recognize their place and function in the relations of production and simultaneously misrecognize the hierarchical nature of these relations. Ideology is both a cognitive and a material determination of subjectivity, both "the imaginary relationship of individuals to their real conditions of existence" and a relationship which is lived, "inserted into material practices governed by material rituals which are themselves defined by the material ideological apparatus."[6]

As later theorists have shown, several of Althusser's formulations need to be revised and developed further if they are to prove useful in a materialist cultural history with a political project of social transformation. These revisions must begin with Althusser's dichotomy between scientific knowledge and ideological misrecognition. He uses these epistemological categories to distinguish between Marxist and non-Marxist social theory, ultimately reducing them to the opposition between "truth" and "falsehood." The result, however, is to privilege Marxist "science" with an unmediated access to reality which transcends social determinations and removes scientific knowledge from historical change. In Tony Bennett's words, "Rather than conceiving of particular ideologies, particular works of literature and particular sciences which, according to their nature and the uses to which they are put, may be either progressive or regressive in their political implications, each being mapped out as an arena of class struggle, Althusser's position implied that class struggle takes place between the eternal verities of science, the eternal falsehoods of ideology, and the eternal equivocations of literature."[7]

Yet Althusser does in fact lay the groundwork for a materialist epistemology in his attack on empiricism. Here he argues that knowledge is not an immediate apprehension of reality, but a complicated productive process in which existing conceptual materials are transformed according to a problematic, the systematic assumptions and procedures that govern intellectual labor in a particular discipline. This means that an unbridgeable gap exists between the "real object" and the "object of knowledge" which is constructed to represent it. Reality is never available except in the form of an intellectual construct, and since the production of knowledge is a social practice, this construct can be seen as an ideological representation, i.e., determined by, and intervening into, the contradictions of its social conjuncture. The ideological determinations of intellectual labor can be located in its conceptual materials, its problematic, and its social effects. With the view that knowledge is always ideological, the status of the "imaginary" in Althusser's theory of ideology can be redefined: this term does not mean that ideology is a mere fictional representation of its social conditions, but that different ideologies can represent the same conditions differently to serve competing interests. Instances of ideological misrecognition, then, become apparent only from an another, opposing ideological standpoint. It is the project of the Marxist ideology animating the present study to expose hierarchical social relations in opposition to ideologies which may so represent those relations as to question their existence (bourgeois individualism, liberal democracy) or find them natural (patriarchy, racism).

Althusser's theory of the ideological constitution of subjectivity must also be revised: it stresses the dominant ideology, views ideological practices only as *state* apparatuses, and the result is that he excludes social conflict and the possibility of change. As Ted Benton observes, "That agents are distributed to different places in the division of labor (in order for the relations of production to be reproduced) leaves no theoretical room for a discourse and practice of ideology which *resists and opposes* this very process of ideological social reproduction."[8] The range of social practices in any social formation is in fact heterogeneous: each agent is distributed to various places and functions, and social identity is constructed in different and often incompatible interpellations. Social relations, moreover, are conflictual, relations of domination and subordination, and they exist not only between classes, as Althusser stresses, but also between races and sexes. Hence, subjectivity is structured in contradiction, fissured by competing ideologies and social conflicts which are constantly constructing it, but which may also transform it. Althusser's theory of ideology cannot think social transformation because its concept of subjectivity tends to be deterministic rather than determinate, with human action seen as fated rather than contingent on contradictory material determinations. Anthony Giddens' critique offers a materialist theory of human agency which avoids this determinism: he allows for the reflexive monitoring of behavior in the form of the agent's rationalizations for his actions, that self-conscious discourse in which intentions are stated and motives revealed.[9] The agent's self-monitoring does not mean that subjectivity is free of transindividual determinations. Rationalizations for behavior draw on social rules and other ideological cultural materials which reveal the social horizon of the agent's intentions and motives. And, most important, human action always has unacknowledged conditions, like unconscious, ideologically determined motives or social conflicts, as well as unanticipated consequences, like social reproduction or change. The value of Giddens' theory is that it creates the possibility for these conditions and consequences to become conscious and be included in the agent's rationalizations. It is thus more useful in imagining political agency in different social conditions, at different historical moments.

The symptomatic reading construes the agents of textual production and reception as socially determined. Authorial consciousness is the site of contradictory linguistic, psychological, and social determinations that emerge in the text as discontinuities in the cultural materials it puts to work. During the reading process, these discontinuities enlist the reader's consciousness in the determinate contradictions that produced the text, inviting a demystification of the ideologies to which its constitutive materials are allied. Textual production is a self-monitored action for the most part: a writer chooses tropes, genres, conventions, and other formal elements to express intended meanings, and he may rationalize his writing as an expression of his intention. Yet these elements have conditions and consequences which are social and may exceed his self-understanding. The symptomatic reading, therefore, treats textual production not merely as the communication of an authorial message, but also as an ideological cultural practice, in which the text intervenes into its social situation, and textual form is seen as doing the work of ideology.

As Belsey has shown, the concept of determinate subjectivity can effectively mediate between the specific materiality of the text and the ideological determinations of its social situation.[10] The textual work of signification constructs positions of subjectivity for the reader through a variety of formal means, ranging from pronouns and verb tenses to characterization, narrative point of view, dramatic structure, generic expectation. These subject-positions are arranged in a hierarchy of intelligibility, so that the reader gravitates toward the position which offers the greatest coherence of meaning, the most stable knowledge and value, the strongest effect of "truth" or "obviousness"—merely to make sense of the text. This "truth" effect, however, is an illusionism, in which the text seems a transparent window onto reality, and its materiality, the ideology-laden formal means by which it represents the real, all but vanishes to the reader. Here we can see the ideological function of form: the textual positioning of the reader enacts the process of interpellation because the position of intelligibility is also a position in a specific ideology. If this ideology is that of the dominant class or group, the positioning makes hierarchical social relations seem "obvious" and "true," and the reader is subjected to them, i.e., constituted as a subject who aids in social reproduction. Thus, every discursive identity is simultaneously social. The ideological positioning in the text is an imaginary resolution of social contradictions in which the reader recognizes a specific ideological configuration (representations, values, beliefs) as what is true or real, what is good, what is possible.[11] Here another aspect of the imaginary status of ideology comes into focus. Because the ideological resolution includes thinking about social possibility, it can be said to have a *utopian* dimension: in any interpellation "our sense of the mutability of our being-in-the-world and the consequences of change are hereby patterned," writes Göran Therborn, "and our hopes, ambitions, and fears given shape" (p. 18). The text overcomes present problems by casting an image of the perfect society which affirms the collective unity or solidarity of a historically specific social class or group.

The discursive process of ideological interpellation shows that the concept of subjectivity assumed in the symptomatic reading is determinate, not deterministic, contingent on the discontinuous textual work, not the necessary effect of a transcendental principle. The reader is never completely sutured into any one ideological position. Not only the text but reading too is historically specific, and a reading in a later and different ideological configuration may resist or oppose the positioning of an earlier text. Yet even for contemporary readers the subject-positions constructed by the text can never be entirely coherent: the cultural materials which constitute it are varied, and signification is a differential process. Any discourse seeks to fix meaning, but since meaning is relational, constituted by differences along the signifying chain, it is threatened by its very conditions of possibility, vulnerable to polysemy, metaphor, paradox, intertextuality, other forms of semiosis, and it can be fixed only partially, during predication in specific contexts.[12] Because discourse is thus a regularity in dispersion, an ensemble of differential positions, social identity can never be irrevocably fixed: it is the site of different and not always consistent ideological interpellations. These features of discourse make the imposition of obviousness in any text a fragile mechanism which can break down, inviting the reader to expose and interrogate the ideological status of the obvious.

The notion of symptomatic reading conceives of textuality as always potentially demystifying. The text is seen as a skeptical machine which turns the intelligible into the propagandistic, the partial fixation of meaning into the legitimation of social domination, and the reader into a subject-in-process dispersed over the conflicting ideological codes that colonize desire, questioning them, exploring the social contradictions they resolve, dreaming new possibilities for social life. The symptomatic reading is itself an ideological cultural practice, engaged in the production of subjects and the articulation/disarticulation of ideological discourses, and like the texts on which it works, it seeks to resolve real social problems and stimulate utopian thinking. "For hermeneutics," Jameson argues,

> traditionally a technique whereby religions recuperated the texts and spiritual activities of cultures resistant to them, is also a political discipline, and provides the means for maintaining contact with the very sources of revolutionary energy during a stagnant time, of preserving the concept of freedom itself, underground, during geological ages of repression. Indeed, it is the concept of freedom which, measured against those other possible ones of love or justice, happiness or work, proves to be the privileged instrument of a political hermeneutic, and which, in turn, is perhaps itself best understood as an interpretive device rather than a philosophical essence or idea. For wherever the concept of freedom is once more understood, it always comes as the awak-

ening of dissatisfaction in the midst of all that is—at one, in that, with
the birth of the negative itself: never a state that is enjoyed, or a mental
structure that is contemplated, but rather an ontological impatience in
which the constraining situation itself is for the first time perceived in
the very moment in which it is refused.[13]

The utopian desire released by the symptomatic reading is the desire
for freedom from present problems, but it is expressed through the
historical narratives which this reading constructs in its ideological critique of texts, in its exposure of how they mystify their contradictory
social conditions. The ideological resolution performed by the symptomatic reading markedly differs from that of the texts on which it
works by making explicit the social conditions which compel it to preserve a concept of freedom. The symptomatic reading is a political instrument in Marxism's opposition to capitalist social practices, a mobilization of the text against dominant forms of critical reception which
serve as theoretical supports for social reproduction, a strategic reading
which speaks to the social conflicts in the capitalist formation where it
occurs so as to spur revolutionary social change.

Caroline literary texts and their reception especially recommend
themselves for this sort of Marxist cultural intervention. Not only are
these texts implicated in a prerevolutionary conjuncture that witnesses
the triumph of bourgeois social practices, but the dominant reading of
that literature has been informed by bourgeois critical discourse. The
first chapter examines the discourses of two major critics of Caroline
texts: Samuel Taylor Coleridge and T. S. Eliot. The logical tensions and
contradiction in the criticism of these writers show how the theoretical
assumptions of their discourses valorize a concept of the human subject which is determined by the ideology of bourgeois individualism.
The concept of the subject as a free, unified consciousness that transcends the contradictory determinations of history leads both Coleridge and Eliot to privilege authorial intentionality, organic unity, and
illusionistic response, even though differences in the ways each critic
sets to work this concept permit distinctions between a "romantic" and
a "modern" critical discourse. The periodization which these differences establish, however, is here construed not in terms of literary and
intellectual history, but in social terms. With the aid of social commentary in texts like Wordsworth's preface to *Lyrical Ballads*, Coleridge's
Shakespeare lectures, and Eliot's "London Letters" for *The Dial*, the
valorization of the transcendental subject in romantic and modern crit-

icism can be taken as an ideological response, a reactionary solution to the crises of the subject precipitated by the development of capitalism in its market and monopoly phases.

The critique which exposes the ideological determinations of romantic and modern discourse, moreover, is itself determined by Marxist ideology and thus bases its theoretical assumptions on a different concept of the subject, human consciousness as the determinate, contradictory site of social conflicts. And not only does the determinate subject give rise to the symptomatic reading, to the understanding of discontinuities in the text as ideological contradictions which signify beyond authorial intention, but it too responds to a contemporary crisis of the subject, the decentering and fragmentation of consciousness precipitated by consumer capitalism in post–World War II culture. What has been called the postmodern subject suffers a breakdown in the temporal organization of its experience and therefore is also characterized by an inability to construct historical narratives which reflect on present social conditions.[14] By assuming the concept of the historically determinate subject, the symptomatic reading refuses the reactionary solution to this crisis of historicity which would be involved in any valorization of individualism and thus constitutes a revolutionary strategy: the determinate subject enables this reading to expose the ideological resolution and utopian thinking of the texts it examines by developing historical narratives which encourage readers to think the contradictions of their own social situation and imagine new social possibilities.

This is not to say that the transcendental subject is a discursive element which is inevitably reactionary in its ideological functioning. Ideologies do not have any necessary class or group belongingness. The social significance of an ideological discourse rather depends on the specific elements it articulates, its specific form of articulating them, and the specific social conjuncture in which the discourse is deployed. In contemporary Latin America, for example, liberation theology has managed to produce a revolutionary discourse grounded in a concept of transcendental subjectivity by combining Christian metaphysics with historical materialism. In the words of the Brazilian theologian Clodovis Boff, "The theology of liberation seeks to demonstrate that the kingdom of God is to be established not only in the *soul*—this is the individual personal dimension of the kingdom—and not only in heaven—this is its transhistorical dimension—but in relationships among human beings, as well. In other words, the kingdom of God is to be established in social projects, and this is its historical dimension."[15] Although we agree, with Ernesto Laclau, that freeing ideologies from class reductionism "opens the possibility of integrating into a revolutionary and socialist ideological discourse, a multitude of elements and interpellations which have up to now appeared constitutive of bourgeois ideological discourse,"[16] the present study will argue that individualism carries with it theoretical constraints which hamstring any progressive cultural intervention into consumer capitalism. Most notable among these constraints is an inability to think historical difference at a time when historicity is in crisis: in individualistic critical discourses, the transcendental subject leads to a processing of the cultural object as authorial self-expression, product of the authorial or human imagination, container of abstract moral themes concerning the timeless, universal essence of human nature, ultimately removing culture from its specific historical moment and repressing any thinking about historical change.

The second chapter takes up this point in a discussion of the reception of Caroline texts since the nineteenth century, specifically the criticism of leading Caroline playwright Philip Massinger. Here the aim is to show that Massinger has been assigned a marginal position in the canon of English Renaissance drama by such critics as Coleridge, Leslie Stephen, and Eliot because the formal discontinuities in his plays resist the critical operations of an individualistic discourse. Massinger's plays can be seen as the casualty not only of the dominance in criticism of the transcendental subject, but also of the crises of the subject under capitalism which led to that dominance. Once this is established, the chapter goes on to offer a symptomatic reading of Massinger's tragicomedy *The Maid of Honour* based on the determinate subject: discontinuities in characterization, in the tragicomic genre, and in topical allusions are used to argue that the play is an interrogative text which demystifies the competing ideologies of the monarchy and the aristocracy in response to the widening gap between these two social factions during the reigns of the early Stuart kings. This reading seeks to mobilize Massinger's play in opposition to the individualistic discourse which has marginalized it, turning the text into an arena of conflict where what is in question is not just the dominance of that discourse and the readings it enables, but also its ideological determinations.

The remaining chapters offer symptomatic readings of three groups of Caroline texts: drama played in the public and elite theaters, masques produced at court, and lyric poetry written by courtiers.

These readings situate the texts in the prerevolutionary conjuncture of Caroline England. Ideological determinations are exposed through an analysis of discontinuities in characterization, narrative, genre, and topical allusions, among other cultural materials. And these determinations are given historical specificity with detailed reconstructions of social conflicts which rely on post–World War II historians of various ideological standpoints—Whig, Marxist, revisionist—but which aim to project narratives that stress opposition between competing classes and groups in order to represent the conditions of revolutionary social change.[17] These chapters on city comedy, the court masque, and Cavalier love poetry also include symptomatic readings of other critical discourses which have processed the texts, engaging with the *Scrutiny* group, humanist historicism, and the new historicism, interrogating their theoretical assumptions, and challenging their readings as conservative responses to the contemporary crisis of subjectivity.

The title of this study is taken from an often cited poem by the Cavalier poet Thomas Carew (see the epigraph to this introduction), where he argues against English involvement in the Thirty Years War, asserting that Englishmen should rather "use the benefit / Of peace and plenty" in Caroline England by devoting themselves to more pleasurable activities, like "Tourneyes, Masques, Theatres." The symptomatic readings set forth here are designed to expose this notion of the "*Halcyon* dayes" under Charles I as a mystification, both of the social conflicts exacerbated by royal policy and of the ideological functions of the texts. The traditional view of Caroline texts presents them as the escapist and self-congratulatory entertainments of a court aristocracy which eschew any involvement in the social conflicts that would erupt in the civil war.[18] Yet Carew's poem itself reveals that texts cannot be separated from their social context, that in Caroline England they in fact constitute a political intervention by (re)producing ideologies that may either support or oppose the royal government. After an elaborate description of Aurelian Townshend's masque *Tempe Restor'd,* in which Henrietta Maria played the role of "the Queene of Beautie," Carew's poem suggests that such entertainments mystify royal power by dazzling the submissive spectators with "her rare perfections" and thus distracting them from her "high state": "our soules fell at her feet, / And did with humble reverend dutie, more / Her rare perfections, then high state adore." In this way, Carew's poem interrogates its own reference to the "*Halcyon* dayes" under Charles, turning the phrase into an appropriate title for this collection of symptomatic readings because it can stand both for a utopian mystification which legitimizes the absolutist state and for an ideological critique which treats it with demystifying irony.[19] But since we will also be concerned with the reception of Caroline texts, the phrase can be taken in yet another way, as an allusion to the dominance of individualistic critical discourses since the nineteenth century, utopian mystifications which eclipse the social conditions of the text and of their own critical operations on it by situating the first in a timeless, universal realm of Literature and by assuming that the second are performed by transcendental subjects seemingly unaffected by the crises of subjectivity in the capitalist social formations where those operations are performed. It is these "our *Halcyon* dayes" in criticism which this study seeks to challenge through symptomatic readings of critical as well as literary texts.

Chapter One

The Ideology of the Individual in Anglo-American Criticism

The breakdown of individuality today not only helps us to understand its category as a historical feature but also evokes doubt about its positive nature.

Max Horkheimer and Theodor Adorno, *Dialectic of Enlightenment*

I N T H E W A K E of the poststructuralist attack on interpretation by such theorists as Jacques Derrida and Gilles Deleuze, the function of criticism has been increasingly questioned, so that whatever its claims to contribute to the understanding of texts, it no longer enjoys its formerly privileged status. Far from being objective and innocent, criticism can now be seen as a transformative activity mediated by theoretical assumptions that make possible, but also limit, its thinking about the author, the text, and the relations of both to the world. Instead of mirroring a pregiven literary essence embedded in a text by an author and forever available to subsequent readers, criticism metamorphoses the text into an object of knowledge defined and processed from a distinctive, even if unstated, theoretical standpoint. In this sense, the critic's operations do not unobtrusively describe the text, but rather actively *produce* it in a determinate form for dissemination and consumption.

Marxism, although forced by this theoretical development to undertake a rigorous self-examination and redefinition, is required by the premises of dialectical materialism to go a step further and historicize the transformative activity of criticism by arguing that it does not transcend the contingencies of time and place.[1] Like the texts on which it works, criticism is determined by the specific conjuncture of social forces that are contemporary to it, and the assumptions that shape its discourse have connections to current ideologies, to ensembles of social

representations, values, and beliefs that exist at various levels of articulation and consciousness and reflect the competing interests of different social groups. This is not to say that criticism is immediately reducible to the instrument or organ of a given class or class fraction: its
materials and operations have their own specificity and undergo a relatively autonomous development which, taken at face value, seems free
of social determinations. The point is rather to see criticism as a social
practice, active in the (re)production of ideology, functioning in academic and other cultural institutions which constitute centers of power
in any social formation, and therefore resulting in a broad range of
concrete effects. These may include not only the rate of book sales, but
the formation of a canon of authors and texts, not only the authority
of certain interpretations and theoretical assumptions, but the reproduction of dominant ideologies and thereby the maintenance of the
existing relations between classes.

Studying a body of criticism from this point of view will involve
several, quite different tasks. There is first the work of critical analysis:
it will be necessary to reconsider readings and judgments that have
gained acceptance as authoritative at any historical moment and to examine the theoretical assumptions that gave rise to them. Canon formation presents a particularly convenient entry into this analysis because the valuation of specific authors and texts as canonical or
apocryphal gives us a glimpse of a critical discourse in operation; as
Frank Kermode has observed, "The decision as to canonicity depends
upon a consensus that a book has the requisite qualities, the determination of which is, in part, a work of interpretation."[2] Such a critical
consensus is historically specific: it varies from period to period, subject to changes, for example, in the authority of different theoretical
assumptions and in the cultural institutions that support critical practice. Having exposed the theory underlying a specific decision as to
canonicity, therefore, we will go on to perform a work of historical
inscription, tracing a network of affiliations between that theory and
the social formation in which it operates. The goal of these tasks is
both to recognize the specificity and autonomy of a critical discourse
and to think of it as an activity that is socially determined and determining. At the same time, moreover, given the dialectical conception of
criticism assumed in the very posing of this goal, it will be necessary
to initiate an autocritique: admitting that the transformative capacity of
our own critical discourse produces a delimited object-for-criticism, we
are obligated to reflect on the assumptions and social determinations
that seem to have influenced that discourse.

For Marxist criticism, it is imperative that the critical writings of Samuel Taylor Coleridge and T. S. Eliot be made the object of this sort of investigation. Coleridge and Eliot can easily be considered the most crucial figures in the ascendancy of romantic critical theory and its subsequent assimilation into modern critical discourse; and not only have they decisively conditioned the interpretation and evaluation of many authors and texts, including those from the sixteenth and seventeenth centuries, but their influence has coincided with the triumph of capitalism. To mediate between these two historical developments, one literary, the other socio-economic, it seems possible to concentrate on a key theoretical assumption and its ramifications in the work of both critics: this is what I shall call the Individual, the concept of the human subject as a free, unified consciousness that transcends the epistemological limitations of biography and history and is the origin of meaning, knowledge, and action. By the term "individual," I do not mean concrete individuals, the agents who live and sustain social relations. Rather, the term designates a specific way of conceiving the subjectivity of those social agents, and especially their acts of cognition. It has long been noted that the concept of the transcendental subject is a legacy of Enlightenment philosophy which has extensively determined Anglo-American critical thinking since the beginning of the nineteenth century.[3] The line of inquiry to be taken here, however, will seek to explain the dominance in criticism of this concept by regarding it as an ideological response to the socio-economic changes that accompanied the development of capitalism. More precisely, I want to suggest that the valorization of the individual in the criticism of Coleridge and Eliot constitutes a reactionary attempt to resolve the crises of the subject precipitated by the capitalist mode of production during its market and monopoly phases. The idea is not merely to expose the link between the romantic and modern critical tradition and what has become known as "bourgeois individualism," but also to show that the two critical oeuvres which form the landmarks of this tradition function as symbolic acts designed to heal social contradictions which they ultimately perpetuate.

I

It was with the emergence of the expressive theory of poetry in the late eighteenth century that the individual came to dominate English literary criticism. Coleridge's influential version of this theory emphasizes the author and the creative process, but also carries implications

for the nature of the text and of the reader's response. Coleridge conceives of both author and reader as ideally free, unified subjectivities,
who are not thrown into division by determinations that conflict with
their intention and escape their control, and whose coherent thoughts
are framed, whether as producer or consumer, in an equally coherent
text. This assumption is so valorized and beyond question for Coleridge that it ironically and quite unconsciously undoes the unity of his
own writing by producing several contradictions which resist resolution. Some critics have attempted to rehabilitate his theory by explaining away these logical scandals; others have found them disappointing,
indicative of his failure as a theorist.[4] In both of these instances, however, it is clear that the critics themselves assume Coleridge's concept
of the subject: their praise or blame rides on the question of whether
he expressed his ideas with rational consistency. In an effort to disso-
ciate my inquiry from this assumption, I will treat the contradictions
strategically, as an effective heuristic device: they will help us elucidate
the precise way in which the individual figures among the conditions
that make possible Coleridge's critical discourse and simultaneously
put it into question.

   Coleridge's theory of poetry is genetic: the poet's integrated consciousness, under the guidance of his "imagination," is the source of a
highly organized signifying system that expresses truths about the
world.[5] Coleridge asserts that in the creative process the poet experiences an imaginative identification with his materials which is profoundly unconscious. "Genius" is considered "an unconscious activity"
(*BL*, 2: 258), and the "true poet" is one who possesses "a more than
ordinary sympathy with the objects of nature or the incidents of human
life . . . united with a more than ordinary activity of mind in general,
but more particularly of those faculties of mind we class under the
name of fancy and imagination—faculties (I know not how I shall
make myself intelligible) that are rather spontaneous than voluntary"
(*SC*, 2: 50). In Coleridge's theory, the act of poetic composition occurs
in its most desirable form when the poet spontaneously sympathizes
with his text. Thus, if a poet who writes plays or narrative poems fails
to identify completely with his characters, his text is likely to reveal the
notorious "ventriloquism," a "defect" in which "two are represented as
talking, while in truth one man speaks" (*BL*, 2: 109). Wordsworth errs
in this way, since we immediately recognize his "thoughts and diction"
in the speeches that he assigns to his characters. Shakespeare, however,
is the exemplar of maximum identification: his genius was such that

he "made himself all characters . . . for the time, he became Othello, and spoke as Othello, in such circumstances, must have spoken" (*SC,* 2: 14 and 102).

This formulation runs into logical difficulties when Coleridge insists that the poet's unconscious identification with his text is simultaneous with a self-conscious control. The imagination, "that synthetic and magical power" under whose agency the poet creates, is "first put in action by the will and understanding, and retained under their irremissive, though gentle and unnoticed, controul" (*BL,* 2: 12). The creative process is thus voluntary *and* spontaneous; the poet is aware of himself in the act of creation ("understanding") *and* absorbed in his text, unaware of this critical detachment ("unnoticed"). The corollary that Coleridge draws from these contradictions is that the poet's characters have an identity to his individual mind *and* are representative. Shakespeare is summoned to bear the burden of illustration in a series of paradoxical comments. In him we find "a genial understanding directing self-consciously a power and an implicit wisdom deeper than consciousness" (*SC,* 1: 198). Shakespeare produced his "characters out of his own intellectual and moral faculties, by conceiving any one intellectual or moral faculty in morbid excess and then placing himself, thus mutilated and diseased, under given circumstances" (*SC,* 1: 34). Nonetheless, "he drew characters which would always be natural, and therefore permanent, inasmuch as they were not dependent upon accidental circumstances" (*SC,* 2: 110). Shakespeare is "characterless, because characteristic. The poet lost in his portraits contrasted with the poet as a mere ventriloquist; wonderful union of both in Shakespeare" (*SC,* 1: 73).

The questionable logic derives from the pressure that the concept of the individual puts on Coleridge's discourse: it indicates an effort to preserve, at the cost of logical consistency, the author as an autonomous subject who controls the meaning of his text. This is perhaps why Coleridge was anxious that his statement about the spontaneity of the imagination would not be "intelligible": anything that limits the author's command over the production of his text cannot be easily joined to the concept of a free, noncontradictory subject. Hence, the antinomy in his "organic" concept of poetic genius: on the one hand, genius seems to follow the laws of nature ("the *rules* of Imagination" are "the very powers of growth and production" [*BL,* 2: 65]); on the other hand, genius is "the power of acting creatively under laws of its own origination" (*SC,* 1: 198). M. H. Abrams exploits Coleridge's fondness for biological analogies to devise a "solution" for this problem, thereby showing that the individual is a valorized assumption in his own critical discourse. His attempt, however, is less than satisfactory and actually restates the contradiction in the most pointed terms: "Acting . . . under 'laws of its own origination,' achieving works each of which is unique, the genius gives the laws by which his own products are to be judged; yet these laws are universal laws which he himself must necessarily obey, because his composition proceeds in accordance with the order of the living universe."[6]

Similar contradictions emerge in Coleridge's treatment of the reader. The reading experience involves an illusionism, a vicarious participation in the text that Coleridge describes as a "willing suspension of disbelief for the moment" (*BL*, 2: 6). This suspension of judgment is contingent upon "a specific *dramatic* probability [which] may be raised by a true poet, if the whole of his work be in harmony; a *dramatic* probability, sufficient for dramatic pleasure, even when the component characters and incidents border on impossibility" (*BL*, 2: 189). The illusory effect of probability allows the poet to exercise a psychological domination over those who respond to the text: "The consciousness of the poet's mind must be diffused over that of the reader or spectator; but he himself, according to his genius, elevates us, and by being always in keeping prevents us from perceiving any strangeness, tho' we feel great exaltation" (*SC*, 1: 183). Like the author's identification with his materials (and avoidance of ventriloquism), the pleasurable illusion that distinguishes the reader's response is held to be a normative principle: the mark of a "great poet" is "the power of so carrying on the eye of the reader as to make him almost lose the consciousness of words— to make him *see* everything—and this without exciting any painful or laborious attention" (*SC*, 1: 189). Yet since the illusion is an experience in which the reader surrenders his conscious self-mastery and yields his thoughts and feelings to the efficacy of the text, it compromises the autonomous individual, so we find Coleridge making the contradictory assertion—that the reader's will is active in his response. The paradox becomes most apparent when Coleridge compares the dramatic illusion to dreaming: "In sleep we pass at once by a sudden collapse into this suspension of will and the comparative power: whereas in an interesting play, read or represented, we are brought up to this point, as far as it is requisite or desirable, gradually, by the art of the poet and the actors; and with the consent and positive aidance of our own will. We *choose* to be deceived" (*SC*, 1: 116). But how can a spectator aid the poet and the actors with his will when they have persuaded him to suspend it during the experience? If the spectator consents to be "brought up to this point" at the start of his experience, doesn't he abandon himself to the manipulation of production values? Coleridge resists the idea that we do not preside over our own acts of cognition, that we are not free subjectivities, but subject to the power of the text or the performance.

In Coleridge's practical criticism, the individual leads him to disregard another of his normative principles: organic unity. Whenever Coleridge theorizes about the text, he habitually relies on biological analogies: the text is considered a "natural" synthesis of interdependent parts, each of which is so closely connected to the other as to form a unique whole, and none of which can be altered or removed without fundamentally damaging that whole. The reader who responds to this organic unity has a similarly organized experience, feeling "such delight from the *whole,* as is comparable with a distinct gratification from each component *part*" (*SC,* 1: 197), and this supports that "willing illusion" which Coleridge values so highly. Given such emphasis on unity, we would logically expect Coleridge's criticism of a text to examine the interrelationships among the several parts and construct an image of textual wholeness. In practice, however, his tendency is to give enormous stress to one part, characterization. He searches for the unified subjects in the texts he examines, often neglecting or minimizing such other textual features as narrative and genre. In Coleridge's view, characters should be represented as autonomous persons with unique identities, and a premium is placed on psychological consistency and literary decorum. Shakespeare is praised because "he shows us the life and principle of each being with organic regularity," while Fielding's *Tom Jones* is faulted for "forced and unnatural" scenes in which "the whole matter is incongruous, and totally destitute of psychological truth" (*SC,* 2: 131 and 101). In the end it becomes clear that Coleridge's practical criticism deals not with organic wholes, but with fragments; it implicitly discriminates between grades of relevance among the parts of a text, assigning the greatest importance to characterization, and especially to the coherent development of character psychology.[7]

We can't assume that Coleridge's expressive theory, however "natural" it has come to seem since the nineteenth century, provides an objective representation of textual production and reception or of the nature of specific texts. Each antinomy demonstrates that his critical discourse is predicated on the individual, a concept of the subject as a free, unified consciousness identical to itself in all its expressions. "Will," "reconciliation," "organization," "unity," "identity"—these are basic terms in Coleridge's expressive theory, and they entail precise reading strategies and principles of evaluation. Contradictory formulations occur when there is a logical restriction of the subject's freedom and identity or, in the case of organic unity, when the subject as character must be subordinated to other parts of the text. In several of these formulations, "spontaneous," "unconscious," "illusion" become basic terms, and the contradictions look toward a totally opposite concept of the subject as a consciousness divided within itself by psychological and social determinations, a concept that will later underlie, although in very different ways, Freudian psychoanalysis and Marxist social theory and the literary criticism they have made possible. In Coleridge, however, the presence of the individual precludes any significant development of this determinate subject, masking but not resolving the discrepancies in his writing. The individual can thus be seen as a conceptual limit, the site of contradictions that never receive explicit statement or examination, but that nonetheless reveal the privileged assumption in Coleridge's critical discourse.

Certainly the greatest irony here is that Coleridge himself, in both his work and his life, utterly violated that assumption. The contradictions suggest that his own consciousness was riddled with gaps and inconsistencies, that he failed to achieve the unity of mind he attributed to the author in his expressive theory. The fact is that Coleridge's criticism defies any attempt at reconstruction that values his own criterion of unity: it survives mainly in what Thomas McFarland has called "rubble-heap works"—an elliptical literary memoir, fragmentary lecture notes, copious marginalia—and over the course of several decades it underwent a series of radical transformations in which different codes (politics, psychology, religion) shaped his theory.[8] And then there is his checkered career, notorious for its plagiaries and procrastination, full of numerous plans for writing projects that were left unfinished or never really begun. It is tempting to turn, with McFarland, to Coleridge's biography in order to understand his "ruined existence" and connect the divisions in his work with those in his personal life—his estrangements from family, wife, and friends, his drug dependency and hypochondria, his general anxiety. McFarland develops a very plausible psychoanalytic explanation, locating the origin of Coleridge's problems in his childhood relationships to his mother and his older brothers. In this way, Coleridge's privileging of the individual in his writing may be read as a form of unconscious wish fulfillment, an imaginary compensation for his fragmented life or, in McFarland's terms, "an actual incompleteness striving toward a hypothetic unity" (p. 47).

The difficulty with such a psychoanalytic approach, however, is its tendency to recuperate the individual in the end. Having psychoanalyzed Coleridge as a subject split by familial determinations that helplessly reduce him to "the characteristic neurotic form of compulsive repetition" (p. 109), McFarland paradoxically concludes with a paean to his rational control: "Coleridge, I have always felt, is in a special way a hero of existence: though life bore down on him, he fought from the knees. . . . he preserved his life, his reason, and his humanity" (pp. 132–33). The importance of the individual to McFarland's discourse is particularly evident in his habit of generalizing romanticism as "merely the intensification of certain attitudes inseparable from human experience" (p. 43). Thus the romantic fascination with "fragmented modalities" becomes an essential feature of human nature, and the "principle" which "allows us to maintain inner coherence despite the chaos of such fragmentation" is Kant's "apperception, . . . the 'transcendental unity of self-consciousness,' the abiding and unchanging 'I'" (p. 44). Because much modern scholarship assumes the transcendental subject, romanticism is loosed from its historical moorings and regarded as the bearer of eternal verities, perhaps the most significant of which is that very concept of the subject. As Jerome McGann has pointed out, "the idea that poetry, or even consciousness, can set one free of the ruins of history and culture is the grand illusion of every romantic poet," and "this idea continues as one of the important shibboleths of our culture, especially—and naturally—at its higher levels."[9]

We don't want to deny the value of psychoanalysis in understanding the dominance of the individual in romantic critical discourse, but rather to prevent it from setting up individualism as the ultimate horizon of that understanding. Since individualistic approaches have so far had the power to distract attention from other determinations, there is a need to emphasize the concept of the individual as a historical phenomenon, rooted in the socio-economic changes that transformed late eighteenth-century England. This view has received a few incisive statements, but it has found wider acceptance only recently because of an underlying complicity between modern criticism and romanticism.[10] It requires a new formulation, therefore, one which may gain in persuasiveness by confessing from the outset that the social context of a cultural product (here a critical discourse) "is not immediately present as such, not some common-sense external reality, nor even the conventional narratives of history manuals, but rather must itself always be (re)constructed after the fact."[11] Empirical history is accessible only through textual forms which constitute an interested transformation of it, but which can still yield a precise description of the transforming process; we can focus on how the text actively reorganizes a historical moment without forgetting that it is articulating its own *context* for us and thus guiding our understanding of its relations to history. Instead of attempting a historical reconstruction which claims "objectivity" and then measuring it against the "distortions" of romantic texts, we will examine how specific texts create their own versions of history by considering the efforts of Wordsworth and Coleridge to address contemporary social developments in their criticism. Their observations explore the relationship between writing and reading, giving particular attention to the psychological effects of the literary text on readers whom they define as affected by historical change. The passages, rarely if ever discussed by critics, are striking for their presupposition of the two conflicting concepts of the subject we have already encountered elsewhere in Coleridge's theoretical work, one transcendental, the other determinate.

This is most clear in the programmatic preface to *Lyrical Ballads* (1800), a piece that can be considered a collaboration between Wordsworth and Coleridge whose composition the former seems to have controlled.[12] In its celebrated version of the expressive theory of poetry, the poet is clearly conceived as an autonomous individual:

> All good poetry is the spontaneous overflow of powerful feelings; but though this be true, Poems to which any value can be attached, were never produced on any variety of subjects but by a man who being possessed of more than usual organic sensibility had also thought long and deeply.

To explain this account of the poet, Wordsworth asserts that human cognitive acts are self-willed unions of thought and feeling ("our continued influxes of feeling are modified and directed by our thoughts"), which transcend biographical and social determinations in offering a knowledge of "general representatives" where "we discover what is really important to men." The poet's "more than usual organic sensibility," a precursor of Coleridge's more elaborate theory of imagination, carries with it a certain power over other "men": because it enables the production of unified texts ("the feeling therein developed gives importance to the action and situation and not the action and situation to the feeling"), the poet can exercise a beneficent effect on the reader: "The understanding of the being to whom we address ourselves, if he be in a healthful state of association, must necessarily be in some degree enlightened, his taste exalted, and his affections ameliorated." Wordsworth proceeds to make this psychological effect the basis of a social mission for the poet, and explicitly for the authors of *Lyrical Ballads*: it is the authors' "organic sensibility" that "distinguishes these Poems from the popular Poetry of the day," a feature of "general importance" because it shows that

> the human mind is capable of excitement without the application of gross and violent stimulants; and he must have a very faint perception of its beauty and dignity who does not know this, and who does not further know that one being is elevated above another in proportion as he possesses this capability. It has therefore appeared to me that to endeavor to produce or enlarge this capability is one of the best services in which, at any period, a Writer can be engaged; but this service, excellent at all times, is especially so at the present day. For a multitude of causes unknown to former times are now acting with a combined force to blunt the discriminating powers of the human mind, and unfitting it for all voluntary exertion to reduce it to a state of almost savage torpor. The most effective of these causes are the great national events which are daily taking place, and the encreasing accumulation of men in cities, where the uniformity of their occupations produces a craving for extraordinary incident which the rapid communication of intelligence hourly gratifies.

This is a glance at the Napoleonic wars and the economic reorganization of England during industrialization, the emergence of mass production and the routinization of the work process, with a nascent communications industry to support and extend the cycle of exchange. Wordsworth's dire cultural diagnosis seems to be echoed by Coleridge, some ten years later: in a lecture note Coleridge expresses "regret" about the "ever-increasing sameness of human life," observing that the "dead palsy of the public mind" renders "men" unable to judge "by actual experience" any cultural product manifesting "the laws of association of feeling and thought, the starts and strange far-flights of the assimilative power" of the imagination (*SC,* 1: 185).[13]

These transitions from creative process to reader response to social context may appear seamless in my exposition, but they in fact rest on contradictory assumptions. With both writers, the use of social developments to explain reader psychology signals a shift to an entirely different concept of the subject: whereas the poet enjoys an autonomy from the social formation which allows him to preserve his "organic sensibility" or "assimilative power," the contemporary reader's consciousness is likely to be the determinate effect of social upheavals over which it is powerless; while the psychological difference between poet and reader is repeatedly described as one of degree ("more than usual organic sensibility"), in effect it is a difference of kind. Neither Wordsworth nor Coleridge faces the question of how the poet completely circumvents the oppressive weight of history borne by his contemporaries; instead they vacillate between idealistic assertions of the individual and grim topical allusions that implicitly contradict their assertions with contrary evidence. Both writers construct metaphysical hierarchies, founded on the "organic sensibility" or "assimilative power," in which "one being is elevated above another in proportion as he possesses this capability" (Wordsworth) and only the artist of "genius" is able to "force his way out of the crowd, not of the vulgar, but of the aristocracy of the intellect, and presume to join the almost supernatural beings that stood by themselves aloof" (Coleridge).

These rhapsodic claims are of course typical of the romantic glorification of the poet. But their status as a period or cultural commonplace should not prevent us from noticing how they take on the whine of special pleading in the context of certain social observations. Wordsworth, pointing to the negative consequence of the current "tendency in life and manners" on "the literature and theatrical exhibitions of the country," laments that "the invaluable works of our elder writers, I had almost said the works of Shakespear and Milton, are driven into neglect by frantic novels, sickly and stupid German tragedies, and deluges of idle and extravagant stories in verse." The incredulous tone with which he mentions the "neglect" of the canonized "elder writers" seems to take for granted that the "works" of transcendental subjects should be timeless and universal; Wordsworth's statement, however, actually confesses the increasing marginality of those writers. Similarly, Coleridge's rhapsody appears in a deflating inquiry into "the dependence of genius on the taste of the public," in which he aims to elucidate the socially determined forms of psychological "disease most preclusive of tragic worth." Even the "valued advantage of the theater" to be "a delightful, yet most effectual remedy" for the popular mental "palsy" is undermined by contemporary theatrical conditions, which have Coleridge wishing, "if only the actors were what they have been" (*SC*, 1: 184–85).

In such references to English cultural trends, it is evidently assumed that the poet's autonomy is relative to the social formation in which the composition and consumption of his texts take place, and this flaw in the logic transforms the typical romantic assertion of the individual into what Raymond Williams has acutely described as a "defensive reaction" that "is evidently compensatory: the height of the artists' claim is also the height of their despair. They defined, emphatically, their high calling, but they came to define and to emphasize because they were convinced that the principles on which the new society was being organized were actively hostile to the necessary principles of art."[14] It is important to add that a compensation grounded on the "principles" of romantic critical discourse can only be imaginary because it means asserting the free, unified subject in the face of contradictory social determinations. There is a general tendency in romanticism to posit an opposition between human "nature" and social "manners," as Wordsworth does, insisting, for example, that there exist "certain inherent and indestructible qualities of the human mind," while stating that social "causes" can "blunt the discriminating powers of the mind" and "reduce it to a state of almost savage torpor."[15] In Wordsworth and Coleridge, specifically, the romantic presupposition that the subject has an integrity apart from history results in a repression—apparently unconscious to some extent and discernible only through the blind spots in their writing—of the contrary awareness that history is constitutive of the subject, of its intellectual and emotional horizons, its mode of address to the world, its psychological makeup.[16] Both writers fail to see, for example, that their very social mission is determined by a historical situation which is not of their making and is eluding their control. In this sense, their valorization of the individual can be read as a symbolic act designed to resolve the contemporary social contradictions that were dividing the consciousness of poet and reader alike.

The imaginary status of this "solution" becomes clear when the writers themselves comment briefly on the impossible idealism of their social mission, although of course without ever being driven to abandon or revise their privileged assumption. In a statement that seems both a standard rhetorical gesture of modesty and an anxious glance at reviewers' attacks on the first edition of *Lyrical Ballads* (1798), Wordsworth admits that his "effort" is "feeble" when compared with "the magnitude of the general evil" and wishfully predicts that "the time is approaching when the evil will be systematically opposed by men of greater powers and with far more distinguished success." Coleridge thinks that "a conceivable and possible, tho' hardly to be expected, arrangement of British theaters" might introduce the "wisdom and intuition" of Shakespeare "into the heads and hearts, into the very souls, of the mass of mankind," but then he begins to waver: "It seems to me a pardonable enthusiasm to steal away from sober likelihood and share so rich a feast in the faery world of possibility! Yet even in the sober cheerfulness of a circumspect hope, much, very much, might be done—enough, assuredly, to furnish a kind and strenuous nature with ample motives for the attempt to effect what may be effected" (*SC*, 1:186–87). In such passages, the individual is imagined as the heroic savior of human consciousness against the degrading contradiction of social change, but he will not materialize until some unspecified future time; in the present, there can be no more than a hope for "men of greater powers" or "a kind and strenuous nature."

The individual is the conceptual means by which romantic critical discourse "takes a stand" with respect to contemporary social developments; it functions as an ideology, investing a real relation between social agents with an imaginary one "that *expresses* a *will* (conservative, conformist, reformist or revolutionary), a hope or a nostalgia, rather than describing a reality."[17] Since, however, the real is available only in textual forms, the point is not that romanticism is "false" or "distorted," but that like all discourse, its social representations rework the real from a specific ideological standpoint. The romantic ideology must be seen as fundamentally conservative, even conformist, in its response to historical change; for although the autonomy of the individual, as Williams points out, "offered an immediate basis for an important criticism of industrialism,"[18] it is paradoxically a theoretical presupposition for the capitalist mode of production. In liberal economic and political theory, the concept of the transcendental subject has been known as "bourgeois individualism," an ideology that "sets agents up as individuals/subjects, free and equal, and presents them as it were in a presocial state."[19] Bourgeois individualism can be considered the effect of specific historical changes ("the product on one side of the dissolution of the feudal forms of society, on the other side of the new forces of production developed since the sixteenth century" [Marx]), but it also

serves as a necessary condition for the reproduction of capitalism because its constitution of subjects as autonomous individuals "allows for
the functioning of those juridical-political structures which permit the
labor contract (buying and selling of labor power), capitalist private
property (N.B. the role of this ideology as the *condition of existence* of
the juridical relation of property), the generalization of exchange, competition, etc."[20] For romantic critical discourse, this means that the ideology which enables it to oppose the social and psychological consequences of the industrialized mass production and urbanization that
characterize market capitalism simultaneously enables it to act as a
theoretical support for that mode of production. The romantic reaction
is also a capitulation, although a profoundly unconscious one, not only
because ideology imperceptibly "slides into all human activity" and "is
identical with the 'lived' experience of human existence itself,"[21] but
also because it is the specific effect of the ideology of the individual to
conceal the conditions under which consciousness exists by asserting
the free, unified subject.

The conservatism of romantic critical discourse can be glimpsed in
the precise way it rewrites the text as an object-for-criticism. Assuming
the historical transcendence of the imagination, this discourse delimits
poetry as, in Coleridge's words, a "vivid reflection of the truths of nature and of the human heart" (*SC*, 1: 148) and thus inevitably eclipses
two historical moments: the past in which the text was produced and
which it brings into existence, although reorganized, for subsequent
readers; and the present that determines the valorization of the ideology of the individual in romantic critical theory and practice. This historical amnesia is also characteristic of liberal economic theory (among
other bourgeois discourses): as Marx notes in the *Grundrisse,* "Smith
and Ricardo still stand with both feet on the shoulders of the eighteenth-century prophets [e.g., Defoe and Rousseau, both of whom are
mentioned earlier in this passage], in whose imaginations this eighteenth-century individual . . . appears as an ideal, whose existence they
project into the past. Not as a historic result but as history's point of
departure. As the Natural Individual appropriate to their notion of human nature, not arising historically, but posited by nature" (p. 83).
Romantic critical discourse cannot (or may refuse to) discern this fundamental resemblance to other bourgeois discourses because it initiates
an increasing specialization of writing, a division between "culture" and
"society" or between "art" and "politics" (or "economics") which in
England, as has often been observed, seems to follow the romantic

disillusionment with the aftermath of the French Revolution.[22] E. P. Thompson's account acknowledges the function of ideology as an imaginary compensation for a real social situation: "How far is it possible for men to hold on to aspirations long after there appears to be no hope of inserting them into 'the real world which is the world of all us'? If the social context makes all insertion seem impossible—if all objective referents for these hopes are cruelly obliterated—if the attempt to live out the ideals appears to produce their opposite—if *fraternité* produces fratricide, *égalité* produces empire, liberty produces liberticide—then aspirations can only become a transposed interior faith" (p. 174).

Since the individual is the key article in this "interior faith," we can better describe the two social functions of romantic criticism, one utopian, the other ideological. By assuming the historical transcendence of the imagination, this discourse claims for itself an autonomy by virtue of which it can criticize the social formation where it operates and imagine a different, future formation where its values may be realized. Yet insofar as the assumption of transcendence effaces the social determinations of its critical materials and operations, this discourse cannot think its legitimating relationship to the capitalist formation it so abhors and therefore cannot offer a penetrating critique of social problems. The ideology of the individual is reproduced again and again in romantic critical discourse, both in axiomatic statements of the expressive theory of poetry and in the textual analyses that the theory informs. When during the nineteenth century this discourse is finally institutionalized in belles lettres criticism—for example, in the work of Matthew Arnold or Leslie Stephen—it achieves a cultural ascendancy that can only contribute to the dominance of bourgeois ideology and hence the reproduction of capitalism. Romantic critical discourse, despite its utopian aspirations, eventually plays into the hands of that industrial captor of the public mind whom it was initially intended to vanquish.

II

Eliot's assimilation of romantic critical theory has been recognized by a growing number of critics who have not taken his antiromantic pronouncements at face value. His criticism, especially the early essays and lectures, can now be seen as a distinctively modern transformation of romantic theories of imagination and literary history.[23] What will be emphasized here, however, are the conflicting concepts of the subject assumed in this transformation: Eliot's critical discourse puts forward several theoretical points that appear truly antiromantic in their opposition to the romantic valorization of the individual, but his formulations of them are filled with contradictions in which the individual reemerges to prevent a complete theoretical break. Once again, such blind spots will be treated as a heuristic device which, in this case, exposes the individual as the conceptual limit of Eliot's discourse.

In Eliot's "impersonal" theory of poetry, the poet is conceived as a subjectivity divided by determinations that exist outside it, and that, during the creative process, escape its conscious control. "The more perfect the artist," Eliot states in "Tradition and the Individual Talent" (1919), "the more completely separate in him will be the man who suffers and the mind which creates."[24] The cognitive acts of this creative mind are not autonomous ("no poet, no artist of any art, has his complete meaning alone" [p. 4]); rather, they depend upon an adherence to the Western literary "tradition" so that "the present is directed by the past" (p. 5). For the poet, such an adherence entails a self-denial, a surrender of identity, for "the mind of Europe—the mind of his own country—[is] a mind which he learns in time to be much more important than his own private mind" (p. 6). This division of the poet's consciousness by literary history means a move away from the genetic orientation in romantic theories of composition to an emphasis on the materiality of the text as a "medium." In Eliot's often quoted assertion, "The poet has, not a 'personality' to express, but a particular medium, which is only a medium and not a personality, in which impressions and experiences combine in peculiar and unexpected ways" (p. 9). The creative process of combination, moreover, is a deeply unconscious state in which the poet is released from his personal consciousness and subsumed in a "medium" and a "consciousness of the past." Eliot underscores the automatism of this psychological process by describing it with scientific analogies, particularly chemical terms and reactions: "the poet's mind" is "the transforming catalyst," "a receptacle for seizing and storing up numberless feelings, phrases, images, which remain there until all the particles which can unite to form a new compound are present together" (p. 8).

With the mention of "seizing," however, we have almost imperceptibly shifted to a different concept of the subject: like Coleridge's notion of the involuntary, unconscious "genius," Eliot's "impersonal" theory also and quite paradoxically assumes that the poet is a free, unified consciousness that directs its cognitive acts and textual production. Thus, on the one hand, Eliot displays a romantic fascination with biological metaphors for the unconscious by remarking that "the historical sense compels a man to write not merely with his own generation in his bones, but with a feeling that the whole of the literature of Europe from Homer and within it the whole of the literature of his own country has a simultaneous existence and composes a simultaneous order" (p. 4). On the other hand, however, when he refers to specific manifestations of this "historical sense," the passive compulsion becomes active and conscious selection: "Some can absorb knowledge, the more tardy must sweat for it. Shakespeare acquired more essential history from Plutarch than most men could from the whole British Museum" (p. 6). If we had earlier assumed, with Eliot, that even Shakespeare wrote with a subliminal awareness of the entire Western literary tradition up to the Renaissance, this example conversely shows that he was likely to indulge a personal preference for certain authors like Plutarch, that what matters is less the "order" of tradition than the autonomy of the individual as exhibited in his choices and capacity to "absorb knowledge." This contradictory view of Shakespeare bears a striking resemblance to Coleridge's paradox, that Shakespeare had "a genial understanding directing self-consciously a power and an implicit wisdom deeper than consciousness," with the proviso, of course, that for Eliot the self-abnegating "implicit wisdom" is synonymous with the poet's "historical sense" as well as with his dependence on a material "medium."

Eliot's recuperation of the romantic expressive theory is clear near the end of his programmatic essay: although he aims to raise the flag of antiromanticism in an attack on Wordsworth's famous definition of poetry, the passage ripples with inconclusive reversals that imply a basic agreement with the object of the attack. The poet's "experiences," Eliot begins,

> are not "recollected," and they finally unite in an atmosphere which is "tranquil" only in that it is a passive attending upon the event. Of course this is not quite the whole story. There is a great deal, in the writing of poetry, which must be conscious and deliberate. In fact, the bad poet is usually unconscious where he ought to be conscious, and conscious where he ought be unconscious. Both errors tend to make him "personal." Poetry is not a turning loose of emotion, but an escape from emotion; it is not the expression of personality, but an escape from

personality. But, of course, only those who have personality and emotions know what it means to want to escape from these things. (Pp. 10–11)

In the end, the poet (and perhaps his select readers as well) becomes a transcendental subject whose "escape from personality" is actually an indirect self-expression, based on a knowledge that originates with him alone ("only those who have personality and emotions know" it). Eliot's poet, like Coleridge's "genius," has "the power of acting creatively under laws of its own origination" (*SC*, 1:198). And just as Coleridge asserts the cognitive autonomy of "genius" after restricting it to the unconscious workings of the imagination, Eliot smuggles the individual back into his discourse by setting the poet free from the psychological ("unconscious"), textual ("medium"), and historical ("tradition") determinations with which he had so decisively distinguished his theory from romanticism.

The valorization of the individual in Eliot's critical discourse underlies the influential theory of literary history he formulated as the "dissociation of sensibility." The consciousness or "personality" that Eliot finds expressed in the work of certain seventeenth-century English poets has the freedom and unity implicit in such romantic concepts of the subject as Wordsworth's "organic sensibility" and Coleridge's "assimilative power" of the imagination: Eliot's version, in "The Metaphysical Poets" (1921), is that "their mode of feeling was directly and freshly altered by their reading and thought" (p. 246). As was the habit of his romantic predecessors, Eliot proceeds to generalize this psychological reading of specific texts into a theory of poetic composition and a metaphysical hierarchy of "sensibility" that discriminates between the extraordinary poet and "the ordinary man":

A thought to Donne was an experience; it modified his sensibility. When a poet's mind is perfectly equipped for its work, it is constantly amalgamating disparate experience; the ordinary man's experience is chaotic, irregular, fragmentary. . . . in the mind of the poet these experiences are always forming new wholes. (P. 247)

The poet's unified sensibility, like Coleridge's imagination, first seems to operate automatically (in the "metaphysical" poets it is "a mechanism of sensibility which could devour any experience" [p. 247]) as well as at profoundly unconscious biological levels ("One must look into the

cerebral cortex, the nervous system, and the digestive tracts" [p. 250]).
Yet when Eliot actually describes this sensibility in the act of creation,
the poet has complete command over the production of his texts: "The
poets in question . . . were, at best, engaged in the task of trying to find
the verbal equivalent for states of mind and feeling. . . . The [modern]
poet must become more and more comprehensive, more allusive, more
indirect, in order to force, to dislocate if necessary, language into his
meaning" (p. 248).

This notion of the poet's comprehensiveness derives from Eliot's
"impersonal" theory of poetry: the unified sensibility consists of "feeling . . . altered" not only by "thought," as in the romantic expressive
theory, but also by "reading" which links the individual poet to the
literary tradition. "Marvell's best verse," unaffected by the psychic dissociation, "is the product of European, that is to say Latin, culture"
("Andrew Marvell" [1921], p. 252). An understanding of Marvell on
the basis of the "impersonal" theory of poetry would lead to the conclusion that his "historical sense" involves a displacement of him ("the
man who suffers," his "personality" and "experience") as the origin of
his text. Eliot's conception of Marvell, however, leads in the opposite
direction, returning to the poet and reiterating the central paradox of
"Tradition and the Individual Talent." Although defined as "the product" of "culture," Marvell remains a transcendental subject to whom the
determinations of literary history are merely counters manipulated in
the creative process: according to Eliot, Marvell's unified sensibility
gives his poetry the "quality" of "wit" (an "internal equilibrium," "a
tough reasonableness beneath the slight lyric grace"), and such poetic
qualities "are conscious and cultivated [;] the mind which cultivates
one may cultivate the other" (pp. 252, 263). In Eliot's psychohistorical
theory of "dissociation," the poet of unified sensibility is simultaneously
a part of and apart from tradition: his consciousness is the determinate
effect of literary history only when he transcends it and incarnates the
individual, possessing the optimal degree of self-consistency and self-
mastery.

The individual is the conceptual limit of Eliot's critical discourse,
the boundary beyond which his thinking cannot pass without issuing
into contradiction or breaking off altogether; as a result, any extended
development of theoretical points that assume a radically different concept of the subject is precluded. Eliot's provocative references to the
materiality of the textual "medium" form one such casualty. The "impersonal" theory of poetry leads Eliot to articulate a notion of the opac-

ity of language, in which literary texts are viewed not as referential but as constructed out of "conventions" and "rhetoric," materials which are mechanically productive of such illusionistic effects as the "real" presence of an author's or character's personality or the outside world. In this productive process, the author is decentered as the source of the text and instead becomes its effect. In "Four Elizabethan Dramatists" (1923), Eliot states as his "point of view" that drama "will have its special conventions of the stage and the actor as well as of the play itself," for "it is easier to present the effect of something in a firm convention" (p. 94). Several years earlier, in "Rhetoric and Poetic Drama" (1919), Eliot had remarked on the conventional quality of the "conversational style": "At the present time there is a manifest preference for the 'conversational' in poetry—the style of 'direct speech,' opposed to the 'oratorical' and the rhetorical; but if rhetoric is any convention of writing inappropriately applied, this conversational style can and does become a rhetoric" (p. 26). Here Eliot regards the contemporary fascination with the rhetorical effect of "direct speech" as "a vice of manner" (the "convention" is "inappropriately applied"), but this is a practice he wants to supplant by positing "a rhetoric of substance also, which is right because it issues from what it has to express" (p. 26). The peculiar effect of this "rhetoric of substance" is a transparency that effaces the very existence of language as a material medium and produces the illusion of the real presence of the referent or what is signified by that medium. In an unpublished lecture delivered in 1933, Eliot spoke of this illusionism as "that at which I have long aimed, in writing poetry; to write poetry which should be essentially poetry, with nothing poetic about it, poetry standing naked in its bare bones, or poetry so transparent that we should not see the poetry, but that which we are meant to see through the poetry, poetry so transparent that in reading it we are intent on what the poem *points at,* and not on the poetry, this seems to me the thing to try for."[25] The "rhetoric proper to Shakespeare at his best period" has a transparency which distracts us from the productive operations of language given to characters (their "rhetorical speeches") and instead focuses our attention on the subjectivities constituted by those operations:

The scene from *Julius Caesar* is right because the object of our attention is not the speech of Antony (*Bedeutung*) but the effect of his speech upon the mob, and Antony's intention, his preparation and consciousness of the effect. And in the rhetorical speeches from Shakespeare

which have been cited, we have this necessary advantage of a new clue
to the character, in noting the angle from which he views himself. But
when a character *in* a play makes a direct appeal to us, we are either the
victims of our own sentiment, or we are in the presence of a vicious
rhetoric. ("'Rhetoric' and Poetic Drama," p. 28)

The closing account of reader response reminds us of how close
Eliot's theory is to romantic discourse: his condemnation of the defective "direct appeal" clearly assumes Coleridge's concept of ventriloquism, in which the illusionistic "suspension of disbelief" is shattered
because the reader perceives an implausibility, an inconsistency. And
just as Coleridge found that this "suspension" occurs during an experience evoked by an organically unified text, Eliot argues that the transparency is produced by a union of material signifier ("rhetoric of substance") and conceptual signified ("what it has to express"): when the
rhetoric is not "inappropriately applied" and the union is achieved, the
signifier seems to vanish, and we succumb to the illusion that we are
in the presence of the signified; when there is an inconsistency in the
application of the rhetoric, such as a "direct appeal" to the reader, the
signifier becomes opaque, we see it as the producer of the illusion, and
we sense that "we are in the presence of a vicious rhetoric." Eliot of
course does not have Saussure's rigorous theory of the linguistic sign,
but his concept of the conventional or rhetorical nature of literary language, as Antony Easthope has suggested, does look toward later developments in semiotics[26] and marks a definite theoretical advance over
Coleridge: Eliot does not concentrate narrowly on reader psychology,
but also takes account of the productive operations of language. The
result is that Eliot, unlike Coleridge, is not reluctant to characterize a
text or performance as actively determining the consciousness that experiences it ("we are [made] . . . the victims of our own sentiment").

It is Eliot's enthusiasm for the effect of transparency, however, that
paradoxically limits the extent of his advance because it takes his discourse back to the romantic valorization of the individual. Like Coleridge, Eliot tends to search for the unified subjects in the texts he examines, elevating the coherent development of character psychology to
a normative principle. Thus, in "Hamlet and His Problems" (1919),
Shakespeare's play is considered "most certainly an artistic failure" because of a discontinuity in Hamlet's characterization: "Hamlet (the
man) is dominated by an emotion which is inexpressible, because it is
in *excess* of the facts as they appear" (pp. 123, 125). In several of Eliot's

formulations, furthermore, the productive operation of language, its property as a material medium, is abruptly and inexplicably elided, so that the text no longer produces an effect of transparency, but is rather a transparent expression of the poet's personality. Note the sudden shift in the last sentence of this passage:

> There is in fact no conversational or other form which can be applied indiscriminately; if a writer wishes to give the effect of speech he must positively give the effect of himself talking in his own person or in one of his roles; and if we are to express ourselves, our variety of thoughts and feelings, on a variety of subjects with inevitable rightness, we must adapt our manner to the moment with infinite variations. ("Rhetoric and Poetic Drama," p. 26)

The "impersonal" theory of poetry, which assumes "conversational" and other forms, suddenly jumps to an assumption of poetic self-expression, and the poet, initially considered the determinate effect of language, is now installed as the transcendental origin of a text that expresses his thoughts and feelings "with inevitable rightness." The same sort of turnaround happens in "Four Elizabethan Dramatists" in equally brief space: "No artist produces great art by a deliberate attempt to express his personality. He expresses his personality indirectly through concentrating upon a task which is a task in the same sense as the making of an efficient engine or the turning of a jug or a table-leg" (p. 96). It is evident that Eliot has here abandoned the theory of "impersonality," since it would require him to eliminate self-expression from such a "task" by perhaps asserting that the materials forming those products resist (or at the least transform) any communication of the producer's personality.

Although Eliot's references to the material effects of language are stated with axiomatic force in the more theoretical essays, he tends to contradict them in his critical practice by developing a series of psychological readings where the text becomes diaphanous. The "objective correlative" presented in "Hamlet and His Problems" is a formalistic concept ("the only way of expressing emotion in the form of art") which assumes the conventionality of language ("a set of objects, a situation, chain of events which shall be the formula for that *particular* emotion" [pp. 124–25]). In "Tradition and the Individual Talent," the "various feelings" experienced in a response to a text are similarly endowed with materiality by "inhering for the writer in particular words or phrases or images" (p. 8), not in his psychology. When Eliot discusses a specific body of writing, however, the "formula" and the "words or phrases or images" begin to dissolve, leaving a clear image of the writer's "emotion" and "feelings" (p. 49). As Edward Lobb has noted, "Even the most cursory reading of the Elizabethan essays will show that Eliot tries, in each instance, to isolate the personal element in the dramatist's work."[27] Eliot assigns such importance to transparency in poetry and drama that the materiality of this linguistic effect is disregarded and the poet again becomes a transcendental subject, visible through the text as its origin.

Eliot's valorization of this concept of the subject also determines the nature of his reflections on the critical activity itself. On the one hand, he seems to assume that criticism actively transforms the text into an object-for-criticism on the basis of a historically specific critical theory; on the other hand, criticism is conceived of as an unobtrusive and unmediated reproduction of the essential significance of the text. Thus, Eliot opens "Four Elizabethan Dramatists" with the assertion that "what I wish to do is to define and illustrate a point of view toward the Elizabethan drama, which is different from that of the nineteenth century," and "furthermore, I believe that this alternative critical attitude is not merely a possible difference of personal bias, but that it is the inevitable attitude for our time" (p. 91). One year earlier, however, in "The Function of Criticism" (1923), Eliot wrote that "the critic's task" is "the elucidation of works of art and the correction of taste" (p. 13), an essentialist project in which "the elucidation of works" apparently transcends the limitations of time and place and is therefore granted an absolute authority over other kinds of "taste."

In "Shakespeare and the Stoicism of Seneca" (1927), Eliot continues this vacillation. He notes, disapprovingly, that contemporary critics overlay Shakespeare's texts with determinations that are not "the truth of Shakespeare" or the "real Shakespeare" (p. 107). There are a number of eminently "personal" versions ("one of the chief reasons for questioning Mr. Strachey's Shakespeare, and Mr. Murry's, and Mr. Lewis's, is the remarkable resemblance which they bear to Mr. Strachey, and Mr. Murry, and Mr. Lewis respectively"). And there are versions in which "we have had Shakespeare explained by a variety of influences," such as Montaigne and Machiavelli, whose work is itself vulnerable to misrepresentation ("the real Machiavelli [is] a person whom Elizabethan England was as incapable of understanding as Georgian England, or any England, is" [p. 109]). Eliot's disapproval seems to imply that it is possible to reproduce the essential truth of Shakespeare's text, in opposition to the fictive transformations of the other critics. Yet although he actually goes so far as to put into question this possibility ("About any one so great as Shakespeare, it is probable that we can never be right" [p. 107]), Eliot does not see any inconsistency in his subsequent decision to "propose a Shakespeare under the influence of the stoicism of Seneca" (pp. 109–10) and then perform the very same critical activity he had just challenged. He justifies his own proposed "influence," exempting himself from his previous critique of Lytton Strachey, J. Middleton Murry, and Wyndham Lewis, by claiming the authority to act as final judge for Shakespearean criticism and by resorting to a seemingly self-effacing anti-intellectualism that in the context of his essay is in effect self-aggrandizement: "I wish merely to disinfect the Senecan Shakespeare before he appears. My ambitions would be realized if I could prevent him, in so doing, from appearing at all" (p. 109). Yet the "stoicism" that Eliot finds in Shakespeare's texts, what he describes as "the attitude of self-dramatization assumed by some of Shakespeare's heroes at moments of tragic intensity" (p. 110), is in fact the illusionistic effect of real presence he so extols in Shakespeare's characterizations, so that the "influence" he proposes would qualify as a "personal bias," despite his disclaimer that "I am not under the delusion that Shakespeare in the least resembles myself" (pp. 108–9).

These logical scandals, like the others we have formulated in Eliot's critical discourse, rest on conflicting concepts of the subject: at certain times, Eliot presupposes that the critic's consciousness is constituted by personal and historical determinations that motivate him to rewrite the text in a specific way; at other times, the critic, usually Eliot himself, enjoys an autonomy in which his knowledge of the text is free from the "errors" induced by "personal bias" and history. These assumptions likewise splinter Eliot's practical criticism, where the text is delimited now as an expression of the poet's personality, now as the product of its historical period, now as the container of eternal verities. "What every poet starts from," states Eliot, "is his own emotions," yet "the great poet, in writing himself, writes his time"; although the poet's work is the product of biographical and social determinations, with Dante and Shakespeare "the essential is, that each expresses in perfect language, some permanent human impulse . . . something universal and impersonal" ("Shakespeare and the Stoicism of Seneca," p. 117). In these abrupt shifts, Eliot couples an antiromantic insistence on the priority of social context with a recuperation of romantic expressive theory, eclipsing the past moment which determined the production of the text and the present moment which determines its reception; the result is that both poet and critic are implicitly characterized as free, unified subjects who, as in Wordsworth and Coleridge, are privileged with a knowledge of the timeless and universal truths of human nature. Yet insofar as Eliot sees the critical activity as the promulgation of these truths and "the correction of taste," he assumes that human subjectivity admits historical differences. In "The Metaphysical Poets," Eliot asserts that the dissociation of sensibility occurred at a specific historical moment, "between the time of Donne or Lord Herbert of Cherbury and the time of Tennyson and Browning," but he wonders "whether [the metaphysical poets'] virtue was not something permanently valuable, which subsequently disappeared, but ought not to have disappeared" (pp. 247, 245).

Eliot occasionally examines the social determinants of the dissociated sensibility in early twentieth-century poets and readers, suggesting that his critical discourse, like that of the English romantics, can be understood partly as an ideological response to contemporary social developments. This is clearest in the "London Letters" he wrote for *The Dial*. These acerbic pieces, combining social commentary with literary criticism, are remarkable for the continuity they establish between romantic and modern critical discourse, since Eliot's observations, like those of Wordsworth and Coleridge, explore the psychological effects of capitalism on writing and reading. It is evident, moreover, that although these two discourses articulate and respond to the capitalist mode of production at quite different stages of organization and development, their social representations are decisively mediated by the same conservative assumption, the individual.

Eliot seems most disturbed that "the insurgent middle class" has achieved an economic, political, and ideological hegemony which, although challenged in various ways, is not at all likely to "topple":

> At the very moment when the middle class appears to be on the point of perdition—beleaguered by a Coalition Government, the Three Trades-Unions, and the Income Tax—at this very moment it enjoys the triumph, in intellectual matters, of being able to respect no other standards than its own. And indeed, while its citadels appear to topple, it is busy strengthening its foundations. Year by year, royal birth-day by royal birth-day, it gains more seats in the House of Lords; and on the other hand, if it rejects with contumely the independent man, the free

man, all the individuals who do not conform to a world of mass-production, the Middle Class finds itself on one side more and more approaching identity with what used to be called the Lower Class. Both middle class and lower class are finding safety in Regular Hours, Regular Wages, Regular Pensions, and Regular Ideas.[28]

Eliot's topical references describe the middle class's economic base not as the increasing industrialization of urban manufacture that confronted the romantics over a hundred years before him, but as a monopolistic centralization and concentration of capital, an advanced rationalization of the work process, and a burgeoning mass communications industry. Nevertheless, he finds that these social developments have virtually the same deleterious impact on human psychology and cultural activity that Wordsworth and Coleridge deplored: "The atmosphere of literary London," Eliot observes in another "Letter," is marked by a "particular torpor or deadness . . . facilitated by conditions which are universal as well, . . . by the newspapers, the reviewing of books, the journalistic life; by the actual and by every proposed economic system, which gives so high a place to Security—whether in the form of gilt-edged bonds or old-age pensions—and so low a place to adventure and contemplation."[29] In Eliot's view, "the social evolution" underlies the "dulness" and "extreme lack of culture" for which he denounces the anthologies of Georgian poetry edited by Harold Monro and read by segments of the middle class:

> a poetry which takes not the faintest notice of the development of
> French verse from Baudelaire to the present day, and which has perused
> English literature with only a wandering antiquarian passion, a taste for
> which everything is either too hot or too cold; there is no culture here.
> Culture is traditional, and loves novelty; the General Reading Public
> knows no tradition, and loves staleness. (*D* 70, p. 451)

In Eliot's "London Letters" it seems clear that the consciousness of the middle and lower classes is the determinate effect of social "conditions" which dominate them: their "Regular Ideas" mean that they are possessed of the notorious dissociated sensibility, a cognitive degeneration in which feeling is not freely directed by thought ("adventure and contemplation") and by reading ("culture," "tradition"). At the same time, however, Eliot just as clearly argues from an assumption that he is a free, unified subject that escapes the ravages of historical change to recognize the value of "culture" and condemn the "torpid indifference" of his middle- and lower-class contemporaries. This assumption emerges when Eliot offers an illustration of "culture": the mention of French symbolist poetry shows that what he is championing in place of the "staleness" of the Georgian anthologies is not some impersonal "historical sense," as we might have expected, but a selective revision of the Western literary tradition which, like the example of Shakespeare choosing Plutarch in "Tradition and the Individual Talent," appears to be quite personal; "its governing principle," as Terry Eagleton has remarked, "seems to be not so much which works of the past are eternally valuable, as which will help T. S. Eliot to write his own poetry."[30] At one point, Eliot himself suggests that his comments on the Georgian anthologies may indeed presume the canonization of his personal preferences (an admission he would openly make much later in his career), but the force of the remark is to put his judgment beyond question by assigning this criticism to the "multitude" who wear the epistemological binders of history: "I am prepared to be accused, so unconscious is the humour of the multitude, of self-advertisement" (D 70, p. 451).[31] The paradox here is that Eliot excepts himself from one transindividual determination (the psychic dissociation of monopoly capitalism) by implying that he is the product of another (the literary tradition) which actually restores him to the status of the individual, of the unified sensibility that transcends contradictory determinations. This logical sleight of hand indicates that the valorization of the individual in Eliot's concept of tradition is a symbolic act that "resolves" the social contradictions dividing the consciousness of Georgian poets and readers, including Eliot himself: by installing his poetry and criticism in the "ideal order" of "existing monuments," he not only compensates for his marginality in relation to middle-class cultural hegemony, but also represses the fact that his writing is determined by such contemporary social developments; "culture" and "unification of sensibility" become Eliot's slogans because he faces an "extreme lack of culture" and a "dissociation of sensibility." Eliot responds to the crisis of the subject under monopoly capitalism by making his own bid for cultural hegemony with a peculiarly monopolistic concept of tradition that covertly recuperates the autonomy of the subject.

Eliot's critical discourse thus functions as an ideology, an imaginary compensation for a real historical situation, and since it performs this function by valorizing the individual, like romanticism, its ideological standpoint can be seen as a conservative alignment with the very class whose "triumph, in intellectual matters," it was intended to challenge.

This is evident when Eliot observes that the psychological degradations of the capitalist mode of production ironically cause a social leveling for the dominant class; for although critical of the bourgeoisie's crucial role in the deplorable "social evolution," he seems to sympathize with the anxiety provoked by its *déclassement*: "The Middle Class finds itself ... more and more approaching identity with what used to be called the Lower Class. . . . In other words, there will soon be only one class, and the second Flood is here" (*D* 70, p. 451).[32] Eliot's wish to prevent the loss of class difference—to maintain, in effect, the social status of the bourgeoisie—also appears in his concern that individualistic values are on the wane: he laments the "complexity of causes, which seems to make the English poet take refuge in just those sentiments, images, and thoughts which render a man least distinguishable from the mob, the respectable mob, the decent middle-class mob"; and there are approving but vague references, first to "the independent man, the free man, all the individuals who do not conform to a world of mass-production" (*D* 70, p. 451), and then later to "a truly independent way of looking at things, a point of view which cannot be sorted under any known religious or political title" (*D* 72, p. 511). Eliot's social commentary, it seems, takes the bourgeoisie to task for failing to measure up to its own ideology of individualism; and, in this light, it is his critical discourse that becomes the guardian of bourgeois ideology by staging a rehabilitation of the autonomous subject.

Eliot's reliance on a transindividual and authoritarian concept of tradition to compensate for the psychic dispersal under monopoly capitalism may appear to contradict the ideology of individualism, but in fact this antinomy is typical of bourgeois discourse. In liberal political theory, as Nicos Poulantzas has pointed out, the free and equal individuals constituted by bourgeois ideology

> do not seem able in one and the same theoretical movement to be unified and attain their social existence except by means of gaining political existence in the state. The result is that the private individual's freedom suddenly appears to vanish before the authority of the state which embodies the general will. . . . Rousseau's characteristic position should be noted: "Man must be as independent as possible from other men and as dependent as possible on the state." It is even clearer in the classic example of the physiocrats, fierce partisans of *laissez-faire* in the economic and equally fierce partisans of political authoritarianism: they called for the absolute monarch to embody the general will and interest.[33]

Just as liberal political theory asserts that private agents must accept the authority of the state in order to maintain their freedom, Eliot's critical theory asserts that individual poets must surrender their selves to the authority of the literary tradition in order to achieve self-mastery ("There is accordingly something outside of the artist to which he owes allegiance, a devotion to which he must surrender and sacrifice himself in order to earn and to obtain his unique position" ["The Function of Criticism," p. 13]). Both discourses act as theoretical supports for the reproduction of capitalism by setting up free subjects and uniting them in a transindividual institution that is said to represent the "general will of the people" or the "ideal order" of the "existing monuments," and that thus conceals the socio-economic conditions under which the institution exists. In liberal political theory, the capitalist state is relatively autonomous from economic relations, and it is because of this theoretical division of politics from economics that the state is assumed to be representative of the general interest, not merely that of the economically dominant classes: "This state presents itself as the strictly political, public *unity* of the particular, private, economic antagonisms of the ensemble of 'society'. . . . economic antagonisms which the state claims to have the function of surmounting by unifying [private] agents within a 'popular-national' body" (Poulantzas, p. 276). In Eliot's critical theory, there is a similar mystification: the tradition presents itself as a strictly literary, ideal unity of individual authors and texts ("The mind of Europe . . . does not superannuate either Shakespeare, or Homer, or the rock drawing of the Magdalenian draughtsmen" ["Tradition and the Individual Talent," p. 6]); yet this notion of the autonomous realm of Literature masks the often conscious revisionism performed by modern poets and critics like Eliot in response to the social dislocations produced by such economic developments as monopoly capitalism. As Robert Weimann has observed, "It was only by ignoring the actual needs and modes of reception as a process of consciousness in history that Eliot could define the quality of the individual talent as formal and impersonal."[34]

Eliot's critical theory encourages the same historical amnesia we have seen in other bourgeois discourses, including romanticism, and thereby continues the specialization of writing, the division between "culture" and "society," that began to occur early in the nineteenth century. When Eliot's theory is later assimilated by the New Critics and the *Scrutiny* group and institutionalized in academic literary study, textual production and criticism come to be viewed predominantly as ac-

tivities performed by the transcendental subjects of bourgeois individualism, untouched by the specific historical determinations that
occasionally come under examination even in Eliot's critical practice.[35]
Eliot's bid for cultural hegemony was highly successful, and modern
critical discourse fulfills and sustains the utopian function of the romantic valorization of the individual by announcing the appearance of
a new class of intellectuals whose self-avowed autonomy permits them
to criticize the cultural degeneration of the middle and lower classes
and to preserve the absolute values of the literary tradition. As with the
romantic movement, however, because this discourse is so resolutely
individualistic, success is achieved at the cost of reproducing bourgeois
ideology and hence contributing to the hegemony of the class that Eliot initially considered responsible for the most undesirable social
developments.

III

The foregoing analyses demonstrate that articulating the concept of
subjectivity assumed in a body of criticism is a productive method of
performing an ideological critique: the individual can be considered a
fundamental determinant of critical discourse since the romantic movement—a theoretical assumption which ruptures the logic of the critical
texts it makes possible, links them with the dominant, bourgeois ideology during two periods of decisive social change, and includes
among its concrete effects the reproduction of capitalist social formations. Hence it would be naive to presuppose that the knowledge this
discourse gives us can be assigned a truth value simply on the basis of
its objectivity or adequacy to the essential truth of a literary text. As an
intellectual operation programmed by the theoretical assumptions and
ideological tendencies of a specific historical conjuncture, criticism
stands in a peculiarly active relation to the real object, overlaying its
resistant but malleable materiality with a distinctive set of determinations. These determinations show that when any critical discourse
processes a text, it is simultaneously offering an ideological solution to
real social problems and expressing utopian aspirations for social life.
Since these points apply to my own discourse as well, it is now time to
reflect in greater detail on the assumptions and social forces that have
shaped it.

The best entry into this self-examination may well be what some
period specialists are likely to find a conspicuous absence: my ideolog-

ical critiques of romantic and modern criticism have deliberately omitted any consideration of the specifically political theories put forth by
both Coleridge and Eliot later in their careers. The lateness of their
forays into political discourse is certainly an important ground for their
exclusion here: both speculated on the ideal role to be played in government by religious and cultural institutions decades after they had
formulated their critical theories and produced their influential works
of practical criticism. This is to say not that their political writing has
no connection to their literary criticism, but rather that it is a later
development which, given their advocacy of rigid class hierarchies and
authoritarian social institutions, constitutes a deepening of their initial
conservatism and consequently a transformation of the bourgeois ideology signified by their critical discourse.

But this distinction between kinds of discourse already suggests
another, methodological reason for omitting this political material from
the present context: my discussion takes as its point of departure Althusser's theory of the social formation as a complex ensemble of social
practices which are mutually determining, but relatively autonomous,
and therefore develop unevenly. In capitalist social formations, the increasing specialization of discourse increases the autonomy of these
practices, so that, as we have seen, intellectual "disciplines" are established and "literature" is separated from "politics" and "economics." In
this sense, the effort of both Coleridge and Eliot to make literary criticism a highly specialized activity has partly dictated the approaches
that will be taken here to their own criticism. The uneven development
of social practices means that any ideological critique of romantic and
modern critical discourse must respect their specificity by distinguishing between political commentary and literary criticism while elucidating assumptions they may share with other discourses. The discursive
specificity drives the analysis to the level of implicit assumption, neces-
sitating the use of symptomatic reading, because there are not likely to
be many explicitly stated common themes between these specialized
discourses: Eliot's political theory, by developing key Coleridgean ideas
like the cultural elite or "clerisy," has a closer thematic relationship to
Coleridge's apology for the status quo, *On the Constitution of the Church
and State,* than to the *Biographia Literaria.*

With Althusser's theory of the social formation comes a more crucial theoretical assumption in my discourse: the determinate subject.
This basic tenet of materialist social theory is an assumption which not
only departs radically from the bourgeois individualism of romantic

and modern critical discourse, from the individualistic notions of un-constrained intentionality, organic unity, and illusionistic response, but also gives rise to the method of symptomatic reading with which that discourse has been processed here: the analysis of textual discontinu-ities as ideological contradictions which have a historical significance beyond, and perhaps even in opposition to, authorial intention. As with romantic and modern criticism, moreover, the symptomatic read-ing can be historically situated in the development of capitalism, so that the concept of the determinate subject, like its transcendental counterpart, can be understood as both an effect of, and a response to, a contemporary crisis of subjectivity: the decentering and fragmenta-tion of consciousness precipitated by what has been called consumer or late capitalism.

A distinctive feature of this post–World War II phase of the capi-talist mode of production is the enormous and unprecedented extent to which each step in the productive process is industrialized. As Er-nest Mandel has argued, "This new period was characterized, among other things, by the fact that alongside machine-made industrial con-sumer goods (as from the early 19th century) and machine-made ma-chines (as from the mid-19th century), we now find machine-produced raw materials and foodstuffs. *Late capitalism, far from representing a 'post-industrial society,' thus appears as the period in which all branches of the economy are fully industrialized for the first time;* to which one could further add the increasing mechanization of the sphere of circulation (with the exception of pure repair services) and the increasing mecha-nization of the superstructure."[36] The industrialization of circulation (the cycle of commodity production and exchange) and of other social practices and institutions, especially those engaged in cultural produc-tion ("the superstructure"), has meant an influx of capital into increas-ingly sophisticated communications technology which is most evident in the expansion of the advertising and entertainment industries. As a result of this advanced stage of technological development, the mysti-fying process of commodification characteristic of capitalism—the "commodity fetishism" whereby the social relations that lie behind products and services are masked by the commodity form, by exchange value—can penetrate more deeply into the consciousness of social agents, giving them a new vulnerability to the ideologies of individu-alism in the media (e.g., the "self-made man" stereotype in *Rocky* (1976) or *Dallas*; the "Marlboro Man" advertisements; the myths of "success" and "self-improvement").[37] It is the technological aspect of consumer capitalism that seems to be most important in the emergence of a distinctively postmodern culture where subjectivity is decentered and fragmented.

The nature of this postmodern subject becomes clear when contrasted with the romantic and modern crises of subjectivity, since in all three cases mass communications plays an instrumental role. For Wordsworth, the industrialized "uniformity of . . . occupations" numbed the "organic sensibility" and caused "a craving for extraordinary incident which the rapid communication of intelligence hourly gratifies," wherein the nascent communications industry was represented as a psychological relief from, and therefore as a palliative which maintained, the mode of production. For Eliot, a more developed rationalization and routinization of the economy provoked an equally numbing "dissociation of sensibility" which manifested itself in "finding safety in Regular Hours, Regular Wages, Regular Pensions, and Regular Ideas" and was "facilitated by the newspapers, the reviewing of books, the journalistic life," so that the media was seen as actively constituting social agents as class subjects. For Jean Baudrillard, however, the mechanization of the media has advanced so far in the post–World War II period that they no longer operate as an instrument of socialization, but rather produce an "implosion of the social in the masses" by transforming communication and, indeed, the very process of signification:

> There are no longer media in the literal sense of the term (I am talking above all about the electronic mass media)—that is to say, a power mediating between one reality and another, between one state of the real and another—neither in content nor in form. Strictly speaking, this is what implosion signifies: the absorption of one pole into another, the short-circuit between poles of every differential system of meaning, the effacement of terms and of distinct oppositions, and thus that of the medium and the real.[38]

Baudrillard's examples of this implosion are taken from such media as film and television, where he finds "only a perpetual game of question/answer, an instrument of perpetual polling," and consequently a collapse of the communicative poles of sender/receiver, interviewer/respondent, pollster/polled, resulting in "a total circularity of signalling" and an implosion of meaning: the receiver has always already absorbed the code of the sender, because "the answer is called forth by the question, it is designated in advance," or "the ones questioned always pretend to be as the question imagines and solicits them to be."[39] Even though the intention of media discourses like advertising and public relations is plainly opinion manipulation, they produce an effect of implosion on consciousness which is actually much more extreme than such an account of their intention would imply: what distinguishes this effect from, say, the mind control suggested in Eliot's attitude toward journalism is that it is "an absolute manipulation—not passivity, but the *non-distinction of active and passive*" (*S*, pp. 57–58). Thus, not only is the subject dislocated as the transcendental origin of meaning, knowledge, and action because its cognition is infiltrated by codes, but reality becomes indistinguishable from, and recedes beyond, the coded representations or simulacra reproduced by both the media and the viewer.

Max Horkheimer and Theodor Adorno locate a similar decentering of the subject in the entertainment industry. The Hollywood film, they note, operates through an "identification with a manufactured need," creating and depending on "worn grooves of association" in the viewer, and this too coincides with a deferral and confusion of reality: "Because of his ubiquity, the film star with whom one is meant to fall in love is from the outset a copy of himself."[40] Under the mechanization of mass communications in consumer capitalism, the "ever-increasing sameness" and "staleness" which Coleridge and Eliot had lamented in nineteenth- and early twentieth-century culture give way to an erosion of stylistic distinction and semantic difference ("Every detail is so firmly stamped with sameness that nothing can appear which is not marked at birth, or does not meet with approval at first sight" [*CI*, p. 128]), whereby reference and representation are neutralized, meaning and history drained away, only to be replaced by simulacra that engender a fascination with the medium, the model, the code. Baudrillard points out, following Marshall McLuhan, that this fascination derives to a large extent from the very nature of the electronic media—"the very style of montage, of découpage, of interpellation, solicitation, summation"—with their tendency to shatter the subject's experience into discrete moments of intensity, a phenomenon most noticeable in film: "The images fragment perception into successive sequences, into stimuli toward which there can be only instantaneous response" (*S*, pp. 123, 119). Film montage interpellates the subject by eliciting a series of instantaneous responses in which the ideological codes of the images are naturalized, made invisible, routine, unconscious. The fragmentation of the subject by such media isolates and intensifies the present, leading to a disjointed experience of time and a failure to imagine historical development as more than a serial arrangement of hypnotic simulacra. In Jameson's exploration of postmodern subjectivity, this breakdown of temporality has immediate consequences for cultural production: "If, indeed, the subject has lost its capacity actively to extend its pro-tensions and re-tensions across the temporal manifold, and to organize its past and future into coherent experience, it becomes difficult enough to see how the cultural productions of such a subject could result in anything but 'heaps of fragments' and in a practice of the randomly heterogeneous and fragmentary and the aleatory."[41]

At this point, the relationship between postmodern culture and the symptomatic reading can be more easily perceived. The stress on textual discontinuity which characterizes this reading indicates that the Althusserian assumptions on which it rests, particularly the concepts of social formation and determinate subjectivity, are partly determined by the postmodern experience of the subject—both as effects and as calculated responses which transform that experience. The postmodern subject, decentered and fragmented by diverse media simulation, emerges in the practice of symptomatic reading as a splintering of author and text into heterogeneous cultural materials mediated by ideology and as an insistence that these ideological materials always intervene between text and reality, that paradoxically the text can be related to history only through difference and deferral, only through its relationship to ideology. Even if determined by the postmodern subject, the symptomatic reading aims to solve the breakdown of temporality which is part of its experience; based on the thoroughgoing historicization required by dialectical materialism, this kind of reading not only locates discontinuities in the text, but analyzes them as the effect of social conflict in a specific historical conjuncture. Hence, the symptomatic reading, by assuming the socially determinate subject, is also a calculated response to the contemporary crisis of subjectivity: it eschews the reactionary solution to this crisis which would be involved in any valorization of individualism that eclipses the social determinations of consciousness (just as my representation of the cultural consequences of consumer capitalism avoids any individualistic categories like the "organic" or "unified sensibility"), and it thereby constitutes a revolutionary strategy that drives a wedge through interpretive cruxes and forges social contexts in which to understand them.

To some critics, this may well appear "subjective" and, when older texts are under discussion, "anachronistic." Both charges, however, do not stand up to examination: on the one hand, they presuppose an essentialist notion of criticism which privileges the individual and assumes an unmediated access to the unified meaning of the text; on the other, they ignore the fundamentally historicist character of Marxist discourse. The symptomatic reading, as I have tried to show in my treatment of Coleridge and Eliot, can take into account the discursive and historical specificity of the text, yet without disregarding the fact that its own critical activity is a transformative appropriation which reflects the historical conjuncture of the critic. This reading "should not lose sight of the fact that the problematic underlying the analysis of the text is *external* to it," as Chantal Mouffe points out, "and that the unity of the text is often established along quite separate lines from the problematic itself."[42] Thus, in order to struggle against individualistic critical operations and the crisis of historicity in contemporary culture, the symptomatic reading insists on the irreducible historical difference of the text while admitting that its representation of the text's historical situation is guided by the capitalist formation where the reading occurs.

This intervention against reactionary social practices also encompasses such other cultural manifestations of consumer capitalism as the new theories of textuality in poststructuralist discourse. Like the symptomatic reading, these theories reflect the decentering and fragmentation of the subject through media simulation. There is in fact a close resemblance in the textual operations of the symptomatic reading and the several varieties of deconstruction on the current critical scene, such as Derrida's "grammatology," Roland Barthes's opposition of "writerly" to "readerly" texts, or Deleuze and Guattari's "schizoanalysis": what they all have in common is a notion of the text as a fragmented simulacrum, in which the process of signification is skewed, meaning destabilized, reference and representation highly mediated by the heterogeneous multiplicity of materials the text assimilates and the processes by which it transforms them. Like the symptomatic reading, moreover, these deconstructive operations reveal their grounding in the contemporary crisis of subjectivity through their own critique of the transcendental subject. Barthes's programmatic formulation of "the death of the author," for example, shows how the poststructuralist theory of textuality displaces authorial intentionality: "A text is not a line of words releasing a single 'theological' meaning (the 'message' of the Author-God), but a multi-dimensional space in which a variety of writings, none of them original, blend and clash. The text is a tissue of quotations drawn from the innumerable centers of culture."[43]

Much poststructuralist discourse differs from the symptomatic reading, however, by refusing any rigorous historicization of the texts on which it works or of its own textual operations. The "death of the author" assumes a concept of the determinate subject, but the determinations are solely textual, not social; textual discontinuities point to "the innumerable centers of culture," to intertextuality, unlimited semiosis, not to discursive forms seen as social practices. As Weimann has trenchantly put it, the poststructuralist theory of textuality, suffering the crisis of historicity in postmodern culture, discourages attempts to raise the question, "Does 'the absence of the subject' (in the form of a sovereign creator) allow for some highly mediated and multideterminant individual form of historical *activity* through which social conglomerates, cultural institutions, ideological apparatuses, etc., can assert themselves as historical *Subjekt?*"[44] In some of its most extreme forms, poststructuralist textuality has engendered a formalist fetishization of the text, and the textual operations performed by the reader, as "*free play,* . . . a field of infinite substitutions in the closure of a finite ensemble" (Derrida), or the "bliss" of "the text that imposes a state of loss, . . . that discomforts" (Barthes), or "the process of desiring-production" where "the value of art is no longer measured except in terms of the decoded and deterritorialized flows [of desire] that it causes to circulate beneath a signifier reduced to silence, beneath the conditions of identity of the parameters, across a structure reduced to impotence" (Deleuze and Guattari).[45] It is here that a reactionary individualism reminiscent of the romantic capitulation to market capitalism seems to creep back into poststructuralist discourse, since the valorization of transgression, whether located in the discontinuous materials of the text itself or in the transformative operations of criticism, can be understood as a recuperation of subjective freedom, a personal liberation from the ideological codes that territorialize desire, a self-indulgence. This is especially apparent in the American appropriation of Derrida's writing, as Frank Lentricchia has suggested, for it can be questioned whether "the American Derridean's desire to experience the joy of freedom [is] any more than a reflection (and tacit acknowledgment), as it was for Lionel Johnson, Ernest Dowson, and the younger Yeats, of a situation in which that kind of freedom is denied all around, a situation in which oppression, not freedom, characterizes social existence."[46]

It is in order to combat the reactionary tendencies of poststructuralist discourse, then, that the symptomatic reading must be developed and implemented: it too acknowledges the power of language and textuality to derail authorial intention, dispersing subjectivity across a range of simulacra, but it situates the cultural production of the decentered, fragmented subject in history, admitting that "history" is here construed in the Marxist terms of modes of production and social conflict and always reconstructed vis-à-vis the specific historical conjuncture of the historian. Because of their shared historical ground and shared assumptions, it remains important for the political project of Marxist discourse to engage poststructuralism, to profit from its theoretical breakthroughs and rigor, but not without failing to note that its questionable response to the contemporary crisis of subjectivity is ultimately a capitulation to consumer capitalism. This engagement can have a strategic function, as Jameson indicates:

> We may admit the descriptive value of the poststructuralist critique of the "subject" without necessarily endorsing the schizophrenic ideal it has tended to project. For Marxism, indeed, only the emergence of a post-individualistic social world, only the reinvention of the collective and the associative, can concretely achieve the "decentering" of the individual called for by such diagnoses; only a new and original form of collective social life can overcome the isolation and monadic autonomy of the older bourgeois subjects in such a way that individual consciousness can be lived—and not merely theorized—as an "effect of structure" (Lacan).[47]

Until this new consciousness can be lived in a new form of collective social organization, one of the theoretical elaborations most supportive of the invention of this collectivity is a historicization of cultural practices, an opening up of cultural production and reception to an awareness of historical determinations, of those collective forces which shape the lives of concrete individuals and which require the force of collective consciousness to be transformed. It is this historical awareness that the symptomatic reading seeks to promote against individualistic forms of historical reconstruction and the ahistorical tendencies of poststructuralism—yet to do this it relies on poststructuralist theories of textuality and subjectivity which reflect the breakdown of temporality in postmodern culture, the schizophrenic experience where the "present of the world or material signifier comes before the subject with height-ened intensity, bearing a mysterious charge of affect," and where "the past as 'referent' finds itself gradually bracketed, and then effaced altogether, leaving us with nothing but texts."[48] The symptomatic reading, in its deconstructive textual operations, in its pursuit of formal discontinuity and dense intertextuality, seeks to mobilize the schizophrenic ideal of poststructuralist discourse against the privatization which this discourse seems ever ready to undergo in its appropriation by contemporary American criticism. Symptomatic reading is a Marxist poststructuralism which turns deconstructive textual strategies into ideological critique, processing the linguistic and cultural heterogeneity of the text as ideological contradiction, transforming the privatized bliss of textual dissemination into utopian imagining, a free play over different possibilities for social life, but an ideological play that is not free of the postmodern situation.

Chapter Two

The Marginalization of
Philip Massinger's Plays

The difficulty lies not in understanding that the Greek arts and epic are bound up
with certain forms of social development. The difficulty is that they still afford us
artistic pleasure and that in a certain respect they count as a norm and as an
unattainable model.

Marx, *Grundrisse*

IT MAY SEEM strange that the criticism of Philip Massinger's plays
should be recommended for the sort of historically grounded study
of textual reception and canon formation suggested in Marx's statement. Massinger is hardly regarded as a first-rate playwright, he has
failed even to become a "norm" of what to avoid in writing plays, and
the shadow of neglect has long obscured his work for all but the most
diligent of scholarly specialists. Yet the very strangeness of proposing a
materialist inquiry into Massinger's reception (and the readiness with
which we may sense this strangeness) can also serve to defamiliarize
the reigning view of his texts, to make visible the immense and unnoticed power which this view has exerted over us, and to expose and
question the determinations and effects of its dominance.

For nearly two centuries, Massinger's plays have elicited a succession of devastating negative judgments that have assigned him a marginal position in the canon of English Renaissance drama. During the
nineteenth century, invidious comparisons with canonized authors like
Shakespeare and Jonson quickly became a routine feature of commentary on Massinger. And whereas plays by such "minor" authors as Mar-
lowe, Kyd, Tourneur, Webster, and Ford have held an intense fascination for modern readers, provoking comment and allusion in diverse

kinds of writing, Massinger has occasionally been omitted from "authoritative" surveys of Renaissance drama. Nor have sympathetic appraisals done much to improve his reputation: as his most recent editors lament, the terms of the praise have been so ineffectual, so unwilling to confront the opposing arguments, that he "has even suffered a little from his advocates."[1] Today Massinger continues to appear on reading lists in university courses and is readily available in an impressive variety of well-annotated editions, but rarely are his plays examined in dissertations, articles, or books, and almost never are they revived in student or professional productions. After reviewing these points we might easily conclude—without much exaggeration, I think—that Massinger is virtually unread in academic institutions and unknown to the theatergoing public.

This tale of Massinger's apocryphal status is not intended to set the stage for an extravagant attempt to elevate his reputation. Indeed, it would be difficult to argue that his treatment has been uniquely "unjust" since many other writers have suffered a similar fate; among Massinger's contemporaries, Richard Brome comes most readily to my mind.[2] Moreover, to suppose that Massinger's "essential" value has been somehow unrecognized or misunderstood ignores the problem that a body of writing can easily support conflicting readings and estimations, and that different critical opinions are based not merely on different kinds of textual evidence, but also on the different theoretical assumptions which process that evidence. Assertions of essential value, in other words, elide that transformative critical operation by which a text is produced in a determinate form, and thus they not only fail to account for the opposing judgment in an incisive way, but tend to lack an awareness of their own status as acts of appropriation. What makes Massinger worthy of special attention is the specific determinations that have so decisively influenced the understanding and evaluation of his work: the critics who have played an important part in his neglect are those "major" writers who have also had a considerable impact on the romantic and modern critical tradition—Coleridge and Eliot. This suggests that any study of Massinger's poor reception must take into account the ideology of Anglo-American criticism, both the social conditions which it resolves in an imaginary way and the theoretical assumptions that inform that solution. More specifically, the history of Massinger's marginalization is simultaneously the history of the dominance in criticism of the transcendental subject. Hence, Massinger's plays can be viewed as one, specifically literary casualty of those crises of the subject that were precipitated by the development of capitalism and in turn led to the valorization of bourgeois individualism in romantic and modern critical discourse.

In arguing this view of Massinger's predicament, I will emphasize interpretive cruxes that the bourgeois reading discovers in his texts. My discussion will concentrate on how the textual features of Massinger's plays prove recalcitrant to the reading strategies and normative principles of an individualistic discourse and are therefore processed as defects deserving of blame. Although the specific terms of the analyses and evaluations do vary somewhat from critic to critic, the reception of Massinger since the nineteenth century has been consistently less than hospitable because his texts seem to resist any reading which privileges a concept of the subject as a free, unified consciousness. Having recognized that the individual is a romantic legacy that has banished Massinger from the pantheon of Renaissance playwrights, we can try to shake off the tyranny of this ideology by beginning a different reading of Massinger's plays—one, however, that seeks not to install them in a new canon constructed on the basis of different theoretical assumptions, but to be more aware of those assumptions and their implication in larger, social issues. "A politically motivated criticism," as Tony Bennett has observed, "must aim to mobilize the text, to re-determine its connections with history by severing its existing articulations and forging new ones, actively politicizing the process of reading."[3] Treated in this strategic manner, Massinger's plays become a site of conflict, where what is in question is not just the dominance of a specific critical discourse and the readings it enables, but the ideological determinations of that discourse, its status as a cultural intervention into the competing class interests of its social conjuncture. The mobilization to be initiated here, then, aims to combat the bourgeois ideology of individualism with a symptomatic reading of Massinger's plays which speaks to the crisis of subjectivity under consumer capitalism by taking as its key theoretical assumption the socially determinate subject.

I

Coleridge's reading, rooted in his expressive theory of poetry, moves easily from the evidence of the texts to Massinger the author. For Coleridge, Massinger did not sufficiently identify with his literary materials. He exemplifies the "Vein of *satire* on the *times*,"[4] so he often reveals a critical distance from his characters instead of the desired sympathy that Coleridge approves in Shakespeare: "Massinger, and all, indeed, but Shakespeare, take a dislike to their own characters, and spite themselves upon them by making them talk like *fools* or *monsters*" (*MC*, p. 95). In Coleridge's description of this defect, it seems clear that Massinger is found guilty of ventriloquism:

> Massinger's Sylli [in *The Maid of Honour*] comes forward to declare him-
> self a fool, *ad arbitrium auctoris,* and so the diction always needs the
> *subintelligitur* (the man looks *as if he thought* so and so) expressed in the
> language of the satirist, not of the man himself. . . . The author mixed
> his own feelings and judgments concerning him, but the man himself,
> till mad, fights up against them and betrays, by the attempt to modify
> them, an activity and copiousness of thought, image, and expression
> which belongs not to Sylli, but to a man of wit making himself merry
> with his own character. (*MC*, pp. 94–95)

Massinger's satiric impulse prevents him from surrendering himself in the creative process, from participating in his text unconsciously and therefore imperceptibly; he deliberately "mixed his own feelings and judgments" in Sylli's characterization, showing his hand in the character's verbal excesses and excluding the development of a unique identity. Thus, Massinger's characters do not have the psychological consistency of unified subjects: they tend to be inadequately motivated ("utter want of preparation, as in Camiola, the Maid of Honour" [*MC*, p. 95]) and given to sudden extremeties of behavior ("unnaturally irrational passions . . . as in Mathias in *The Picture*" [*MC*, p. 96]). It is evident that Massinger's ventriloquism violates Coleridge's evaluative criterion of organic unity: "The *dramatis personae* were all planned *each by itself;* but in Shakespeare the play is a *syngenesia*—each [character] has indeed a life of its own and is an *individuum* of itself, but yet an organ to the whole—as the heart, etc., of *that* particular whole" (*MC*, p. 95). Massinger's characterization is an example of what Coleridge elsewhere calls "mechanic form," as "when on any given material we impress a predetermined form, not necessarily arising out of the properties of the material" (*SC*, 1: 198).

This lack of organic unity, apparent in other textual features as well, has an adverse effect on responses to Massinger's plays: instead of inviting an unconscious participation, they provoke an unpleasurable detachment. The incoherent development of the characters does not create a fixed position of identification ("From the want of character, of a guiding point, in Massinger's characters, you never know what they are about" [*MC*, p. 95]), and the dramatic structure is occasionally alien-

ating because "the comic scenes in Massinger not only do not harmonize with the tragic, not only interrupt the feeling, but degrade the
characters that are to form any part in the action of the piece so as to
render them unfit for any *tragic interest*" (*MC*, p. 96). The disunity leads
not to the willing suspension of disbelief, but to a sense of improbabil-
ity that shatters any dramatic illusion: Massinger is faulted for the "im-
propriety, indecorum of demeanour in his favourite characters, as in
Bertoldo [in *The Maid of Honour*], who is a *swaggerer*, who talks to his
sovereign what no sovereign could endure, and to gentlemen what no
gentleman would answer but by pulling his nose" (*MC*, p. 94).[5]

Coleridge concludes that Massinger "is not a poet of high imagination" (*MC*, p. 96), and it is not difficult to see that the individual underlies this verdict. In Coleridge's expressive theory, it is chiefly "a more
than ordinary activity of the mind in respect of the fancy and imagination" that characterizes the transcendental subjectivity of the poet
(*SC*, 1: 147); Massinger's satiric impulse, however, is the sign of a weakened imagination which at one point Coleridge considers the determinate effect of the playwright's social position: "the continued flings at
kings, courtiers, and all the favorites of fortune" make Massinger seem
"like one who had enough of intellect to see the injustice of his own
inferiority in the share of the good things of life, but not genius enough
to rise above it and forget himself—envy demonstrated" (*MC*, p. 95).[6]
There is a paradox in Coleridge's social psychology that shows Massinger is censured because he cannot be described as a free, unified subject: his conscious control of the creative process (critical distance from,
as opposed to imaginative identification with, his text) is actually an
unconscious lack of self-control, a socially induced "envy" which made
him resort to satire. Coleridge sees Massinger as a candidate for the
ideal "aristocracy of the intellect," but one who finally cannot be admitted because his exclusion from another, social aristocracy in early
Stuart England caused the mentally debilitating dissatisfaction that
soured his writing; only a "genius" like Shakespeare can transcend the
influence of contemporary social developments and "forget himself" in
poetic composition. This reading of Massinger demonstrates that Coleridge's discourse is systematic, even if punctuated by logical discrepancies: the valorization of the individual in the expressive theory of
poetry entails that Coleridge's practical criticism will rely on Massinger's biography both to rewrite the disunity of his texts as the expression of a determinate subject and to judge them inferior to the organic
plays which Shakespeare freely crafted from his organized consciousness. The transcendental thinking of individualism has so shaped Cole-

ridge's discourse that the concept of the determinate subject emerges only to be repressed: on the one hand, the texts he finds defective are those that can be explained with reference to history, yet historical determinations, enlisted as a way to understand Massinger's plays, never manage to displace his imagination as the final horizon of Coleridge's reading.

Despite the predominantly negative tenor of Coleridge's comments, he includes a list of Massinger's "characteristic merits," most of which concern his language. Although on this occasion the discussion turns away from authorial psychology to focus on the verbal medium of the text, the change of emphasis is still governed by the privileged assumption of romantic discourse. Thus, Coleridge's pursuit of the unified subjects in Massinger's plays leads him to comment on the illusionistic effect of transparency by which subjectivity is constituted in language: Massinger's "rhythm and meter are incomparably good, and form the very model of dramatic versification" because they are "flexible and seeming to rise out of the passions" and because "the emphasis" and "the acceleration or retardation of the voice in the pauses" are "all which the mood or passion would have produced in the real Agent" (*CS*, p. 678). Coleridge's praise implies a view that the smoother or more varied the pattern of metrical stresses, the more conversational the verse, and the greater the illusionistic effect of transparency, of the character's presence. This anticipates Eliot's more general reflections on the textual medium and involves the same significant shift in assumptions that occurs in the modern critic: Coleridge assumes that transparency is an illusion ("seeming") produced by language ("rhythm and meter"), but then elides the materiality of that productive process by judging the effect valuable wholly because of its presumed approximation to reality ("the real Agent").

Although existing only as fragmentary lecture notes and marginalia,[7] Coleridge's reading of Massinger became the standard one during the nineteenth century, a development that attests not only to the immense authority he acquired as both theorist and critic, but also to the firm entrenchment of romantic critical discourse in the belletristic criticism of Victorian periodicals. For critics like Walter Bagehot and Leslie Stephen, as for their predecessors, the valorization of the transcendental subject functioned as a conservative ideological solution to the developing social contradictions of industrial capitalism, yet these contradictions had reached a degree of exacerbation unknown to the romantic critics: "the professionalization of knowledges, warring of ideological standpoints and rapid expansion of an unevenly educated reading public" forced the Victorian "man of letters" to assume a contradictory role, "at once source of sage-like authority and canny popularizer, member of a spiritual clerisy but plausible intellectual salesman," thus compensating for the social constraints on his critical activity by claiming for himself a cultural authority based on an individualistic autonomy of judgment, his privileged access to the eternal verities of "a general humanism."[8] The social constraints that delimited the belletristic critic's role and led to a more defensive adherence to individualism resulted in a further demotion for Massinger. This is apparent in Leslie Stephen's essay "Massinger," first published in the *Cornhill Magazine* in 1877.[9] True to his social function as informed popularizer, Stephen displays a familiarity with several previous estimates of the playwright, including the typically romantic censures of Charles Lamb and A. W. Ward.[10] But Stephen clearly aims to deepen Coleridge's comments, sometimes quoting the earlier critic and repeatedly echoing his words.

Stephen's reading, also rooted in the expressive theory of poetry, is much more psychologistic. Whereas Coleridge thought Massinger a "satirist," Stephen goes further along the same tack to discover "a moralizer by temperament" (p. 348), who is likewise diagnosed as the victim of a diminished imagination: "It is probably this comparative weakness of the higher imaginative faculty which makes Lamb speak of him rather disparagingly. He is too self-conscious and too anxious to enforce downright moral sentiments to satisfy a critic by whom spontaneous force and direct insight were rightly regarded as the highest poetic qualities" (p. 352). Massinger's "self-conscious" morality is an imaginative "weakness" that prevents him from identifying unconsciously with his texts. When Massinger creates a villainous character, he "cannot throw himself into the situation; and is anxious to dwell upon the obvious moral considerations" (p. 360). Stephen's discussion marks a definite descent in Massinger's reputation because he finds ventriloquism even in the extortioner Overreach of *A New Way to Pay Old Debts,* a role that had been a considerable theatrical success in the early nineteenth century, especially in Edmund Kean's version: "It is equally plain that here, too, Massinger fails to project himself fairly into his villain. His rants are singularly forcible, but they are clearly what other people would think about him, not what he would really think, still less what he would say, of himself" (p. 367).[11]

Stephen shows how Massinger's ventriloquist development of char-

acter "from the outside" results in inconsistencies that violate the criterion of organic form: "His plays are apt to be a continuous declama-
tion, cut up into fragments, and assigned to the different actors. . . .
The villains will have to denounce themselves, and will be ready to
undergo conversion at a moment's notice, in order to spout openly on
behalf of virtue as vigorously as they have spouted in transparent disguise on behalf of vice" (p. 368). Like Coleridge, Stephen is concerned
with the impact of Massinger's disunified texts on the reader, noting
that they are apt to evoke an alienating, not a sympathetic, experience.
Massinger's "want of vital force" (p. 380), the atrophy that his moralizing temperament inflicts on his imagination, does not encourage the
illusionism valued so highly in romantic discourse, but rather produces
distancing implausibilities: "Massinger's heroes and heroines . . . mor-
alize rather too freely. We do not want sermons, but sympathy, when
we are in our deepest grief; and we do not feel that any one feels very
keenly who can take his sorrows for a text, and preach in his agony
upon the vanity of human wishes or the excellence of resignation" (pp.
379–80).

The romantic valorization of the individual leads Stephen, like
Coleridge, to explain his notion of Massinger's inferiority by characterizing him as a determinate subject, one whose impoverishment of
imagination is the psychological effect of social developments under
the early Stuart kings; Stephen's contribution is to elaborate on the
earlier critic's allusions to Massinger's social status by adding a fuller
discussion of his biography. Stephen asserts that although in prerevolutionary England "the drama reflected in the main the sentiments of
an aristocratic class alarmed by the growing vigor of the Puritanical
citizens" (p. 342), it registered different responses depending on the
personality of the playwright in question: "The difference between
Fletcher and Massinger, who were occasional collaborators and apparently close friends . . . was probably due to difference of temperament
as much as the character of Massinger's family connection" (p. 343).
The mention of Massinger's "family connection" seems to refer to S. R.
Gardiner's argument that Massinger's plays are political allegories
which comment on current issues, domestic and foreign, from the
standpoint of the Earls of Pembroke, formerly his father's employers
and later his patrons.[12] But Stephen doubts this reading and prefers to
see Massinger's "stage" as the representative of a more general decline
of feudal values filtered through his melancholic temperament: "Its
chivalry is a survival from a past epoch, not a spontaneous outgrowth
of the most vital elements of contemporary development, [and its] sit-

uations . . . are wanting in the imaginative unity of the great plays, which show that a true poet has been profoundly moved by some profound thought embodied in a typical situation" (pp. 354–56). Not only does Stephen's valorization of the individual evaporate the linguistic materiality of the text, transforming it into a transparent representation of the playwright's psychology, but there is a characteristic inconsistency in his use of history: although he insists on the importance of Massinger's class position to understand his plays, the psychologistic explanation is ultimately given priority over historical determinants, the "typical situation" over the cultural "survival."

Because the "vital elements of contemporary development" are what Stephen defines as the emergent mercantile and manufacturing interests ("the Puritanical citizens" [p. 342]), the individualistic assumptions in his negative judgment of Massinger reflect an allegiance to liberal political theory as well as an assimilation of romantic critical discourse. Stephen's history of Renaissance drama rests on the Whig version of English history, developed by such historians as Macaulay and Gardiner, in which the revolution is seen as the "Puritan" struggle for religious and constitutional liberty against a tyrannical king who fostered a decadent aristocratic culture.[13] Hence, Stephen's opinion that "the stage, which represented the tone of aristocratic society, rightfully perished with the order which it flattered" because it "was one of those evil growths which are fostered by deeply-seated social corruption, and are killed off by the breath of a purer air" (p. 337). Stephen's conclusion appropriately alludes to Milton: "the old strenuous spirit" which is said to be missing in Massinger's plays, the "spirit" of human freedom and unity, may have "gone elsewhere—perhaps to excite a Puritan imagination" (p. 381). Massinger is implicitly convicted on two counts, one aesthetic (his texts lack organicity because of his weak "spirit"), the other political (he's a reactionary royalist), and both are determined by bourgeois ideology. The learned and tendentious qualities of Stephen's essay reflect the Victorian man of letters' social function in the face of a fragmented, ideologically various public, what Eagleton has described as "a didactic, covertly propagandist posture towards his readership, processing knowledge in the act of providing it."[14] Stephen's reading of Massinger is the work of a bourgeois cultural critic who defensively responds to a social conjuncture in which bourgeois ideology is threatened by reaffirming it in the marginalization of a reactionary playwright.

By the end of the nineteenth century, bourgeois critical discourse had retreated from this threatened situation, becoming the dominant approach to literature in the academy and the literary reviews of the modern movement. Both kinds of critical activity sought refuge from the commodified culture of the mass readership in an intense specialization, whether the technical research of professional scholarship or the theoretical speculations of an avant-garde aesthetic program, whereby they compensated for the decisive diminution of their social function by clinging all the more resolutely to individualistic assumptions (e.g., in the development of literature as a "transcendental object of enquiry" or in the defense of the "strong personality").[15] The romantic reading of Massinger was at this point given institutional authority, and his plays assigned the marginal position in the canon of Renaissance drama which they continue to occupy. Edmund Gosse's chapter in his "University Extension Manual," *The Jacobean Poets* (1894), recapitulates terms from the standard estimation: "Variety of interest is secured, but sometimes at the sacrifice of evolution, and the personages act, not as human creatures must, but as theatrical puppets should."[16] Eliot's essay "Philip Massinger" (1920), which as a "little magazine" contribution is as specialized as Gosse's academic "manual," initiates a new episode in the history of Massinger's reception, particularly since his approach rests on a modern transformation of romantic critical discourse. Eliot makes the modern move of calling attention to the conventionality of Massinger's texts, their relationship to the literary tradition, but his reading turns out to be ultraromantic: it eclipses history entirely by explaining Massinger's plays solely with reference to authorial psychology.

Although occasioned by the publication of A. H. Cruickshank's unfavorable monograph on Massinger—the first devoted to the playwright—Eliot's essay is not properly a review but a critical statement which puts to work his current theoretical ruminations on tradition and the history of sensibility. Eliot accepts Cruickshank's "recognition" of Massinger's "inferiority" (p. 182), asserting that it is enough "to elucidate" Cruickshank's "most important judgment": "Massinger, in his grasp of stagecraft, his flexible meter, his desire in the sphere of ethics to exploit both vice and virtue, is typical of an age which had much culture, but which, without being exactly corrupt, lacked moral fiber."[17] Since Cruickshank's terms show his conformity to the nineteenth-century Massinger ("flexible meter," "lacked moral fiber"), it seems clear that by taking up those terms Eliot grounds his reading on a romantic valorization of the individual manifested in an esteem for transparent verse that reflects the poet's consciousness. Yet, as we saw in Eliot's theoretical essays, the individual can be realized only in tradition, in a historical sense, so he proceeds to open up Cruickshank's mention of "culture" by examining "Massinger's indebtedness" to earlier writers (p. 182). Eliot discusses "parallel quotations from Massinger and Shakespeare collocated by Mr. Cruickshank" and adds two of his own parallels between Massinger and Webster, concluding that Massinger's method of borrowing indicates a dissociated sensibility: with Massinger, "we end a period where the intellect was immediately at the tips of the senses. . . . The verse practiced by Massinger is a different verse from that of his predecessors; but it is not a development based on, or resulting from, a new way of feeling. On the contrary, it seems to lead us away from feeling altogether" (pp. 185–86). Eliot rewrites Cruickshank in terms of the dissociation theory: "if Massinger's age, 'without being exactly corrupt, lacks moral fiber,' Massinger's verse, without being exactly corrupt, suffers from cerebral anemia," a condition in which his "feeling . . . is simple and overlaid with received ideas" (p. 187). Eliot later defines the "received ideas" generally as "morals," demonstrating that the problem is Massinger's moralistic temperament: "What may be considered corrupt or decadent in the morals of Massinger is not an alteration or diminution in morals; it is simply the disappearance of all the personal and real emotions which this morality supported and into which it introduced a kind of order" (p. 189).

Eliot follows the romantic critics by attributing the disunity of Massinger's writing to his psychic dissociation:

> Mr. Cruickshank, Coleridge, and Leslie Stephen are pretty well agreed that Massinger is not master of characterization. . . . a character, to be living, must be conceived from some emotional unity. A character is not to be composed of scattered observations of human nature, but of parts which are felt together. Hence it is that although Massinger's failure to draw a moving character is no greater than his failure to make a whole play, and probably springs from the same defective sensitiveness, yet the failure in character is more conspicuous and more disastrous. A "living" character is not necessarily "true to life." It is a person whom we can see and hear, whether he be true or false to human nature as we know it. What the creator of character needs is not so much knowledge of motives as keen sensibility; the dramatist need not understand people; but he must be exceptionally aware of them. This awareness was not given to Massinger. (P. 188)

Eliot apparently restricts the creative process to the artist's unconscious when he gives priority to "keen sensibility" over consciously applied "knowledge." Yet the passage abruptly slides into the typical romantic paradox of the conscious unconscious when he asserts that the artist creates character from an "awareness" of "motives," however intuitive. Eliot assumes Coleridge's account of poetic composition as "the balancing and reconciling of opposite or discordant qualities" like "self-possession and judgment with enthusiasm and vehement feeling" (*SC*, 1:150) and thus censures Massinger because the playwright does not possess subjective freedom and coherence. The psychological inconsistency of his characters mirrors his lack of "sensitiveness," his inability to participate vicariously in their actions because of the disjunction between his "defective" emotions and his "received" morality. And so Massinger's texts do not sustain the dramatic illusion: in Massinger's case, it is specifically the morality that turns repulsive: "He inherits the traditions of conduct, female chastity, hymeneal sanctity, the fashion of honor, without either criticizing or informing them from his own experience. . . . As soon as the emotions disappear the morality which ordered it [*sic*] appears hideous. . . . When Massinger's ladies resist temptation they do not appear to undergo any important emotion; they merely know what is expected of them; they manifest themselves to us as lubricous prudes" (pp. 188–89). Because Massinger could not give organic form to the traditional morality, because he "could not vivify it" and "fit it into passionate, complete human characters," there is a loss of plausibility for the reader, and the values appear "absurd" and "ridiculous" (p. 189). Eliot treats Massinger's "morals" as textual materials, "traditions" and "conventions" which the playwright inherits; yet this sense of their materiality is subordinated to Eliot's insistence that the moral "traditions" should also be transparent, should contribute to the illusory presence of the characters, and that this does not happen with Massinger because of the emotional atrophy of his sensibility: "Massinger dealt not with emotions so much as with the social abstractions of emotions. . . . He was not guided by direct communications through the nerves" (p. 190). As in Eliot's theoretical remarks on poetic language, the idea that subjectivity is a determinate effect of the textual "form" given to "traditions" is here contradicted and repressed by the dominant theme of the essay, that Massinger's plays are primarily a form of self-expression.

Although Eliot's concept of tradition leads him to associate Massinger with the values of a specific historical period—"the Elizabethan morality" (p. 189)—he departs from both Coleridge and Stephen by making no effort to sketch the social determinations which divided the playwright's mind and texts. Eliot's discussion has so deeply assimilated the genetic bias of romantic expressive theory that to explain Massinger's inferiority, he goes no further than the man himself: "He might almost have been a great realist; he is killed by conventions which were suitable for the preceding literary generation, but not for his. Had Massinger been a greater man, a man of more intellectual courage, the current of English literature might have taken a different course. The defect is precisely a defect of personality" (p. 195). The author possesses "his own" viewpoint or "personality" apart from the determinations of history, and it is only the inherent strength of this "personality" which decides whether it continues to be transcendental, freely manipulating inherited "conventions" to express a uniquely "new view," or is conversely determined and, like Massinger, "killed by them." Eliot distinguishes Massinger from his contemporary Ford in these very terms, finding that the latter was able to maintain (in some unspecified way) his subjective integrity: "Even in so late and so decayed a drama as that of Ford, the framework of emotions and morals of the time is only the vehicle for statements of feeling which are unique and imperishable: Ford's and Ford's only" (p. 189). Ford's "statements of feeling" can be paradoxically "unique and imperishable" because Eliot's concept of the strong personality, like Wordsworth's "organic sensibility" or Coleridge's "assimilative power" of the imagination, transcends the determinants of the social formation in which it exists.

But an unanswered question returns to worry Eliot's argument, especially since nineteenth-century critics sought to answer it: why did Massinger suffer from "a defect of personality"? The conspicuous absence of any attempt to address this issue is symptomatic of the advanced specialization of Eliot's (and, generally, modern) critical discourse, its tendency to annihilate the historical moment in which textual production occurs and to establish "culture" as an "ideal order" autonomous from "society": not only does Eliot fault Massinger for the psychic limitations that disfigure his texts, but the omission of any reference to biography or history presupposes that those limitations originated with the playwright himself, perhaps in biology, in his genetic makeup—"Had Massinger had a nervous system as refined as that of Middleton, Tourneur, Webster, or Ford, his style would be a triumph" (p. 187). Eliot's reading of Massinger clearly privileges the historical transcendence of the subject assumed in bourgeois individualism, but by confining itself to Massinger's psychology, it pushes that assumption to an extreme unprecedented in the history of Massinger's reception.

Eliot's authority as a poet and critic, as well as the continuing ascendancy of bourgeois discourse in scholarly publishing and in literary magazines like his own *Criterion,* meant that his essay sounded the death knell for Massinger's modern reputation. The first sign of Massinger's apocryphal status is the lack of editions: after Arthur Symons' two-volume selection in the Mermaid Series (1887), a substantial group of Massinger's plays was not published until the complete scholarly edition of Edwards and Gibson (1976). Eliot's negative verdict seems to have had a similar effect on criticism and scholarship, for not only has there been a dearth of belletristic assessments of Massinger's plays since his essay, but they were soon being neglected by scholars as well. In 1940, on the centenary of the playwright's death, the anonymous tribute in the *Times Literary Supplement* lamented that "to-day the candidate for Honors in English Literature, taking the cue from his examiners, sets him in the class of those who can be safely neglected, knowing that, at most, one of his plays will be mentioned in an 'omnibus' question."[18] This, however, was not a tribute that would stimulate a revision of Massinger's reputation, since it too made the now commonplace judgment that "he is never sufficiently excited by his characters to wonder why they behave as they do."

In 1957, T. A. Dunn, the author of the second and last book-length study of Massinger, could observe that "there has been virtually no important or significant criticism of Massinger during the past thirty years," although Dunn's "hope to have done something by this study towards asserting Massinger's right to a serious reconsideration" was simultaneously contradicted by his opening remark that Massinger "is not, it must be admitted, a great, or even always a very good, dramatist."[19] Dunn accepts the bourgeois reading without qualification, favorably quoting Coleridge and Eliot and providing detailed discussions of additional textual evidence which he processes with the same individualistic assumptions. Thus, Dunn concludes that Massinger's plotting is defective because of "his endeavoring to plot in accordance with his moral or thematic purpose, rather than in accordance with his story. . . . even had Massinger not had this didactic-moralistic bias, his rigidly critical attitude to life and his somewhat stiff and unbending turn of mind would always have prevented him from relinquishing to his characters the right to speak for themselves. . . . His ideas are prose-concepts, springing not from Feeling but from Intellect" (pp. 65, 141, 266). What is most remarkable about Dunn's approach is that it depends so much on romantic expressive theory; it is as if the advent of the New Criticism, or even Dunn's own research in literary history, had done nothing to pry Massinger's plays away from his personality by suggesting other determinants of their meaning: "To discover more about Massinger the Man," writes Dunn, "it is to the plays that we have to turn, for it is there that his real biography is written" (p. 52). In 1973, Robert Fothergill was still denouncing Massinger's "limitations" in fundamentally the same terms as the romantic and modern critics: "On the one hand, the clarity of his satiric insight seems to be impaired; on the other, the range of felt life in the plays is too narrow and impoverished."[20]

II

The criticism of Massinger's plays manifests a remarkable homogeneity: the successive judgments give different emphases to different theoretical and critical points, ultimately in response to the changing social position of the critic's activity, but it is clear that Massinger has been marginalized because his texts do not conform to the individualistic assumptions of bourgeois critical discourse, namely, unconstrained intentionality, organic unity, and illusionistic response. It is now time to turn to some of the textual features that have gotten Massinger such rough treatment from nearly two centuries of critics. The features themselves are not in question here, since like earlier critics I find them to be interpretive cruxes, places where plot or characterization suddenly goes awry. Even if it may well be true that these features were less (or not at all) problematical for seventeenth-century playgoers and are conspicuous only from a romantic, modern, or postmodern perspective, the many readers who have responded negatively to them can be treated primarily as "informants," following Michael Riffaterre's procedure for textual analysis: "The segments of the text which cause his reactions, the informant will call in turn beautiful or unaesthetic, well or poorly written, expressive or flavorless; but the analyst will use these characterizations only as clues to the elements of the relevant structure."[21]

My analysis will differ from the ones put forth by my informants, however, by processing these elements on the basis of a different concept of the subject: in place of the individual, I assume the determinate subject constituted by conflicting social developments, economic, political, and ideological. This assumption shifts the ground of textual analysis away from Massinger the author (a historical figure whose biography, in any case, contains gaps that lay a shaky foundation for individualistic constructions) and situates it in the social conjuncture in which his plays were produced and which can be detected in them only obliquely, through their uneven assimilation of materials mediated by specific class interests. Hence, the discontinuities which so many critics have perceived in Massinger's texts can be read as symptoms not of his diseased imagination, but of a relation to ideology, to an imaginary, class-specific resolution to social conflicts. This symptomatic reading foregrounds considerations that an individualistic discourse minimizes or jettisons altogether during textual analysis, i.e., the linguistic materiality and historical specificity of the text. Decentered from the author's consciousness and displaced from a transcendental realm of human truths or literary tradition, the text is regarded as an active transformation of various raw materials, the social representations, genres, conventions, tropes which come to it always already allied to ideologies and which, during the textual work of assimilation, can be modified to signify different ideological standpoints. The text is treated, then, less as a transparent medium of communication than as a material process in which the arrangement of signifiers can produce such effects as transparency, or the illusionistic presence of a character.

The often noted inconsistency in Massinger's characterization, its tendency to dispel such illusionism, particularly invites treatment by the symptomatic reading. In the first scene of *The Maid of Honour* (1621?), for instance, Bertoldo, a Maltese knight who is the bastard brother of the Sicilian king Roberto, creates a position of intelligibility from which to evaluate the social and military pretensions of two wealthy citizens' sons, Anthonio and Gasparo. The viewer or reader quickly gravitates toward Bertoldo as he wittily exposes the heirs' inexperience and naïveté when asked to "shew [them] / the difference betweene the city valour, / And service in the field" (1.1.69–71).[22] The bitter climax to Bertoldo's satire reveals the values at stake in his characterization:

> Bertoldo.   I remember you
>   When you came first to the Court and talkt of nothing
>   But your rents, and your entradas; ever chiming
>   The golden bells in your pockets, you believ'd
>   The taking of the wall, as a tribute due to
>   Your gaudy clothes; and could not walk at mid-night
>   Without a causelesse quarrell, as if men
>   Of courser outsides were in duty bound

To suffer your affronts: but, when you had beene
Cudgell'd well, twice or thrice, and from the doctrine
Made profitable uses, you concluded
The soveraigne meanes to teach irregular heyres
Civility, with conformity of manners,
Were two or three sound beatings.

Anthonio.   I confesse
They did much good upon mee.

Gasparo.   And on mee—
The principles that they read were sound.

Bertoldo.   You'll finde
The like instructions in the Campe.

                                              (1.1.91–107)

If we rely on Antony Easthope's theory of poetic discourse,[23] it is not difficult to see the material basis for Coleridge's account of Massinger's blank verse as "flexible and seeming to rise out of the passions": the meter is varied enough to give the sense of natural speech, and by frequently enjambing the lines and compelling the reader to read (or the viewer to listen) for syntactic continuity, Massinger's poetry strictly maintains the linearity of the signifying chain, insisting on a coherent meaning that distinguishes clearly between speaker and listener, "I" and "you." As a result, Bertoldo's speech produces the illusionistic effect of a speaking voice, creating a stable subject-position, a position, it must be remembered, which is potentially one of identification because from it the values underlying Bertoldo's satire become intelligible, become in fact "true" and "obvious"; we see immediately what the heirs were unable to see, that they reduce military exploits to street brawls because they mistakenly equate the social prestige accruing to the aristocracy with the profit accumulation of the bourgeoisie. The material features of the text which work to make this meaning transparent construct a position of identification which entails rejection of the heirs' bourgeois enterprise, but approval of Bertoldo's aristocratic linking of honor with military distinction. This demonstrates that the construction of subjectivity through characterization enables the text to function as an ideological practice: the position of intelligibility is simultaneously a position in ideology, because in constituting subjectivity the text produces what Althusser describes as the ideological effect, imposing "obviousnesses, which we cannot *fail to recognize* and before which we have the inevitable and natural reaction of crying out (aloud or in the 'still, small voice of conscience'): That's obvious! That's right! That's true!"[24] The subject-position constructed in Bertoldo's characterization, insofar as it makes obvious the attitude that military service distinguishes nobility from commoners, is determined by the ideology of degree, the feudal representation of a rigid class hierarchy founded on birth.[25]

Degree is feudal because of its historical origins: it is the conservative hierarchical ideology which emerged to legitimize the feudal mode of production during the medieval period. In its first, decisive formulations at the beginning of the eleventh century, it is called the Three Estates: "Here below," writes Gerard, Bishop of Cambrai, "some pray, others fight, still others work." The historian Georges Duby has defined the basic ideological "principle": "The order of the entire world is based on diversity, on the hierarchical disposition of ranks, on the complementarity of functions. The harmony of God's creation results from a hierarchized exchange of respectful submission and condescending affection" (p. 34). The "creation" is a divinely ordered hierarchy of metaphysical essences, a "chain of being," so that "class division and seigniorial oppression were. . . . justified by a natural inequality residing in impurity," i.e., sin (p. 166). In the feudal ideology, aristocratic and clerical exploitation of agrarian labor is eclipsed by a metaphysically grounded notion of social responsibility, a social virtue, "charity," in which the dominant classes are assigned social obligations as well as privileges: "Just as the function of the pure was to pray for their fellows, and that of the valiant to risk their lives in defense of all, so the function of those whose value consisted in their weariness was to win the bread of other men in the sweat of their brow. This toil they offered in exchange for the salvation of their soul and the security of their body. Justifying themselves, but in the same stroke justifying the seigniorial mode of production as well" (p. 158).

Although degree represents the feudal class hierarchy as timeless and transcendental, like any ideological discourse it underwent various transformations determined by the particular historical conjuncture of social forces into which it intervened. As Duby shows, it was during the twelfth and thirteenth centuries, when the hegemony of the feudal aristocracy was consolidated in Europe, underwritten by its alignment with monarchy, that knighthood was juridically redefined as innate nobility, and social rank seen as a question of birth, not merely military specialization. Degree became the ideology of a hereditary class, legitimizing aristocratic exploitation of the land by distinguishing class members from the clergy (from "those attributes whose source lay in anointment and in an alliance between monarchical and sacerdotal power") and from an expanding bourgeoisie, whose commercial activity forced a redefinition of the third estate so that merchants and craftsmen displaced agrarian workers to a lower ideological ranking.

During the Renaissance, the feudal equation of birth with social prestige and landed property was adapted to a new set of class relations and economic practices, and the hierarchical social representation was refined, often extending beyond three or four rankings.[26] Degree now became an ideological resolution to the contradictory situation of the aristocracy with the rise of the absolutist state, which maintained aristocratic domination and exploitation of the land but simultaneously threatened them by stimulating the land market and developing mercantile and manufacturing interests.[27] In seventeenth-century England, Keith Wrightson notes, "the establishment and maintenance of gentility depended upon the acquisition and retention of landed wealth. Birth, a genteel life-style and activity in places of authority were secondary criteria, buttressing the fact of substantial landownership" (p. 27). Degree remained a feudal ideology, even with the emergence of absolutism, increased social mobility, and commodity exchange, because its ideological function remained the legitimation of the feudal class hierarchy and aristocratic power. In *Basilikon Doron* (1599), James I's political advice to his successor, Prince Henry, is informed by the ideology of degree ("the whole Subjects of our countrey (by the ancient and fundamentall policie of our Kingdome) are diuided into three estates"), and following the medieval formulations which institutionalized knighthood, the nobility is ranked after the clergy but assigned a preeminence ("the Nobilitie, although second in ranke, yet ouer farre first in greatnesse and power, either to doe good or euill, as they are inclined").[28] This reference to aristocratic morality reveals James's absolutist wrinkle on the feudal ideology: his exposition of the Three Estates is also a criticism of each class for "some speciall vices," class-specific behavior which is "not proceeding from the Princes order," whereby he reduces the trifunctional model to a binary opposition— monarch and subjects—legitimizing royal power (pp. 22–23).

In Massinger's play, Bertoldo's contempt for the bourgeois heirs can be seen as an attitude determined by the feudal ideology of degree, particularly at a time when the political and economic domination of the aristocracy is threatened. Bertoldo displays his nobility not only by valuing military specialization, but by demonstrating an honorable concern for the obligations that accompany the privileges of social rank. Hence, he detests the heirs' lack of social responsibility, their maltreatment of their social inferiors, "as if men / Of courser outsides were in duty bound / To suffer your affronts."

Yet as we have come to expect from examining Massinger's critics, Bertoldo's characterization is not entirely consistent. As the first scene unfolds, another, different subject-position is created, and a conflicting ideological determination begins to operate. Bertoldo's brother King Roberto enters to receive a petition for military support from the ambassador of the Urbinese duke Ferdinand: the duke's "ambition to incroach upon / His neighbours territories" (1.1.116–17) made him woo the Princess of Siena, but after "being deni'd [her] favours," he deviated from "a noble way" in an attempt "to force affection, by surprisall of / Her principall seat" and is now held captive by another Maltese knight, Gonzaga, "the honor of his Order," who has taken up the Princess' cause (1.1.122–26). Since the ambassador's exposition follows so closely upon Bertoldo's validation of the aristocratic code of honor, the duke's behavior appears to demand a negative judgment which, in Bertoldo's silence, Roberto subsequently verbalizes, creating the position of intelligibility from which the petition can be seen as warranting refusal:

> Since injustice
> In your Duke, meets this correction, can you presse us
> With any seeming argument of reason,
> In foolish pitty to decline his dangers,
> To draw'em on our selfe? Shall we not be
> Warn'd by his harmes? The league proclaim'd between us,
> Bound neither of us farther then to ayde
> Each other, if by forraigne force invaded,
> And so farre in my honour I was tied.
> But since without our counsell, or allowance,
> He hath tooke armes, with his good leave, he must
> Excuse us, if wee steere not on a rocke
> We see, and may avoyd.
>
> (1.1.145–58)

At first Roberto's characterization also seems determined by the ideology of degree: not only does he respect the aristocratic ideal of "honour"—here in the form of the personal integrity evinced in keeping his word—but he recognizes the duke's "captivity" as a "correction" that shows "Heaven is still just" (1.1.127–28), thus voicing a belief in the providential order on which the feudal hierarchy is based. As Roberto proceeds, however, it becomes clear that he constitutes the related but somewhat different ideology of absolutism, that Renaissance transformation of degree in which the hierarchical distribution of social prestige and power favors the king over the aristocracy; hence, the social structure represented in Roberto's speech consists of only two classes, "Monarchs" and "subjects," eclipsing the existence and political agency of an intermediate group of aristocrats:

> Let other Monarchs
> Contend to be made glorious by proud warre,
> And with the blood of their poore subjects purchase
> Increase of Empire, and augment their cares
> In keeping that which was by wrongs extorted;
> Guilding unjust invasions with the trimme
> Of glorious conquests; wee, that would be knowne
> The father of our people in our study,
> And vigilance for their safety, must not change
> Their plough-shares into swords, or force them from
> The secure shade of their owne vines to be
> Scorch'd with the flames of warre, or for our sport
> Expose their lives to ruine.
>   (1.1.158–70)

Roberto's self-image as "the father of our people" whose "study, / And vigilance" aims to ensure his subjects' "safety" reflects the patriarchal representations of kingship in absolutist ideology, particularly as it is expressed in the early Stuart kings' political documents. In a speech to Parliament during 1610, for example, James I dwells on the "principall similitudes that illustrates [*sic*] the state of Monarchie," indicating that "Kings are also compared to Fathers of families: for a King is trewly *Parens patriae*, the politique father of his people"; in *Basilikon Doron*, he develops the analogy in terms which Roberto's speech also uses, asserting that "a good King" cares for the "well-fare and peace of his people; and as their naturall father and kindly Master, thinketh his greatest contentment standeth in their prosperitie" (pp. 307, 19).[29] When, through the proximity of Bertoldo's validation of the aristocratic code and the transparency of Roberto's blank verse, the text conspires to make the king's refusal of the ambassador seem the obvious and right course to take, we have in effect been subtly dislodged from the ideological position of the feudal aristocracy and installed in the ideology of the absolutist state.

It is at this point that the text puts these ideologies into conflict, opening discontinuities in the characterizations and dispersing the incompatible subject-positions it has constructed. After the exchange between Roberto and the ambassador, Bertoldo steps forward to oppose the king's decision and urge him to war, offering a series of arguments all derived from the aristocratic values that underpin degree: he publicly reproaches Roberto for preferring "your ease before your honour" (1.1.182–83) and asserts that the military expedition can reinforce a weakened class hierarchy by enriching the nobility with the spoils of victory ("Silke . . . to make distinction / Betweene you, and a Peasant, in your habits" [1.1.198–99]) and by renewing the commitment of decayed "younger brothers" to "the glory of the warre" so that they can "redeem our mortgag'd honours" (1.1.217–19, 236). The ideological conflict between Bertoldo and Roberto generates competing and irreconcilable concepts of honor: from the viewpoint of degree, Bertoldo is right to seek opportunities to distinguish himself in battle, and Roberto has dishonored himself by choosing peace, "the nurse of drones, and cowards" in Bertoldo's construction (1.1.188), whereas from the viewpoint of absolutism, Roberto has honored the provisions of his defensive league with the Urbinese duke and is right to pay heed to his fatherly responsibility for his subjects' "well-fare and peace," as James would put it.

Under the pressure of this conflict, both Bertoldo and Roberto lose their coherence as positions of intelligibility, and we can see that the discontinuities in each of their characterizations are symptomatic of ideological contradictions which are concealed—however briefly—by the illusionistic effect of transparency. Bertoldo's esteem for the noble profession of arms had made him the champion of honor, but his military support of the Urbinese duke is paradoxically shown to neglect this aristocratic ideal. Ferdinand's cause is branded dishonorable merely by the chivalrous Gonzaga's defense of the princess; but it is also this knight who later informs Bertoldo, after he is defeated and captured with the duke's army, that he has lost his membership in the Maltese brotherhood by breaking his oath "to guard / Weak Ladies from oppression, and never / To draw thy sword against 'em" (2.5.78–80). Indeed, insofar as Bertoldo joins an imperialistic war motivated by Ferdinand's ruthless "ambition" and his own "hope of gaine or glory" (2.5.81), his characterization seems to undergo an almost complete reversal, in which a concern for honor comes to serve the drive for profits that he had satirized in the city heirs. This reversal exposes contradictions in the ideology of the feudal aristocracy: at first Bertoldo's aristocratic code of honor validates degree by drawing a sharp class distinction between the nobility and the bourgeoisie; but then his very adherence to this code compels an opposition to absolutism which violates degree and is allied with bourgeois self-aggrandizement. Bertoldo's move asserts his autonomy from the social hierarchy and clearly poses a threat to the state. When Roberto's "absolute answer" to the ambassador's petition goes no further than allowing volunteers to aid the embattled duke, Bertoldo hastily departs "without taking of his leave," provoking the king to call his action "a wilfull scorn / Of duty and alleageance" (2.1.2, 7–8). Yet Roberto himself does not remain a stable subject-position: there are discontinuities in his characterization which likewise expose contradictions in absolutist ideology. The patriarchal representation of absolutism which justified Roberto's refusal of the Urbinese ambassador legitimizes a centralization and concentration of power in which the monarch relies on government agents who pursue their self-interests and lack any sense of fatherly care for his subjects. Roberto violates the very principle of class hierarchy which supports his hegemony by displacing nobility like Bertoldo with the opportunistic upstart Fulgentio, "a Gentleman, yet no lord" who "hath some drops / Of the Kings blood running in his veines, deriv'd / Some ten degrees off" (1.1.23–25); and by resorting to court favorites to exercise his authority, Roberto is simultaneously abusing it, since he winds up aiding Fulgentio in his coercive "amorous project / To the fair, and rich *Camiola*" (2.1.43–44). Roberto's policies maintain the absolutist state in the face of aristocratic opposition, but they also contradict his ideology and therefore raise doubts about the legitimacy of his power.

The significance of the discontinuous characterizations in *The Maid of Honour* can be understood with the aid of Catherine Belsey's concept of the "interrogative" text, a kind of writing which "refuses a single point of view, however complex and comprehensive, but brings points of view into unresolved collision or contradiction," so that "no authorial or authoritative discourse points to a single position which is the place of the coherence of meaning."[30] The first scene of Massinger's play constructs two different subject-positions and then throws them into conflict, distancing the audience from the ideology of each position and compelling an interrogation of the social contradictions which those ideologies conceal—the contradictory social conditions that make possible two distinct kinds of class power, aristocratic and monarchical.

Bertoldo's support of Duke Ferdinand and Roberto's elevation of Fulgentio create inconsistencies that shatter the effect of transparency momentarily produced by the characterizations and prevent the ideologies
of degree and absolutism from hiding the conditions of existence of
the aristocracy and monarchy, particularly their reliance on bourgeois
values and practices to assert and maintain their power against one
another.

Massinger's text thus interrogates the ideologies of the two dominant classes in the absolutist state, and it accomplishes this demystifying critique by deconstructing their representations of subjectivity. The
identities of characters like Bertoldo and Roberto are initially defined
by their fixed positions in the metaphysical and social hierarchies of
degree and absolutism: they are assigned a position of metaphysical
subjection to God in the providentially ordered chain of being and a
position of social subjection to the classes or groups ranked above and
below them (in both ideologies the dominant agents—king and aristocracy—have responsibilities as well as privileges in relation to their
social inferiors). By virtue of the ideological positions they constitute
in the text, these characters appear coherent, transcendental subjects,
endowed with an essential nature that exists apart from the determinations of their immediate social situation. As a result of the discontinuities that the textual work opens in their characterizations, however,
Bertoldo and Roberto are decentered from their ideological positions
and transformed into determinate subjects in process, characters whose
essence dissolves in inconsistent actions determined by the contradictions of the class struggle in which they are locked. Hence the determinate subject can be viewed as subversive of the transcendental
concepts of subjectivity that underlie the ideologies of degree and absolutism as well as bourgeois individualism, although of course differently in each case. The common assumption in these ideologies is the
concept of the human subject as a coherent essence that transcends the
determinate contradictions of history; with degree and absolutism, this
essence is defined in metaphysical and social hierarchies, whereas with
individualism, it is independent of any hierarchies but nonetheless defined by the equally transcendental property of freedom. The determinate subject is, in contrast, immersed in the flux of history, the site of
contradictory determinations that threaten to destabilize both the ideological practices that constitute subjectivity and the social institutions
in which those practices operate. As Jonathan Dollimore has shown,
these different concepts of the subject circulated in Renaissance culture,

particularly in the drama, where discontinuous, socially constructed identities cast doubt on any notion of transcendence.[31]

Since the determinate subject can be an instrument of ideological subversion in a text where subjectivity is also represented as transcendental, its appearance can be taken as a symptom of an ideological conflict in the social formation where the text was produced. Belsey states that "at times of crisis in the social formation, when the mode of production is radically threatened, for instance, or in transition, confidence in the ideology of subjectivity is eroded,"[32] and interrogative texts like Massinger's appear, reflecting the decentered subjectivity of social agents, their slippage between different and opposing ideological positions. *The Maid of Honour*, then, would seem to reflect the class struggle in the hegemonic bloc of early seventeenth-century England, specifically the conflict between the aristocracy and the Jacobean government. Yet the relationship between Massinger's text and its historical ground must not be thought in terms of resemblance, as a specular reflection or homology, in which the narrative is a historical allegory: since social developments enter the text indirectly, through the complex process by which it transforms ideology-inscribed cultural materials, the relationship between text and history can never be more than a staggered, differential one, overdetermined by the uneven patterns of development which occur in cultural production and other social practices (e.g., economic, political, legal) because of the specificity of their materials and the processes by which those materials are transformed. Thus, it becomes necessary to recognize that the emergence of the determinate subject in *The Maid of Honour*, while reflecting a class conflict under the early Stuart kings, is in the first instance an effect of the assimilation of a particular dramatic form, tragicomedy, which includes among its defining features discontinuous characterization. Eugene Waith describes the "protean characters" of tragicomedy as "combinations of irreconcilable extremes," noting that "in every case the character, conceived as an extreme type, is subordinate to the situation and often changes radically to suit the requirements of the plot."[33] Although Waith's description is phrased in purely formal terms, it reveals the importance of the determinate subject to tragicomedy by indicating that the character's identity does not transcend, but is shaped by, the abrupt changes in its relationships to other characters, the numerous contingencies of "situation" and "plot," the generic necessity to give a comedic closure to a tragic action.

This suggests that Massinger's assimilation of the tragicomic form

can be useful as a way to define more precisely the ideological significance of *The Maid of Honour.* Because textual materials like genres already involve an ideological refraction of a given conjuncture of social
forces, a later text in a different conjuncture may so appropriate them
as to harmonize with or contradict their ideology and thereby signify a
different one.[34] As Fredric Jameson has pointed out, the existence of
these possibilities means that to specify different modes of appropriation, we must develop a concept of intertextuality which can encom-
pass both resemblances and differences between a text and the materials on which it works. Hence Jameson's recourse to a "negative"
intertextual construction which can "register a determinate and signifying *absence* in the text, an absence that becomes visible only when
we reestablish the series that should have generated the missing term."
Thus, we must be attuned to discontinuities not just *within* the text,
among the materials it puts to use, but also *between* the text and earlier
uses of those materials; these discontinuities are "determinate and signifying" in the sense that they can be read as symptoms of the text's
ideological operation on social forces. To understand more fully the
subversiveness of the determinate subject in Massinger's play, we must
take into account its appearance in the tragicomic form developed by
Beaumont and Fletcher. Here our aim is, first, to elucidate how Massinger's play puts to work and transforms the discontinuous characterization of tragicomedy and, second, to read this generic transformation as
determined by a new social conjuncture. *A King and No King* (1611) is
distinctive enough to exemplify Beaumont and Fletcher's handling of
the genre, and similar enough in theme to Massinger's *The Maid of
Honour* to illuminate their differing treatments of the dominant classes
under absolutism.[35]

Beaumont and Fletcher's protean character is Arbaces, the king of
Iberia who, as the play opens, has just defeated the Armenian army and
captured their king, Tigranes. Arbaces describes himself in absolutist
terms as the divine right monarch whose victory has been providentially ordained ("this sole arm propp'd by divinity" [1.1.128]) and who
nurtures a paternal care for his subjects ("Now are my joys at full, /
When I behold you safe"; "I will be a father to you" [2.2.76–77, 135]).
This absolutist ideology never becomes transparent, however, because
the extremity and wild vacillation of Arbaces' moods fail to create a
coherent subject-position. In the first scene, in fact, his speeches tend
to self-destruct, disintegrating into inconsistencies often made explicit
by the other characters:

> *Tigranes.*   You should have kept your temper
> Till you saw home again, where 'tis the fashion
> Perhaps to brag.
> *Arbaces.*   Be you my witness, Earth,
> Need I to brag? Doth not this captive prince
> Speak to me sufficiently, and all the acts
> That I have wrought upon his suffering land?
> Should I then boast? Where lies that foot of ground
> Within his whole realm that I have not past
> Fighting and conquering? Far then from me
> Be ostentation. I could tell the world
> How I have laid his kingdom desolate
> With this sole arm propp'd by divinity,
> Stripp'd him out of his glories, and have sent
> The pride of all his youth to people graves,
> And made his virgins languish for their loves,
> If I would brag. Should I, that have the power
> To teach the neighbor world humility,
> Mix with vainglory?
> *Mardonius.* [Aside]   Indeed, this is none?
>   (1.1.117–34)

The critical remarks of Tigranes and the Iberian captain Mardonius highlight the way Arbaces' speech deviates widely and unconsciously from its intention: it is a series of boasts punctuated with denials that he is boasting. The fluent blank verse could easily create the effect of a stable "I," a powerful voice that decisively establishes the intelligibility of absolutism, but the repeated appearance of those denials undermines the meaning and forestalls this effect, making Arbaces seem incoherent, out of touch with his language and the situation in which he is speaking. Hence no subject-position is constructed for the audience who is distanced from Arbaces and invited to interrogate how the absolutist ideology thematized in his speech masks the social conditions of his power.

Beaumont and Fletcher's text points to this masking operation through the skewed relationship between the character's exaggerated speech and its immediate situation. As Arthur Mizener has observed, the typical discontinuity in Beaumont and Fletcher's characterization is produced by a speech "written primarily to exploit a feeling which contrasts with, parallels, or resolves the patterned sequences of emotions which have . . . been exploited in the speeches which form its context."[36] We shall rewrite Mizener's suggestive mention of "resolves" to argue that the wayward speeches of Beaumont and Fletcher's characters have an ideological function: just as ideology offers a resolution for social conflict by "hiding the real contradictions and . . . *reconstituting* on an imaginary level a relatively coherent discourse which serves as the horizon of agents' experience,"[37] the speech which departs from "the patterned sequences" of the "context" permits the protean character to smooth over or resolve the social contradictions figured in those "sequences." Arbaces' recourse to absolutist ideology in his extravagant speech offers an imaginary solution to the doubt raised about the legitimacy of his power: he must deny Tigranes' charge that he is boasting because, according to the correspondences between the body politic and the microcosm which are often enlisted to justify absolutism, his excessive pride signifies not the restraint of kingly reason, but the unruly passion of someone much lower in the social hierarchy; as Tigranes neatly puts it, "Had Fortune thrown my name above Arbaces', / I should not thus have talk'd, for in Armenia / We hold it base" (1.1.114, 116–17).[38] By concentrating power in the king, furthermore, Arbaces' absolutist rant conceals the enormous extent to which his victory relies on the military service of the aristocracy and even on the workings of chance. The noble Mardonius makes explicit this concealment when he frankly responds to Arbaces by asking, "Was not that bragging and a wrong to us / That daily ventur'd lives?" (1.1.280–81). And it is also Mardonius who, shortly before the king enters, suggests that the defeat of the Armenians may have been an accident, the unexpected result of a retreat hastily ordered by the cowardly captain Bessus: "thou meant'st to fly," he tells Bessus, "and, thy fear making thee mistake, thou ran'st upon the enemy; and a hot charge thou gav'st, as, I'll do thee right, thou art furious in running away, and I think we owe thy fear for our victory" (1.1.69–73).

The peculiarities of Arbaces' speeches, like the discontinuities in Roberto's characterization, expose the contradictory social conditions under which the absolute monarch's power exists, but which are resolved by absolutist ideology. *A King and No King,* however, differs from Massinger's play by sparing the aristocracy from this sort of ideological critique. This is apparent both in the characterization of Mardonius and in the comedic closure of the text. Mardonius constructs the first position of intelligibility for the audience, one which remains stable during the entire play: through his satire of Bessus' cowardice in the opening scene, the values which become "obvious" are those enshrined in the aristocratic code of honor, and this ideological effect is later confirmed when Bessus, after pretending to military distinction for two acts, reveals in a soliloquy that he is in fact an ignoble upstart, who "came to town a young fellow without means or parts to deserve friends" (3.2.9–10). It is through Mardonius that degree is validated and absolutism demystified, since his critical remarks make the king's eccentric behavior intelligible and point to the ideological operation in his speeches. When Arbaces enters boasting in his exaggerated, distracted manner and Mardonius says in another of those cutting asides, "Thy valor and thy passions sever'd would have made two excellent fellows in their kinds" (1.1.172), we "naturally" question the king's right to rule because the honorable captain has made transparent the ideological correspondence between reason and nobility in which psychology is enlisted to underwrite the feudal class hierarchy.

A similar but much more spectacular privileging of the aristocracy can be seen in the plot resolution through which the text manages the discontinuities in Arbaces' characterization. The doubts regarding the legitimacy of his power are answered by the revelation that he is not actually a king, but a high-ranking nobleman, the son of the Lord Protector Gobrias who gave Arbaces at birth to the royal family in a plot with the apparently infertile queen Arane. Wishing "to bring an heir" to maintain her aged husband's hold on the throne, Arane feigned a pregnancy, and when she "perceiv'd / This hope of issue made her fear'd and brought / A far more large respect from every man, / And saw her power increase," she decided to have the infant Arbaces pose as her son (5.4.202, 214–17). Yet the revelation of Arbaces' true identity does not necessarily mean that he will lose his title and power; on the contrary, in a turn of events planned all along by Lord Gobrias, Arbaces is now able to rule as the legitimate monarch by marrying Queen Arane's real daughter Panthea, formerly thought to be his sister and the object of incestuous longings which had nearly driven him to suicide. Thus, the discontinuity of Arbaces and the coherence and stability of Mardonius can simultaneously discredit absolutist ideology and preserve the class relations represented by degree, while the plot resolution, engineered by a nobleman, constructs a political alignment between the monarchy and the aristocracy in which the latter becomes the hegemonic class.

The interrogative nature of Massinger's *The Maid of Honour* refuses any such ideological solution. The text puts to work the discontinuous characterization of tragicomedy by extending it to every ideological position, managing the discontinuities that fissure the leading characters by exacerbating rather than resolving them. Not even Camiola, the maid of the title, escapes this subversive treatment: it is she who is exploited to heal the class conflict figured in Bertoldo and Roberto, but her own discontinuities show her instead to be determined by the contradictions of that conflict. Described as "an heyre / Sprung from a noble familie" (1.2.138–39), Camiola is immediately established as the protectress of the aristocratic code of honor against the infractions of personal desire: although attracted to Bertoldo, she justifies her refusal of his overtures by insisting, through analogies characteristic of degree, that he ranks above her in the social hierarchy ("One aerie with proportion, nere discloses / The eagle and the wren" [1.2.141–42]) and by urging him to respect the vow of celibacy required of every Maltese knight and thereby submit to the divine providence which orders that hierarchy ("When, what is vow'd to heaven, is dispensed with, / To serve our ends on earth, a curse must follow" [1.2.153–54]). In this way, Camiola's first appearance constructs a coherent position of intelligibility that reaffirms the feudal ideology after Bertoldo's questionable support of the Urbinese duke. Later, however, when Fulgentio attempts to coerce her into marriage with Roberto's backing, she loses her coherence in a sudden shift to a quite different ideology by taking a Stoic stance that in fact asserts the autonomy and self-consistency of bourgeois individualism: "Though the King may / Dispose of my life and goods, my mind's mine owne," she tells Fulgentio, "And shall never be yours. . . . I am still my selfe, and will be" (2.2.168–70, 177).[39] Camiola's actions grow more individualistic when Bertoldo is defeated and captured by Gonzaga: she decides to pay Bertoldo's ransom provided that he enter a "solemne contract" to marry her (3.3.206), whereby she not only contradicts her initial concerns about his honor, but pursues her erotic interests through the sort of contractual arrangement which typifies bourgeois enterprise and equalizes the partners, regardless of their positions in the social hierarchy. The discontinuities in Camiola's characterization bear a close resemblance to those we have seen in Bertoldo and are symptomatic of the same ideological conflict: at first the means by which the ideology of degree is made transparent, she is subsequently involved in a struggle against absolute monarchy in which she becomes allied with bourgeois values and practices.

Hence, at the end, having lost her integrity as a subject-position, Camiola fails to produce the ideological solution effected by Gobrias in Beaumont and Fletcher's play. In fact, the last scene shows another inconsistency in her action: after leading the characters (and the audience) to believe that she will marry Bertoldo, she summons a friar to perform the ceremony but abruptly announces her decision to enter a convent, recommending that Roberto "pardon" Fulgentio "And to his merits love him, and no further" and urging Bertoldo to "reassume your order; and in fighting / Bravely against the enemies of our faith / Redeeme your mortgag'd honor" (5.2.283–84, 287–89). Camiola's turn to the religious life would seem to rehabilitate and stabilize her protean character, to establish her devotion to the divine providence that ratifies the ideologies of absolutism and degree, so that her counsel to Roberto and Bertoldo might be "obvious" enough to legitimize the absolutist state while asserting the feudal class hierarchy. Yet the surprising reversal in her marriage plans and the very logic of her counsel prevent the emergence of any coherent ideological position. The situation that would come about if her recommendations were followed would reconcile the conflict between Roberto and Bertoldo only by excluding the aristocracy from the power structure, by removing the possibility of its political intervention into the absolutist state: Bertoldo's renewed commitment to the Maltese knighthood may restore the social prestige of his class rank, while perhaps satisfying his drive for profits in imperialistic wars against religious "enemies," but Roberto will apparently continue to favor upstarts like Fulgentio on the individualistic basis of their "merits," and it will be the king alone who judges their worthiness. This should not be read, however, as a confirmation of absolutism; on the contrary, the play ends not with a new political alignment in which the monarchy dominates the aristocracy, but with a stalemate in which these two classes remain in substantially the same situation of potential conflict as when the play opened. Indeed, Camiola's advice that Bertoldo "redeeme" his honor through arms ironically echoes his rebellious argument in favor of Duke Ferdinand's imperialism, suggesting once again that any form of aristocratic militarism which is not in the service of the state can pose a threat to it.

To account for the development of tragicomedy from Beaumont and Fletcher to Massinger, we must ultimately confront the changing class alignments in the seventeenth century; Massinger's transformation of the form, his radical extension of discontinuous characterization to every ideological position in the text, can be taken as symptomatic of the deepening conflict between the early Stuart kings and the aristocracy. Beaumont and Fletcher's *A King and No King* intervenes into an earlier social conjuncture where the prestige and power of the aristocracy are being markedly eroded by the Jacobean court. During the sixteenth century, noblemen were gradually dissociated from the military vocation they cultivated in the medieval period and were encouraged by the Tudor monarchy to pursue careers of government service which were extremely lucrative as well as powerful and prestigious.[40] The result was a relatively stable alignment between monarchy and aristocracy and a consolidation of royal power, especially during the early and middle years of Elizabeth's reign. Segments of the nobility were converted to commercial activities which included investment in mercantile and manufacturing ventures as well as capitalist estate management, and they became dependent on the monarchy for such rewards as patents of monopoly, wardships, pensions, and the offices which gave them a role in the state appropriate to their class rank. This is to say not that there existed no aristocratic opposition to Elizabethan policy—courtiers should not be seen as resting with comfortable satisfaction inside the fold of monarchical authority and patronage—but rather that, as Perry Anderson has observed, "factional rivalries within the higher nobility now mainly took the form of corridor intrigues for honors and offices at court," and the rare revolts like Essex's conspiracy were mounted by disappointed office-seekers who were in severe financial straits.[41]

Under James, however, the always delicate economic and political alignment between aristocracy and monarchy was progressively weakened, since, as Lawrence Stone puts it, "after 1603 the peerage had to face the invasion of Scottish place-seekers and the growing competition for posts from an educated and ambitious gentry."[42] The court was quickly dominated by James's Scottish favorites and two English factions led by the Howard family and Robert Cecil, Earl of Salisbury, so that royal gifts were not equitably distributed and many noblemen were excluded from office, their desire for power and profit frustrated. At the same time, the extravagance of the Jacobean court and the reliance on the sale of titles as one means to finance the enormous expenditure contributed to a decline of respect for both king and aristocracy and alienated the old peerage from the new. Beaumont and Fletcher's play responds to these social contradictions not by mirroring them but by seeking to overcome them, by developing an imaginary solution which serves aristocratic interests: through its demystification of the ideology of absolutism and valorization of degree, through the hegemony it ultimately assigns to noblemen like Gobrias and Arbaces, *A King and No King* expresses the wish that the aristocracy would regain their social prestige and assume control of the state.

From this perspective, it becomes necessary to revise John Danby's provocative and influential assertion that Beaumont and Fletcher are "James's unconscious agents . . . capturing the Great House literature for the courtier, writing for adherents of a Stuart king rather than for Tudor aristocrats."[43] The notion that Beaumont and Fletcher's audience solely or even largely consisted of royal "adherents" suggests that Danby's reconstruction of Jacobean history collapses the aristocracy into monarchical authority, erasing the constant shift for power between them, whether at court or in Parliament, and therefore performing the same function as the harmonious class hierarchy represented in James's absolutist ideology. The historical conjuncture I have sketched above, particularly the widening gap between the court and the aristocracy, allows for the existence of an aristocratic ideological position distinct from, even if related to, that of the monarchy: as Poulantzas has remarked, "We can establish the possibility of a whole series of dislocations between the dominant ideology and the politically hegemonic class or fraction."[44] In early Stuart England, these dislocations were registered in relatively autonomous cultural institutions like the elite indoor theaters and in those class fractions in the hegemonic bloc— aristocratic and bourgeois—that frequented them, for it has now become clear that the audiences of those theaters, although predominantly "privileged" in their social status, included opponents as well as supporters of royal policy.[45]

Danby's view of a seamless hegemonic class, moreover, is coincident with his failure to recognize that Beaumont and Fletcher's plays subvert the ideology of absolutism in the critical discontinuities of the dethroned Philaster as well as of Arbaces, yet privilege degree through the coherence of aristocratic characters like Dion as well as Mardonius and Gobrias. It is this ideological mechanism that points to the staggered, compensatory relationship between text and history, to the attempt of *A King and No King* to resolve the conflict between monarchy and aristocracy by imagining an alignment in which the latter becomes the politically dominant fraction. Thus, it is not quite that Beaumont and Fletcher were, as Danby states, "unconsciously fighting a rearguard action on behalf of the Court, compensating with advances in Blackfriars for the retreats in Westminster" (p. 181), but that by demystifying the ideology of absolutism and valorizing degree, their texts could act as an imaginary compensation for aristocrats who were seeking to share the crown's power and profits, whether through the competition for court office or through political maneuvers against royal policy conducted by themselves in the House of Lords and by their bourgeois associates and clients in Commons.

The exact date of Massinger's *The Maid of Honour* remains in doubt, but it seems evident that it was produced several years after the Duke of Buckingham's rapid rise to power, perhaps in 1621, and continued to be popular throughout the 1630s.[46] Hence, it intervenes into a more polarized conjuncture of social forces than that of Beaumont and Fletcher's play, one where Buckingham's self-aggrandizing distribution of royal patronage increased aristocratic alienation from the court and more closely aligned segments of the nobility with the gentry and with mercantile and manufacturing interests. This alignment is most clearly seen in the decisive development of a parliamentary opposition, in both Lords and Commons, to the pro-Catholic appearance of James's pacifist foreign policy and the economic policies of his ministers. Between 1619 and 1624, the opposition threw the Jacobean government into a political crisis by impeaching Buckingham's clients and court allies and by drawing up measures which sought to force the king to defend the Protestant cause on the Continent and to restrict the fiscal expedients developed by government officials like the Lord Treasurer Lionel Cranfield.[47] It is this polarization of classes that underlies the interrogation of ideologies in Massinger's play: the historical situation in which segments of the aristocracy join with bourgeois groups in city and country against the royal government and its aristocratic and bourgeois agents precipitates the ideological contradictions signified in the discontinuous characterizations.

The relationship between the text and its historical ground is not a one-to-one correspondence, but is rather mediated by its distinctive transformation of a generic convention, the protean characters of tragicomedy, so as to expose the operation of two opposing ideologies: we can see how the discourses of absolutism and degree are designed to solve the contradictory conditions under which the monarchy and the aristocracy exist and conduct their struggle for power. The discrepancies between Bertoldo's support of aristocratic imperialism (Duke Ferdinand) and the code of honor that underpins degree, and between Roberto's reliance on bourgeois opportunism (Fulgentio) and the patriarchal representations of kingship in absolutism, reflect a social conjuncture in which both the aristocracy and the absolutist state are allied with various bourgeois groups against one another. In *The Maid of Honour,* the discontinuous characterization of tragicomedy is pushed so far that there is no single privileged discourse comparable to the valorization of degree in Beaumont and Fletcher's *A King and No King,* and the ideological contradictions that emerge in the conflict between Bertoldo and Roberto have a symmetry (the absolutist state and the aristocracy both contradicted by, and dependent on, the bourgeoisie) that points to the increasing condensation of the social conflicts near the end of James's reign. Massinger's play fails to offer a coherent ideological solution to these conflicts because they are nearly fused into what Anderson has described as the "characteristic pattern" of revolts against the absolutist state, "an overdetermined explosion in which a *regionally* delimited part of the nobility raised the banner of aristocratic separatism, and was joined by a discontented urban bourgeoisie and plebeian mobs in a general upheaval. Only in England, where the capitalist component of the revolt was preponderant in both the rural and urban propertied classes, did the Great Rebellion succeed."[48] This revolutionary situation does not fully materialize until deep into Charles I's reign, after the opposition against Buckingham and the royal government climaxes in the dissolution of Parliament and the king resorts to a number of economic and religious innovations that antagonize large segments of the propertied classes. Still, it is evident that in contrast to the court factionalism against which Beaumont and Fletcher championed the interests of the aristocracy, the class conflict to which Massinger's play responds is so divisive and complicated in its divisions that it makes an unqualified adherence to any one ideological position impossible and instead invites a demystification of each ideology.

We can deepen this consideration of how the social conjuncture of *The Maid of Honour* determines its interrogative nature by examining its topical allusions. Since S. R. Gardiner's essay on the "political element" in Massinger, critics have often noted how the play appears to treat political issues through resemblances in the opportunism of Buckingham and Fulgentio and in the pacifism of James and Roberto.[49] Yet these allusions have been processed in readings that bear the mark of an individualistic critical discourse: the text is reduced to a reconstruction of Massinger's biography, principally his ties to the earls of Pembroke through his father's employment as their business agent and through his own status as the pensioner of Philip Herbert, Earl of Montgomery and later fourth Earl of Pembroke. As a result, it is argued that *The Maid of Honour* expresses the Pembrokes' opposition to Buckingham's self-serving machinations at court and to James's failure to support Protestantism in the Thirty Years War. The problem with this author-oriented reading, however, is that it totally elides the crucial mediation of literary form: the topical allusions in a text never give unmediated access to history or even an interested version of it which is simply conditioned by a single ideological position; the formal elements which constitute a text may so complicate its assimilation of historical references as to transform them into an ideological signification of reality and then to expose that signification as ideological. With Massinger's play in particular, the discontinuous characterization derived from tragicomedy undermines the allusions, simultaneously disclosing and questioning their relationship to a specific ideological position.

Bertoldo's commitment to a foreign war entails an opposition to Roberto's pacifist position which seems to allude, even if in a general way, to the militant Protestantism of English aristocrats frustrated by James's reluctance to defend their religion on the Continent. But the inconsistencies in Bertoldo's character show that very commitment to be a mystification of the contradictory conditions of aristocratic power, specifically a feudal legitimation of a conversion to bourgeois practices, and hence the allusion does not yield an ideologically consistent commentary on Jacobean politics which can be assigned to an alienated aristocracy. It is this ideological dislocation that prompted Philip Edwards' incisive critique of the readings initiated by Gardiner: "Massinger carefully points to the dishonorableness of the military adventure which Gardiner's thesis makes Massinger approve of."[50] A similar critique can be made of any attempt to regard the characterization of Fulgentio simply as an expression of aristocratic resentment against Buckingham. Portrayed as "the state Catamite" whose "revenue lyes / In . . . the Kings eare" (1.1.25–26, 270), Fulgentio does indeed suggest the homosexual relationship between James and Buckingham during the latter's accumulation of enormous wealth and power. Still, by the end of the play, an effort is made to rehabilitate the "maid of honour" Camiola in order to reinstate Fulgentio as the king's agent, a turn of events which in effect displaces the aristocratic opposition to Buckingham that seemed initially to underlie the character and reasserts the absolutist ideology that had masked government corruption, both in Roberto's Sicily and James's England.

Perhaps the most dislocating treatment of topical allusions in *The Maid of Honour* occurs in its interrogation of Elizabethanism. By "Elizabethanism," I mean the nostalgia for Elizabeth's reign which is signified in various cultural products under the early Stuart kings. As Martin Butler describes it, this "cult of the memory of Elizabeth" was fundamentally "an emotional concern for *values*—opposition to Spain and the Pope, support for international Protestantism, aggression abroad, unity at home in a church properly reformed under a godly prince—the values of the old national myth of England's greatness which Elizabeth was supposed to have been furthering."[51] Since to many the Stuarts seemed to have abandoned these values, the Elizabethanism expressed in such texts as biographies of the queen, sermons, and histories of England was implicitly a response to dissatisfaction with the royal government. In this sense, it can be seen as an ideological solution to the polarized class conjuncture during the early seventeenth century, one which seeks to resolve social conflicts that proved too difficult for Church and Parliament, but which does so by serving the interests of the propertied classes aligned against the king. Hence, in Massinger's play, it is appropriate that the nostalgia for Elizabeth's reign is given to Bertoldo, the character who constitutes an allusion to the aristocratic opposition to the Jacobean government. Here the Elizabethanism takes the form of a Sicilian admiration for England intended to persuade Roberto to offer military support to Duke Ferdinand:

> if examples
> May move you more then arguments, looke on *England,*
> The Empresse of the European Isles,
> And unto whom alone ours yeelds precedence;
> When did she flourish so, as when she was
> The Mistress of the Ocean, her navies
> Putting a girdle round about the world;
> When the *Iberian* quak'd, her worthies nam'd;
> And the faire flowre Deluce grew pale, set by
> The red Rose and the white? Let not our armour
> Hung up, or our unrig'd *Armada* make us
> Ridiculous to the late poore snakes our neighbours
> Warm'd in our bosomes, and to whom againe
> We may be terrible: while we spend our houres
> Without variety, confinde to drinke,
> Dice, Cards, or whores.
>
> (1.1.220–35)

The fact that Bertoldo is given this Elizabethanism, however, inevitably undermines its ideological determination. Because of the inconsistencies in his characterization, the nostalgia for Elizabeth's reign which at first reflected the aristocratic disapproval of James's pacifist foreign policy is subsequently exposed as another mystification of aristocratic power: Bertoldo's speech is actually an effort to justify a dishonorable war in which a militaristic, self-aggrandizing aristocracy poses a threat to the absolutist state. What seemed an allusion determined by an anti-absolutist ideology is transformed by the interrogative nature of Massinger's text into a tacit legitimation of absolutism.

III

The foregoing analysis of Massinger's *The Maid of Honour* processes some of the same discontinuities as the individualistic readings. Yet because it assumes the socially determinate subject and the notion of textuality projected by that assumption, it offers a symptomatic reading where authorial intention is decentered and fragmented by the text's discontinuous appropriation of cultural materials and by its interrogation of the ideologies to which those materials are allied. This skewing of intentionality is perhaps most clear in the topical allusions: they can easily be taken as evidence of Massinger's intention to comment on social developments from the viewpoint of the Jacobean aristocracy, but they are nonetheless overtaken by the interrogative textual work which subverts and demystifies their ideological significance. Seen as an interrogative text, Massinger's play exposes the hermeneutic weakness of such categories of romantic and modern criticism as organic unity and the illusionistic effect of transparency, calling into question their valorization of the transcendental subject and recommending the more productive categories of postmodern criticism, particularly textual discontinuity and the construction of subject-positions which have been developed in poststructuralist theories of textuality.

Yet the recommendation of these critical categories cannot be based solely on their explanatory power, on the density of meanings they uncover in the text. Since they are here employed in the service of a Marxist analysis, they must be made capable of yielding a historical knowledge which takes into account the text's as well as their own place in history. For the contemporary Marxist critic, then, the problem becomes how such a dialectical approach can share some of the assumptions of poststructuralist textual theory, yet transform them by confronting their implication in the contemporary crisis of historicity, apparent not only in their antihistorical formalist tendencies, but also in the radical relativism that treats history as a coded representation, a simulacrum, or, as Hayden White has argued, a product of "linguistic determinism," where "there can be no such thing as a nonrelativistic representation of historical reality, inasmuch as every account of the past is mediated by the language mode in which the historian casts his original description of the historical field prior to any analysis, explanation, or interpretation he may offer of it."[52] Contemporary Marxist discourse, because it insists on the linguistic materiality of the text, can agree with this determinism of historical representations, but without excluding their social determinants and by making a resolute effort to preserve the historical difference of the represented object, the ways in which it deviates from the field delimited by the historian's discourse and determined by his social conjuncture. If any implementation of the materialist dialectic in literary history entails the assumption that every critical act is always a transformation of the text dependent on our experience of the present, we must clarify the sense in which the symptomatic reading, grounded in the decentering and fragmentation of the subject under consumer capitalism, can *at the same time* be a historicization that maintains the irreducible historical difference between its own critical operations and Massinger's play.

The profoundly historicist dimension of the symptomatic reading can be revealed by contrasting its operation with those of an individualistic discourse. Coleridge's judgment of Bertoldo as "a *swaggerer,* who talks to his sovereign what no sovereign could endure, and to gentlemen what no gentleman would answer but by pulling his nose" (*MC,* p. 94), shows the critic seeking to identify with a consistent subjectivity in order to experience its illusionistic presence, thereby neglecting the productive materiality of the text, its construction of subject-positions. Hence, Coleridge is somewhat rudely distanced by the incoherence of Bertoldo's characterization—particularly his wavering adherence to the aristocratic code of honor—and driven to occupy the positions constituted by King Roberto or the chivalrous Gonzaga: the judgment that declares Bertoldo a swaggerer is demanding a greater respect for honor and class distinction and therefore assumes the ideological representation of a rigid class hierarchy, a characteristic feature of the ideologies of degree and absolutism. Coleridge's individualistic discourse (and perhaps also his own conservative leanings toward a hierarchical social organization) thus leads to what might be called a deferential reading: it entertains a deference to the text which would surrender without resistance to the material production of subject-positions, would gladly occupy them and thus valorize their ideological burden; in this way, however, Coleridge simultaneously defers the historical specificity of the text, avoiding its immersion in a seventeenth-century situation, failing to think its characters as the textual construction of positions in historically specific ideologies.

This is of course the kind of historical thinking which the symptomatic reading performs in processing Massinger's play. But since the historicity of the reading depends on its assumption of the determinate subject, a conceptual reflex of the contemporary crisis of subjectivity, it would seem ultimately another ahistorical reading, affirming only an identity it has located in a historically alien object, making the contradictory determinations of Bertoldo's character an allegory of the semantic implosions and schizzes of desire that characterize the postmodern subject. To prevent this erasure of historical difference, however, the symptomatic reading adopts an attitude toward the text that is not deferential, but differential, that resists the textual construction of subject-positions and demystifies their ideological determinations, insisting on the historical specificity of the ideologies, on their functioning in a different social formation structured by a different mode of production, fractured by different social conflicts. Thus, it can be argued that we are able to recognize and demystify the ideologies at work in the play, because we live in a late capitalist social formation where degree and absolutism no longer obtain and where individualism has been eroded by a crisis of subjectivity; the mystifying function of these ideologies becomes visible to us not only because the text interrogates them, but because the differences in our historical conjuncture permit us to perceive the interrogation.

The key concept in this Marxist historicism, as Jameson has shown, is that of the mode of production, the unique combination of productive forces and class relations of production which determines the varied roles of economic, political, and ideological practice in the continued existence of a social formation. Each mode of production "designates not merely a specific type of economic 'production' or labor process and technology, but also a specific and original form of cultural and linguistic (or sign) production (along with the determinate place of the other traditional Marxian superstructures of the political, juridical, the ideological, and so forth)."[53] The feudal mode of production, for instance, is defined by transparent relations of personal dependence (between serf and lord, layman and cleric) that assign a dominant role to political and religious ideologies which mystify these relations as "natural" or "sacred."[54] It is possible for criticism to enter into a relation of simultaneous identity and difference with a text produced in the past because the concept of mode of production is a differential one: not only does it take such specific forms as slavery, feudalism, capitalism, and communism, but "every social formation or historically existing society has in fact consisted in the overlay and structural coexistence of *several* modes of production all at once, including vestiges and survivals of older modes of production, now relegated to structurally dependent positions within the new, as well as anticipatory tendencies which are potentially inconsistent with the existing system but have not yet generated an autonomous space of their own."[55] This concept carries implications both for the object of historical study and for the cognitive activity of the historian: on the one hand, if every social formation is a contradictory "overlay and structural coexistence of *several* modes of production," then social practices such as ideological and cultural production will be fissured by contradictions between residual elements from earlier ideological and cultural forms and emergent elements from distinctively new ones; on the other hand, if this sedimentation of modes of production varies with each historical conjuncture, then "every act of reading, every local interpretive practice, is grasped as the privileged vehicle through which two distinct modes of production confront and interrogate one another," a confrontation which illuminates the historical difference between past text and present reading because through the critical act the past "judges us, imposing the painful knowledge of what we are not, what we are no longer, what we are not yet."[56]

Thus, the symptomatic reading of Massinger's play examines it as a determinate effect of the social contradictions generated by the transition between two modes of production—feudal and capitalist: the formal discontinuities reflect the contradictory social practices by which aristocratic privilege and the absolutist state were both supported and limited by bourgeois enterprise, engaging the early seventeenth-century viewer and reader in these contradictions through the demystification of the ideologies of degree and absolutism by a nascent individualism. The extent to which a seventeenth-century response to the text would be reactionary or revolutionary, the nature of the ideological resolution with which the spectator or reader processed the textual discontinuities can be suggested by studying the political economy of the theater, as Richard Burt has argued, or by reconstructing the audience in as much detail as possible and speculating about responses on the basis of family ties, class position, economic and political commitments.[57] If we rely on the important step in this direction taken by Butler's provocative treatment of early Stuart social history, his view that "the theater audiences, while not lacking strong links with the court, were themselves drawn from those same parliamentary classes from which the political challenge to Charles in 1640 would come,"[58] it becomes evident that an interrogative text like Massinger's which brings different ideological positions into unresolved conflict must be considered a determining factor in the development of a social consciousness which led to the parliamentary revolution, thereby propelling the transition between modes of production that produces the very ideological contradictions in the text. The ideological tendencies of a particular viewing or reading experience in the seventeenth century can of course vary widely, but the extreme discontinuity of such texts as Massinger's, their representation of subjectivity as an unstable site of social contradiction, has the effect of pointing to the possibility and perhaps imminence of social change, even if they fall short of recommending it or finally elicit a conservative horror. It is the latter kind of response that can be glimpsed in Coleridge's initially strange judgment that Massinger was "a Democrat," "a decided Whig":[59] antimonarchical characters like Bertoldo seem to have focused Coleridge's reactionary fear of revolution so much that he did not recognize Bertoldo's aristocratic valorization of degree, however much it was contradicted by the character's swaggering.

But we must not forget that this symptomatic reading, although it forges a historical context for *The Maid of Honour,* is also an effect of the contemporary phase of the capitalist mode of production and its constitution of a distinctively contradictory form of subjectivity. In order to prevent our historicization of this reading from making it seem no more than a relativistic eclipse of the past, in order to preserve the historical difference of the text, we will suggest that any exposure of its interrogative nature is simultaneously an exposure and interrogation of us, whereby we learn "a lesson of privation," as Jameson puts it, "which radically calls into question the commodified daily life, the reified spectacle, and the simulated experience of our own plastic-and-cellophane society," so that "the primacy of collective ritual or the splendor of uncommodified value, or even the transparency of immediate personal relations of domination, at once stigmatize the monadization, the privatized and instrumentalized speech, the commodity reification of our own way of life."[60] Massinger's play differs from the symptomatic reading strategies that process it because its social conjuncture is a transitional stage between the feudal mode of production and the productive relations of capitalism, a stage wherein hierarchical ideologies like degree and absolutism which imagine a collective social organization are being challenged by the emergence of individualism. The social conjuncture of the symptomatic reading is, in contrast, a late phase of capitalism in which a nascent collectivist ideology constituted by the concept of the socially determinate subject challenges and demystifies the individualism in Anglo-American critical discourses. Because a symptomatic reading of Massinger's play highlights this difference in social conjunctures, it can make us aware of a collective form of social life different from our own atomization, can impress on us the disintegrative effects of capitalism even when the oppressive "personal relations of domination" in feudalism provide the model of collectivism, and can therefore create a hope for the reimagination and reemergence of a collective model in the future, one without the oppression characteristic of capitalism as well as the feudal mode of production.

This, then, must be figured into the history lessons which the following chapters are intended to develop, even as they are occupied in (re)constructing the social and literary history of another time. They examine several literary forms from the Caroline period—primarily city comedy, the masque, and lyric poetry—reading them symptomatically by reconstructing the increasing fusion of social contradictions which exploded in civil war and by elucidating the ideological solutions which individual texts provide for those contradictions. Throughout, the symptomatic readings focus on formal discontinuities, on the textual work and its appropriation of raw materials, whether these may be other literary forms or topical allusions. But since Caroline England is a prerevolutionary social conjuncture in which the political hegemony of the bourgeoisie and the dominance of the capitalist mode of production are ultimately realized, and the residual social practices of feudalism are gradually subordinated and marginalized, the readings offered here can be seen as implicitly probing the capitalist social formation in which we live, confronting us with its absences and lacks, with the way our own social practices stifle a collective form of life, suggesting the possibility of social change. The importance and urgency of recognizing this "lesson of privation" can perhaps be established by referring to contemporary social developments, to forms of economic exploitation or racial and sexual discrimination, and juxtaposing them with forms of social responsibility projected in feudal ideologies. In a discourse as specialized as that of academic literary history, however, it may be more effective to note that the historicity of the following readings, their claim to respect the historical difference of the texts they process, depends in the long run on evoking and stressing the collective social models which are decisively threatened in those texts and in their social ground.

Chapter Three

Transformations of City Comedy

They were never lucky enough to resolve their contradictions, or to disguise them with the help of institutions artfully devised for that purpose. On the social level, the remedy was lacking . . . but it was never completely out of their grasp. It was within them, never objectively formulated, but present as a source of confusion and disquiet. Yet since they were unable to conceptualize or to live this solution directly, they began to dream it, or to project it into the imaginary.

Claude Lévi-Strauss, *Tristes Tropiques*

S INCE L. C. KNIGHTS'S pioneering study *Drama and Society in the Age of Jonson*, it has been recognized that the genre of Renaissance drama known as "city" or "citizen" comedy constitutes a response to social developments in early Stuart England. Set mostly in London, city comedies develop a distinctive set of character types (e.g., the usurer, the prodigal) and narrative structures (mainly intrigues and confidence games) in order to comment on the socio-economic changes that accompanied the rise of capitalism. Knights's sociological reading has dominated the reception of these texts since the thirties, even when subsequent critics took somewhat different approaches by offering formalist inquiries into generic and other textual materials or empirical research into the history of Jacobean London.[1] It is only recently, however, with the possibility of a materialist critique of the magazine which Knights co-founded, *Scrutiny,* that the determinants and effects of his critical discourse can be understood and more decisively combated.[2] For what has become clear is that the *Scrutiny* group responded to the crisis of subjectivity they saw as a consequence of monopoly capitalism with an oppositional discourse that ultimately reaffirms the individualistic assumptions which support that mode of production. Since these assumptions are fundamental determinants of Knights's sociology

99

of city comedy conditioning both his analyses of particular plays and
his reconstruction of their historical ground, we will first consider the
ideological function of his approach and then challenge it with a symptomatic reading of the genre.

I

The *Scrutiny* group explicitly articulate their critical project as an
educational initiative designed to resist the deleterious effects on the
subject wrought by capitalist productive means. In *Culture and Environment* (1933), F. R. Leavis and Denys Thompson develop a pedagogy of
social criticism, in which the advanced rationalization and mechanization of the work process, the mass production of commodities, and
the development of the mass media to sustain the cycle of production
are viewed as determining a "standardization and levelling-down outside the realm of mere material goods."[3] They argue that consciousness
is rendered passive, fragmented by atomized social relations and incapable of discriminating language use and value judgment, compelled
by "meaningless" work with "no fulfillment of the personality" to seek
"compensation" in cultural forms like the media, which "discourage all
but the most shallow and immediate interests, the most superficial,
automatic and cheap mental and emotional responses" (pp. 68–69, 99,
102).

This loss of subjective freedom and unity, while reflecting new technological advances in manufacturing and communications, bears a
close resemblance to the modern dissociation of sensibility earlier diagnosed by Eliot, and like him, the *Scrutiny* group find their solution
in a concept of "tradition." Their version of this concept, however, is
social as well as literary, not just a canon of texts, but a set of cultural
values fostered in a specific kind of social formation.[4] Hence, they construct a history of England in which a precapitalist and preindustrial
"organic community," located in the medieval village or in other predominantly rural periods and areas, gave coherence to consciousness
and enabled its self-realization in transparent language and moral action. "What we have lost," Leavis and Thompson assert, is "an art of
life, a way of living, ordered and patterned, involving social arts, codes
of intercourse and a responsive adjustment, growing out of immemorial
experience, to the natural environment and the rhythm of the year"
(pp. 1–2). These cultural values represent "our spiritual, moral and
emotional tradition"; but since their social context has been "destroyed"

by the "machine" economy and they are not conveyed by the "debased" language of the media, we can have access to them in "literature alone," by preserving "the literary tradition" through "a tradition of taste, kept alive by the educated (who are not to be identified with any social class)" (pp. 3, 81–82).

The key concepts in *Scrutiny's* discourse—"organic community," "tradition," "the educated"—form antinomies in which the dislocations of subjectivity under monopoly capitalism are given an imaginary resolution which valorizes the individual. This ideological function can be seen, first, in the metamorphosis of the organic community from a historically specific concept to a transhistorical one. The view that only an earlier, homogeneous social formation could nurture the cultural values of tradition assumes the socially determinate subject, but Leavis and Thompson proceed to argue that these values can be cultivated in the exceedingly heterogeneous formations of the present, whereby the organic community is released from its specific historical moment and its values assigned to a timeless human essence: "The loss of the organic community was the loss of a human naturalness or normality" (p. 93). And what initially seems a tradition that differs from Eliot's purely literary concept by comprehending social determinations finally reverts to an "ideal order" of texts, because it is only here that the values of the organic community are still available.

This eclipse of history creates a second antinomy in *Scrutiny's* discourse: the "educated," the cultural elite who preserve and disseminate the traditional values through "literary education," are transformed from determinate subjects into transcendental ones. Leavis and Thompson admit that their project is socially determined, that they are led to investigate "the possibilities of training taste and sensibility" by the cultural crisis accompanying the advances in capitalist production; "it is plain," they insist, "a modern education worthy of the name must be largely an education *against* the environment" (p. 106). Yet in some unstated way they themselves are able to escape the "debilitating" social determinations to reflect on them critically, to recognize the organic community as "a worthy idea of satisfactory living," and to propose as a way to realize this "idea" an educational program that "demands energy, disinterestedness and a firm consciousness of purpose" (pp. 5, 109). How, we may ask, can teaching be directed "*against* the environment" and still possess "disinterestedness"? The logical tension here, as Francis Mulhern observes, is that "the principle of opposition to the course of modern history could only reside in an entity that was somehow not itself implicated in it" (p. 75)—namely, the traditional values of the organic community, but implicitly the transcendental subjectivity of the educated. Setting these values apart from the disruptive changes of history winds up privileging the cultural elite who maintain them, showing that with the *Scrutiny* group, as with Eliot, a corporate, transindividual concept of tradition actually masks a recuperation of the individual. The educated are said to have "a surer taste than any individual can pretend to" because their values originate in a community and continue to exist in a suprapersonal tradition (p. 82); yet the determinate nature of those values paradoxically frees the educated from the fragmenting determinations of the present, endowing them with an organic sensibility and making them so autonomous as "not to be identified with any social class." Although *Scrutiny's* discourse is self-avowedly an answer to historical change—the decay of the organic community—its valorization of the transcendental subject in effect denies history by excluding the social contradictions that create the possibilities for change, the class divisions that existed even in the organic community to cause its decay, and that figure in *Scrutiny's* own opposition to modern social developments by forcing it to attribute a compensatory value to individualism.

Knights's sociological approach to city comedy rests on the individualistic assumptions of this discourse, but he develops their antinomies further in the concepts of history and language which animate his historical research and his readings of the plays. Knights provides empirical evidence for the *Scrutiny* version of English history: "The medieval village was a *community*," he argues, "it functioned as a unit," and "medieval thought was dominated by tradition, the custom of the community."[5] Until late into the Elizabethan period, when the decisive emergence of market capitalism initiated the gradual destruction of the organic community, "national taste was remarkably homogeneous, all ranks spoke, roughly, the same language, and shared the same general sentiments; there was no insuperable bar between 'educated' and 'uneducated'" (p. 141).

Knights's mention of this "insuperable bar" only to eliminate it glances at the atomization of modern social relations, reminding us that his history of the organic community aims to solve this problem by imagining a diametrically opposite social formation. The ideology of his solution becomes apparent in contradictory historical accounts where the transcendental subject is invoked. On the one hand, Knights's assumption that culture is socially determined commits him to detailed research which repeatedly turns up class conflicts in the organic community—"a fundamental opposition between craftsman and trader" in economic practice (p. 24), for example, or the ideological opposition between "most members of the House of Commons," who "tended more and more to express the new commercial opinion," and "the social dramatists," who "owed a great deal to the traditional economic morality inherited from the Middle Ages" and "drew upon traditional opinions and attitudes that were more potent in the Privy Council than in Parliament" (pp. 7, 173–74). On the other hand, however, the ideological function of Knights's discourse requires the organic community to be represented as a social formation without conflict, where class divisions do not fissure consciousness: "The conception of class is misleading when applied to the Middle Ages. . . . the functional groups often cut across lines that we recognize as class divisions . . . medieval man was conscious of *status,* rather than of class; conscious, that is, of his position and function within a local community, rather than of membership in a nation-wide order of more or less equal wealth" (p. 18). The modern crisis of subjectivity drives Knights to view the organic community as the site of a consciousness not riven by the economic, political, and ideological conflicts that he elsewhere discovers between craftsman and trader, Privy Council and Parliament. This is clearly an individualistic move, one whose effect is to privilege the cognition of the members of this community in such a way that their status-oriented social representation is considered not a mystification of competing class interests and class domination, but an adequate image of reality, not a historically specific ideology, but an eternal moral truth: "sixteenth-century social thought—its insistence on degree and vocation, its subordination of private profit to public good, and its suspicion of, if not hostility towards, riches—helps to explain some of the virtues of the cultural inheritance of Shakespeare's contemporaries" (p. 156). Like other *Scrutiny* critics, Knights treats the organic community as a source of transcendental "virtues," apparently forgetting that he also describes these values as merely one ideological possibility among others in the class conflicts of Renaissance England, and without recognizing that they can seem "virtues" in a modern context only because they serve the equally ideological function of articulating an opposition to capitalist social practices.

This ideological function is also evident in the concept of language which Knights formulates in his history of the organic community. He argues that the unified consciousness shaped by this community gives rise to transparent language use in which self-expression and reference are not frustrated by the social determinations that decenter modern subjectivity and make its language inexpressively opaque:

> Today, unless he is exceptionally lucky, the ordinary man has to make a deliberate effort to penetrate a hazy medium which smothers his essential human nature, which interposes between him and things as they are; a medium formed by the lowest common denominator of feelings, perceptions and ideas acceptable to the devitalized products of a machine economy. The luck of the Elizabethan in *not* having such a veil to pierce, in being able to obtain whatever satisfactions were possible at first hand, was of course due . . . to the fact that mass production, standardization and division of labor, although not unknown, were still exceptional and undeveloped. (Pp. 11–12)

The valorization of the transcendental subject that underlies Knights's ahistorical treatment of the organic community makes for a paradoxical account of Elizabethan language. The passage states that for both the "ordinary man" under capitalism and the "Elizabethan," language is a determinate social practice, mediated by economic and cultural production and constitutive of consciousness. Knights emphasizes this materialist dimension of his view by siding with Leavis' "remark that 'Shakespeare did not create his own language'" and by adding that "Shakespeare's English" was a "supremely expressive medium" which "fostered . . . perceptions and general habits of response" (pp. 11, 12). But somehow these determinations vanish from Elizabethan language to enable unmediated communication which grasps "things as they are" and expresses the "essential human nature" of the user. Because Knights links the organic community with a subjectivity free of linguistic and social constraints, the "perceptions and general habits of response" he cites as effects of Elizabethan language are removed from a specific historical moment and installed in an autonomous realm of truth and humanity.

Knights's notion of the transparency of Elizabethan language controls his readings of the plays by projecting a romantic concept of the text in which authorial intention, organic unity, and illusionistic response act as categories of explanation and evaluation. The sociological approach Knights adopts leads him initially to consider textual production as a complicated process wherein the author is subordinated to the cultural materials which the text appropriates: "The poet who is able to draw on a living tradition embodies it in a particular, comprehensible form; and for us to grasp that form is to work our way into those extra-personal conditions which combined with the writer's genius to make his work" (p. 177). Yet when particular plays are discussed, the author emerges as a unified consciousness that exerts complete control over the creative process and expresses itself in an organically unified text. Thus Knights finds that Ben Jonson's "plays have the tightness and coherence of a firmly realized purpose, active in every detail" (p. 185). Quoting a distinctively romantic observation from Eliot's essay on Jonson, Knights describes *Volpone* as a "concentration upon one dominant group of impulses, 'a unity of inspiration that radiates into plot and personages alike'" (p. 201). By the same token, Thomas Dekker is regarded as an inferior writer because he "is never sure of what he wants to do. The moral drive is dissipated by the constant striving after obvious 'effects,' by the recurring introduction of irrelevancies, by the failure to maintain a consistent tone, so that although Dekker is never guilty of tickling his readers' palates with descriptions of vice, one often suspects the journalistic intention" (p. 231). This reliance on romantic expressive theory, coupled with Knights's idealization of the traditional values of the organic community, rewrites the text as a statement of moral truths vivified by the illusionistic effect of transparency: "the best parts" of *The Staple of News* are said to "exhibit Jonson's firm grasp of an humane scheme of values, values which are potently *there*" (p. 223). The discontinuity of Dekker's pamphlets, however, points to his weak "grasp" of this "scheme": his indecisive wavering between the "moral drive" of the organic community and the "journalistic intention" to subordinate morality to the exigencies of the fledgling Elizabethan publishing industry results in texts that provoke the reader's distance and suspicion, not the illusionistic response that entails identification with the values Knights prizes so highly.

The considerable stress Knights places on illusionism as a normative principle comes from his own ideological "scheme," his effort to enlist city comedy in *Scrutiny*'s opposition to monopoly capitalism. He reserves his highest praise for any play that presents "the anti-acquisitive tradition" so evocatively as to make it seem compellingly true or real. Symptomatic of this ideological function is the occasional shift in the focus of his discussions from the text to the "traditional values" that inform it, so that his project becomes not so much preserving those values as "demonstrating" that they are in fact valuable: "The most effective way of demonstrating the value of the inherited standards of the period is to examine those masterpieces of Jonson's in which they are present as a living force" (p. 200). The suggestion that "the *value* of the inherited standards" is not intrinsic but dependent on the transparency of Jonson's text is of course not intended by Knights, because he never sees that this dependence questions the transcendental status of the "standards," reducing their meaning and value to mere textual effects which require critical demonstration in a struggle against capitalist social practices.

The romantic assumptions of Knights's discourse combine with its adversarial stance to produce a canon that reinforces and extends the modern elevation of Jacobean drama initiated by Eliot. Jonson is canonized because "his greatness as a poet makes clear the value of the popular tradition which is only dimly apprehended in the work of lesser men such as Dekker and Heywood" (p. 178). Heywood "wrote at least two plays that have some life in them and do not consist of assembled parts," but "he was incapable of exploring, modifying or making effectively his own the morality of the age" (p. 248). Middleton is given apocryphal status because his plays "present neither thought, nor an emotional attitude to experience, nor vividly realized perceptions. They stake all on the action, [and] do not embody the thought and opinion of the time, since that is irrelevant to the intrigue" (pp. 260–61). Knights's overriding concern for the values of the organic community even enables him to rehabilitate Massinger's city comedies. Yet given the individualistic assumptions of his critical discourse, he can do so only in the very same terms that romantic and modern critics had used to marginalize Massinger: Knights explicitly reverses Eliot's negative evaluation by arguing that "in the figures of Sir Giles Overreach, Luke Frugal and the City Madam and her daughters the Elizabethan social morality is certainly 'vivified'" (p. 291).

Knights's reading of the plays is clearly a deferential one in which he takes their social representations at face value, gravitating toward any subject-position which makes feudal ideology the ground of intelligibility in a text, affirming the moral values which the playwrights formulate in a conservative reaction against social change: "The dramatic treatment of economic problems showed them as moral and individual problems—which in the last analysis they are" (p. 176). The deferential quality of this reading also includes a deferral of the historical specificity of the plays by minimizing the cultural and social materials they assimilate and smoothing out the discontinuous textual work of assimilation. Hence, Knights acknowledges that "one could consider [Jonson's] references (explicit and otherwise) to earlier poets and prose-writers from Chaucer onwards; his avowed interest in the *Vetus Comoedia;* the obvious 'morality' influence in such plays as *The Devil is an Ass* and *The Magnetic Lady;* the popular source of the jog-trot rhythms used for Nano, Androgyno and the Vice, Iniquity. But when we are dealing with a living tradition such terms are hopelessly inadequate, and exploration can be more profitably directed . . . to-wards Jonson's handling of his main themes, lust and the desire for wealth and their accompanying vanities" (p. 188). The recognition that the text appropriates other literary materials creates the possibility of a reading that illuminates the historical difference of city comedy, that situates it in a specific cultural and social formation; yet this gets side-tracked by the transcendental "living tradition" encapsulated in ab-stract moral "themes." Historical markers like topical allusions, even when identified, are similarly set aside. Although Knights devotes fully half of his study to detailed historical research and intersperses his analyses of allusive texts like *The Devil is an Ass* with accounts of Jaco-bean economic practices, he still concludes that "the play goes beyond economics and questions of expediency. Since it is the work of a great artist it cuts beneath the superficial follies, the accidental forms, and goes to the root of the disease, shaping the material in the light of an humane ideal that is implicit throughout" (p. 218).

This romantic glorification of authorial insight and control and its ahistorical emphasis on moral themes join in Knights's readings with that other aesthetic ideal of romanticism—organic unity—to explain away any discontinuities that would point to an ideological conflict in a text. For Knights, city comedy expresses only the "anti-acquisitive attitude" of a feudal conservatism. His tendency to organicize the text is evident in his discussion of Volpone's attempt to seduce Celia. Quot-ing the lengthy speech in which Volpone tries to impress her with his wealth, Knights observes that "there is indeed an exuberant description of luxury . . . and the excited movement seems to invite acceptance. But at the same time, without cancelling out the exuberance, the luxury is 'placed,' [because] the exaggeration . . . is itself sufficient to suggest some qualification . . . The manner of presentation . . . suggests that the double aspect of the thing presented corresponds to a double atti-tude in the audience: a naive delight in splendor is present *at the same time as* a clear-sighted recognition of its insignificance judged by fun-damental human, or divine standards" (pp. 187–88; Knights's empha-sis). Yet if the passage can "invite acceptance" of "luxury," how can there also be a "clear-sighted recognition of its insignificance"? And hence how can Knights go on to argue that the passage exemplifies "an equanimity and assurance" on Jonson's part "that springs . . . from the strength of a native tradition" (p. 188)? Is the "attitude in the audience" really "double" or just a (Dekker-like) moment of confused indecision finally resolved? Knights's reading locates subtle shifts of tone and reference in Volpone's speech, but without admitting that they offer the reader no coherent ideological position: Volpone's "exuberance" constitutes a valorization of bourgeois enterprise which is undermined when the competing feudal ideology fissures the text to produce a critical sense of "exaggeration"; yet this "exaggeration" can in turn support only a restricted valorization of the conservative economic morality because the effect is produced "without cancelling out the exuberance." Knights's romantic critical categories blank out the recalcitrant materiality of the text, neglecting those textual materials and discontinuities that would allow him to open up city comedy to the social developments he reconstructs.

This sort of historical amnesia, so typical of bourgeois discourse, limits the effectiveness of Knights's study in *Scrutiny*'s educational initiative against monopoly capitalism. While we may share his anticapitalist stance and his militant conception of criticism as a strategic cultural intervention into specific social conjunctures, it remains important to acknowledge that the transcendental subject so informs the weapons of his intervention—his history of the organic community and his reading of city comedy—as to make them theoretically complicit with the mode of production they are designed to oppose. The very idea of the organic community, moreover, would seem to make *Scrutiny*'s critical project attractive to contemporary Marxist discourse, to its mobilization of texts through historical readings that stimulate thinking of collective forms of social life as alternatives to the crisis of subjectivity under consumer capitalism. But the individualistic assumptions that underlie historical reconstructions such as Knights's discourage any consideration of the social contradictions that are the conditions of political action at any historical moment. As Mulhern notes, the organic community "was a spiritual entity, incarnated not in social structures but in 'tradition.' And the principal effect of this discourse, manifest equally in its utterances and its practical policy, was a categorical dissolution of politics."[6] Without the capacity to think contradiction in socially determinate forms, to imagine other, conflicting possibilities of social organization, a critical discourse committed to social change cannot hope to promote the cultural conditions for the development of a political agenda. The *Scrutiny* group must be recognized as suffering from theoretical constraints which make its critical project a reactionary model for any contemporary cultural intervention against capitalist social practices.

To avoid those constraints we shall turn instead to the materialist practice of symptomatic reading, mobilizing a body of Renaissance drama against the individualistic discourse that has so far conditioned its reception by foregrounding those cultural and social determinations of textual production which are suppressed in Knights's study. The focus will be the ideologically significant discontinuities within the text and in its assimilation of the cultural materials which constitute it. This will enable a reading of city comedy as an ideological cultural form, a dramatic genre which presents an interested representation of real social contradictions by seeking to manage them with imaginary solutions. Individual plays in this genre can then be seen as reflecting ideological positions in the prerevolutionary conjuncture under the early Stuart kings.

Crucial to the historicity of this reading is its dependence on a generic concept: identifying a large group of Renaissance plays as a relatively coherent genre does the work of mediation between cultural materials and social conflicts. This "mediatory function," as Jameson has pointed out, comprises "the strategic value of generic concepts for Marxism": "The notion of a genre . . . allows the coordination of immanent formal analysis of the individual text with the twin diachronic perspective of the history of forms and the evolution of social life."[7] Jameson formulates a dialectical theory of genre which assumes the provisional, ad hoc quality of generic concepts, yet only on the condition that such concepts be seen as a means of historicizing the analysis, as a critical experiment or temporary "scaffolding" set up solely to bring into view the text's work on its historical ground, in effect "devised for a specific textual occasion." The assumption that generic concepts are not intrinsic but heuristic, not "natural" and inductive but constructed and deductive, indicates Jameson's effort to take into account the postmodern destabilization of the text in poststructuralism and in contemporary aesthetics of discontinuity (e.g., the fiction of Samuel Beckett or William Gaddis, the poetry of John Ashbery or the so-called L = A = N = G = U = A = G = E group). But what Jameson does not adequately stress is that if the contemporary critical scene has made us too sceptical to find generic concepts anything more than "relatively arbitrary critical acts," we are already thinking their occasion as more than "textual": the very act of constructing such concepts needs to be historicized, seen as determined not only by a critical discourse but by its cultural and social conjuncture, and so allowing the possibility of other constructions from other discursive and ideological positions. Thus, among the determinations of the present reading, it is particularly the ahistorical tendencies of late capitalist critical discourses, as well as Knights's romantic categories, that recommend constructing a generic concept for the sake of the historical specificity it can give to an ideological critique of the plays. In a formal analysis of individual texts guided by the notion of a city comedy genre, textual discontinuities read as generic transformations will produce a concept of the ideology of the form at different stages of development, enabling us to understand those transformations as ideological shifts ultimately determined by the changing class allegiances which precipitated the political failure of the royal government. By pursuing this twin diachronic perspective, we can initiate a reading of city comedy that mediates between the material specificity of the plays—their peculiar autonomy as literary texts and dramatic actions—and the social formations in which they are produced and reproduced, i.e., transformed into objects-for-criticism.

II

The social contradictions in Renaissance England mark it as a critical fault line in the history of the West. At the economic level, elements from the feudal mode of production, characterized by relations of economic dependence and predominantly agricultural production for local consumption, coexisted with nascent capitalism, characterized by contractual arrangements between economically independent agents and the production of agricultural and industrial commodities for a market, both national and international.[8] During the sixteenth and early seventeenth centuries, this economic contradiction appeared in England as a significant increase in the size and income of certain lower strata in the social hierarchy, particularly the gentry, the legal profession, merchants, and manufacturers. The sale or gift of monastic and crown lands may have been most important in stimulating the rise of these classes by creating an extremely active land market, but there were also growing opportunities to amass fortunes in overseas trade and industrial manufacturing.[9] In the face of this unprecedented shift in the distribution of wealth, segments of the feudal nobility gradually adapted to commercial activities primarily by managing their estates more efficiently and investing in lucrative business ventures, although some were not above marrying into the families of highly successful entrepreneurs.[10] These economic changes were reflected at the political level not only in the emergence of Parliament as the site of the rising classes' interventions across a range of social practices—economic, legal, religious, etc.—but also in the contradictory functioning of the absolutist state as it sought to sustain its hegemony. As Perry Anderson has observed, "the apparent paradox of Absolutism in Western Europe was that it fundamentally represented an apparatus for the protection of aristocratic property and privileges, yet at the same time the means whereby this protection was promoted could *simultaneously* ensure the basic interests of the nascent mercantile and manufacturing classes."[11]

A similar contradiction can be seen at the ideological level. On the one hand, England was still very much a social formation founded on status, and there continued to be enormous respect for the rigid class hierarchy expressed in the ideology of degree. Thus, members of the upwardly mobile classes often cultivated values associated with the feudal nobility by indulging in conspicuous consumption and by purchasing titles. And what inspired noblemen to supplement the income from their estates with business investments was usually less a commitment to capitalist economic practice and bourgeois values like thrift than a more conservative desire to reinforce their social position by maintaining an aristocratic standard of living.[12] Economic developments, on the other hand, depending on contracts that treated the parties on an equal basis without deferring to status, resulted in social mobility and implicitly assigned great value to personal freedom and individual rights, concepts which had already received religious expression in Protestant theology and Puritan sectarianism and would be formulated in philosophical terms as the ideology of possessive individualism.[13] The competing ideologies, as well as their relations to economic and political practice, can be glimpsed in Christopher Hill's description of how pew assignments differed in Anglican and Puritan churches:

> Ecclesiastical officers, from bishops to churchwardens, occupied themselves with seeing that members of the parish were seated in due order of social precedence. The purchase of the right to build or occupy a specially grand pew was beginning, but social status was still at least as important in the allocation of seats as cash paid. In the voluntary sects

it was normal for pews to be rented; the remaining seats, equal in status, were available for the first comer.[14]

The passage shows, in a remarkably concise way, that the differences in
pew assignments are highly mediated by the more global social contradictions I have been describing. Even the most practical details of early
Stuart church organization can be seen as a complex, uneven process
of overdetermination, wherein contradictory social practices produce
effects in each other which, however, tend to be visible only in the
specific terms of each practice. The pew assignments reflect principally
ideological conflicts, differences in church government and theology,
which are mediated by political and economic practice: the hierarchical
social representation that underwrites the hegemony of the royal government is enforced by the "ecclesiastical officers" of the Anglican
Church, whereas the possessive individualism that overdetermines the
"voluntary sects" permits commercial relations to shape religious ob-
servance according to a liberal democratic model of social life which is
potentially subversive of church and state. The seating of the different
congregations concretizes the multiple, contradictory determinations
of seventeenth-century social practices, but only in the peculiar terms
of church organization and hence relatively autonomous from those
other practices.

This process of overdetermination can also illuminate dramatic
texts, like city comedy, which have a properly representational mode of
address to the world: city comedies represent the social contradictions
of early Stuart England through dramatic forms highly mediated by
various cultural and social determinations. Mediation complicates mimesis, making the latter an activity that is more transformative than
imitative: representation, as Weimann has cogently described it, "constitutes the image or transcription of a social or individual situation,
not through the 'objective' recreation or repetition of that situation (or
that speech, text, thought), but through the assimilation or appropriation of it in terms of the needs, interests, and perspectives of the representing activity or mode of literary production."[15] Any effort to construe these "needs, interest, and perspectives" and examine their
transformative work in the social representations of city comedy must
begin with the formal aspects of the text and the class-specific ideologies inscribed in them. We will concentrate on the generic conventions
of city comedy, the recurrent character and plot types that construct
positions of intelligibility for the reader. The forms and ideologies at

stake in the overdetermined representations of the genre can be suggested by Jonson's *The Alchemist* (1610).[16]

The opening quarrel between the cozeners consists of a string of increasingly provocative epithets and tirades which immediately raise questions about identity, effectively turning Face and Subtle into volatile subjects in process. A captain wearing a sword and a doctor in reach of his scientific instruments clash on stage, as is clear from Jonson's direction for Dol in the marginal note at 1.1.115: "*Shee catcheth out Face his sword: and breakes Subtles glasse.*" Yet within the first hundred lines or so the personal and social messages signified by their costumes are quickly skewed by the dialogue: their insults build to an identification of them as servant and vagrant, petty thief and confidence artist. The *in medias res* opening propels the reader or spectator to make sense of the quarrel, but the extremely discontinuous form of the exchanges, the shifting back and forth between the most elliptical yet surprising bits of information, suspends any closure on a single identity, provoking instead scepticism and suspicion with each revelation. If the dialogue between Face and Subtle can be said to create a stable position of intelligibility, however momentary, it must be the acute sense of class status which they express in their repeated assertions of social superiority over one another. "Why, I pray you, haue I / Beene countenanc'd by you? or you, by me?" Face asks Subtle, while Subtle notes that Face would have "beene lost / To all mankind, but laundresses, and tapsters, / Had I not beene" (1.1.21–22, 85–87). Insofar as we search for a position from which the cozeners' criticisms of one another can be understood, we assume the feudal concern that social distinctions have been violated, and that one or both of these characters have refused the status assigned them by the class hierarchy. This is not to say that the military and medical professions signify nobility or aristocracy; actually, they did not enjoy much social prestige during the Jacobean period. As Lawrence Stone notes in *The Crisis of the Aristocracy,* "Active personal occupation in a trade or profession was generally thought to be humiliating."[17] The point is rather that the quarrel assumes the equation of class position with self-worth which characterizes the aristocratic ideology that legitimized feudal class relations. In this sense, the text offers an initial valorization of degree.

The quarrel, however, has an almost immediate dislocating effect on this ideological position. It is in fact each cozener's purpose to deconstruct the other's hierarchical representation of their relationship by exposing the contradictions in the superior status he arrogates to him-

self. Subtle unmasks Face as "once (time's not long past) the good, /
Honest, plaine, liverie-three-pound-thrum, that kept / Your masters worships house here in the *friers,* / For the vacations" (1.1.15–18).
Face reveals Subtle as a vagrant whose failed con games keep him
impoverished:

> *Face.* When all your *alchemy,* and your *algebra,*
>   Your *mineralls, vegetalls* and *animalls,*
>   Your coniuring, cos'ning, and your dosen of trades,
>   Could not relieue your corps with so much linnen
>   Would make you tinder, but to see a fire;
>   I ga' you count'nance, credit for your coales,
>   Your stills, your glasses, your *materialls,*
>   Built you a furnace, drew you customers,
>   Aduanc'd all your black arts; lent you, beside,
>   A house to practise in—
> *Subtle.*   Your masters house?
> *Face.* Where you have study'd the more thriving skill
>   Of bawdrie, since.
> *Subtle.*   Yes, in your masters house,
>   You, and the rats, here kept possession.
>   Make it not strange. I know y'were one, could keepe
>   The buttry-hatch still lock'd, and saue the chippings,
>   Sell the dole-beere to the *aqua-vitae*-men,
>   The which, together with your *christ-masse* vailes
>   At *post and pair,* your letting out of counters,
>   Made you a pretty stock, some twentie marks,
>   And gaue you credit, to conuerse with cobwebs . . .
>   (1.1.38–57)

Face tries to establish his ascendancy over Subtle by setting himself up
as the generous aristocrat who defines his relationship to the fraudulent
alchemist as a philanthropic gesture. The driving linearity of Face's
blank verse, the effortless way the periods and catalogues slip into a
patronizing tone, work to make his noblesse oblige seem almost "natural," but then Subtle punctures the whole aristocratic demeanor by
forcing us to see how it conceals Face's origins as the pilfering servant.

The discontinuous characterization of the cozeners disperses their
identities across so many positions in the class hierarchy, collapsing
each position they assume into contradictory social conditions that demystify their superior self-images and turn any social representation
based on degree into a fiction designed to mask their illicit profit ac-

cumulation. They use the social representations of the feudal ideology in an instrumental way, as roles ("captain," "doctor") adopted to achieve a financial aim. And they appear as social agents who exist apart from the class hierarchy (the vagrant Subtle and the prostitute Dol) or who are released for a definite period from a position in the lower strata (Face) because a social superior is absent. This social autonomy means that once all the revelations have been made and all the class pretensions stripped away, the cozeners come before the reader in the bourgeois representation of "free and equal individuals related to each other as proprietors of their own capacities and of what they have acquired by their exercise."[18] Since Subtle and Dol are not allotted specific functions by the class hierarchy, and Face's position as servant is disrupted by the plague that drove his master from London, they are free of any relations of economic dependence and can engage their labor in profit-making ventures: their confidence games, in Dol's construction, constitute a form of commercial activity based on an egalitarian contract, the "venter *tripartite* . . . All things in common . . . Without prioritie" (1.1.135–36). And indeed their dealings with their victims are dramatized as transactions: several unsuspecting characters seek to purchase Subtle's varied services since they have been tricked into believing that he can conjure up the Queen of Fairy, tell fortunes, provide the philosopher's stone, and give instruction in the practices and entertainments of gentlemen in London.

This analogy between fraud and business can be taken as a moral satire on profit accumulation, but only from the conservative perspective of degree, which is conceptually constrained to think freely competitive agents morally suspect because socially subversive. Yet the text signifies this satiric representation just as Dol's contract metaphor sets up another, competing perspective on bourgeois enterprise: her intervention into the quarrel resolves any confusion about the cozeners' identities by establishing possessive individualism as the position from which their actions can be understood and evaluated. Dol reconciles Face and Subtle by arguing that they are free and equal subjects, not their socially superior self-representations, and impresses on them the necessity to shake hierarchy from their thinking if their business arrangement is going to continue:

> You will accuse him? You will bring him in
> Within the *statute*? Who shall take your word?
> A whoreson, upstart, apocryphal captain,

Whom not a puritane, in black-*friers,* will trust
So much, as for a feather! And you, too,
Will giue the cause, forsooth? You will insult,
And claime a primacie, in the diuisions?
You must be chiefe? as if you, onely, had
The poulder to proiect with? and the worke
Were not begun out of equalitie?
The venter *tripartite?*

(1.1.125–35)

Dol's individualistic solution to the quarrel can be welcomed as "right" because it gives coherence to the cozeners' actions after all the narrative uncertainty generated by their discontinuous characterization; the reader can accept what she says as "true" because it defines a direction for the narrative to take. But even as Dol fixes this new ideological determination in the cozeners, her speech opens up contradictions in it: the cozeners tend to live out, in the imaginary, the hierarchical social representation to which their individualism is opposed. Face's threat to denounce Subtle under "the *statute* of *sorcerie*" entails reassuming his class position as the "Honest" servant, although, as Dol reminds him, he no longer commands the "trust" of this position with his neighbors (nor with the reader at this point). Subtle must be reminded of the contract that binds them into a democratic collective, a "*republique*" in Dol's words (1.1.110), where they receive equal pay for equal work instead of the exploitative relations he asserts with his "claime" of "primacie." The contradictory ideologies at work in the cozeners become evident when we notice that Dol's efforts to stop the quarrel include puffing them up with titles and class epithets like "Sovereign" and "General," which are in fact her terms of endearment for them, whereas after the reconciliation Face uses the same tropes with Dol in an entirely demystified way, as ironic, pseudogallant flattery that glances at the men's domination of her:

at supper, thou shalt sit in triumph,
And not be stil'd Dol Common, but Dol Proper,
Dol Singular! The longest cut, at night,
Shall draw thee for his Dol Particular.

(1.1.176–79)

Despite their freedom from the class structure, the cozeners turn repeatedly to hierarchy: it not only threatens to erupt in their disproportionate economic demands, but characterizes their sexual exploitation of Dol, transforming the democratic relations suggested by her "*republique*" metaphor into a wistful imaginary solution for the problems of their situation. Metaphors like "*republique*" and "venter *tripartite*" used to describe the cozeners' criminal conspiracy can signify their individualism, their characterization as the transcendental subjects of bourgeois economic and political practice, but not without simultaneously revealing the contradictory conditions of these individuals. Far from transcending social determinations, the cozeners can realize their personal freedom only through the egalitarian contract, which permits them to conduct their commercial activity, but which transfers their right to profit over to the group. The discontinuous development of the cozeners in this opening scene operates on a key ideological contradiction in Jacobean England by interrogating the two opposing ideologies, showing how their assumption of the transcendental subject, defined either by its place in a "natural" class hierarchy or by its "natural" autonomy, represses the determinate nature of their actions: the relations of domination which Face and Subtle construct over one another and over Dol and the relations of mutual dependence which enable their profitable con games.

The cozeners constitute a generic convention of city comedy, a recurrent character type which is developed from earlier dramatic and literary forms, like the clever slave in Greek New Comedy and in Plautus' plays and the confidence artists in Robert Greene's pamphlets on London crime.[19] An examination of how these cultural materials are transformed in the interrogative textual work of *The Alchemist* can clarify the ideological contradictions in the character type and initiate a diachronic perspective on the city comedy genre. The Plautine clever slave shapes Face's role as the scheming servant quite directly: Jonson based the opening scene on the quarrel which opens the Latin playwright's *Mostellaria* (usually translated as *The Haunted House*).[20]

The slave Tranio, the model for Face, is being reproached by his colleague Grumio for leading a prodigal and dissolute life with the son of their master, who as the play begins has not yet returned from traveling abroad for several years. Grumio, an older, more conservative slave, warns the arrogant Tranio that his behavior warrants punishment, beatings as well as hard labor, because it undermines the master-slave hierarchy: "I expect you know you're going to be sent out to the mill yourself before long," says Grumio, "Better make the most of your time now, my lad. Drink and be merry, waste your master's goods and make a ruin of your master's fine young son. Drink with your friends all day and night, Greek fashion. Buy your women and set them free. Live like lords, with hangers-on feeding their bellies at your expense."[21] Grumio insists on the legal status of slaves as property, on the slave-owner's total ownership of the slave, while Tranio has all along been denying this status: he has in fact dislodged father and master as the figure of authority in this patrician family.

The quarrel reveals the ideological subversion operating in the Plautine clever slave: Tranio's corruption of his master's son challenges the *virtus Romana,* the ideology of the aristocratic oligarchy that ruled Rome during the Republic. This ideology assumes a rigid class hier- archy where birth and political or military achievement gain admittance to the dominant class; yet since aristocratic hegemony did not have a legal or constitutional rationalization in Republican Rome, it was rein- forced by patriarchal values in state and family, like the *mos maiorum* (forefathers' custom or precedent) and *pietas* (obedient respect for an- cestral gods, the fatherland, fathers, and husbands).[22] During the pe- riod of Plautus' popularity, roughly the beginning of the second century B.C., this ideological ensemble was further implemented in sumptuary legislation proposed most notably by Cato the Censor to reinforce the cohesiveness of the aristocracy: limitations on conspicuous consump- tion not only controlled class membership, but somewhat relaxed the economic and political conflicts among aristocratic factions by discour- aging the competitive display of wealth and foreign culture. Cato's or- ations specifically attacked the aristocratic fetish for Hellenistic culture, arguing that it deviated from traditional Roman values and led to moral depravity.[23] Thus, Tranio's subversiveness can be described more pre- cisely: it is not just that his aristocratic behavior overturns the class hierarchy by repressing his property status, but also that his dissipation with his master's son violates the sacred patriarchy of state and family by cultivating what aristocratic ideologues like Cato felt were immoral Greek customs.

This ideological subversion, however, is finally limited by the dis- continuities in Plautus' characterization of the clever slave. The quarrel between Tranio and Grumio differs from the one between Jonson's coz- eners most significantly by interrogating only the slave's subversion, not the aristocratic ideology which is its object. This qualified interro- gation is achieved first through Grumio, who quickly unmasks Tranio's socially superior attitudes as class pretensions, making "obvious" the slaveowner's perspective:

Tranio. You're jealous, Grumio, if you ask me; jealous because I'm doing well and you're not. It's only natural. It's natural for me to keep women and you to keep cows; me to have a good life, you to have a mucky one.

Grumio. Gallows-meat, that's what you are, and what you soon will be, if I know anything about it—hustled through the streets under a yoke, with goads through your guts, when the master comes home.

(Pp. 27–28)

Tranio's aristocratic self-image is repeatedly exposed as a mystification of its contradictory conditions, namely, his property status and his master's temporary absence, but these exposures never really bring into question the hierarchical social representation of the Roman aristocracy. On the contrary, both self-image and exposure are made from this same ideological standpoint. Tranio's preference for leisure over labor makes the aristocratic assumption that class rank is "natural," that he enjoys a transcendental right to leisure which distinguishes his status from that of the chattel slave Grumio (the Latin reads: "*decet* med amare et te bubulcitarier, / me uictitare pulchre, te miseris modis" [1.1.50–51; my emphasis]). And as soon as we agree with Grumio that this right is not due to Tranio, only to his master, the text has made us concerned with class distinctions, attuned to any infringment of them, ready to judge ridiculous any social pretense entertained by a slave who in Roman law lacked rights of any sort, including those over his own person. Plautus' Latin is particularly effective in this ideological positioning of the reader: Grumio's references to the master underscore Tranio's subservience by avoiding the all-purpose term of authority *dominus* in favor of the more specific *erus,* signifying "a man in relation to his servants" (as when Tranio is described as a "master's ruin" [p. 26]—"erilis permities" [1.1.3]).[24]

The clever slave's aristocratic self-image can thus contribute to the valorization of the class hierarchy even as he turns it upside down by presenting a different basis for determining rank: as Erich Segal has pointed out, Plautine comedy "creates a new—albeit temporary—aristocracy, in which wit, not birth distinguishes the ruler from the ruled" (p. 105). The slave is admitted to this temporary aristocracy of "wit" by the ingenious schemes he develops; but while these schemes sustain his inversion of the class hierarchy, the goals he sets for them ensure his eventual return to the lower strata. The clever slave never challenges his property status: he never seeks manumission or money to buy his freedom. The omission of such goals removes the threat of social disorder from the slave's schemes, bearing out George Duckworth's observation that "even the cunning and unscrupulous slaves act out of faithfulness to their masters," whether father or son.[25] Tranio sets about to deceive his master only in order to delay the discovery of the son's dissipations and his own part in them. This Tranio succeeds in doing, through the most masterful machinations in which the slave becomes the position of intelligibility over his deceived master and the spectator or reader participates in the ideological subversion, in the slave's domination of the aristocrat. But how subversive can this position be when the slave can only imagine every aristocrat he deceives as his slavelike property ("the asses are saddled . . . most mule-drivers saddle mules, but I'm saddling human mules") and is always ready to indulge himself in grandiose aristocratic fantasies: "Alexander the Great and Agathocles, so I've heard tell, were the two top champion wonder-workers of the world. Why shouldn't I be the third—aren't I a famous and wonderful worker?" (p. 63). It is the clever slave's "wit" that allows him to develop schemes in which he dominates his master, but his dominance remains an imaginary one because the "wit" is mediated by the hierarchical thinking of the *virtus Romana* and ultimately turns out to be inconsequential. Instead of confronting the property relations which the aristocratic ideology mystifies, Tranio joins in their mystification by striking aristocratic poses. After all of Tranio's plots collapse, he remains impudent right up to the end, but his goal is only to resume his place with his master's forgiveness.

Drawing on David Konstan's materialist approach to Roman comedy, we can read the limited subversion of the Plautine slave as an ideological mechanism which managed the social stress caused by the Second Punic War and the economic expansion that accompanied Roman imperialism. "In a period when foreign campaigns, the rise of slavery on a mass scale, and growing class divisions among the citizens threatened the solidarity of the Roman community," Konstan argues, "comedy portrayed a natural harmony in the society, in which its members, despite contrary impulses, were ultimately united through the fundamental bond of kinship" or, in the case of slaves, membership in a household.[26] This ideological function can be perceived in the discontinuities that mark the conclusion of the *Mostellaria*. The head of the household forgives both his son and his slave, but they do not really abandon their erring ways: the father asserts that his son "can go on, now I'm here, as he did when I was away, with his girls, his drinking, and whatever he likes. As long as he is sorry for having wasted all that money, I'm satisfied," while Tranio cheekily reminds his master that any reprieve will be only temporary because "i'm sure to do something wrong tomorrow; then you can punish me for both crimes" (pp. 83, 84). The continuation of the son's dissipations and the slave's insubordination, instead of weakening the authority of the paterfamilias, in effect reinforces it by demonstrating the need for his close supervision of his inferiors. And the general pardon at the end, by reaffirming the patriarchal values of the *virtus Romana,* provides an ideological solution to the disruptive social changes wrought by Roman conquest, particularly the increase in aristocratic wealth and consumption and the enormous influx of foreign slaves.

The conservative ideology of Plautine comedy is also reflected in the theatrical conditions in Republican Rome, a consideration which offers an opportunity to distinguish the present reading of the *Mostellaria* more sharply from Segal's view that the clever slave is radically subversive. To explain this subversiveness, Segal cites the fact that drama was performed during a yearlong schedule of festivals, suggesting that festival and drama are cultural practices which are "saturnalian," which share a "holiday" inversion of "everyday" values.[27] But our ideological critique of the clever slave requires us to emphasize the conservatism of these cultural practices, the role they play in social control and reproduction. This role becomes evident in the intermittent quality of the festivals and their restriction to carefully defined blocks of time: there was an annual total of only seven or eight days reserved for dramatic performances.[28] Moreover, a new festival that included drama was instituted during the Second Punic War with the specific intention "to keep up public morale."[29] The clever slave participates in this conservative ideological apparatus as a dramatic form whose discontinuities show that its brief "holiday" inversion of "everyday" ideological positions actually strengthens them.

Jonson's cozeners are determined by two historically different ideologies which transform the clever slave type by increasing its subversiveness. The cozeners' discontinuous characterizations, like Tranio's, interrogate a hierarchical model of social life, degree in their case, but their crucial difference from the slave is that they construct a conflicting ideological position from which to do this—individualism. Whereas the "wit" of Tranio's schemes merely inverts the Roman class hierarchy by allowing him to occupy the dominant aristocratic position, the cozeners' profit-making schemes threaten the feudal order by defining them as free and equal subjects whose class rank fluctuates with the particular scheme they devise and the profit they accumulate. Face's individualistic actions question degree most clearly when his master Love-Wit returns in the final scenes, which are also modeled on Plautus' *Mostellaria*. Face tries to conceal the evidence of his crimes by deceiving Love-Wit that the house is haunted. This ploy works for Tranio, even if it is finally discovered, but for Face it fails quickly, and the servant's efforts to evade punishment must go beyond the slave's impudent "wit" by proposing a new contract with his master, wherein Love-Wit is assigned the cozeners' ill-gotten gains and even Dame Pliant, the wealthy widow whom Face had himself planned to marry. Love-Wit's acceptance of the offer destabilizes the master-servant relationship because the contract equalizes him and Face, establishing the contradictory conditions in which class distinctions between "master" and "servant" must now exist between them. These conditions are neatly signified after the contract is realized, and the widow wed, in the contented Love-Wit's assertion "I will be rul'd by thee in any thing, Ieremie" (5.5.143). His use of "Ieremie" indicates that Face has returned to his servant status (the line responds to Face's request for permission to serve pipes and tobacco indoors), so that he is no longer "Captain Face" or "General" as in the con games, but "Ieremie butler" as the neighbors know him (5.1.27). Yet the notion of a master who would "be rul'd" by his servant glances at the restructuring of the feudal hierarchy which occurs when the contract dislodges both of them from their class positions. In the closing lines, Face explains the abrupt turn of events at Love-Wit's return, but his identity changes yet again, the faithful servant giving way to the free agent speaking from outside the class structure, the actor standing outside his dramatic role: "My part a little fell in this last *Scene,* / Yet 'twas *decorum*" (5.5.158–59). The ending thus does not resolve the ideological conflict created by the individualistic contract so much as accommodate commercial activity (Face's "part" as cozener) to the feudal hierarchy (the social "decorum" of his deference to his master) by implicating a member of the gentry in his servant's crimes. This accomodation functions as an unstable device to contain the two competing ideologies: it preserves yet compromises the traditional class distinctions by limiting yet permitting an illicit form of profit accumulation. Class distinctions now enable bourgeois enterprise, which in turn acts as a new economic support for aristocratic hegemony. This alignment, however, simultaneously demystifies the individualistic assumption of transcendental freedom and the social and metaphysical rationalizations of the feudal hierarchy.

The confidence games which take up much of the action in *The Alchemist* present another such strategy of containment, but one where the textual positioning powerfully engages the viewer or reader in the ideological conflict posed by the cozeners. As each scheme gradually unfolds, the cozeners construct a position of identification which, unlike the positions offered by their duped victims, shares in the "true" knowledge of the action. This positioning makes us complicit in the cozener's profit-making, as critics have noticed,[30] inviting us to evaluate the weaknesses of each dupe, cozener-like, and even to desire the success of each scheme. Thus, it also constitutes an ideological position that validates the cozeners' bourgeois enterprise and represses the contradictory conditions of their individualism which were disclosed in the opening scene. Yet no sooner does the reader applaud the cozeners' cleverness than this position is skewed by the fundamental resemblance that emerges between cozener and dupe: both are represented as threats to the feudal class hierarchy. This discontinuity can be illustrated by the entrance of Dapper, the law clerk who plans to leave the legal profession because he aspires to be a fashionable gentleman adept at gambling:

> *Dapper.* Captaine, I am here.
> *Face.* Who's that? He's come, I think, Doctor.
> Good faith, sir, I was going away.
> *Dapper.* In truth,
> I'am very sorry, Captaine.
> *Face.* But I thought
> Sure, I should meet you.
> *Dapper.* I, I'am very glad.
> I had a sciruy *writ*, or two, to make,
> And I had lent my watch last night, to one
> That dines, to day, at the shrieffs: and so was rob'd
> Of my passe-time. Is this the cunning-man?
> *Face.* This is his worship.
> *Dapper.* Is he a Doctor?
> *Face.* Yes.
>
> (1.2.1–9)

Since we are privy to the cozeners' plans, Dapper's excuse for his lateness acquires an ironic subtext, becoming an unwitting indication that

he is a prime candidate for the confidence game: not only is this suggested by his use of "rob'd" to describe his thoughtless loan of his
watch, but his mention that he possesses such a rare and expensive
object and is acquainted with a person who "dines" with a government
official like the sheriff reveals his socially superior self-image and hence
his vulnerability to cozeners masquerading as a captain and a doctor.
Yet once we view Dapper as an appropriate victim because he nurtures
an illusory conception of his social standing, the text has subtly shifted
our ideological standpoint to degree, the confidence game turns into a
conservative satire on the rising classes in Jacobean England, and we
recognize, retrospectively, that both dupe and cozeners are poseurs,
motivated by the same pursuit of wealth and social prestige. Indeed,
since we have already witnessed the cozeners' class pretensions during
their quarrel, it becomes difficult to determine whether Face's repeated
reference to Dapper's lateness is intended to bait the dupe or expresses
the disgruntlement of a captain who feels that his rank has been
slighted. The confidence games are thus the locus of an ideological
conflict: by positioning us with the cozener and exposing the dupe as
obtuse and ridiculous, they can elicit simultaneously our approving
acceptance and critical rejection of profit accumulation; they offer a
means both to champion possessive individualism and to condemn
violations of degree.

It is in the confidence games that we can see how city comedy
appropriates the Elizabethan pamphlets on London crime to develop
the cozener type. Subtle and Dol in particular are modeled on the
teams of vagrants and prostitutes which recur among Robert Greene's
con artists or "cony-catchers." Face's reference to Subtle's "tricks / Of
cosning with a hollow cole, dust, scrapings" (1.1.93–94) is a rather
specific allusion to a section appended to Greene's *A Notable Discovery
of Cozenage* (1591) where colliers are shown cheating their customers
by selling sacks filled with "small willow-coals, and half dross."[31] The
ideological conflict presented by the confidence games in *The Alchemist*
can also be found in Greene's cony-catching pamphlets, so that the
differences in their representation of profit accumulation offer us the
opportunity to describe more precisely the subversiveness of Jonson's
cozeners and of the generic convention they form.

Critics have long noted that Greene's pamphlets are riddled with
discontinuities. Walter Davis finds that each text is fissured into "two
styles" which "are each emblematic of different voices and different values," namely "the periodic moralizing style and the paratactical narra-

tive style," and he subsequently concludes that these "voices" are those "of two men, or of two sides of the strangely divided mind of Robert Greene."[32] We shall depart from Davis's individualistic reduction of this discontinuity to authorial psychology by arguing that the two "styles" or discourses point to an ideological conflict: the discrepancy between the pamphlets' announced project of moralistic muckraking and social reform, on the one hand, and their engagingly suspenseful narrative, on the other, signifies a subversion of a conservative social representation that potentially maintains the existing class hierarchy and the property relations which support it.

The moralizing discourse reflects the ideology of degree. Hence, the most prevalent theme in the moralizing is the condemnation of cony-catching as a social disorder in which citizens are dislodged from their class positions. In *A Notable Discovery of Cozenage,* the effect of cony-catching is a collapse of the hierarchical relationships in which the victims are inserted:

> The poor farmer simply going about his business or to his attorney's chamber is caught up and cozened of all. The servingman, sent with his lord's treasure, loseth ofttimes most part to these worms of the commonwealth. The prentice, having his master's money in charge, is spoiled by them, and from an honest servant either driven to run away or to live in discredit forever. The gentleman loseth his land, the merchant his stock, and all to these abominable cony-catchers. (P. 171).

The moralizing discourse constitutes concrete individuals as economic agents in the class hierarchy: the "farmer," "servingman," "prentice," and so forth are defined solely by the function they are assigned by the relations of production. The cony-catchers, however, resist the subject-constitution of degree; they are viewed as posing a special threat to the social structure because they have distanced themselves from it in both thought and action. Since they "are in religion mere atheists" (p. 174), they refuse to assume a place of metaphysical subjection to God in the providentially ordered chain of being on which the feudal hierarchy is based; and since they have the habit of "preferring cozenage before labour and choosing an idle practice before any honest form of good living" (p. 164), they refuse to assume a position of social subjection to an employer in which they can contribute to the reproduction of class relations. This theme of idleness enables us to define more specifically the ideology of the moralizing discourse because it is also a presupposition in the repressive Elizabethan statutes on vagrancy: as A. L. Beier has observed, "The main schemes, the statutes of 1576 and 1597 [which recommend the House of Correction for "idle" offenders], still assume that vagrants were trying to avoid work. . . . And the writers of the rogue literature perpetuated the image of vagrant crooks willing to do anything to avoid honest labor."[33] Since the moralizing in the pamphlets contains the same representation of vagrancy that justified the intervention of the royal government, usually in the form of imprisonment, corporal punishment, and forced labor, it can be described as a discourse mediated by a specific form of the ideology of degree that supported Elizabethan absolutism.

The narrative discourse, in contrast, reflects the ideology of possessive individualism. Hence, whereas the subjectivity of the citizens in the moralizing discourse is determined by their position in a social hierarchy, the narrative characterizes the cony-catchers as free subjects who are the origin of meaning, knowledge, and action. The cony-catchers are motivated primarily by a desire for profit accumulation; "The two ends I aim at," we hear one say, "is gain and ease; but by what honest gains I may get, never comes within the compass of my thoughts" (p. 174). Greene's individualistic treatment of the criminals becomes apparent when contrasted with More's deterministic representation of the thieves in *Utopia*: the cony-catchers are not influenced by social developments beyond their control, like displacement by the enclosures; instead they seem to transcend social determinants and freely choose to acquire money through confidence games. As a result, they have a demystifying and purely instrumental attitude toward the ideology of degree: the roles they play in their cony-catching plots usually require them to select and act out a specific position in the social hierarchy. The so-called "verser," for instance, is described as assuming "the countenance of a landed man" (p. 160); in *The Second Part of Cony-Catching* (1592), the cony-catchers, "apparelled like very honest and substantial citizens, come to bowl, as though rather they did it for sport than gains, and under that colour of carelessness, do shadow their pretended knavery" (p. 205). The cony-catchers treat degree not as a providentially ordered social structure which shapes the course of their lives, but as a mere device to be used at will.

The two discourses in the cony-catching pamphlets construct rather different subject-positions, thereby enlisting the reader in the ideological conflict they articulate. The moralizing discourse, in its insistence that the text is the product of an author who intends to influence the reader, foregrounds this author as the position of intelligibility, the "I" who stands in for Greene and describes his "book" as "written faithfully to discover these cozening practices" (p. 158). When occupying the place of this subject, the reader is aligned against the cony-catchers and constituted as a patriotic citizen who values the metaphysical and social hierarchies of degree and who accepts as "true" and "obvious" the representations of the cony-catchers mediated by the feudal ideology and Elizabethan absolutism. "Ah, gentlemen, merchants, yeomen and farmers," writes the moralizing author after describing a scam worked by a prostitute and her pander, "let this to you all, and to every degree else, be a caveat to warn you from lust, that your inordinate desire be not a means to impoverish your purses, discredit your good names, condemn your souls, but also that your wealth got with the sweat of your brows, or left by your parents as patrimony, shall be a prey to those cozening crossbiters!" (p. 181). In the narrative discourse, however, the author is subordinated to, and virtually indistinguishable from, the cony-catchers, who are consequently foregrounded as the position of intelligibility. When occupying the place of this subject, the reader is aligned with the cony-catchers, is privy to their complex machinations against the conies, and accepts the individualistic representation of the cony-catchers as "true" and "obvious." We read that "as soon as they see a plain country fellow, well and cleanly apparelled, either in a coat of homespun russet, or of frieze, as the time requires, and a side-pouch at his side—'There is a cony,' saith one" (p. 162), and the narrative secures our complicity by generating suspense and leading us to expect the successful completion of the crime. Thus, for the reader, the transition from moralizing to narrative discourse entails a sudden and unannounced shift to a different position of intelligibility and consequently to a different ideological position: a valorization of feudal degree gives way to a subversive valorization of bourgeois individualism, and the reader who had previously been harangued to consider cony-catching "egregious cozenage" is now cajoled to see it as a "merry jest" (p. 171).

Yet with texts as discontinuous as these pamphlets we may question whether individualism remains the privileged ideology. And indeed we learn that the cony-catchers are disrespectful not only of the providentially ordained class structure, but also of bourgeois enterprise: "They are given up into a reprobate sense and are in religion mere atheists, as they are in trade flat dissemblers" (p. 174). There are occasions in the narrative, furthermore, when suddenly, almost imperceptibly, another shift in the subject-position occurs, so that the individualistic discourse is subverted. In *A Notable Discovery of Cozenage,* for example, one confidence game involves making the cony believe that he is cheating an innocent bystander who is actually another cony-catcher; here the text constructs a position of intelligibility from which possessive individualism in the form of the cony's drive for profits is regarded explicitly as "greediness" (pp. 164, 165, 167), and hence the reader is encouraged to accept a judgment that maintains the static class hierarchy of degree by condemning profit accumulation. *The Second Part of Cony-Catching* similarly uses the confidence games to attack bourgeois individualism: a cony-catcher "who had apparelled himself marvellous brave, like some good well-favoured gentleman," deceives a maid that he has become her "suitor" so as to gain access to her master's property; yet since "she began to think better of herself than ever she did before, and waxed so proud that her other suitors were counted too base for her," the reader who had initially accepted the valorization of the cony-catcher's individualism is now invited to view it as a punishment for social pretensions which violate the feudal class hierarchy (pp. 224–25). At such points in the pamphlets, a subject-position in an individualistic discourse abruptly and paradoxically is transformed into a position in the ideology of degree, and the confidence games that had been seen as a threat to the social order now serve to strengthen that order. Because the positioning in the pamphlets is so contradictory, no discourse or ideology is privileged, and the reader moves from one position of intelligibility to the other, compelled to question both in the movement.

Even in this brief examination it becomes quite clear that Jonson's cozeners owe much to Greene's cony-catchers, that both character types are determined by the same ideological conflict, and that their positioning of the reader is equally unstable. What will be emphasized here, however, are the differences between them, the most striking of which is the virtual absence of feudal moralizing in *The Alchemist*. The moralizing discourse which establishes the occasion for the cony-catching pamphlets can be glimpsed in a much abbreviated form in Jonson's prologue, which advertises his intention to expose London crime ("No clime breeds better matter, for your whore, / Bawd, squire, impostor" [ll. 7–8]) in order to "better men" (l. 12). Because of this abbreviation of the moralizing, the cozeners' confidence games become the principal means by which violations of the feudal class hierarchy can be criticized and frustrated; but since the cozeners do not create a stable ideological position for the reader, since their confidence games can validate individualism and degree at the same time, the textual work contradicts the didactic intention stated in the prologue and puts into play another morality, another ideology. This radical destabilization of the feudal moralizing means that *The Alchemist* must be seen as more subversive than the pamphlets: Jonson's cozeners transform Greene's cony-catchers by creating more textual space for the valorization of bourgeois enterprise.

This is borne out by the discontinuous treatment of Surley, the only character who sees through the cozeners' schemes before Love-Wit's return. Surley's criticisms of the alchemical discussions between Subtle and the duped Sir Epicure Mammon strongly resemble the moralizing discourse in the cony-catching pamphlets: not only does he express his scepticism of alchemy by asserting that he "would not willingly be gull'd" (2.1.78), but he describes Subtle's specialized terminology as "canting" or thieves' jargon and indicates the cozeners' deception of Mammon with a metaphor that refers to traps set for rabbits: "The hay is a pitching" (2.3.42, 71). Exasperated by Mammon's unquestioning respect for the "doctor," Surley explicitly likens alchemy to cony-catching by arguing that the former "is a pretty kind of game, / Somewhat like tricks o' the cards, to cheat a man, / With charming" (2.3.180–82). Yet, unlike the authorial moralizing in the pamphlets, Surley's exposures never manage to set him up as a spokesman for the feudal ideology because they are grossly contradicted by his own individualistic reliance on cony-catching. Surley's criminality is revealed by Mammon, who tells his friend that the gold-generating philosopher's stone will obviate the need for the profit-making schemes on which he had formerly depended:

> You shall no more deale with the hollow die,
> Or the fraile card, No more be at charge of keeping
> The liuery-punke, for the yong heire, that must
> Seale, at all houres, in his shirt. No more,
> If he denie, ha'him beaten to't, as he is
> That brings him the commoditie.
>
> (2.1.9–14)

Surley resorts both to cheating at gambling and to commodity swindles, in which a prodigal gentleman is persuaded (here by a prostitute) to pawn his inheritance for a loan that includes both cash and worthless commodities; the device is yet another allusion to Greene's pamphlets and is exploited by other cozeners in city comedy.[34] We can see Surley's cony-catching technique in action, moreover, when he poses as a Spanish count in order to steal the wealthy Dame Pliant away from the cozeners and persuade her to marry him. Here his acquisitiveness leads him to propose a contract with the widow on the basis of his claim to having prevented Face and Subtle from staining her "honor": "Your fortunes may make me a man, / As mine ha' preseru'd you a woman" (4.6.13–14). Thus, Surley's insight into the cozeners' schemes can be attributed to his own criminal expertise, for he is characterized not as an upright defender of the feudal order, but as a competitor of the cozeners who like them pursues wealth and prestige. Yet because Surley is not as clever or successful as the cozeners, because his attempt to win the widow is finally defeated by Face and Love-Wit, he actually winds up increasing our admiration for them. Jonson's text so appropriates the cony-catching pamphlets as to privilege the cozeners' individualism, however much this ideological determination is qualified by degree elsewhere in the interrogative textual work. Examining the connection between the pamphlets and the play registers a subversive diminution of feudal moralizing which is symptomatic of how far *The Alchemist* goes toward approving bourgeois enterprise even while dramatizing its disruption of the class hierarchy. Jonson's text, in its processing of various cultural materials, in its discontinuous narrative and characterization, offers a set of distinctly progressive strategies to contain the transition to capitalism.

III

Similar strategies of containment seem to distinguish city comedies from the later years of Elizabeth's reign through the Jacobean period. We can perceive a discontinuity in the treatment of commercial activity which points to the ideological conflict. Businessmen form a character type in the genre, and they are repeatedly portrayed as greedy citizens who enrich themselves by relying on unethical or illegal means, often at the expense of the gentry. Quomodo, the woollen-draper in Middleton's *Michaelmas Term* (c. 1606), deviously gains possession of the prodigal Easy's estate through a fraudulent bond. Meercraft, the projector in Jonson's *The Devil is an Ass* (1616), nearly wins the title to the boorish Fitzdottrel's land after dazzling him with a sham industrial venture. Allwit, a goldsmith in Middleton's *A Chaste Maid in Cheapside*

(c. 1611), leads a life of aristocratic leisure because of his unsavory financial arrangement with Sir Walter Whorehound; as Allwit explains, the knight has

> Maintained my house this ten years,
> Not only keeps my wife, but a keeps me,
> And all my family; I am at his table,
> He gets me all my children, and pays the nurse,
> Monthly, or weekly, puts me to nothing,
> Rent, nor church duties, not so much as the scavenger:
> The happiest state that ever man was born to.
>
> (1.2.16–22)[35]

Even the glowing portrait of the bourgeoisie in Dekker's *The Shoemakers' Holiday* (1599) is not without its darker side. Simon Eyre accomplishes his meteoric rise from master shoemaker to Lord Mayor of London by committing two crimes: he deals with a Dutch skipper who seems to be evading the customs duties, and he impersonates an alderman to impress this foreigner with his "countenance in the city" (2.3.138).[36] As in *The Alchemist,* the businessmen's intrigues are occasionally motivated by the attractions of social climbing. Once Quomodo is confident that he has successfully tricked Easy out of his property in Essex, he takes a moment to fantasize about his new status as landowner:

> Now shall I be divulg'd a landed man
> Throughout the Livery; one points, another whispers,
> A third frets inwardly, let him fret and hang!
> . . .
> Now come my golden days in,
> —Whither is the worshipful Master Quomodo and his fair
> bedfellow rid forth?—To his land in Essex!—Whence comes
> those goodly load of logs?—From his land in Essex!—Where
> grows this pleasant fruit? says one citizen's wife in the
> Row.—At Master Quomodo's orchard in Essex.—Oh, oh, does
> it so? I thank you for that good news, i'faith.
>
> (3.4.5–7, 12–18)[37]

In Massinger's *A New Way to Pay Old Debts* (1621), the extorting usurer Overreach also aims to improve his social position: he hopes that the huge dowry he has ruthlessly amassed for his daughter will attract

Lord Lovell to marry and thereby elevate her to "right honorable" (4.1.129).[38]

The shady deals should not mislead us into thinking that the plays are merely moral condemnations of such vices as greed and lust. Nietzsche's "genealogy" of moral values, by producing "a knowledge of the conditions and circumstances in which they grew, under which they evolved and changed," exposes their social origin and function: Nietzsche argues that "a concept denoting political superiority always resolves itself into a concept denoting superiority of soul," so that the attribution of evil to a social other (sex, race, class) can be seen as reflecting a social hierarchy and constituting a basic ideological category of power and domination.[39] In city comedies, the equation of social mobility with immoral conduct reflects feudal class relations, in which birth and title dictate social position; the immorality identified with bourgeois enterprise is a function of the ideology of degree. Moreover, because some of the intrigues in these plays contain topical allusions, the moral judgment is being delivered on actual incidents in Renaissance England; Richard Levin has pointed out that the commodity swindle in *Michaelmas Term,* for instance, apparently alludes to a case brought before Star Chamber.[40] Since the businessmen we have been examining combine typical characterization, moral condemnation, and topical allusion, they are particularly dense *ideologemes,* representations of a real upwardly mobile class which are mediated by ideology-inscribed cultural forms like the clever slave and the conycatcher and which carry a moral judgment determined by the feudal ideology.[41] Viewed in this way, the repeated association of commercial activity with vice and crime seems to suggest that the plays legitimize the traditional class hierarchy.

Yet the characterizations of the businessmen so position the viewer or reader as to force him to qualify this suggestion. We alone share in the knowledge of their intrigues, just as we are given an insider's look at the cozeners' confidence games in *The Alchemist,* so that their brilliant mastery tends to win our admiration, a response that is not a little encouraged by the naïveté and sheer stupidity with which their victims are usually characterized. "At the center of figures such as Quomodo," notes Brian Gibbons, "is their menace, their evil, their corrupting effect on society; but their threat is at once less sensational and more difficult to dismiss when we see what determination and intelligence they summon in pursuit of their prey. Middleton does not oversimplify the kind of liveliness from which the threat springs."[42] To avoid the individualistic assumptions of Gibbons' author-oriented comment, we must ground the reader's perception of this "liveliness" in the discontinuous textual work and recognize it as an ideological effect of dramatic structure. Because the text presents the businessmen as the position from which the action becomes intelligible, their feudal image as social "menace" is decentered, enabling a valorization of their bourgeois "determination and intelligence." The result of this decentering is that the fortune hunters in city comedy, from Eyre and Volpone to Allwit and Meercraft to Overreach, typically confront us with a paradoxical combination of villainy and virtuosity. As villains, they reflect the reactionary ideology which asserts that their insatiable greed upsets the feudal order; as virtuoso manipulators, they reflect a progressive ideology which affirms their capitalist drive for profits.

A similar discontinuity can be seen in the treatment of another character type in early city comedies, the gentlemen who resort to money-making intrigues frequently in retaliation for the costly deception they suffer at the hands of the businessmen. These gentleman usually win back what is theirs, but the ideological significance of their victory is made ambiguous by the attendant circumstances. Massinger's Welborne regains his property from Overreach, but to do so he devises an elaborate plot that rivals the extortioner's in its ingenuity, and he must rely on the aid of Marrall, Overreach's "creature." Although the gallant Wittipol in Jonson's *The Devil is an Ass* is not cheated out of his land, he succeeds in preventing the hoodwinked Fitzdottrel from losing his. Nonetheless, it is difficult for us to regard Wittipol as wholly honorable after we have watched his effort to seduce Mistress Fitzdottrel and the chicanery he uses to protect her husband. Indeed, Wittipol can help the Fitzdottrels only by joining forces with Meercraft and agreeing to impersonate a "Spanish" lady, a key element in the projector's swindle. The gentleman's ultimate success in these examples seems to be an affirmation of the feudal class structure, but the means by which he achieves it ally him to the greedy businessman who seeks to fleece the gentry, thereby exposing the conflicting ideological determinations that shape the gentleman type.[43] In Middleton's *A Mad World, My Masters* (c. 1606), the ideological conflict is signified by an abrupt dislocation of the textual positioning in the last act. The dissolute Follywit cannot come into his inheritance until the death of his grandfather, Sir Bounteous Progress, so he devises a series of successful swindles to share Sir Bounteous' wealth while he is still living. Follywit's actions are not at first seen as criminal because of the complicity which the

text creates between him and us, who may well agree that the gentleman is only taking what will rightfully be his. Yet Follywit finally loses
his integrity as a position of intelligibility when the two thieves who
have been his accomplices are arrested, underscoring his criminality,
and he unwittingly marries his grandfather's whore.

Middleton's *A Chaste Maid in Cheapside* offers a remarkable variation on this discontinuity: it introduces several gentlemen whose
machinations bear a striking resemblance, but who are not characterized in such a way as to elicit the same sort of judgment from us.
Whorehound agrees to support the Allwits in return for Mistress Allwit's sexual favors and ingratiates himself with the prosperous goldsmith Yellowhammer in order to marry his daughter Moll; Touchwood
Senior is contracted by Sir Oliver Kix to impregnate his childless wife
for a fee, and Touchwood Junior plots to marry Moll without her
father's consent. There are certainly differences in motivation here:
Whorehound is driven by greed and lust, while the Touchwood brothers are impoverished gentry who want to improve their fortunes and
who truly love the women to whom they are married or engaged. All
the same, we should not minimize the financial goals that figure so
prominently in each of these characters' actions. Despite the resemblances between them, however, Whorehound is fatally wounded in a
duel with Touchwood Junior and repents that he is "o'ergrown with
sin" (5.1.74) before he dies, whereas Touchwood Senior so successfully
executes his part of the contract that Kix pledges to support him and
his burgeoning family, and his brother marries Moll to the approbation
of the gentry and citizens present at the wedding. Even Yellowhammer
is won over to the newlyweds' side. The contradiction in the representations of Whorehound and the Touchwood brothers indicates that,
like Jonson's Love-Wit, Middleton's gentlemen function as an intricate strategy of containment: their membership in the gentry maintains
the feudal veneration of status, while the conflicting treatments of
their resourceful money-getting at once reject (in Whorehound) and approve (in the brothers) the emerging capitalist ethos of possessive
individualism.

The ideological tension produced by such accommodations inevitably complicates the endings of early city comedies. The bourgeois
optimism that pervades Dekker's *The Shoemakers' Holiday* runs into
logical difficulties when the king appears in the final scene. The king
not only grants Eyre's request to pardon the deserter Lacy, but goes so
far as to bless the gentleman's marriage to Rose, a citizen's daughter,

silencing the opposition of the lovers' status-conscious parents with the egalitarian remark that "love respects no blood, / Cares not for difference of birth and state" (5.5.105–6). At the same time, however, we are never allowed to forget the traditional class hierarchy: Lacy is knighted to "redeem" the "honour which he lost in France," and the king can appreciate Eyre only as a stereotypical commoner, insisting that he "be even as merry / As if thou wert among thy shoemakers" (5.5.113–14). This inconsistency in the king's actions turns the ending into an ideological standoff, in which the royal power whose legitimacy depends on degree simultaneously transgresses and reinforces class distinctions.

Middleton's plays have frequently been faulted for their implausible resolutions. In *Michaelmas Term,* Levin takes issue with the abrupt metamorphosis of Easy from a gullible prodigal to an efficient operator who recovers his land from Quomodo and even marries the swindler's wife: "We are never wholly convinced that we should rejoice in the defeat of those whose cleverness has been the principal source of our pleasure, or in the victory of one of the weakest and least interesting characters in the play."[44] What underlies Levin's disapproving response is the skewed positioning in the text. Plausibility is an effect produced when characters are coherently developed and the viewer or reader is able to occupy a stable subject-position from which the plot resolution can be seen as "true" or "right," i.e., intelligible because consistent with the characters' actions. The discontinuities in Middleton's characterization, however, make such subjective stability impossible: after being complicit with Quomodo and his collaborators for much of the play, we are more than likely to resist the text's effort to evoke our identification with Easy, whose ultimate success will therefore seem unsatisfying and implausible. A sudden turnaround also puts into question the ending of Middleton's *A Trick to Catch the Old One* (c. 1606). After our participation in the cunning schemes and in the obvious delight with which the rakish gentleman Witgood regains his estate from his miserly uncle Lucre, eludes his persistent creditors, and marries the niece of the wealthy businessman Hoard, it becomes difficult to identify with his final repentance, and we may not just regret it, but doubt Witgood's self-consistency, his sincerity. R. B. Parker has concluded that in Middleton's "early comedies, the difficulty of reconciling his immoral characters with a moral denouement results in a split of tone and the use of such theatrical devices as *deus ex machina,* court scenes, or unmotivated masques."[45] Yet it will be useful to remind ourselves that because these formal discontinuities are disruptive of the subject-positions constructed in the texts, they prevent the development of a single, unified ideological standpoint: we can read the "difficulty" of Middleton's city comedies as a symptom of the considerable pressure put on them to endorse the personal freedom to accumulate wealth without overriding class distinctions founded on birth.[46]

IV

It seems apparent that early city comedy comprises an ambivalent response to the contradictions in English society. The repeated attempt to "solve" them produces a number of discontinuities that ultimately stem from an ideological conflict: the Elizabethan and Jacobean plays exhibit an approving interest in the rise of capitalism by applauding its high energy and calculation, but they still cling to the feudal order and the moral values that uphold it. During the reign of Charles I, however, city comedy undergoes a fundamental transformation. Fewer professional playwrights are working in the genre, and those who do take it up so assimilate its conventions as to generate an entirely different solution to social contradictions. Late city comedy continues to come to terms with commercial activity and social climbing in London settings; what has changed is the ideological significance of its response. We can detect a renewed esteem for the ideology of degree that is extremely guarded in its attitude toward bourgeois enterprise.

Perhaps the clearest indication of this change is the treatment of businessmen: they tend to support the traditional class hierarchy rather than threaten it. Crasy, the usurer in Brome's *The City Wit* (c. 1629), is a notable departure from the ruthless villains in the earlier plays: he actually goes bankrupt because he has refused to follow the deceitful practices of a Quomodo or an Overreach; "All was but my kind heart in trusting" is how he accounts for his financial ruin (1.1).[47] Crasy decides that "what my willing honesty hath seem'd to loose, my affected deceits shall recover" (1.1), and he works a series of confidence tricks that dupe his untrustworthy debtors into repaying him and deflate their aristocratic airs, whereby the complicit viewer or reader is positioned in the ideology of degree. Brome's text contains an allusion to *The Alchemist* that calls attention to his transformation of the city comedy genre: Crasy enlists the aid of the prostitute Dol Tryman and her younger brother Geffrey Crack, establishing a "covenant" with them or, as Crack puts it, an "Indenture Tripartite, and't please you, like *Subtle, Dol,* and *Face*" (3.1). Unlike Jonson's trio of swindlers, however,

Crasy is trying only to recover his own money, and at the end he promises his victims that "what, by my sights, I got more than my due, / I timely will restore again to you" (5.1). By relying on deceit and consorting with a prostitute, Crasy has of course besmirched his motives which are otherwise commendable from the viewpoint of the feudal ideology, yet the text absolves him with its emphasis on his morality and with a twist in the plot. Thus, at one point, Crasy pauses to express his scruples: "in despite of the Justice that provok'd me, my Conscience a little turns at these brain-tricks" (5.1); and not only does Tryman repent her "old course" (3.1), but she turns out to be Crasy's faithful apprentice Jeremy in disguise. This startling discovery comes as a surprise to Crasy as well as us, sacrificing plausibility by undermining the usurer's function as position of knowledge in order to maintain his innocence against the moral suspicion provoked by all his subterfuges.

Sir John Frugal, the merchant in Massinger's *The City Madam* (1632), also reveals a rehabilitation of the typical businessman in early city comedy. Like Crasy, he does not depend on deception to "increase his heap," but restricts himself to "where the law gives him" (1.2.141–43).[48] He is kindhearted instead of miserly or grasping: when he confronts several debtors who are late in repaying his loans, he is touched by his brother Luke's plea for leniency and decides to "give 'em longer day" (1.3.113). Sir John heartily agrees with Lord Lacy's feudal pronouncement that "a fit decorum must be kept, the court / Distinguished from the city" (3.2.154–55), and so the only intrigue in which he engages is intended to cure his wife and daughters of their social pretensions: with the help of the lord, his son Sir Maurice Lacy, and the country gentleman Mr. Plenty, he masquerades as a savage Indian from the New World in order to stop the women from ridiculously following court fads and living too far above their station. Sir John remains undefiled by this intrigue not just because he has sterling motives and aristocratic accomplices, but because it is a reworking of the "disguised duke" plot that animates such plays as Marston's *The Malcontent* (1603) and Shakespeare's *Measure for Measure* (1604).[49] Like Duke Vincentio, Sir John makes a hasty and inexplicable departure at the beginning, yet subsequently returns, his identity concealed, to spy on his household and correct the wrongs he finds there. Notwithstanding this basic similarity, however, Sir John is a merchant, not a duke, a knighted commoner not a nobleman by birth, and this discontinuity in Massinger's appropriation of the conventional plot betrays the effort to ennoble him.

It has been argued that such transformations should be read as the emergence of a progressive attitude in city comedy, a mature willingness to embrace capitalist values.[50] Yet if we examine them carefully against earlier plays in the genre, it seems more likely that they are symptomatic of a conservative reaction, in which bourgeois enterprise is represented as an activity that reproduces the feudal order. In early city comedy, the ideological representations of businessmen reflect possessive individualism, even if frequently overdetermined by a reactionary moral judgment: the validating positions of intelligibility consist of equal competing individuals who freely pursue their self-interest in the acquisition of wealth, respecting the status accorded to rank only in their desire to improve their own class position. In late city comedy, the businessmen are ideologemes that reflect degree: the textual positioning privileges members of a hierarchical community whose personal freedom to acquire wealth is constrained by a conflicting impulse to avoid any conduct that challenges the hierarchy. The capitalists in the Caroline plays are committed not so much to the profit motive as to the feudal ideology with all its moral restrictions. This paradox, implicit in the generic transformations we have considered, constitutes a new, more illusory strategy of containment: it magically resolves the real threat posed to the traditional class structure by the rise of capitalism.

We can develop this point further by observing that Caroline city comedies displace the emphasis usually given to the villains in the early form of the genre: when bourgeois characters are now portrayed as greedy or socially subversive, they often inhabit the margins of the play in greatly abbreviated roles and are finally defeated or else reformed. In Nabbes's *Covent Garden* (1632), as soon as the innkeeper Mrs. Tongall meets the foolish gentleman Dungworth, she begins to calculate: "I must project a profit out of the accident; a new Gowne, or a Beaver, or some composition with a bond of assurance. when I procure him a good wife. Perhaps hee shall have my Daughter *Jynny*" (1.2).[51] Yet most of the action is concerned with the honorable city justice Sir Generous Worthy and his family, and Tongall is never given the opportunity to operate on Dungworth; instead she inexplicably latches onto the nonentity Littleword, who has only a single word of dialogue in the text and does not prove to be profitable for her. In contrast to the subject-positions created by the earlier treatments of commercial activity, we don't identify with Tongall: our attention is rather drawn to Sir Generous, under whose supervision the pretentious upstarts Warrant, Spruce, and Dungworth are humiliated. In Brome's *The Damoiselle* (c. 1637), similarly, Vermine is merely *described* as a rapacious usurer who beggars the gentry "by the strong hand of Law, Bribes, and oppression" (1.1); for the most part, he actually functions as the gullible victim of the gentleman Dryground, whose well-intentioned schemes bring about Vermine's reformation.[52]

Nabbes's *The Bride* (1638) seems to introduce a credible villain in Raven, who plots to be made the heir of his uncle, the wealthy merchant Goodlove. Yet whenever Raven tries to remove the only obstacle in his path, Goodlove's son Theophilus, he is foiled by accidents or Theophilus' superior strategy. On one occasion, Raven arranges to have his unarmed cousin assaulted by a gang of "blades," but Theophilus valiantly—and somewhat miraculously—overpowers them all. On another occasion, Raven successfully persuades Theophilus to yield to his love for his father's fiancée and run off with her on the day of the wedding; instead of disinheriting his son, however, Goodlove suddenly announces that he had long known about Theophilus' affection for the young woman and in fact had intended to have them married. As these examples suggest, the twists in the plot incline toward the ridiculously improbable, discouraging any identification with Raven and signaling an ideological pressure to stigmatize profit accumulation by condemning his covetous attempt on his uncle's fortune. Here the energy and intelligence of the earlier businessmen in the genre are reduced to a ludicrous, and therefore easily dismissible, ineptness. The laughter provoked by Raven's inability to direct the action for his ends is an efficient way to minimize real social contradictions.

Massinger's Luke Frugal remains the only villain who dominates a considerable part of a Caroline city comedy, and indeed critics have frequently noted how much he resembles the colossal Overreach. Nonetheless, it is possible to observe how ideology diminishes his characterization. The overweening ambition that drives Overreach gives way to Luke's monstrous greed. Whereas Overreach seeks to better his social position, Luke succumbs to a crazed obsession with mere wealth: his rallying cry is not "right honorable," but "All human happiness consists in store" (4.2.133). This transformation is accompanied by a corresponding meanness of behavior. Overreach is fond of aristocratic displays that dazzle Lady Allworth's cook Furnace:

> This Sir Giles feeds high, keeps many servants,
> Who must at his command do any outrage;

Rich in his bait; vast in his expenses
Yet he to admiration still increases
In wealth, and lordships.
                                                (2.2.110–14)

Luke, however, is a miser who enjoys the "dainties" at a banquet in his
honor because they are "unpaid for" (5.3.15–16) and decides to sell his
brother's family as sacrifices for an Indian cult since "they are burden-
some to me, / And eat too much. And if they stay in London, / They
will find friends that to my loss will force me / To composition"
(5.1.56–59). These differences give us a glimpse of the feudal ideology
at work, decreasing Luke's power to create a position of identification
for the audience and encouraging our esteem for the generous, more
effective, and more conservative Sir John. Luke's control of the action,
however short-lived, certainly does not make him as inconsequential
as Nabbes's Tongall or Brome's Vermine; yet the enormity of his crimes,
especially his readiness to accept the Indians' offer, does not complicate
moral judgments in quite the way that the virtuosity of the earlier villains did.

The same reactionary ideology that rehabilitates or displaces the
conventional bourgeois characters in Caroline city comedies also transforms the gentlemen: they too become advocates of the traditional class
hierarchy. When Bornwell, the landed knight in Shirley's *The Lady of
Pleasure* (1635), chastises his wife Aretina for aping the aristocratic
practice of conspicuous consumption, we are positioned in the ideology of degree by his concern not only about the possibility of his financial ruin but about the immodest height of her aspirations: "you make
play / Not a pastime but a tyranny," he tells her, "and vex / Yourself and
my estate by it" (1.1).[53] Bornwell's intrigue completely reverses the libertinism that forces such gallants as Witgood and Welborne to turn to
their profitable confidence tricks: unlike them, he does no more than
pose as a prodigal and *pretend* to dissipate all his wealth so that he can
shock his wife out of her wasteful spending. Lord Lacy in *The City
Madam* can be considered another laundered version of the earlier
gentlemen. He creates a position of intelligibility as the representative
of feudal values whose sly "inventions" successfully reform Sir John's
arrogant wife and daughters and who counsels Luke on the standard
of living appropriate to the family of a prosperous merchant. A gap in
the text exposes the ideological operation in Massinger's treatment of
Lacy: near the end, we suddenly learn that he has "pawn'd" his land to

Sir John, but in contrast to Lacy's predecessors in the genre, the question of whether this was due to his dissolute past or his mismanagement is conveniently left unanswered, and the force of the revelation is to provide more evidence for Luke's inhumane avarice—it is he who brings it up in an effort to silence Lacy's opposition to his deal with the Indians. Lacy's conduct is so far beyond reproach in the play that he even has qualms about calling Luke a "villain": "Heaven forgive me /For speaking so unchristianly, though he deserves it" (5.2.85–86). As we saw with the honest usurer Crasy, Lacy's bad conscience signals the textual work of rehabilitating the character type.

When a gentleman in a Caroline comedy is motivated primarily by a desire to make money rather than preserve the feudal order, we can nevertheless perceive an ideological pressure to absolve him and contain his commercial activity. Thus, Moneylack in Brome's *The Sparagus Garden* (1635) is introduced as a knight who wasted his estate in "riotousnesse" and caused his wife such anguish that "her long night watches at home shortened her dayes, and cast her into her grave" (1.3). Yet when Moneylack's father-in-law upbraids him about his sordid past, the knight's language abruptly shifts to transparent verse to register a note of sincere repentance: "sir, I wish my life might have excus'd / Hers, farre more precious: never had a man / A juster cause to mourne" (1.3). Moreover, Moneylack's attempts to recoup his losses aim not for the land and wealthy wives sought by a Love-Wit or Follywit but for "small parcells of ready money" (4.10), and we cannot avoid the impression that despite his "tricks" and "discoveries," he does not substantially enrich himself, that his motive is not greed but necessity.

The intrigue by which he and two accomplices empty the pockets of the provincial Tim Hoyden contains another of Brome's allusions to the trio of swindlers in *The Alchemist* (2.2), thus indicating how far Moneylack's characterization diverges from the conventional rake in the early plays. Tim is a "Yeomans sonne" who resembles the naive Kastril: as soon as he appears, he announces himself as an easy mark by informing Moneylack, "I have foure hundred pounds sir; and I brought it up to towne on purpose to make my selfe a cleare gentleman of it" (2.3). Like the ruses of the "venture *tripartite,*" Moneylack's deception of Tim constitutes a biting satire of social climbing, which, along with his victim's obtuseness, positions us in degree and goes some way toward extenuating the questionable nature of the deed. This extenuation culminates at the end when Moneylack's crime is discovered: instead of implicating his "Lungs," the shopkeeper Brittleware, he shoulders all the blame and pledges to Tim that he will "give . . . all the satisfaction that I can" (5.13). Moneylack's admission of guilt has the paradoxical effect of a redemption that ultimately confirms the traditional class hierarchy: we are asked to believe that although his poverty compels him to rely on illicit acts, he still has the honorable scruples of a gentleman. Love-Wit in *The Alchemist* cannot sustain such a belief because he makes off with the loot and the widow at the end. Love-Wit's assertion of his superior class position in his dealings with Face actually undermines feudal values, reducing them to a mystification of the gentleman's individualism. Brome's text develops a conservative accommodation of commercial activity that removes the subversiveness it had in the earlier form of the genre. Moneylack's "project" frustrates a character's move to raise his social status and concludes with a penitent restitution of the ill-gotten gains.

The conservatism of late city comedy also results in a transformation of the critical attitude toward the court taken by some of the earlier plays. This becomes clear after we first observe that both forms of the genre articulate their criticism in feudal terms, with the court represented as a site of social climbing and profit accumulation. The provincial Andrew Gruel in Middleton's *Michaelmas Term,* a predecessor of Brome's Tim Hoyden, is portrayed as an upstart courtier who tries to strengthen his tenuous class status by marrying Quomodo's daughter Susan. Andrew, like Tim, is satirized on the basis of degree. The text repeatedly ridicules his social pretensions by indicating his lower-class origins: he writes an offensively illiterate letter to Mrs. Quomodo; his mother and his pander remind us that he is "a tooth-drawer's son" (1.1.251, 2.1.140); he loses Susan to the decayed gentleman who is his chief rival; he is ultimately forced to marry the woman he had tried to prostitute, the daughter of a Northamptonshire "hay-tosser" (3.1.23).

While the Caroline plays contain this sort of satire on upwardly mobile courtiers, their feudal rehabilitation of the genre intensifies their reaction against the bourgeois values at court by shifting it from a satiric subplot to a moralistic main plot and by proliferating the court connections of the character types. Whereas in early city comedy the businessmen and gentlemen who set up positions in possessive individualism seem to act on their own initiative, with the help of agents but almost never depending on courtiers to conduct their financial ventures, the Caroline transformation frequently presents an alignment of these characters against the court, positioning us in an effort to reinforce the feudal class hierarchy. In Jonson's *The Devil is an Ass,* the brief references to the court's involvement in Meercraft's projects, such as his pursuit of a royal patent of monopoly for "a new kind of fucus (paint for ladies)," heighten the sense of his virtuosity, increase his control over the conned Fitzdottrel, and validate his commercial activity (3.1.372). In Massinger's *The City Madam,* conversely, Sir John Frugal's wife and daughters express their social aspirations by emulating court culture, but the audience is never allowed to share their disrespect for class rank: it is made questionable right at the outset, where a conversation between Frugal's apprentices constructs the position from which the women will be satirized:

> Goldwire.   there was some shape and proportion
>   Of a merchant's house in our family; but since
>   My master, to gain precedency for my mistress
>   Above some elder merchants' wives, was knighted,
>   'Tis grown a little court in bravery,
>   Variety of fashions, and those rich ones:
>   There are few great ladies going to a masque
>   That do outshine ours in their everyday habits.
> Tradewell. 'Tis strange my master in his wisdom can
>   Give the reins to such exorbitancy.
>
>   (1.1.20–29)

The "wisdom" at issue is the feudal ideology; Sir John demonstrates that he can exercise this "wisdom" by plotting with Lord Lacy to teach the women that "a merchant's house" is not "a little court." From the progressive standpoint of an early city comedy like *The Devil is an Ass,* the court has an exciting gold-rush atmosphere where money-making schemes collapse class distinctions and extend the social power of individualism; from the reactionary standpoint of late city comedy, court life encourages a lamentable decay of feudal values, in which bourgeois self-interest compromises degree.

In Shirley's *The Lady of Pleasure,* the honorable Celestina, widow of an "honest knight" (1.1), portrays courtiers as aristocrats on the make, racing to marry wealth regardless of class rank:

> No widow
> Left wealthy can be throughly warm in mourning,
> But some one noble blood or lusty kindred
> Claps in with his gilt coach and Flandrian trotters,
> And hurries her away to be a countess.

> Courtiers have spies, and great ones with large titles,
> Cold in their own estates, would warm themselves
> At a rich city bonfire. . . .
> No matter for corruption of blood—
> Some undone courtier made her husband rich,
> And this new lord receives it back again.
>
> (2.2)

Here the prodigal gentleman who wastes his inheritance in early city comedy is turned into the "undone courtier" whose dealings on the marriage market undermine the social hierarchy by neglecting "corruption of blood," thereby striking at the metaphysical foundation of aristocratic status, the identification of worth with birth. This feudal criticism of the court is implicit in the quarrel between Aretina and Bornwell which sets Shirley's main plot in motion: she urges Bornwell to seek court office, but he regards any service to the absolutist state as morally questionable:

> *Aretina.* A narrow-minded husband is a thief
> To his own fame, and his preferment too;
> He shuts his parts and fortunes from the world,
> While, from the popular vote and knowledge, men
> Rise to employment in the state.
> *Bornwell.* I have
> No great ambition to buy preferment
> At so dear a rate.
> *Aretina.* Nor I to sell my honor
> By living poor and sparingly.
>
> (1.1)

The quarrel presents competing definitions of "perferment" and "honor." What Bornwell rejects is preferment based on "the popular vote and knowledge"; the preferment he would approve is based on class rank, whereby birth determines worth for "employment in the state." The absolutist state disregards the innate nobility on which the class distinctions of degree are grounded in favor of "fame," whereby popularity, command of other classes' attention, determines worth. Similarly, Bornwell defines "honor" as spiritual superiority, while Aretina defines it as a material social practice, conspicuous consumption: he argues that she can spend less "with safety of / Your birth and honor, since the truest wealth / Shines from the soul, and draws up just admirers" (1.1). From Bornwell's feudal perspective, to seek court office means selling one's honor by measuring it not in metaphysical terms but in social ones, as Aretina tends to do. The commercial metaphor for compromised honor reappears at the end, again associated with court culture; Celestina uses it to rebuff a lord's sexual overtures:

> Lord.   there is a spacious dwelling
> Prepared within my heart for such a mistress.
> Celestina. Your mistress, my good lord?
> Lord.   Why, my good lady,
> Your sex doth it no dishonor
> To become mistress to a noble servant
> In the now court Platonic way. Consider
> Who 'tis that pleads to you; my birth and present
> Value can be no stain to your embrace.
>   (5.1)

Celestina's response is to stage a lesson in the ideology of degree: she agrees to prostitute herself to the lord's "birth and present / Value" if he sells his coat of arms to "a chapman," forcing him to realize that "honor" is "that which grows and withers with my soul, / Beside the body's stain" (5.1), that the social prestige of the court should be founded on morality. Martin Butler describes Celestina's conservative attitude toward court life: "She is not so much attacking the court as defending the *status quo* (the system of honor) which is unbalanced by the lord's exceeding of his place. The lord's failure to match his 'worth' to his 'status' (the two ideas suggested by 'honor') disrupts and nullifies the system; Celestina's riposte suggests that the system is prescriptive and that, to deserve his status, the lord must recognize the responsibilities, as well as the privileges, that it confers."[54] For Butler, Shirley's text conceives of Caroline England as a "harmoniously balanced society," where the court and gentry like Bornwell and Celestina each have "their *place*" (p. 175). What needs to be emphasized, however, is that this is a reactionary social representation which values the traditional class hierarchy over what is presented as the court's individualistic approach to social relations, the unrestrained pursuit of self-interest, whether in the form of profit accumulation or sexual promiscuity. The criticism of the court in late city comedy must not be taken as progressive or revolutionary in its ideological standpoint: the plays rather present a feudal response to the contradictory workings of the absolutist state, the economic, political, and ideological cultural practices which protect feudal privilege while integrating bourgeois interests in Caroline England.

V

The conservatism evident in such generic transformations can perhaps explain the considerable emphasis placed on maintaining the integrity of the family in late city comedy. The conservative image of the family during the Renaissance conceives of it as a patriarchal institution that reproduces feudal class relations and the absolutist state. It is characterized by age and sex hierarchies which are overdetermined by the ideology of degree through repeated analogies between the head of the household and such figures of authority as the king, government officials, clergy, teachers, and shop masters. This sort of analogical thinking gave rise to the patriarchalism in political speeches and treatises by writers like James I and Sir Robert Filmer: as Gordon Schochet has shown, arguments in favor of absolute monarchy could hold "that because political power was merely an extension of natural and paternal authority, the obligation of the subject to obey his sovereign was identical to the unquestioning obedience a child owed its father."[55] The patriarchal image of the family was disseminated in courtesy books on the proper behavior of wives and children and in religious instruction, particularly interpretations of the Fifth Commandment. In the *Shorter Catechism* (1644) of the Westminster Assembly of Divines, for example, this commandment is given a generalized reading that draws feudal class distinctions:

> Q[uestion] 64. *What is required in the fifth Commandment?*
>
> A[nswer]. The fifth Commandment requireth the preserving the honour, and performing the duties, belonging to every one in their severall places and relations, as Superiors, Inferiors, or Equals.
>
> Q. 65. *What is forbidden in the fifth Commandment?*
>
> A. The fifth Commandment, forbiddeth the neglecting of, or doing anything against, the honour and duty which belongeth in their severall places and relations.[56]

This feudal image of the patriarchal family is in itself highly authoritarian, yet it also mediates between paternal authority and political domination, between family and state. The scene of biological reproduction contributes to social reproduction, not just because it maintains the population at relatively stable levels, but because it leads to the internalization of familial duties that can strengthen the power structure in society at large, whether it be aristocratic hegemony or absolute monarchy.

It is important, however, to avoid confusing this image of the family with real family life during the Renaissance. The image no doubt determined lived experience to some extent by encouraging the obedience of wives and children and the submission of dominated classes; but since social agents are always dispersed over a range of different ideological positions (political, religious, familial, sexual, etc.), and since the relative unity of ideological discourses admits a wide margin of logical inconsistency, no single ideological interpellation hermetically seals the subject off from other possibilities for action. S. D. Amussen's examination of patriarchal political theory and family life in the provinces demonstrates that the theory "provided a means to maintain order when it was most threatened," but also notes that "the general acceptance of the gender order stands in marked contrast to the attitudes toward the class order," which show more conflict because "systems of ranking," although consistently hierarchical, were shifting "from the more traditional one of status to a more 'modern' one based on wealth and, eventually, class."[57] During this period, furthermore, the patriarchal image of the family had conflicting meanings—one dynastic, linked closely to feudal aristocracy and absolutism in its concern with maintaining the continuity of lineal descent, class position, and political power; the other affective, linked closely to bourgeois liberalism in its individualistic conception of the family as a "private" space of emotional fulfillment and morality, autonomous from the "public" space of social practices like economic exchange and political action.[58] Although the Renaissance image of the family remained consistently male-dominated in its articulation of sexual roles, this contest in meaning meant that patriarchalism could be made to support conflicting political ideologies: Christopher Hill has observed that "during the revolutionary period even radical theories were often still expressed in patriarchal forms," even if this necessitated a significant transformation of the feudal and absolutist meanings we have outlined above.[59] In view of such divergences, we must be careful how we use the patriarchal image of the family to interpret the drama. Specifically, we would do well to heed Levin's warning about the use of cultural history to cen-

sure the behavior of a character that is favorably portrayed in the text;
as Levin aptly puts it, "The ideas of the time have become a club with
which to clobber the character."[60] Our materialist approach will be
guided by the discontinuous textual work, and we will focus on the
ideological shifts implied in different treatments of the patriarchal image and their different patterns of positioning.

In early city comedy, violations of familial duties occur with remarkable frequency, and over and over again we are led to identify with
disobedient children who ignore the restrictions of a parent or guardian. The texts so work on us that we would be quite disappointed if
the miserly Hoard managed to prevent the marriage of his niece to the
resourceful Witgood, or if Moll Yellowhammer were forced by her dim-
witted father to marry the insatiable Whorehound instead of Touchwood Junior, or if Margaret bowed to Overreach's ambitious plot to wed
her to Lord Lovell rather than young Allworth. In *The Shoemakers' Holiday,* our sympathies lie with Lacy and Rose's love, even though her
father and his uncle seek to keep them apart, and we would not like to
see Rose seduced by the glib Hammon, whom her father approves: her
momentary interest in him seems a betrayal of Lacy. In Jonson's *Bartholomew Fair* (1614), the gentleman Winwife appears a much more
acceptable match for Grace Wellborn than the gull Cokes, whom her
guardian Justice Overdo is trying to foist on her to gain control of her
inheritance.

In discussing the pitfalls of the "ideas-of-the-time" approach, Levin
adduces still more examples and is certainly right to assert that "the
unsuitability of the suitor favored by the parents could almost be called
a convention of this drama."[61] For our purpose, however, it will be
necessary to add that in early city comedy the ideology of this convention is progressive. The patriarchal image of the family is the casualty
of the strained accommodation that these plays develop for commercial
activity: they try neither to minimize the subversiveness of capitalism
nor to disrupt the feudal order, and the result of this tension is that the
family is usually shattered by a domineering bourgeois parent, who
alienates his daughter, and by an ingenious gentleman, who schemes
to wed her. Because the child's disobedience is made a position of identification for the audience, we can read it as a means simultaneously to
"punish" the parent and "reward" the gentleman; and since in most
cases both men regard marriage as a way to acquire wealth and improve
or stabilize their social rank, the violation of familial duties functions
as a containing strategy that can both reject and approve the emerging
capitalist economic practices.[62] Yet the mere willingness to jettison the

authoritarian family and the pleasure of any validating identification with this willingness can leave no doubt that generally there is more approval than rejection.

Late twentieth-century audiences may be especially receptive to the transgressions of the family in early city comedy. The development of capitalism in the intervening centuries ensured the cultural dominance of the bourgeois image of the patriarchal family, which, because of its affective, liberal meanings, introduced new emphases on privacy and individual psychology and conceived an opposition between the individual and society.[63] In this sense, we are primed for the plays to position us in their transgressions because the family is typically violated by love matches, in which the disobedient child expresses personal emotions that conflict with and escape paternal authority. Whereas desire is collective in the feudal image of the patriarchal family, the child internalizing the father's wishes and respecting the social hierarchy, here it is atomized into a kind of emotional competition between father and child, in which the child opposes the father's social aspirations with her private wishes. The characterizations do not have any psychological complexity, of course, and patriarchy, although momentarily threatened by a daughter's disobedience, is ultimately recuperated in her marriage, with her internalization of the gentleman's desire to disobey the father. All the same, we can notice an acceptance of individualism: the subversive pursuit of self-interest distinguishes the child's private emotional life as well as the father's (and the gentleman's) money-making.

Late city comedy, in accordance with its conservatism, transforms this conventional treatment of the family by stressing reconciliations, whether between husband and wife or father and child. And not only do many plots turn on the restoration of age and sex hierarchies among the family members, but this is often enmeshed with an effort to protect the feudal order. Sir John Frugal laments, "What's wealth, accompanied / By disobedience in a wife and children?" (2.3.46–47), and his intrigue enables him at once to reassert his patriarchal authority and to enforce the traditional class distinction between city and court. When the "noise" of Bornwell's seeming prodigality finally moves his unfaithful, spendthrift wife to repent, "I throw my own will off, / And now in all things obey yours," he responds comfortingly that "the sums are safe, and we have wealth enough, / If yet we use it nobly" (5.1), demonstrating in his use of "nobly" that their standard of living will be more modest but nonetheless suited to his status as a knight.

The plot of Brome's *The Damoiselle* involves a similar, but much more complicated, turn of events. At the beginning, we learn that the prodigal Dryground has "already spent a faire Estate," and although he had an affair with Elianor, the sister of the decayed gentleman Brookall, he "deny'd / Her promis'd Marriage" and "turned her off with Childe" (1.1). Dryground's machinations, however, issue from his repentance: he uses them to make amends for his faults, and they do so in a way that simultaneously reestablishes the patriarchal family and bolsters the class structure. Thus, he reforms the "riotous" Wat, the son of the usurer Vermine, and this reformation persuades Vermine both to cancel Dryground's debt to him and to return the land he had wrested from Brookall by making it the dowry of his daughter Alice, whom Dryground has matched with Brookall's equally destitute son Francis. At the end, Dryground himself renews his affection for the jilted Elianor, promising to rescue her from a life of crushing poverty, and Wat professes a desire to marry Phillis, Elianor and Dryground's illegitimate daughter. The outcome of this intricate plotting is a group of reconciliations and marriages that disarm the threat of capitalism and uphold the ideology of degree: because Dryground intervenes in Vermine's family by disciplining Wat and arranging Alice's marriage, an oppressive usurer gives up his profitable but socially disruptive practices, and the beggared gentry are put on a firm financial footing appropriate to their rank. In this way, the text's validation of patriarchalism coincides with a reactionary accommodation of commercial activity, one which depends on a bourgeois character's rather improbable willingness to suppress his profit motive and use his wealth to support the gentry.

The fact is that the ideological pressure to maintain the authoritarian family is so strong in the Caroline plays that characterizations often disintegrate into inconsistencies and plot twists border on implausibility. Nabbes's *The Bride* opens with Theophilus urging his father, Goodlove, to abandon his intention to marry a young woman: Theophilus seems a dedicated son, sincerely concerned that Goodlove may be ridiculed for his May–December marriage, and that his age will lead to his wife's dissatisfaction and eventually to her infidelity. Yet Theophilus' motives are impugned by his subsequent admission that he himself loves the girl, and we see him suddenly elope with her. At this point, the text goes into reverse and the work of rehabilitation begins: Goodlove unexpectedly announces that he had prior knowledge of, and approves, his son's affection. Theophilus remains unaware of the revelation until the end, and his unawareness actually contributes to his redemption: on his elopement he is tormented with guilt, and, much to the girl's consternation, he vows not to marry her until he can win their fathers' blessing. The shifts in Theophilus' characterization and the contrivance that keeps him in the dark about his father's real intentions show the ideology of patriarchalism at work shaping the text: through their agency, a son's disobedience is magically transformed into a submission to paternal authority.

A similar trick absolves Brittleware's unruly wife Rebecca in Brome's *The Sparagus Garden.* Rebecca is upset that she has not yet become pregnant, so she decides, "I must have my longings before I can be with child" (2.2). These "longings" both challenge her disapproving husband's authority and reveal her social pretensions: in a vision of aristocratic luxury and lasciviousness, she speaks of wanting "to have a couple of lusty able bodied men, to take me up, one before and another behind, as the new fashion is, and carry me in a Manlitter," and she plans to visit the chic "sparagus garden," which Moneylack describes as "a pallace of pleasure, and daily resorted and fill'd with Lords and Knights, and their Ladies; and Gentlemen and gallants with ther Mistresses" (2.2). Given Rebecca's apparent violation of the family hierarchy, we can only be shocked to learn near the end that she is in f :ct a submissive wife who was trying merely to rid her husband of his bothersome fear that he will be cuckolded: "I confess the ends of all my longings, and the vexations I have put him to were but to run jealousie out of breath" (5.7). It is really Brittleware's jealousy that disrupts the hierarchical relations in his marriage, since it leads him to an unjust suspicion and hence to a too severe exercise of his authority over his wife. Yet although those relations are strained in the play, their legitimacy is never questioned; instead, what seemed a wife's subversion of the patriarchal family and the feudal class structure turns out to be a reinforcement of them.[64]

Through such abrupt reversals, the validation of feudal patriarchalism in Caroline city comedy creates a position of identification for the audience. Whereas in the early form of the genre we would be disappointed with marriages that do not transgress familial relations, in the later form we identify with marriages that restore the age and sex hierarchies among the family members. We can define the ideological significance of this generic transformation by rewriting Northrop Frye's description of comedy from a Marxist perspective. Frye has pointed out that the reconciliations and weddings at the end of comedy signal the appearance of a "new society . . . that the audience has recognized all along to be the proper and desirable state of affairs. . . . the normal response of the audience to a happy ending is 'this should be,' which sounds like a moral judgment. So it is, except that it is not moral in the restricted sense, but social."[65] As valuable as these formal observations are (and will be to my point), their usefulness is limited by Frye's reification of the text: his fundamental assumption that literary production enjoys a strict autonomy from other levels of social practice forces him to suppress the ideological implications of our crucial identification with the "new society" of comedy.[66] What needs to be recalled here is the web of conservative ideological determinations woven around the patriarchal image of the family during the Renaissance. In early city comedy, the society we are made to desire is essentially a capitalist one in which families are broken by possessive individualism; in the later plays, we are made to desire a feudal society characterized by deference to patriarchal authority and social status.

The transformations which differentiate Caroline city comedy make their most provocative appearance in Brome's *The Antipodes* (1638).[67] The presentation of Doctor Hughball and his associate Lord Letoy inventively rehabilitates the conventional businessman and gallant of the early plays. Here the representatives of the bourgeoisie and the nobility do not disrupt society with an individualistic economic struggle, but rather engage in a cooperative enterprise which reproduces hierarchical social relations. In contrast to the imposter Subtle and his alchemical scam, the legitimate Hughball is actually a practitioner of medicine, what we would recognize today as psychiatry, although his class-conscious modesty never "endures the name / Of doctor" (1.1.93). His ingenious therapies constitute a conservative ideologeme of commercial activity: unlike Quomodo or Overreach, he provides services "upon good terms" (1.2.54), and when he successfully cures a patient's madness, he at the same time safeguards the traditional class structure and the patriarchal family. Thus, he has taught a wasteful gentleman to be thrifty after the latter "fell mad / For spending of his land before he sold it: / That is, 'twas sold to pay his debts," and he has helped a lady "to find a way to love her husband," who "was seven years in search of it, and could not, / Though she consum'd his whole estate by it" (1.1.31–33, 54, 56–57). Lord Letoy's intrigues specialize in reconciling family differences, and in the course of the action, he saves the relationships of two couples: with the aid of the dramatic production Letoy mounts at his city residence, the distracted Peregrine is finally led to consummate his marriage to Martha, the "wand'ring look" of Joyless' wife

Diana is tested and her fidelity found "invincible," and Joyless is rid of his insane jealousy (1.6.19, 5.6.1).

Letoy's values distinguish him from the prodigal Mammon or Welborne and the pretentious Aretina:

> let others shine
> Abroad in the cloth o' bodkin; my broadcloth
> Please mine eye as well, my body better.
> Besides, I'm sure 'tis paid for (to their envy).
> I buy with ready money; and at home here
> With as good meat, as much magnificence,
> As costly pleasures, and as rare delights,
> Can satisfy my appetite and senses
> As they with all their public shows and braveries.
> They run at ring and tilt 'gainst one another;
> I and my men can play a match at football,
> Wrestle a handsome fall, and pitch the bar,
> And crack the cudgels, and a pate sometimes.
> (1.5.30–42)

Letoy voices a concern to maintain a standard of living that is suited to his noble rank, but that does not exhaust his wealth or drive him to forsake the simple pleasures of his country estate for the conspicuous consumption of the court. He offers a position in the feudal ideology of a conservative rural aristocracy critical of court culture. Yet there is a revealing discontinuity in this positioning: Letoy is reminded by the herald painter Blaze that when he visits the city, "your house in substance is an amphitheater / Of exercise and pleasure" (1.5.52–53), which mimic the cultural practices of the Caroline court: "For exercises," Letoy proudly asserts, there is "fencing, dancing, vaulting, / And for delight, music of all best kinds; / Stageplays and masques are my nightly pastimes, . . . my own men are / My music and my actors" (1.5.54–57). The contradiction in Letoy's characterization, between the "choice home delights" of the country aristocrat and the city opulence of a court habitué, exposes an ideological operation by which he is absolved of any objectionable conduct, and a criticism of the court evanesces. Although he is said to "live more like an emperor" (1.5.28–29), we also learn that "where another lord undoes his followers, / I maintain mine like lords. And there's my bravery" (1.5.63–64). Here his lavish expenses are portrayed not as wasteful, as the prodigality of so many earlier gentlemen was, but rather as an expression of the noble ideal of generosity, a "bravery" which, in preventing the ruin of "his followers," acquires a moral justification.[68] In this way, the text opens up and smooths over an inconsistency in his actions: a questionable similarity to the very "public shows and braveries" that provoke his criticism of the court gives way to a respect for the feudal class structure and the values associated with it, and noblesse oblige is called on to mystify conspicuous consumption. This ideological operation suggests that the text is managing an anxiety about class distinctions, an uncertainty about the social role of the aristocracy, which, however, can be resolved only in terms of degree. When Letoy first appears, his membership in the feudal nobility is given an emphasis that exceeds the demands of the plot and hints at an unstated need for verification: he is seen inquiring with the herald painter about "mine arms and pedigree," which have been traced "full four descents beyond / The conquest" (1.1.7–8).

The play that Hughball and Letoy stage to cure Peregrine's madness further complicates Brome's transformation of conventional motifs. The scenes in the play-within-the-play seem to function as a broad satire of contemporary social developments, although some may well be more specific topical allusions. The symptomatic reading will construe them as generic transformations by exploiting their differential relationships to material from early city comedy.[69] One antipodean episode bears a strong resemblance to Middleton's *A Chaste Maid in Cheapside*: a gentleman has fathered a child on his wife's servant and entered into a contract whereby he is required to impregnate a citizen's wife for a fee. Other residents of Anti-London include "projectors," who in their crack-brained schemes recall but fall far short of Meercraft's insidious plausibility, and a "feather man" who, unlike such aggressive tradesmen as Yellowhammer or Tapwell in *A New Way to Pay Old Debts,* refuses to accept any payment for his work. Many scenes introduce characters who subvert the traditional class distinctions or the roles dictated by the age and sex hierarchy of the patriarchal family, recalling very generally the violations of degree and patriarchy that appeared so frequently in the earlier plays. We see courtiers, for example, who act like beggars and talk like "watermen," old men who are sent back to school by their sons, and a masculine "Buff Woman" who itches for a fight and whose husband teaches needlepoint.

As critics have noted, the therapeutic value assigned to these incongruities and inversions implies a theory of comedy in which Brome's text dramatizes the proper response to itself: just as Peregrine becomes so engrossed that he recognizes the absurdity of the action and in this recognition regains his mental health, the audience should become so engrossed in *The Antipodes* that the behavior not merely of the antipodeans but of the two Joyless couples as well is seen as absurd and to be avoided.[70] Keeping in mind the intertextual connections between the play-within-the-play and early city comedy, we can go further to comment on the ideological significance of this therapy. By branding the earlier conventions absurd, Brome's text revises or "cures" their progressive ideology and registers a more "healthy" conservatism which it tries to get the audience to endorse. *The Antipodes,* in Ian Donaldson's words, "does not explore or challenge orthodox ideas about social relationships, but takes it for granted that these ideas are not in dispute."[71] Letoy's dramatic production sets up a position of intelligibility for the ailing couples which is ultimately feudal and patriarchal, enabling their psychological readjustment to a reality defined by a conservative representation of family and class relations. And as soon as the viewer or reader begins to judge and correct the characters' responses to the action, overseeing their ideological education with varying degrees of amusement and complacency, he is himself participating in the educational process, positioned as a virtual functionary of Letoy's (and Brome's) ideological cultural apparatus.

Brome's text demonstrates an awareness that cultural products like books and plays create subject-positions for the consumer to occupy and in fact constitute subjectivity: Peregrine is maddened by reading travel literature, made rational by a dramatic production. Brome's text, however, shows no awareness that its own positioning is ideological; on the contrary, whereas Sir John Mandeville's *Voyages and Travailes* are treated as false, the source of insanity and divisiveness, *The Antipodes* is implicitly presented as true or right, a recipe for mental health and social harmony. Through Letoy's production, Brome's text dramatizes the very operation of ideological subjection which it itself performs, although this self-reflexivity never demystifies the operation. The text contains two structures of ideological subjection which are so symmetrical and simultaneous that the audience is encouraged to respond deferentially, to occupy the ideological position which makes sense of the complicated action, rather than develop the sustained self-consciousness that would expose the ideology as a mystification and permit a critique of the patriarchal family and the feudal order. It is usually Letoy who joins the two ideological operations by offering the conservative standpoint from which the multiple levels of action become intelligible. When, for example, Diana sees an elderly gentle-woman dominating her husband in the play-within-the-play, she applauds the antipatriarchal switch of sexual roles, but it is clear that her response has been purposely evoked by Letoy, as part of his plan for curing Joyless:

> *Diana.* In truth, she handles him handsomely.
> *Joyless.*   Do you like it?
> *Diana.* Yes, and such wives are worthy to be lik'd
>   For giving good example.
> *Letoy.*   Good! Hold up
>   That humor by all means.
>   . . .
>
> *Diana.*   It seems the husbands
>   In the Antipodes bring portions, and
>   The wives make jointures.
> *Joyless.*   Very well observ'd.
> *Diana.* And wives, when they are old and past childbearing,
>   Allow their youthful husbands other women.
> *Letoy.* Right. And old men give their young wives like license.
> *Diana.* That I like well. Why should not our old men
>   Love their young wives as well?
> *Joyless.*   Would you have it so?
> *Letoy.* Peace, Master Joyless, you are too loud.
>   (2.7.29–32, 44–51)

The scenes in Letoy's play-within-the-play position Diana in a subversive "humor" in order to increase Joyless' suspicion of her, so that in a climactic recognition of her impeccable virtue, the husband will admit his misjudgment of her and be relieved of his oppressive jealousy. Letoy is running two shows, two ideological subjections, at once: he directs a production for his guests and directs his guests in a production for Brome's audience, and both productions are overdetermined by conservative ideologies. The ending confirms Letoy's nobility, the identity between his social rank and moral worth, but as with his first appearance in the play, we get a glimpse of the feudal values functioning effectively but under strain: his cure of Joyless proves successful, and he announces that he is really Diana's father, but at her birth gave her to another family because he suspected his wife's fidelity. His production, it turns out, is also a device to renew his relationship to his daughter and atone for his own destructive jealousy by doing his socially reproductive work with Doctor Hughball. The "new society" that becomes the object of audience desire in *The Antipodes* is characterized by a backward-looking feudal patriarchalism which has been weakened somewhat by an extravagant court aristocracy and tyrannical husbands, but which is nonetheless recommended as the true representation of social and family life.

VI

We can sum up the differences between early and late city comedy by relying once again on Frye's formal description. Asserting that the basic comedic premise is the obstruction of desire, he points out that "there are two ways of developing the form of comedy: one is to throw the main emphasis on the blocking characters; the other is to throw it forward on the scenes of discovery and reconciliation" (p. 166). It follows from this distinction that the "forward" emphasis is likely to focus attention on what we might call the enabling characters, those who succeed in bringing about the plot resolution. Frye's skeletal account must be revised before we can apply it to a subgenre like city comedy, but it will nonetheless prove useful. We can perceive that early city comedy stresses both blocking and enabling characters and establishes certain similarities between them: businessmen and gentlemen work confidence tricks for their private gain, disrupting family as well as class relations; yet the businessmen are typically portrayed as obstacles that must be overcome by the gentlemen. Later city comedy, in contrast, tends to rehabilitate the earlier businessmen and gentlemen, transforming them both into upright enabling characters who devise intrigues to reproduce the class hierarchy and its elementary unit, the family. This fundamental difference in mode of development corresponds to a shift in ideology. Early city comedy signifies a progressive affirmation of capitalism by valorizing the subversive profit accumulation of the blocking and enabling characters, even though such activities are often represented as immoral and illicit and defeated or given up at the end. Late city comedy, however, signifies a conservative reaction in which the social dangers of the new economic relations are defused and the rehabilitated enabling characters uphold the patriarchal family and the feudal class structure. In both forms of the genre, individual plays are fissured with discontinuities (thematic contradictions, inconsistent characterizations, narrative improbabilities) which allow us to view the text as an arena where these competing ideologies struggle for dominance.

Yet an important problem remains: how can we account for the generic transformations and the ideological shift they imply? It seems clear that the broad social developments we have used to delimit the ideology of city comedy will not provide an answer to this question: since they are global determinants of cultural production during the entire period, they are unable to explain a precise change in the evolution of a dramatic subgenre. To develop such an explanation, we need to examine the specific conjuncture of social forces in Renaissance London, the historical context in which the drama emerges and on which it comments. A significant dislocation of those forces occurred during the early seventeenth century, a change in political alignments, and we can read the ideological shift in city comedy as a response to this change.

The mercantile and manufacturing interests in London were traditionally allied to the crown since it granted them the trading charters and patents for industrial monopolies on which their profit accumulation depended. This alliance was further buttressed by the businessmen's role in government fiscal policy. It was they who collected customs duties and other royal revenues either by leasing these domestic concessions directly from the crown or by subleasing from courtiers who had been rewarded with them. Enjoyed by a small minority, the lucrative privileges that flowed from the monarch inevitably excluded or in some way hurt a considerable portion of the business community, and during the reign of James I, the privileged few were increasingly attacked by the House of Commons as a barrier to free trade and a cause of such improprieties as extortion. Thus, "in the 1621 parliament," as Robert Ashton has observed, "monopolists, customs farmers and members of export-import cartels were all indiscriminately lumped together for abuse."[72] Under James, the city remained aligned with the crown, and the economic practices of both were opposed by a parliament that represented the interests of the excluded businessmen, particularly those from the western counties and the outports.

In 1624, however, the MPs passed a measure that signaled the beginning of a momentous change in this situation: they outlawed all monopolies with the exception of those granted to corporations or designed to encourage technical innovations, and so they avoided any interference with the London-based trading companies whose charters permitted them to monopolize commerce in a specific commodity and region (Ashton, pp. 116–20).[73] By 1629, this rapprochement between Parliament and the chartered companies had been consolidated and a new power bloc developed in which the leading sector of the business community was allied with the parliamentary opposition against the king and against the domestic concessionaires who farmed the royal revenues. An important factor in this development was the series of fiscal expedients to which Charles I resorted in order to raise money. By exploiting loopholes in the Statute of Monopolies and relying on such unpopular devices as forced loans and the levying of impositions without parliamentary approval, the crown not only continued to alienate the MPs and their provincial constituents, but now incurred the hostility of urban merchants. These strained relations worsened during the 1630s when, in the absence of Parliament, the Caroline government issued a steady stream of monopolies, resurrected dormant taxes, and extended the ship money tax from the coastal counties to the entire nation.[74] When the Long Parliament met in 1640, the traditional alliance between the crown and the business community had been destroyed: the king confronted a Commons that represented the grievances of both merchants and landowners against the government and its concessionaires, and that challenged the constitutionality of the royal prerogative in economic and other matters.

The evolution of city comedy can be seen as an ideological reflection of the changing political alignments that seriously threatened and eventually undermined not just the king's hegemony, but the traditional social hierarchy. Early city comedy responded to a nonantagonistic conjuncture which was certainly characterized by conflicting classes and class fractions, but in which these conflicts were displaced across a range of contradictory social practices and held in uneasy equilibrium: city businessmen were both private citizens pursuing their economic self-interest and agents of government fiscal policy; country gentlemen were investors as well as farmers, leisured aristocrats as well as courtiers who received royal favors in the form of industrial and commercial patents. Such contradictory social roles and relations, in which feudal privilege and bourgeois interest merged in institutions like the joint stock company and the absolutist state, appear in the earlier plays as an ambivalent fascination with nascent capitalism because its threat to the feudal order, although latent, was not yet disruptive enough to test class allegiance and warrant an unqualified condemnation or approval. Early city comedy entered the play of social possibilities by assimilating various cultural materials and interrogating their different ideologies, class and sexual, aristocratic and patriarchal, feudal, bourgeois, or absolutist, parliamentarian, Puritan, and royalist, exploring the alternatives for social change. Late city comedy, however, responded to a polarized conjuncture in which social contradictions had condensed into extremely antagonistic conflicts: large segments of the business community and the country aristocracy joined together to oppose government fiscal policy which they felt was oppressive and unconstitutional.[75] The plays reacted to this potentially revolutionary situation by producing a conservative solution to the conflicts: they reveal their allegiance to the ideology of degree by expressing the wish that there be no economic struggle between classes, that the court not encourage profit accumulation and sexual immorality, that the feudal class structure remain intact, grounded on the patriarchal family. The generic transformations of the later plays are the chinks through which we can glimpse this conservatism and, farther beyond, the explosive political alignments that decisively determined it.

The ideology of late city comedy can be described more precisely if we compare it with other social practices which intervene into the same prerevolutionary situation: the parliamentary proceedings in 1628–29 which articulate an opposition to the Caroline ideology of absolutism and to the fiscal and religious policies of the royal government. When Parliament impeached Roger Manwaring for the absolutist sermons he delivered before the king, *Religion and Allegiance* (1627), the ideological terms of John Pym's speech were distinctly feudal, yet obviously antiabsolutist, designed to free capitalist economic practice from the royal prerogative. Manwaring's sermons relied on the divine theory of kingship to justify Charles's fiscal expedients: "To kings . . . nothing can be denied (without manifest and sinful violation of law and conscience) that may answer their royal estate and excellency, that may further the supply of their urgent necessities."[76] Pym's impeachment speech, however, argues in favor of the economic "liberty of the subject" by presenting absolutism as a threat to feudal class relations: Pym says that to alter the "ancient and fundamental law" by which "the subject was exempted from taxes and loans not granted by common consent of Parliament" would upset the "mutual relation and intercourse" between classes in the "old" hierarchical "form of government"—"that which doth actuate and dispose every part and member of a state to the common good; and as those parts give strength and ornament to the whole, so they receive from it again strength and protection in their several stations and degrees."[77] Pym's challenge to government fiscal policy paradoxically transforms degree into an ideological weapon of bourgeois enterprise: the absolutist state is seen as the constitutional innovator because it destroys the "concord and interchange of support" in feudal class relations by setting up economic controls; economic liberalism, in contrast, is seen as "issuing from the first frame and constitution of the kingdom," valorized by custom, a right immemorial. Here Pym's feudal social representation turns progressive, serving the interests of the city businessmen who protested Charles's impositions, forced loans, and monopolies, and attacking the central contradiction in the absolutist state: by using the royal prerogative as a means to shield its own bourgeois enterprise, absolutism represses the social responsibility attached to that privilege in absolutist ideology. Pym criticizes the absolutist state by measuring it against the hierarchical social representation on which it depends and finding it deficient.

Late city comedy contains a feudal critique of the court, but it lacks the burden of bourgeois ideology in Pym's speech and so remains extremely conservative. This becomes most apparent if we consider the different treatment of topical allusions in earlier and later plays in the genre. Bornwell in Shirley's *The Lady of Pleasure* rejects court office because the royal government does not have the properly feudal respect for aristocratic birth and moral worth, yet he echoes Charles's proclamation forbidding the gentry's residence in London when he chides Aretina because they have "against mine own opinion / Quitted the country, and removed the hope / Of our return, by sale of that fair lordship / We lived in" (1.1).[78] Jonson's allusion to a similar proclamation during James's reign is much more interrogative of royal policy. In *The Devil is an Ass,* the projector and confidence artist Meercraft tries to interest the country gentleman Fitzdottrel in a royal patent for land drainage, whereby the government is implicated in the very commercial activity and crime it sought to control by banning gentry like Fitzdottrel from the city. Meercraft makes clear that this is a project "Whereof the *Crowne's* to haue his moiety, / It if be owner [of the land]; Else, the *Crowne* and Owners / To share" (2.1.46–48).

Early and late city comedy also treat court culture differently. In *The Lady of Pleasure,* Celestina criticizes courtiers for their disregard of class distinctions and their sexual immorality, but she seems to have absorbed the mystifications of Charles's reign in the masques when she commends the "truth" and "love of innocence, which shine / So bright in the two royal luminaries / At court" (4.3). *Bartholomew Fair,* in contrast, implicitly challenges the idealized representations of court morality in the masques by alluding to wardship, the fiscal expedient by which the government sold the administration of the estates of minors who were heirs of deceased royal tenants.[79] Justice Overdo's relation-ship to Grace shows that he participates in this "common calamity": Winwife asks her how she came to be Overdo's ward, and she explains, "he bought me, Sir; and now he will marry me to his wiues brother, this wise Gentleman, that you see, or else I must pay value o' my land" (3.5.271–76). Since Overdo is both a royal officer and the owner of a royal ward, Grace's predicament exemplifies the contradictory social conditions that lie behind the metaphysical rationalizations of absolut-ist ideology, thereby questioning the legitimacy of royal authority.

In late city comedy, the interrogation of royal policy and culture is usually contradicted by submission. Both Bornwell and Celestina ques-tion Caroline absolutism, but they remain subjected to its hegemony. The royal proclamation which Bornwell tacitly accepts coerced the ar-istocracy to maintain their country seats in order to strengthen the central administration's control over provincial government. Similarly, Celestina is positioned by court culture in the personal and political myth which the masques created for the king and queen to legitimize their rule. The feudal critique of the court in Shirley's text is thus a capitulation to the absolutist state.

Pym's feudal social representation, however, turns out to be subver-sive because it projects a historical myth designed to rationalize parlia-mentary privilege and question the constitutionality of the royal pre-rogative. The lawyer Sir Edward Coke, Lord Chief Justice under James I, then a leader of the parliamentary opposition against the Caroline government, developed the historical myth on the basis of the common law: the fundamental law and ancient constitution of England were custom, unwritten and immemorial, the accumulated wisdom of Eng-lishmen independent of sovereigns and any legislative bodies, inter-rupted momentarily by the Norman Conquest, but restored by Magna Carta and parliamentary statutes. Coke's vision of a medieval utopia, where personal liberties were unthreatened by monarchs, resulted in his "liberalization" of the common law, as Christopher Hill notes, "adapting it to the needs of a commercial society."[80] Coke's codification of the common law in his voluminous legal reports and political writ-ings was a bourgeois mobilization of the feudal past to serve a political confrontation with the royal government in the seventeenth century. "Magna Carta is such a fellow that he will have no sovereign," said Coke; "the common law hath so admeasured the prerogative of the King that he cannot take or prejudice the inheritance of any." Pym's speech at the Manwaring impeachment uses Coke's common-law arguments against the royal government by stating that the subject's exemption from taxes which lack parliamentary approval "was not introduced by any statute, or by any charter of princes, but was the ancient and fundamental law, issuing from the first frame and constitution of the kingdom." And Pym elaborates on the historical myth, just like Coke, by adding that the law was "of that vigor and force as to overlive the Conquest, nay, to give bounds and limits to the Conqueror."

This interested use of the Conquest appears in a wide variety of prerevolutionary discourses and genres, not only in political treatises and parliamentary speeches, but also in a late city comedy like Brome's *The Antipodes,* throwing into relief the ideological differences between them. Dating the constitution back before the Conquest, even suggesting, as Pym does, that William the Conqueror did not in fact conquer England but obtained the crown by composition with Englishmen, had a strategic value for the parliamentary opposition because it made the common law immune from sovereignty and set up Parliament as the protector of common-law liberties against the Caroline government's appeals to the royal prerogative. Arguments for the pre-Conquest antiquity of the common law constituted progressive political interventions in the prerevolutionary period: "as Parliament laid claim to new powers," J. G. A. Pocock observes, "these were represented as immemorial and included in the fundamental law."[81] Brome's text, in contrast, makes a conservative use of such historical arguments when it dramatizes Letoy's concern about his aristocratic pedigree. Blaze tells Letoy that the herald has traced his family "full four descents beyond / The conquest . . . and finds that one / Of your French ancestry came in with the Conqueror" (1.5.7–11). By establishing the antiquity of Letoy's family and demonstrating that the Conquest altered but did not break the continuity of the family line, the herald validates the lord's nobility and sets him up as the protector of the class and sexual hierarchies of feudal patriarchalism in the text. The conservative ideology of late city comedy is different from what Hill calls the *formal* conservatism of the parliamentary opposition: "Coke's stand was [that] there must be great consideration before anything of novelty is established, to provide that it is not against the law of the land. But he was looking in the direction in which history was to advance" (p. 246). Whereas the Parliaments in 1628–29 show that a feudal social representation can paradoxically be forward-looking, overdetermined by possessive individualism and economic liberalism, late city comedy expresses a reactionary feudal nostalgia that looks back to a more stable period when the hegemony of the feudal aristocracy was not threatened by the absolutist state and bourgeois values.

The increasing conservatism of city comedy during the early seventeenth century should not lead us to conclude that the Caroline stage was a rearguard cultural institution. The sheer variety of the drama produced at the public and elite theaters offered many conflicting ideological positions for the audiences and therefore encouraged the imagination of different models for social life. Strongly interrogative texts like Massinger's tragicomedies continued to be written and produced, and the most subversive of early city comedies were revived. *The Alchemist* was performed in 1631 and 1639, *The Antipodes* only once, in 1638.[82] Butler notes that in the Caroline period "the theaters were staging politically dangerous material with increasing frequency and freedom," and "each company without exception ran into trouble with the royal authorities for touching on sensitive issues."[83] Parliament closed the theaters in 1642 not because the drama was aligned with the court in its aesthetics or politics, but because the public theaters had always been viewed as places of potential social disorder, and now both they and their elite counterparts had recently turned into forums for social criticism and political statement. Closing the theaters was a strategic ideological intervention made by a parliamentary opposition who were very much aware that social change was imminent, but who had also decided to control it by limiting its possibilities.

Chapter Four

Topical Allusion and Textuality in the Court Masque

Each time men speak about the world, they enter into a relation of exclusion, even when they speak in order to denounce it: a metalanguage is always terrorist.

Roland Barthes, "Taking Sides"

T HE HISTORY of the canonization of the court masque is at once the history of recent developments in American Renaissance studies. The critical revaluation of this genre can be traced in Stephen Orgel's seminal work, beginning with *The Jonsonian Masque* (1965) and culminating in *The Illusion of Power: Political Theater in the English Renaissance* (1975). Here it becomes clear that the masque was a site where the humanist historicism of the fifties and sixties gradually metamorphosed into the politicized and theoretically self-conscious forms of literary scholarship now known as the new historicism. In the late seventies and early eighties, when Renaissance studies were absorbing research into anthropology and poststructuralist textual and social theory, Orgel's increasing tendency to relate Renaissance culture not so much to "society" as to royal "power" was shared by a number of other critics, notably Stephen Greenblatt and Louis Adrian Montrose, and there developed various projects of historical research that sought to embed Renaissance texts in power relations, often on the basis of anti-humanist concepts of subjectivity.[1] These developments ensured that an obviously propagandistic form of royal culture like the masque would be among the privileged objects of sophisticated new historicist readings. Perhaps the most striking example of this latest transformation of the genre is Jonathan Goldberg's poststructuralist treatment of Jacobean culture, *James I and the Politics of Literature* (1983).

Alongside the shifting theoretical assumptions during this twenty-year canonization of the masque, there appear points of continuity in the ways the politics of the genre has been articulated: individual texts are inserted in historical narratives, documents and illustrations relating to performances are adduced, topical allusions are identified, webs of intertextual connections between Renaissance culture and royal discourse are woven, and more often than not royal ideology is replicated, with the contradictory conditions of royal "power" glimpsed or even exposed only to be mystified in a deferential reading that resists the ideological significance of the discontinuous textual work and occupies the subject-position produced for the king. This deference to royal ideology shows, in particular, that the canonization of the masque is concealing its own dubious politics: as an intervention into the subjective fragmentation and historical amnesia of postmodern culture, it can only be considered ineffectual because in both its humanist and new historicist versions it puts to work transcendental concepts of subjectivity and language which limit its thinking about historical change. For any materialist critical project, therefore, the recent reception of the masque is also a site where the conservatism of bourgeois cultural practices can be countered. Using the work of Orgel and Goldberg, we will examine the shifting assumptions with which two kinds of post–World War II historicism have processed the masque and argue the value, political as well as theoretical, of a symptomatic reading of the genre.

I

In a preface to the 1981 reprint of *The Jonsonian Masque,* Orgel recalls that when he wrote the study "its purpose was frankly polemical: to take Ben Jonson's court masques as seriously as Jonson took them, and to read them in the light of his insistence that the soul of the form was poetry."[2] Taking the masques seriously was what relatively few Renaissance critics did in the immediate postwar period, because the texts, even those written by a canonical writer like Jonson, were regarded as the ephemeral, self-congratulatory entertainments of royalty and aristocracy, too close to obvious political interests, undeserving of the historical research (literary, philosophical, iconographical, social) which was being lavished on canonized texts—Jonson's plays and non-dramatic poetry, for example. This is why Orgel is defensive about his project—"the masque rightly demands less attention from the student of literature" (p. 3)—and why he justifies it by minimizing or even repressing the social affiliations of the genre, effectively transforming the Jonsonian masque into something that can be held more lasting and serious, into "poetry," or "literature," i.e., a container of human aesthetic and moral values that simultaneously reflect and transcend their historical moment. "The masque for Jonson was defined by certain basic requirements," Orgel states in his 1964 preface, "requirements, on the one hand, of his own sensibility and, on the other, of the expectations of his audience. This is my subject: the changing relationship between the masque as spectacle or revel and the masque as literature" (p. vii). The transcendental subject emerges not only in the view of the author as struggling against, and overcoming, both social and formal determinants of the creative process, but also in the shift from authorial "sensibility" versus social "expectations" to "literature" versus "spectacle or revel," a skewed parallelism of critical categories which in effect redefines the social issues raised by the text as mere problems of form.

Orgel's critical orientation can be called humanist historicism informed by the formalist emphasis on lyric poetry in the New Criticism. Jean Howard describes it as the prevailing critical orthodoxy against which the new historicism reacted, "weary . . . of teaching texts as ethereal entities floating above the urgencies and contradictions of history and of seeking in such texts the disinterested expression of a unified truth rather than some articulation of the discontinuities underlying any construction of reality."[3] Humanist historicism announces its project as the historical appreciation of culture, but the history it writes rests on a transcendental concept of subjectivity, a transhistorical essence termed human nature, and as a consequence it projects familiar individualistic textual strategies. Thus Orgel relies heavily on records of authorial intention, assigning this intention priority over the social situation of textual production, construing the text as a coherent expression of intended meanings. The formal problem which Jonson so admirably solved for Orgel was "to unify the disparate parts of the masque" and thereby to absorb its social function into an organic literary whole in which the social can ultimately be transcended: "More than any other masque writer, Jonson was able to treat those external requirements as poetic ones, to make of the demands of the occasion a vital element of a complex work of art" (p. 62). Organic unity, here as in romantic and modern criticism, leads to an illusionistic effect in which human moral truths are vivified or made to seem real. For Orgel, this humanist meaning-effect occurs particularly in later masques, beginning with *Pleasure Reconciled to Virtue* (1618), where Jonson is able to develop solutions for his central formal problem: "In any real world, it is a complicated business for a man to keep his virtue, and with a full sense of those complexities the masque concludes, pointing the way back to Jonsonian drama and poetry. . . . All the masque can do, Jonson seems to say, is to offer a moment in which a vision of an ideal becomes a poetic and dramatic experience—becomes, in other words, a reality" (p. 185).

The ideological standpoint of this reading of the genre can be clarified with Jameson's critique of the Continental historicism from which Orgel's theoretical assumptions derive in part.[4] Jameson describes the methodology of humanist cultural historians like Erich Auerbach and Erwin Panofsky as a "historical and cultural aestheticism": processing "texts as expressions of moments of the historical past, or of unique and distant cultures," humanist historicism is an "aesthetic appreciation and recreation" of its objects, "and the diversity of cultures and historical moments becomes thereby for it a source of immense aesthetic excitement and gratification." Humanist historicism rewrites past culture in terms of German *Lebensphilosophie,* argues Jameson, a philosophical anthropology "in which the infinite multiplicity of human symbolic acts is the expression of the infinite potentialities of a nonalienated human nature. The experience of historicity then restores something of this richness to a present in which few enough of those potentialities are practically available to any of us." Humanist cultural history thus compensates for the subjective dislocations of the present by (re)constructing moments in which the human imagination is said to be most coherent and free of specific determinations, in which the human essence is considered most self-expressive and least alloyed, and "sensibility" is least dissociated or, as Orgel puts it in his conclusion, least affected by "stagnation":

> When a culture accepts the conventions of art without understanding them, the sensibility of the age is in danger of stagnation. The mind then responds not to aesthetic experience, but to mere formulas, automatically; and the time is ripe for the artist to revitalize both his tradition and his culture through a reinterpretation of the forms of art. Essentially this is what Jonson is doing with the masque. Though he is working on a small scale—the form is unusually rigid, and the audience unusually limited—the problems he encounters are basically the problems of all art. (P. 188)

Orgel's humanist pursuit of "aesthetic experience" in Renaissance culture is a historical project that ultimately cuts the text off from history: Jonson's masques are the revitalized products of the "sensibility of the age" because they present an imaginative solution to "the problems of all art." Why the "time" was "ripe" for that solution isn't specified because Jonson's texts are seen as the cultural site where the human imagination transcends historical "time." Yet since Orgel's concluding statement addresses timeless, universal problems in human culture, it can also take on another, self-reflexive application—as a reference to his challenge of the marginalization of the masque in Renaissance studies, his revision of the judgment that the genre is too formulaic, too deeply implicated in a decadent royal culture, lacking in the profound (and disinterested) moral meanings and stronger illusionism of canonized texts. Orgel's polemical revaluation of the masque offered an understanding which canonized the formulas, which gave them intellectual coherence and moral profundity and presented them as sources of aesthetic pleasure, revitalizing his own tradition and culture with a reinterpretation of the forms of art, gathering critic, text, and reader into the transcendental realm of the human imagination.

Following Jameson's critique of humanist historicism, however, we can situate this revaluation more specifically in its historical moment by considering why the time may have been ripe for Renaissance studies to undergo this revitalizing restitution of a body of texts. Continental historicism functioned as an individualistic resolution for the social displacements and catastrophes that have accompanied the development of monopoly capitalism in this century: amid the rise of the industrial metropolis, mass economic practices and mass political movements, mechanized communications and warfare, the increased specialization of labor and the intensified privatization of social life, humanist historicism produced a compensatory cultural history with a transcendental psychology, "the notion of some full development of human potentialities," in Jameson's words. Auerbach writes *Mimesis* (1946) in Istanbul during World War II, "where the libraries are not well equipped for European studies," hoping his book will "contribute to bringing together again those whose love for our western history has serenely persevered."[5] He explicitly likens the method and thesis of his historical research—"basic motifs in the history of the representation of reality . . . must be demonstrable in any random realistic text"—to the work of "those modern writers who prefer the exploitation of random everyday events," exemplified by Virginia Woolf's *To the Lighthouse*

(1927). Both humanist historicism and modern fiction, in Auerbach's account, bear witness to the same social and ideological dislocations in the period between the first and second world wars, notably "the violent clash of the most heterogeneous ways of life and kinds of endeavor" that accompanied "the spread of publicity and the crowding of mankind on a shrinking globe." And both critic and novelist reflect their social ground with "a method which dissolves reality into multiple and multivalent reflections of consciousness," a method which is at once "a mirror of the decline of our world" and its imaginary resolution: "It is precisely the random moment which is completely independent of the controversial and unstable orders over which men fight and despair; it passes unaffected by them, as daily life. The more it is exploited, the more the elementary things which our lives have in common come to light." Auerbach's humanist cultural history so operates on random historical moments as to erase their and its own historical specificity, discovering a common humanity to overcome the social contradictions that he and his sympathetic contemporaries have in common.

Orgel's canonization of the masque, his approach to Renaissance culture as a rich expression of the human imagination, carries the ideological burden of humanist historicism into the consumer capitalism of the sixties, where the subjective stagnation of postmodern culture poses a different, more advanced threat to the reception of the Western cultural tradition. The disintegrating spread of publicity develops into the precession of commodified simulacra, in which representations become conventional or formulaic and responses automatic, and past cultural monuments are vulnerable to displacements and infiltrations from other areas of contemporary culture (e.g., popular forms and themes). In the era of media-produced attitudes tied closely to economic circulation, an academic specialization like Renaissance studies may withdraw farther into the humanist restoration of random historical moments by reinforcing the canon in which human subjectivity is thought to be free and unified. This canon reinforcement may include the continued marginalization of texts which, like Massinger's plays, resist individualistic critical categories and operations or which, like the masques, can be reduced too quickly to conspicuous consumption and narcissistic propaganda, to values that resemble the commodification of culture in the present. Orgel's inflection on humanist historicism seeks to overcome the postmodern crisis of subjectivity by taking still another route: he revises the canon, but in its own terms, offering a humanist reading of Jonson's masques which demonstrates that all along they too were monuments of the imagination, even though minor ones, less monumental than his plays and nondramatic verse. This reaffirmation of the humanist canon, like Auerbach's, elides the historical difference of the texts and defers to their transcendental values. In Orgel's case, however, this deference means a valorization of royal ideology. The moral values in the masques are treated as human "ideals," not ideological mystifications of royal power.

Orgel's attention to the politics of the genre did not emerge until his collaboration with the art historian Roy Strong, *Inigo Jones: The Theater of the Stuart Court* (1973), and his later, independent statement, *The Illusion of Power.*[6] Here the individualistic assumptions of humanist historicism are enlisted in a more politicized treatment of the masque which nonetheless removes its historical specificity, transforming royal ideology into a timeless, universal moral truth. At certain points, Orgel demonstrates a sense of the materiality of cultural forms, the textual work of producing illusionistic effects which position subjectivity. At other points, however, this textual work evaporates to provide free access to reality, a transparent self-expression, and the texts are seen as coherent representations of royal thinking. "Charles was not merely being entertained by his masques; the form was an extension of the royal mind . . . Masques are the expression of the monarch's will, the mirrors of his mind" (pp. 43, 45). In *Neptune's Triumph for the Return of Albion* (1623), "the whole action is presented as a serene extension of the royal will. This is a political myth, an accurate record of the way James viewed his government in his last ten years" (p. 77). Orgel indicates the ideological contradictions in the form: "Philosophically it is both Platonic and Machiavellian; Platonic because it presents images of the good to which the participants aspire and may ascend; Machiavellian because its idealizations are designed to justify the power they celebrate" (p. 40). But these contradictions usually vanish, the Platonized representations of royal power are expounded and emphasized, royal thinking is always coherent, read as didactic, offered for the imitation of Orgel's reader: "Masques are not magical talismans, they are analogies, ideals made apprehensible, so that we may know ourselves and see what we may become" (p. 56). In this statement, the editorial "we" is simultaneously the royal plural, positioning Orgel's reader in royal ideology, deferring to the Platonized politics of the masque, its representation of moral "ideals" as transcendental human values, and thereby participating in its mystification of the contradictory social conditions of the early Stuart governments.

Orgel's valorization of royal ideology is articulated in opposition to

Puritan attacks on theater for its immorality and its wasteful cost, but he generalizes the enemy as the "democratic imagination," which "sees only flattery in this sort of thing" and threatens to marginalize the masque by questioning the serious attention he wants to pay to royal culture: "That such forms of expression should now seem to us at best obscure, at worst insincere, says much for the success of the Puritan revolution" (pp. 40, 88). The ideological paradox of Orgel's reading, however, is that his retreat from the "democratic imagination" is influenced by Whig histories of the seventeenth century, specifically their tendency to read the Jacobean and Caroline periods in terms of too simply defined, stereotypical social oppositions leading to a bourgeois revolution against the monarchy (king and Parliament, Roundhead and Cavalier, court and country, Laudian and Puritan).[7] To challenge the bourgeois demystification of the masques, Orgel assumes the binary oppositions of Whig historiography, but transforms them by rehabilitating the bourgeois ideologeme of royal culture: the moral ideals presented in the masques are not flattery or insincerity, but rather reflect the thinking by which Charles ruled ("Much Caroline legal and political history has the quality of a court masque"), although it remains true that Charles's "idealism was politically naive" (pp. 88–89). As R. Malcolm Smuts has pointed out, Orgel's "analysis rests on an implicit assumption, rooted in Whiggish historiography, that the personal rule was an unrealistic attempt to prevent the natural evolution of a more equal relationship between Crown and Parliament."[8] Both Whig historiography and Orgel's canonization of the masque assume the political incompetence of the royal government, and as a result, they eclipse the complexity and effectiveness of government activities, its implementation of various fiscal expedients and religious policies, its success at law enforcement and tax collection. Orgel's rehabilitation of royal culture, however, is much more repressive of these social conditions because he also turns the ideological mystifications of the texts into moral ideals, valorizing "the royal point of view, whereby the complexities of contemporary issues were resolved through idealizations and allegories, visions of Platonic realities" (*Inigo Jones*, 1:51). Orgel's politicization of the masque in his subsequent work is deeply conservative because it discourages thinking about historical change: its humanist assumptions about subjectivity and textuality and its Whig historiography underwrite a valorization of royal ideology which eliminates the possibilities for contest and subversion in royal culture and frees the masque from the social conflicts which condensed around government policy to precipitate revolution.

It is not, however, until Jonathan Goldberg's new historicist reworking of Orgel's treatment that the canonization of the masque reaches its
most reactionary extreme.[9] Goldberg assumes the poststructuralist notion of the text as a fragmented simulacrum, where meaning is destabilized by the differential process of signification, and representation is
highly mediated by the discontinuous materials it puts to work: "I aim
at exploring the contradictions inherent in language and the power and
limitations conveyed by ruling contradictions" (p. xi). Reality is always
already overtaken by textualized forms. Thus, Goldberg reduces royal
power to representation, and Jacobean England to a discursive formation mediated by royal discourse: "Political reality, ordinary events, and
staged ones are all matters of representation; in the early seventeenth
century, representation was governed by the notion of the king's two
bodies" (p. 177). "Governed" is a key word here because it exposes the
valorization of royal ideology which controls how Goldberg processes
textual discontinuities: they are not read as contradictory ideological
determinations, competing social representations which would suggest
models for social life beyond those imagined by Jacobean absolutism;
they are rather the "sustaining" contradictions of royal ideology. All
texts are transformed into royal simulacra, all textual politics is conservative: "Employing royal language, poets turned the tables on the
monarch, appropriating power against power by engaging the most
radical potential that resides in language, its own multivalent, self-
contradictory nature. This does not make the king's poets subversives
or revolutionaries; on the contrary, royalists all, they followed the king's
prescriptions, pursuing his sustaining contradictions" (p. 116). Goldberg's repeated reference to the "sustaining contradictions" of royal language shows that his appropriation of poststructuralist theory is limited
by his valorization of royal ideology: if language is radically indeter-
minate, as theorists like Derrida and Barthes argue, if the differential
process of signification can not only sustain meaning but break it
down, then textual discontinuities can be read as rupturing royal discourse and subverting Jacobean absolutism, even if the project of the
text, as in the case of the masque, is to celebrate the king and legitimize
royal power.

In Goldberg's deferential reading of the masque, the valorization of
royal ideology coincides with shifts to transcendental concepts of subjectivity and language. Although poststructuralist textual theory requires Goldberg's description of royal discourse as simultaneously
transparent and opaque, he still exploits Orgel's assertion of masque
transparency, here revised to accommodate new theoretical assump-

tions which privilege difference: "The masque then mirrored the royal mind in its self-division" (p. 126). Poststructuralist theory, with its attack on transcendental subjects positioned in metaphysical hierarchies, would find paradoxical the statement that "in Jonson's masques, to celebrate the king means to reveal their shared status as writing" (p. 59): to ground the king's power in language instead of God can only be a celebration that also functions as a desecration and demystification of royal power. Goldberg's reading, however, smooths over the contradictory determinations of royal consciousness by turning it into a transhistorical essence—the text: "The king, too, has the permanence of a text. The masque as text, the masque that reproduces and represents the performance in an unchanging form, assumes the ideal form of the king, the 'lively' statue of Bishop Williams's funeral sermon, standing eternally. . . . nothing less than the eternal life of the text" (p. 59). Revealing his theoretical lineage in New Critical formalism, Goldberg valorizes royal ideology by reifying the text, erasing the historical specificity of its discontinuities, eclipsing its contradictory social conditions, repressing the potential for social change.

This is most clear in his remarks on an extremely topical masque, Jonson's *The Gypsies Metamorphosed* (1621):

> However good-humored, however unthreatening, Jonson's presentation of the court as the country's pickpocket and of the royal favorites as a band of stylish thieves is a revelation that expresses a widely shared contemporary sentiment, which was often less obliquely expressed. Jonson could always claim that his identification of courtiers and gypsies was all in play, that no analogy was really being affirmed. An impartial eye would see that antimasques are as much a version of the court as apotheoses are, but Jonson could count on James's partial reading. (P. 130)

Goldberg's poststructuralist valorization of royal ideology also gives a partial reading, the king's: what James does not read in the masque does not matter, in the long run, does not exist. Although the reference to "contemporary sentiment" clearly offers an opportunity to open up the text to its contradictory social situation, to see in the masque the conflicting ideological positions of other social classes and groups in Jacobean England, Goldberg closes on royal ideology, inexplicably aligning the "contemporary sentiment" with "an impartial eye," giving contemporary dissatisfaction with the royal government an objectivity which prohibits any identification of it with specific class interests. Goldberg's reading does not go beyond the king's partial reading to imagine other social representations, and so the precession of royal simulacra in Jacobean culture has a static quality: texts don't develop, time doesn't pass, every subject is determined by royal discourse.

In this timeless realm, however, the critic magically recuperates his subjective freedom, his control over his cognitive acts, by submitting to the royal text: "To do justice to the text, one must submit to it. Only by submission are discriminatory differences clear and acts of judgment possible" (p. 7). Yet how can these discriminations be clear when they are circumscribed by royal ideology? Aren't the critic's judgments doing the king's justice? Goldberg's poststructuralist reading of Jacobean culture manifests the tendency of American new historicism to read the Renaissance in postmodern terms, yet without confronting the epistemological questions raised by this kind of reading and without recognizing the critic's different historical situation, in effect assuming that the critic is a subject who transcends his moment.

The ahistorical tendencies of the new historicism are partly due to its reliance on the work of anthropologists like Clifford Geertz. Geertz is attractive to Renaissance studies informed by poststructuralism because he uses a textual model for ethnography, whether he is studying Balinese cockfights or Javanese political pageantry. Geertz's use of this model is occasionally self-conscious. In *Negara: The Theater State in Nineteenth-Century Bali* (1980), for example, he observes that his "model" of the "theater state" is "abstract," "a conceptual entity, not an historical one," "a simplified, necessarily unfaithful, theoretically tendentious representation," but also "a guide, a sort of sociological blueprint, for the construction of representations."[10] Later, however, he finally ignores this admission and represses the historical specificity of his textual model of politics by claiming to find it in "the life that swirled around the punggawas, perbekels, puris, and jeros of classical Bali" (p. 135). Elsewhere Geertz tends to minimize the cultural and historical difference between his own assumptions and those of his object by making anachronistic comparisons of ideological representations from fourteenth-century Java and from Elizabethan and Jacobean England and by offering what Vincent Crapanzano has called "blurrings of his point of view, his subjectivity, with that of the natives, or more accurately, of the constructed native."[11]

Goldberg follows Geertz's example by arguing that "from his ethnography [in *Negara*], Geertz proceeds to pose some theoretical consequences that may well apply to the ritual played out in the king's progress through the streets of London" (p. 32). The result is that, like Geertz, Goldberg erases the historical differences between nineteenth-century Bali and seventeenth-century England, stressing the sameness between the ideological representations of Oriental despotism and Jacobean absolutism and ultimately discovering his own poststructuralist assumptions in absolutist ideology: "In opposing Husserl, it may be that Derrida raises terms that more resemble those of renaissance thought than Husserl's do" (p. 151).

In "Blurred Genres: The Refiguration of Social Thought" (1980), Geertz suggests the conservatism of the textual model when he notes that although it constitutes a transformation of contemporary social science, it does not itself encourage thinking about social change. The textual model abandons the "goal" of earlier social science "to find out the dynamics of collective life and alter them in desired directions," choosing instead an "anatomization of thought" that betrays its loss of social and cultural authority: "If the social technologist notion of what a social scientist is is brought into question by all this concern with sense and signification, even more so is the cultural watchdog notion of what a humanist is. The specialist without spirit dispensing policy nostrums goes, but the lectern sage dispensing approved judgments does as well. The relation between thought and action in social life can no more be conceived of in terms of wisdom than it can in terms of expertise" (p. 523). The problem is that no relation between thought and social action can be conceived at all if cultural studies withdraw into "the anatomization of thought"; then the textual model will have overriden the boundaries between academic disciplines while simultaneously reconstructing them along different lines, reaffirming the cult of the sage or expert with a new specialization, a sophisticated notion of textuality, which does not question its relations to its social ground. Geertz's naturalization of the textual model in studies of Bali and Java bears a clear resemblance to media simulation, that process by which the dense sedimentation of codes in media representations are naturalized and the simulacra mask their cultural and social conditions. It is perhaps this resemblance that has done most to erode the authority of the humanist and social scientist by locating scholarship in the continuum of commodified representations. Yet Geertz's "Blurred Genres" omits any consideration of postmodern culture as a whole, focusing instead on changes in two academic disciplines, the humanities and the social sciences. The essay contains the loss of authority suffered by these disciplines not only by remaining within the precincts of academia and omitting any larger, cultural reference, but also by the very tone of its prose: as Adams and Searle note, "Geertz's account of the 'refiguration' of social thought uses the mild rhetoric of worry and ironic amusement, where one might say the same things in the mood of crisis" (p. 514).

The confluence of poststructuralist textuality and Geertz's textual model in Goldberg's reading shows that far from resisting such aspects of postmodern culture, Goldberg celebrates and succumbs to them in a blissful fetishization of the royal text, tracing the infinite substitutions of its finite ideological ensemble, but installing them and the critic's operations in a transcendental space free of social determinations. Jameson points out that the privileging of indeterminacy in the ideology of the text is symptomatic of social life under consumer capitalism, "an atomized society, whose fragmented sub-groups and the resultant multiplicity of 'codes' inflect its art gradually in the direction of just such multipurpose objects, which may be translated into a whole series of private languages in succession."[12] The theoretical complexity and interdisciplinary research of Goldberg's readings reflect these cultural developments, mimicking but simultaneously containing them by valorizing royal ideology, making it the private language of king and critic,[13] never distinguishing, as Alan Sinfield has noted, "strategies of containment from the political pressures they might be trying to manage or conceal."[14] Developing such "pressures"—the contradictory social conditions of academic criticism as well as of royal power—would enable Goldberg's reading to preserve the historical specificity of the text and avoid any valorization of royal ideology or poststructuralist theory which conceals the differences between Renaissance and postmodern culture and thereby removes the capacity of these differences to stimulate thinking about the limits and potentialities of the present.

The discontinuous textual work can be more rigorously historicized if we draw Sinfield's distinction by studying topical allusions, all the while acknowledging that although allusions can be said to anchor a literary text in history, they soon prove to be an unsteady mooring once we begin to investigate the textual operation by which they are transformed. Because the text assimilates different ideological cultural materials, its references to historical figures and events can never be mirror reflections of reality, only interested representations, giving us history mediated by various genres, conventions, tropes, and the competing ideologies to which they are allied. A symptomatic reading which identifies topical allusions and analyzes their assimilation in the textual work can disclose a text's politics, its relation to the ideologies of its specific social conjuncture, finally enabling us to arrive at a penetrating articulation of its place in history. We must not assume, however, that the history reconstructed in a reading of topical allusions is itself free of ideological mediation. The crucial task of historical identification is always an ideological critique of the text from a different ideological standpoint: identifying an allusion means fixing a historical referent in order to expose a disjunction between referent and allusion, an inadequacy between the real and its representation. Establishing the historical referent initiates a differential reading, an interrogation of the interested representations in the text on the basis of a historical reconstruction that serves a different interest in a different conjuncture. Establishing the referent involves a historical narrativization in which the critical act becomes an ideological intervention into its own social and cultural formation. The symptomatic reading of topical allusions assumes a materialist concept of history motored by social contradiction; hence, its identification of allusions and examination of how and to what end they are exploited by the text are designed to create a historical narrative which imagines the contradictory conditions and possibilities of social change.

The court masque particularly recommends itself for this sort of cultural intervention: not only has it been long recognized as one of the most politically significant genres in the prerevolutionary period, but it is political precisely because of its extreme topicality.[15] Jonson's preface to *Hymenaei* (1606) points to this feature of court entertainments, but since the preface is intended to excuse their ephemeral nature, historical references are so ghettoized as to mystify their prominent role in the ideological operations of the genre. The first symptom of this mystification is Jonson's wobbly distinction between the "present occasions" and "more removed mysteries" of the masque: "though their voice be taught to sound to present occasions, their sense or doth or should always lay hold on more removed mysteries" (ll. 15–17).[16] This suggestive remark Platonizes the genre, making allegory its distinctive trope, subordinating "the outward celebration or show" to "the inward parts, and those grounded upon antiquity and solid learnings" (ll. 11–14). The term "present occasions" does the work of mystification: it somewhat obscures the political dimensions of court entertainments by conflating true and proper occasions and topical allusions. The Stuart masque is *occasional* in that it was designed to act as a festive celebration, usually of the Christmas season or an aristocratic wedding. But often it *alludes* to royal policies and proclamations, to political theories and issues, to historical developments that actually lay beyond the immediate reason for its creation. By erasing this distinction between occasion and allusion, Jonson's remark conceals the different ideological determinants that operate on a given masque. In the case of the occasion, we can always discern the effects of the feudal ideology of degree, which subordinates the lower classes in English society by reserving for royalty and aristocracy the effusive praise of the songs and speeches and even the privilege of attending the performance; Jonson acknowledges these ideological effects by asserting that "the outward celebration or show . . . rightly becomes them," i.e., figures their social rank (ll. 11–12). In the case of the allusion, however, more specific ideologies may be at work in the text, so transforming historical references as to legitimize a certain royal policy or to question it from the competing positions of dominated classes.

Both the occasion and the allusion demonstrate that the masque has the political function of maintaining the feudal class hierarchy and the king's hegemony. But the imprecision in the term "present occasions," and the Platonic devaluation of "occasions" against a masque's "more removed mysteries," distract from the recognition that the allusion is really part of the "mysteries": the "solid learnings" contribute to an ideological operation by which any reference to current events is framed by varied cultural materials—dramatic genres like comedy, tropes like allegory, political theories like divine right kingship or the ancient constitution—in order to justify royal power or expose its contradictory conditions. By basing an aesthetic for the masque on Platonic metaphysics, Jonson's preface glosses over the materiality of the text, the textual work by which topical allusions are transformed either into *arcana imperii* that cast reality in the king's image, or into political protests that advance the interests of opposing social groups.[17]

Yet Jonson's preface stops this mystification of his court entertainments in the final sentences. The remark which subordinates the "present occasions" of a masque to its "more removed mysteries" follows other, analogous oppositions based on the spirit-matter hierarchy, one of which, "bodies" versus "souls," suggests the physical mortification associated with Christian asceticism: "So short lived are the bodies of all things in comparison of their souls. And, though bodies ofttimes have the ill luck to be sensually preferred, they find afterwards the good fortune, when souls live, to be utterly forgotten" (ll. 5–9). These metaphysical distinctions are suddenly undermined by a food metaphor at the end:

> And howsoever some may squeamishly cry out that all endeavor of learning and sharpness in these transitory devices . . . is superfluous, I am contented these fastidious stomachs should leave my full tables and enjoy at home their clean empty trenchers, fittest for such airy tastes, where perhaps a few Italian herbs picked up and made into a salad may find sweeter acceptance than all the most nourishing and sound meats of the world. (Ll. 17–25)

Here the "more removed mysteries" are paradoxically redefined as "the most nourishing and sound meats," the spirit-matter hierarchy is inverted, and a topical allusion acts as a reminder that Jonson's "solid learnings" have material conditions. Among the "fastidious stomachs" who criticized Jonson's learned approach to the masque was the poet Samuel Daniel, who had himself written court masques, but whom Jonson soon supplanted as the sole masque writer for the Jacobean court.[18] Because Jonson's masques enjoyed royal patronage throughout James's reign, the food metaphor continues to disseminate meaning, further eroding the earlier valorization of the "more removed mysteries": they can be described not only as food for thought, "the most nourishing and sound meats" for the "understanding," but also as thought for food, an "endeavor of learning and sharpness" for the poet's subsistence; similarly, the "clean empty trenchers" of critics like Daniel mean not only that they take an intellectually "empty" approach to the masque, presumably one stressing the "outward celebration or show," but also that they have not received the well-paying annual commissions from court. The allusion to the rivalry between the two poets demystifies Jonson's earlier Platonization of court entertainments by implying that the "mysteries" of the masque do not transcend, but in fact depend on, the "occasions" of textual production, whether they be a royal commission or a historical event, and that such "occasions" are most revealing sites of the ideological operations in a masque.

We shall make this assumption in a study of topical allusions in a Caroline masque. The allusions in James Shirley's text for *The Triumph of Peace* distinguish it as an important intervention into the deepening social conflicts during the years of Charles's personal rule. The memoirs of Bulstrode Whitelocke, a barrister of the Middle Temple who sat on the planning committee for the production, provide an account of the occasion: performed during February of 1634 at the king's suggestion, the masque was one of those court celebrations that traditionally took place during the Christmas season, a royal holiday entertainment which represented the wealth and power of the hegemonic bloc of Caroline England. But Whitelocke also notes that the masque used topical allusions to achieve a political purpose: to express the affectionate loyalty of the Inns of Court to the king and queen by voicing the lawyers' disagreement with the vitriolic and, to the royal government, seditious attack on court theater by their colleague William Prynne; and to inform the king, in the absence of Parliament, that certain royal fiscal policies were illegal.[19] In Whitelocke's account, the masque contains an ideological contradiction, an expression of political allegiance to the royal government and a parliamentary challenge to the government's legal abuses, and he identifies some of the topical allusions by which the masque communicates its political message, particularly a glance at patents of monopoly. We will explore the fate of this ideological contradiction in the discontinuous textual work by identifying another allusion to contemporary issues, one which shapes the entire antimasque—and turns it against Whitelocke's intended message: the interactions among the characters, the changes in scenery, and the various dances all comprise a reference to Charles's prohibition of the gentry's residence in London.[20]

II

During the late sixteenth and early seventeenth centuries, members of the landowning classes increasingly visited the capital city for both business and pleasure. In their younger days many of them had attended one of the Inns of Court to acquire that basic knowledge of the law which they needed to manage their estates and serve their counties as local officials or MPs. Yet since it was not unusual for them to be mired in some sort of litigation against tenants or neighbors, they occasionally returned to the city to be near the courts at Westminster where they made their depositions and inquired about the progress of their suits. As the center of commercial activity in England, London also offered the gentry the opportunity to borrow money from merchants, invest in trading companies and industrial monopolies, sell the products from their farms, and procure those imported luxuries that did not reach the remote markets in their counties.[21] It was in the city, furthermore, that they could find a remedy for any dissatisfaction they may have felt with the routine and solitude of country life. By residing in London for much of the winter or spring, the country gentleman and his wife might indulge in the latest crazes from the Continent, see new plays and masques, enjoy the company of many friends, and move in the most exclusive aristocratic circles. Perhaps the greatest attraction of the city was the dazzling range of things to do, for there was something to please every taste. Whether the visitor from the provinces was interested in learned sermons or dicing, news of foreign wars or court scandals, an audience with an ambassador or a frolic with a prostitute, he would not be disappointed.[22]

Under James I, the gentry's visits to the capital had begun to occur with some regularity, and by Charles's accession, it must have appeared that many were spending a great part of the year in London or even living there permanently. The early Stuart kings viewed this trend as a twofold threat: it could weaken the ascendancy of the feudal ideology, which justified and reproduced the established social order, and ultimately affect their political power by limiting their control over local affairs. They believed that the gentry's residence in London inevitably meant a decay of rural hospitality and a loss of esteem for that feudal ideal of generosity (*largesse*), one of the "virtues" which set the gentleman above the commoner in the class hierarchy.[23] And they were concerned that this could have ominous effects: when gentlemen neglected housekeeping in the country and spent their wealth elsewhere, their customary relief of the poor languished, able workers went unemployed, and there might be a rise in crime as well as riots, if not rebellion. Similarly, the kings feared that when this landed wealth was consumed in prodigal spending on city pleasures, the result might be an increase in social mobility which would upset the traditional class structure.[24] Since the gentry were the backbone of local government, their frequent absences could also have a damaging effect on legal and political practice. Landowning gentlemen were the king's administrative officials in the country: it was they who were appointed by the king to fill such unpaid offices as justice of the peace and high sheriff.[25] Justices of the peace, for example, in addition to their essential role in law enforcement, "were responsible for providing poor relief, some pensions, trade regulations, food supplies, regulation of ale-houses and the collection of local taxes."[26] Anything that interfered with such duties would naturally hinder the implementation of royal policy.

In 1631, after two years of bad harvests had impoverished rural areas and threatened to cause uprisings, Charles and the Privy Council made an effort to increase the administrative efficiency of local government by issuing the Book of Orders, "for the better administration of justice and more perfect Information of His Majesty, how and by whom the laws and statutes tending to the relief of the poor, the well-ordering and training up of youth in trades, and the reformation of disorders and disordered persons are executed throughout the kingdom."[27] The Book's directives apparently improved the operation and supervision of local government, at least in the beginning,[28] and on 20 June 1632 it was reinforced by a proclamation that commanded the landowning classes to maintain their country residences. The opening paragraph of the proclamation lists the adverse consequences which the king and his advisers feared would result from the gentry's extended visits to London; since the passage bears a striking resemblance to the anti-masque of *The Triumph of Peace,* it is worth quoting in full:

> The Kings Most Excellent Majesty hath observed, That of late yeares a great number of the Nobility and Gentry, and abler sort of his People with their Families have resorted to the Cities of *London* and *Westminster,* and places adjoyning, and there made their Residence more then in former tymes, contrary to the ancient usage of the *English* Nation, which hath occasioned divers inconveniences, for where, by their Residence and Abiding in the severall Countries whence their Meanes ariseth, they served the King in severall places, according to their degrees and ranks in ayde of the Government; whereby their Housekeeping in those parts, the Realme was defended, and the meaner sort of People were guided, directed and relieved: but by their Residence in the said Citties and Parts adjoyning, they have not imployment but live without doing any Service to his *Majesty* or his People, a great part of their Money and Substance is drawn from the severall Countries whence it ariseth, and is spent in the Citty in excess of Apparell provided from forreigne parts, to the enrichment of other Nations and unnecessary consumption of a great part of the Treasure of this Realme, in other vain Delights and Expences, even to the wasting of their Estates, which is not issued into the parts from whence it ariseth, nor are the People of them relieved therewith or by their Hospitality, nor yet set on work, as they might and would be, were it not for the absence of the principall Men out of their Countries, and the excessive use of forraigne Commodities; by this occasion also, and of the great Numbers of loose and idle People, that follow them and Live in and about the said Citties, the disorder there groweth so great and the Delinquents become so numer-

ous, as those places are not easily governed by the ordinary Magistrates, as in former tymes; and the said Citties are not onely at excessive charge in relieving a great number of those idle and loose People, that growe to beggery and become diseased and infirm, but also are made more subject to Contagion and Infection; and the prizes of all kinds of Victualls, both in the said Citties are served, are exceedingly encreased, the poorer sort are unrelieved, and not guided or governed as they might be, in case those Persons of Quality and Respect resided among them.[29]

This proclamation is quite similar to those that James had repeatedly issued during his reign. In 1626, Charles himself had tried the same means, but to little effect. To ensure the success of his latest effort, he ordered that any country gentleman in London who did not hold court office and did not have legal business was to be prosecuted in Star Chamber, and in November of 1632, the attorney general brought suits against more than two hundred offenders.[30]

The extensive instructions of the Book of Orders and the stringent enforcement of the proclamation suggest that they were intended to do much more than prevent riots in rural areas. In fact, the economic crisis that prompted these measures also offered Charles an excuse to consolidate his political power and strengthen the autocracy he had instituted with his dissolution of Parliament in 1629. Both the Book and the proclamation were attempts to bring about a radical reform of local government and counteract the perennial danger that country officials would discharge their duties as they themselves thought best, independent of the central administration and perhaps in opposition to royal policy.[31] Charles's interventions in local affairs can be regarded as political practice designed to realize his absolutist aspirations and determined by the paternalistic ideology of divine right kingship.[32]

This becomes more evident when we recognize that his proclamation against the gentry's residence in London may have exaggerated the actual situation. The local historian Alan Everitt has pointed out that whereas the nobility may have made a habit of visiting the city, the gentry were much more closely tied to their estates:

> In the counties which I have studied most of the peers and a few of the baronets frequented the metropolis fairly regularly for part of the year. The great majority of the knights and virtually all the squires, on the other hand, rarely if ever visited it, except to attend an occasional law-

suit (not a circumstance likely to endear it to them), and virtually never possessed a town house at this date. As is well known there were many proclamations during the early seventeenth century banishing the gentry from London back to their native shires. But what these proclamations do not reveal is that in a large county, such as Suffolk or Kent, there might be 750–1,000 gentry, and that at least three-quarters of them were small parochial squires with an average income of less than £300 a year. Such families could obviously never have afforded a metropolitan establishment. They were essentially provincials, though not necessarily by any means the boozy squires of Whiggish legend.[33]

Everitt's contribution to early Stuart historiography, the concept of the insular and isolationist "county community," sought to correct the tendency of Whig historians like S. R. Gardiner to neglect provincial society in favor of the national conflicts that were played out in central institutions during the revolution. Everitt's correction may have erred in the other direction: the "county community" school of local historians which emerged in the wake of his work has since been criticized as unnecessarily narrow in their assessment of the social and cultural life of the country aristocracy, particularly its ideological divisions in the prerevolutionary period. Everitt's remarks on the infrequency of gentry visits to London, however, need no revision: Derek Hirst cites "a 1632 government census [which] found almost 25 per cent of the peerage (though less than 1 per cent of the gentry) resident in London without good reason."[34] The census urges a sceptical approach to the royal proclamation, mindful of a warning that Marx made long ago in *The German Ideology:* we should not be uncritical in our acceptance of the dominant class's construction of contemporary events.[35] Since only a rather small proportion of the gentry traveled to London with any regularity, it appears unlikely that the administrative machinery of the provinces was markedly impaired at the beginning of the 1630s; on the contrary, the Book of Orders reinvigorated county government at this time and enabled a more strict supervision of local affairs. This clearly implies that Charles's proclamation is an alarmist document primarily designed to achieve a political goal: it constitutes a transformation of a real social trend into a serious problem that justifies royal intervention and therefore upholds the king's dominance in English society. The proclamation, like the Book of Orders, was inspired by the fear that the king was losing control over local government and by the ideological conviction that his power should be absolute and "thorough." In the end, however, the paternalism of Charles's policies seems to have produced the opposite result: it was instrumental in alienating those country gentlemen whose support he desperately needed in his constitutional struggle with the Long Parliament in 1640.[36]

III

Shirley's antimasque consists of the interactions of several allegorical characters, one of whom, Fancy, presents a number of dances and changes of scenery. The topical nature of this activity becomes apparent as soon as the characters meet and introduce themselves to one another in the urban setting of the first scene, "a large street with sumptuous palaces, lodges, porticos, and other noble pieces of architecture, with pleasant trees and grounds [which] opens itself into a spacious place, adorned with public and private buildings seen afar off" (p. 263).[37] Opinion, the first antimasquer we see, is a country gentleman visiting London with his wife Novelty who reveals that they belong to the gentry: she grows infuriated when Opinion calls her his wife, and her retort is, "they can but call / Us so i'th'country" (p. 264). Opinion's costume is another indication of his social status: as we might expect of a gentleman who hails from the country, he does not appear in the latest London styles. In contrast to Confidence, the fashionable man-about-town who wears "a slashed doublet parti-colored [and] a broad-brimmed hat, tied up on one side, banded with a feather," Opinion is dressed "in an old fashioned doublet of black velvet, and trunk hose, a short cloak of the same with an antique cape, a black velvet cap pinched up, with a white fall, and a staff in his hand" (p. 257).[38] The antimasque also contains allusions to some of the entertainments the gentry favored on their stays in the city. Opinion is fond of the theater, and he has come to court to see the masque. Later, when the scene is changed to a tavern, the gallant Confidence persuades the ladies to go inside and "accept the wine" (p. 268). Throughout the antimasque, Opinion and his family are accompanied by Jollity and Laughter, two characters whose names refer to the pursuit of pleasure which sometimes brought the landowning classes to London. Similarly, the names of Opinion's wife and daughter point to the gentry's desire for "novel" experiences that differ from their country routines and so are likely to elicit their wonder or "admiration." At one point, Opinion explicitly mentions the occasion for the masque and speaks favorably of the Inns of Court, saying,

I am their friend against the crowd that envy 'em,
And since they come with pure devotions
To sacrifice their duties to the king
And queen, I wish 'em prosper.

(P. 266)

This gesture of camaraderie can be taken as yet another historical reference: apart from the glance at the disrepute into which the lawyers may have fallen because of the Prynne scandal, Opinion's remark more generally alludes to the fact that the gentry were closely associated with the legal profession, both because they customarily sent their sons to study at the Inns and because they were occasionally involved in litigation.

Two of the dances in the antimasque are pantomimes that dramatize specific details in Charles's proclamation. When most of the characters enter the tavern, Opinion stays behind with Fancy who presents "*a* Gentleman, *and four* Beggars" who walk on crutches: "*The* Gentleman *first danceth alone; to him the* Beggars; *he bestows his charity; the* Cripples, *upon his going off, throw away their legs, and dance*" (p. 268). This episode illustrates the "divers inconveniences" which the proclamation attributed to the gentry's residence in London. Since the term "gentleman" was virtually synonymous with landownership at this time, the victim of the confidence trick can be seen as a member of the gentry who has left his estate to spend his wealth in the city instead of the country "whence it ariseth," thereby neglecting his obligation to relieve the rural poor with his generosity. The thieves who pose as beggars, moreover, are apt examples of those "loose and idle People, that follow" country gentlemen to London and either become "Delinquents" or "growe to beggery." Another dance makes a similar use of the proclamation. Here the performers are dressed as "*a* Maquerelle [i.e., a bawd], *two* Wenches, [and] *two wanton* Gamesters" (p. 268). After a brief dance in which they "*expressed their natures*," they leave the stage only to make a later entrance: "*The* Maquerelle, Wenches, Gentlemen, *return, as from the tavern; they dance together; the* Gallants *are cheated; and left to dance in, with a drunken repentance*" (p. 271). Once again, we see the gentry attracting criminals in the city, but in this case, there is also the suggestion that the two gentlemen are squandering their wealth on gambling and prostitutes or, in the words of the proclamation, on "vain Delights and Expences, even to the wasting of their Estates."

The allusions I have identified show that Shirley's antimasque is hardly a transparent window onto Caroline England. There are indeed references to a real historical development—the gentry's occasional visits to London, the first signs of a fashionable "season"—but these are allied to a contemporary account of that development, the royal proclamation. As a result, the antimasque has that same inadequacy to the real which we found in the official document: both texts involve an essentially ideological operation that serves the king's interests by transforming a social trend into a cause for alarm which requires his intervention. The antimasque performs this ideological operation in its own way, with distinctively literary and dramatic materials, and consequently, it achieves a much more complex transformation of reality than the social commentary that opens the proclamation. The portrayal of Novelty, for example, suggests not only the gentry's interest in new experiences that cannot be had in the country, but also a questionable fascination with every passing fad, with newness for its own sake. The allusion simultaneously functions as a criticism, and one which was shared by conservative members of the gentry like the royalist Richard Brathwaite: in his courtesy book *The English Gentlewoman* (1631), Brathwaite noted that in the city there are "some affecting nothing more than what is most nouell and phantasticke."[39] Thus, when Confidence asks Novelty to drink with him, she replies that "It will be new for ladies / To go to th'tavern; but it may be a fashion" (p. 268). In accordance with the critical element in Novelty's characterization, she angers Opinion by returning drunk, and he reproaches her, "these are / Extremes indeed" (p. 273). The two dances we have considered also complicate the proclamation: they exploit a potential irony inherent in it, but never explicitly stated. The argument set forth in the official document is that when a country gentleman resides in London and fails to relieve the poor or employ able workers in his county, he drives these people to the city where they embark on a life of crime, among other things. The irony exposed by Shirley's text is that ultimately this same gentleman may become the victim of the people he has neglected. In this sense, those gentlemen swindled by the beggars and prostitutes in the dances are themselves responsible for the crimes they suffer. For the gentry, the antimasque seems to be saying, living in London is self-destructive, and they have not the slightest awareness of this fact.

A similar lack of self-awareness underlies the interactions between Opinion and Fancy. As a country gentleman, Opinion represents the gentry's attitude toward Charles's personal rule. His somber clothing and the repeated references to him as the "most grave Opinion" who "will like nothing" (pp. 262, 266, 267) further suggest that he stands for the disgruntled Puritan segment of the landowning classes. Not unexpectedly, then, he is critical of the problems he sees in English society under Charles. When Fancy announces that he will present the effects of peace in the antimasque and the dances of urban crime are performed, Opinion launches into a tirade:

> *Opinion.* I am glad they are off:
> Are these effects of peace?
> Corruption rather.
> *Confidence.* Oh, the beggars shew
> The benefit of peace.
> *Opinion.* Their very breath
> Hath stifled all the candles, poisn'd the
> Perfumes: beggars a fit presentment! how
> They cleave to my nostril! I must tell you,
> I do not like such base and sordid persons,
> And they become not here.
> (Pp. 268–69)

Once more there is an irony in Shirley's text which derives from the proclamation. What Opinion does not perceive is that his very presence in London with his family may have caused the "corruption": as a rural landowner, he should be on his estate relieving the poor with his liberal gifts, not in London berating those people who may have turned to crime because of his own negligence. The fact that it is Fancy who presents the "corruption" sets up a psychological allegory that likewise disarms Opinion's social commentary. Because Fancy is "the sole presenter of the antimasques" (p. 257), Opinion's failure of perception is implicitly attributed to his faulty imagination, and his criticisms of Charles's reign are reduced to self-delusion. This also occurs when Opinion asks Fancy to create an antimasque of rare curiosities, "some more quaint variety, some other / Than human shapes . . . baboons / In quellios [i.e., ruffs]" (p. 271). The scene is changed to "*a woody* Landscape," and we see

> *a* Merchant *a'Horseback with his portmanteau; two* Thieves, *set upon him and rob him: these by a* Constable *and* Officers *are apprehended and carried off. Then four* Nymphs *enter dancing, with their javelins; three* Satyrs *spy them and attempt their persons; one of the nymphs escapeth; a noise of hunters and their horns within, as at the fall of a deer; then enter four*

Huntsmen *and one* Nymph; these *drive away the* Satyrs, *and having res-cued the* Nymphs, *dance with them.* (P. 272)

In these episodes, another criticism of Caroline society is undercut by an irony drawn from the proclamation and by the allegorical signifi-cance of Fancy. Because the constable's apprehension of the criminals is presented as a rarity, the suggestion is that law enforcement is not very effective in the provinces. The analogous scene with the nymphs and satyrs makes this problem even worse by hinting that rural crime is never solved in reality, only in pastoral romances! Since it was the gentry who were responsible for provincial government, Opinion's ab-sence from his county means that he may share the blame for such administrative inefficiency. Opinion, of course, is entirely unaware that he or his class may be derelict in their duties, and the allegory asso-ciates his ignorance with Fancy's inventiveness. Thus, an implied criti-cism of Charles's reign is again reduced to a misperception caused by an overactive imagination.

The antimasque of *The Triumph of Peace* is an especially shifty text, and we should not minimize its subtlety: on the one hand, it registers a criticism of the royal government through Opinion's comments on Caroline society; on the other hand, however, the interactions between Opinion and Fancy transform this criticism into an attack on that seg-ment of the gentry which frequented London. The work of transfor-mation relies on both the proclamation and an allegory derived from Renaissance faculty psychology. The use of Fancy to subvert Opinion's social commentary reveals the suspicion with which the imagination was often regarded during the Renaissance,[40] but the text also contains a brief portrait of "the sole presenter" which provides a more specific definition of his function. Significantly, it is Confidence who describes Fancy to Opinion, instilling in the country gentleman an unwise trust in the imagination:

> *Opinion.*   is this gentleman, this Signor Fancy,
>   So rare a thing, so subtle, as men speak him?
> *Confidence.*   He's a great prince of th'air, believe it, sir,
>   And yet a bird of night.
> *Opinion.*   A bird!
> *Confidence.*   Between
>   An owl and bat, a quaint hermaphrodite,
>   Begot of Mercury and Venus, Wit and Love:
>   He's worth your entertainment.

Opinion. I am most
Ambitious to see him . . .
(P. 264)

As a "prince of th'air" with the characteristics of a "bat," Fancy is likely to create images that are not firmly grounded on an observation of reality. His resemblance to an "owl" increases his unreliability by giving it a political dimension: as we learn later in the masque, the owl symbolizes "faction" ("faction or owl's sight, / Whose trouble is the clearest light" [p. 278]), or what we may define as dissension resulting from a biased perception of the obvious. The inference to be drawn from this "quaint hermaphrodite" is that any product of the imagination which purports to be an accurate representation of society is highly suspect. A similar attitude toward the imagination is expressed in the text when the antimasquer Jollity hurries the other characters into the tavern by remarking, "let's leave Opinion behind us; / Fancy will make him drunk" (p. 268). Fancy's genealogy can be taken as another allusion to the Inns of Court, the producers of the masque who "begot" him and the other characters; it also indicates the reason why he should play so important a role despite his negative connotations. The "Wit and Love" belong to the Inns, who chose a sophisticated court entertainment to convey their devotion to Charles and Henrietta Maria. Fancy is the lawyers' offspring because the allegory he signifies allows them to display their loyalty by wittily exploding any criticism of the king's personal rule. Fancy's genealogy produces what may be the greatest irony in the antimasque: as an anticipation of the later attack on the gentry, it shows the lawyers' Machiavellian strategy of criticizing a social group with whom they were closely associated in order to save face with the king.

The sheer elaborateness of the allegory can only remind us of the ideological operation at work in Shirley's text. Opinion and his family are not mirror images of the Caroline gentry; they rather constitute an ideologeme, a representation of a real social class mediated by another class's values. Studying the portrayal of these characters cannot give us any historical knowledge of the gentry, but it can disclose the antimasque's relation to the king's ideology. This relation becomes quite apparent when we observe that the text represses the real conflicts between Charles and the landowning classes: the social criticism assigned to Opinion does not have any resemblance to the gentry's actual complaints about his personal rule. In the years immediately before the performance of Shirley's masque, they were perhaps most annoyed by the king's fiscal expedients, the combination of forced loans, fines, and taxes which he exploited to increase his revenue without the consent of their parliamentary representatives. In particular it was the gentry who were hardest hit by Charles's decision to revive distraint of knighthood, an ancient usage that permitted him to fine all gentlemen with an annual income of £40 or more who were not knighted at his coronation.[41] This was an unpopular measure that could only reinforce the landowners' increasing alienation from the central government. The local commissioners who were appointed to compound with offenders faced the undesirable task of pursuing their neighbors, and the fines could be quite stiff, some ranging as high as £70. Although largely successful in raising money for the crown, the knighthood scheme did encounter resistance in some counties. Sir David Foulis tried to persuade the Yorkshire gentry to refuse payment; in November of 1633, when the preparations for *The Triumph of Peace* were already under way, his efforts earned him a conviction in Star Chamber, and he was punished with a fine, imprisonment, and removal from all of his offices.[42] Elsewhere the commissioners might be deliberately lax in their collections, going so far as to omit names from their rosters.[43]

Shirley's text is strategically silent on such developments. The effect of its allusions to the proclamation is to displace a real reason for the gentry's opposition to the king with a criticism of Caroline society which is actually an ironic attack on them; and as soon as the viewer perceives the multiple ironies, he has been positioned in the royal representation of the gentry. This displacement and the textual positioning which accompanies it reveal the operation of absolutist ideology: it shows that the entire thrust of the antimasque is to discredit the gentry as a political force and ratify the king's autocracy. Since Opinion and the other gentlemen are shown to be utterly incapable of recognizing the "divers inconveniences" which the proclamation imputes to their London visits, it would be imprudent if not pointless for Charles to summon Parliament and submit his policies for the consideration of the provincial MPs; indeed, according to the logic of allegory, the best course would be for him to intervene solely on the basis of the royal prerogative and restore order in the kingdom. The lack of understanding which the allegory ascribes to the gentry in London is a key factor in the ideological operation of the antimasque; this was the very tactic that Charles himself had used in a proclamation issued in 1629 to explain his dissolution of Parliament:

we shall account it presumption for any to prescribe any time unto us for parliaments, the calling, continuing and dissolving of which is always in our own power; and we shall be more inclinable to meet in parliament again when our people shall see more clearly into our intentions and actions, when such as have bred this interruption shall have received their condign punishment, and those who are misled by them and by such ill reports as are raised upon this occasion shall come to a better understanding of us and themselves.[44]

Like this proclamation, the antimasque insists that the gentry who leave their country estates are "misled" and thus justifies the king's exclusion of them from the political process.

IV

We can extend these observations by examining another topical allusion in the antimasque: a group of projectors who seek royal patents of monopoly for their inventions. During the late sixteenth and early seventeenth centuries, patents were issued for a variety of reasons, most of which did not benefit the commonwealth. Patents could be an effective means to promote industrial expansion by protecting new technical processes and assuring fledgling industries a market for their products. More often than not, however, they were used to serve royal financial interests, reward favorites, and advance political power through economic centralization.[45] During Charles's reign, patents were primarily a fiscal expedient designed to raise money for the crown. Without a Parliament willing to vote him the subsidies he needed to cover his expenses, the king and his ministers developed independent sources of revenue through loopholes in the parliamentary statute which prohibited patents to individuals in 1624. Since the statute had excluded new inventions and corporations from its provisions, Caroline monopolists pretended technical improvements and formed partnerships or companies, and in return for the lucrative privileges which the patents granted them, they paid into the Exchequer an annual rent or, in some cases, a fee for each product sold.[46] The Company of Soapmakers of Westminster, for instance, the most notorious monopoly under Charles, was incorporated in 1632 to use a new manufacturing method and was gradually given the exclusive right to produce soap in England. For their patent, the monopolists agreed to pay the king £20,000 per annum.[47]

Because patents were granted for such commonly used products as soap, salt, wine, and logwood, they were destined to have far-reaching effects which ultimately alienated large segments of the population from the crown. The interests of consumers were largely ignored. Monopolists knew that their privileges were unlawful and would doubtless be revoked if Parliament ever met again, so they tried to get rich quick by driving up prices for inferior goods. Merchants suffered because patents frequently prohibited the import of certain materials long used in manufacturing and gave the monopolists the right to search cargoes. Patents similarly disrupted established industries by forcing independent manufacturers to use new materials and methods, to submit their products to tests conducted by the monopolists themselves, and to compound with them for infringements of their privileges.[48] Throughout the autocratic 1630s, Charles enacted monopolies through proclamations, an effective strategy which enabled him to discourage infringers by bringing charges against them in Star Chamber for contempt of the royal prerogative. Late in 1632, for example, the Privy Council instructed Attorney General William Noy to prosecute several independent soapboilers for violating the patent of the Westminster Company. The offenders were prohibited from engaging in their trade, ordered to pay fines ranging from £500 to £1,500 each, and committed to the Fleet. They were still in custody when *The Triumph of Peace* was first performed.[49]

The monopolies were one of Charles's most unpopular financial measures. Because their effects were so complex and extensive, present at the economic, legal, and political levels of Caroline society, the struggle against them was equally complicated. The Privy Council was constantly besieged with petitions to recall certain patents, most of which were upheld.[50] Soon after Noy's death in the summer of 1634, a group of players who were formerly his clients pilloried him in a farce entitled *A Projector Lately Deade,* "wherein they bringe hym in his lawiers robes vpon the stage, & openlye dissecting hym, finde a 100 proclamations in his heade, a bundle of olde moathe eaten records in his mawe, & halfe a barrell of new white soape in his belly."[51] Charles's summoning of Parliament in 1640 unleashed a flood of pamphlets attacking the monopolists' abuses. One anonymous author observed that the Westminster Company "upon pretence of a new Invention of making white soape . . . did procure themselves to bee incorporated."[52] Another noted the independent manufacturers' plight: "No freeman of London, after he hath served his years and set up his trade, can be sure long to enjoy the labor of his trade, but either he is forbidden longer to use it, or is forced at length with the rest of his trade to purchase it as a monopoly, at a dear rate, which they and all the kingdom pay for. Witness the soap business."[53] In *The Discovery of a Projector,* T. Brugis pointed out that although the monopolist claimed that "all the profit [would] acrew onely to his Majestie, and the good of the Common-wealth," his actual intention was "to raise his fortunes on a sodaine," with the result that his products had such "greater faults" as "insufficiency, exceeding dearnesse, and exceeding basenesse, uglinesse, or il-favourednesse."[54] When the Long Parliament began its reform and re-dress of grievances, it expelled any MP who was a monopolist or was associated in any way with a monopoly, and a large number of indus-trial patents were abolished. Sir John Colepeper, who stood for Kent, delivered an eloquent speech which summed up the problems caused by the monopolists, providing an astonishing list of the many goods they controlled:

> These, like the frogs of Egypt, have got possession of our dwellings, and we have scarce a room free from them: they sip in our cup, they dip in our dish, they sit by our fire; we find them in the dye-vat, wash-bowl, and powdering-tub . . . Mr. Speaker, they will not bate us a pin: we may not buy our own cloaths without their brokerage . . . And, some of these are ashamed of their right names; they have a vizard to hide the brand made by that good law in the last parliament of king James; they shelter themselves under the name of a corporation; they make bye-laws, which serve their turns to squeeze us, and fill their purses.[55]

Such representations of Caroline monopolies are plainly political interventions designed to serve the interests of consumers and the manufacturers and merchants whose businesses were hurt by the mo-nopolists' privileges. The petitions, play, and pamphlets speak for most of the dominated classes in English society, not only the more econom-ically advanced sectors, yet to achieve the concrete effectiveness of in-stitutionalized political power, those criticisms would have to wait until the Long Parliament be echoed in speeches like Colepeper's and thereby assimilated into the ideological discourse of the parliamentary opposition against the king. Shirley's representation does indeed allude to issues raised by the monopolies, but we can perceive certain trans-formations which ultimately point to the operation of absolutist ideology.

The antimasque introduces six comic projectors. Three of them refer, in their diverting way, to the customary practice of winning patents by pretending technical improvements in existing products or methods: a "jockey" has developed "a rare and cunning bridle" that can so "cool and refresh a horse, he shall ne'er tire"; a "country fellow" has bought a "flail" which can thresh corn "without help of hands"; and a "physician" has contrived "a new way to fatten poultry / With scrapings of carrot" (pp. 269–70). Clearly, these inventions are wildly improbable, and they appear to be nothing more than foolish get-rich-quick schemes devised by some rather incompetent projectors who are more likely to be duped than to cheat others with their projects. Thus, the countryman "has sold his acres," giving up his living "to purchase him" the labor-saving flail, while the physician, who adheres to incompatible medical principles (he is "a Galenist, and parcel Paracelsus"), once "thriv'd by diseases, but quite lost his practice" by devoting himself to his bizarre studies in animal husbandry. This note of ridiculousness is repeatedly sounded in the antimasque. We can hear it in the remaining projects which are equally implausible during this period of relatively slow technological development: they include a deep-sea diving suit described as "a case to walk you all day under water," a kind of double boiler in which "the very steam / Of the first vessel shall alone be able / To make another pot above seethe over," and two nautical inventions, one to enable "a ship to sail against the winds," the other, "on Goodwin sands, to melt huge rocks to jelly" (pp. 270–71).

The ideological operation at work in this antimasque becomes evident if we consider the different responses it elicited. Whitelocke states that it "pleased the Spectators the more, because by it an Information was covertly given to the King, of the unfitness and ridiculousness of these Projects against the Law: and the Attorney *Noy,* who had most knowledge of them, had a great hand in this Antimasque of the *Projectors*" (p. 20). The implication, of course, is that the antimasque is imputing illegalities to the king, the source of all patents, and this may well have been the intention of some of the lawyers who produced the entertainment. Yet Whitelocke's assurance about the meaning of the antimasque is not warranted by the fact that his and Shirley's collaborator was Charles's attorney general: Noy was responsible for some of the royal government's most questionable fiscal expedients. It is certain that Noy "had most knowledge of" these things, but also that he was a very opportunistic lawyer who had shifted his allegiance from Parliament to the crown: would he incriminate his own work as a government official in a court masque, however "covertly"? Charles himself apparently did not perceive the imputation of illegalities; the evidence we have rather suggests that he was quite pleased with the entire masque: he ordered a second performance of it.[56] It seems more probable, in fact, that the king viewed the antimasque as praise of his wisdom in selecting only those inventions worthy of monopolies. These opposed responses are possible because, once again, Shirley's text registers a potential criticism of the royal government, but so presents that criticism as to defuse it. Here the work of transformation is achieved by the convenient omission of any reference to the many adverse consequences of the monopolies and by the sheer absurdity of the inventions. Furthermore, because the antimasque omits the precise nature of the patents sought by the projectors—i.e., the privileges each patentee will enjoy, the length of time they will be effective, the annual rents or fees to be paid to the king—the political message which the lawyers wanted to communicate is weakened. Hence, Whitelocke's account of the performance, edited and published after the Restoration and some twenty years of political struggle, civil war, and republican experiments,[57] must be taken as an active, and unwitting, politicization of the text, an effort to preserve its political force by reading in the terms of the patents:

> First in this Anti-masque, rode a Fellow upon a little horse, with a great Bit in his mouth, and upon the Man's head was a Bit, with Headstall and Rains fastened, and signified a Projector, *who begged a patent, that none in the Kingdom might ride their horses, but with such Bits as they should buy of him.* Then came another Fellow with a bunch of Carrotts upon his head and a Capon upon his Fist, describing a *Projector* who begg'd a Patent of *Monopoly,* as the first Inventor of the *Art* to feed Capons fat with Carrotts, and that none but himself might make use of that Invention, and have the Priviledge for fourteen years, according to the Statute. (P. 20)

Shirley's descriptions differ from Whitelocke's politicized reading by functioning as a comic displacement of serious issues, whereby the projectors can be seen not as threats to the social order, but as harmless fun, a point that must have been driven home in the performance by their outlandish costumes and dances. The antimasque does indeed satirize Caroline monopolies, yet in contrast to Whitelocke's statement of its intention, the emphasis is on their "ridiculousness" rather than on their "unfitness . . . against the Law." Shirley's representation may have been intended as a legal argument against the royal prerogative, but it can also be read as a mystification of a social problem, a mystifi-

cation that serves the interests of the royal government and those entrepreneurs who received royal patents of monopoly.

This allusion to Caroline monopolies is also mediated by a dramatic
genre, city comedy, so that we can define more precisely the ideological
significance of Shirley's representation by developing an intertextual
construct which reveals generic affinities and discontinuities in the antimasque. Conventions from city comedy can be isolated not just in the
urban setting of the first scene, "the forum or piazza of Peace" (p. 263),
but also in the interactions between the characters. Opinion is a refash-
ioning of a character type in the genre, the country gentleman who,
like Fitzdottrel in Jonson's *The Devil is an Ass,* visits London for business or pleasure and is made the victim of an intrigue in which his land
is sought or his wife's chastity threatened. Just as Mistress Fitzdottrel
must deal with the advances of the young gallant Wittipol, who boldly
carries on his seduction in front of her husband, so Novelty is spirited
away from Opinion's side by the fashionable Confidence, who succeeds
in getting her drunk. Moreover, just as city comedy, reflecting its origins in the cony-catching pamphlets, consistently characterizes London
as a den of iniquity where swindlers prey on unsuspecting or dissolute
gentlemen, so the brief narrative dances in Shirley's antimasque show
a gentleman duped by vagrants posing as crippled beggars. Another of
these dances exploits the conventional prodigal motif from the drama:
the "*two wanton* Gamesters" who are "*cheated*" by "*a* Maquerelle" and
"*two* Wenches" are reminiscent of gentlemen like Witgood in Middleton's *A Trick to Catch the Old One* or Welborne in Massinger's *A New
Way to Pay Old Debts,* both of whom squandered their estates on drinking, gambling, and prostitutes.

In the previous chapter, we saw how early city comedy signifies a
progressive affirmation of capitalism by valorizing the subversive profit
accumulation of businessmen and gentlemen, even though this valorization was overdetermined by a reactionary moral judgment, whereas
late city comedy signifies a conservative reaction in which the two main
character types are so rehabilitated as to uphold the patriarchal family
and the feudal class hierarchy. Shirley's antimasque bears a strong resemblance to the Caroline transformation of the genre. Since only the
lower classes (beggars and prostitutes) contrive fraudulent money-
making schemes, and only the gentry (the charitable gentleman and
the prodigal gallants) are their victims, the antimasque erases one of
the central ideological conflicts in the Jacobean plays—the gentleman's
reliance on the very same schemes that had victimized him—and the
traditional class distinctions are maintained. Similarly, once the viewer

perceives the multiple ironies associated with the gentry's visits to London, the antimasque has enforced a concern with feudal values like noblesse oblige, or the aristocrat's responsibility for his social inferiors, and patriarchal values like male authority and female obedience, thereby affirming the ideologies of degree and patriarchy.

The conservatism of these generic transformations is particularly apparent in the discontinuities between the projectors in the antimasque and those in early city comedy. Meercraft, the projector in *The Devil is an Ass*, exhibits the mixture of villainy and virtuosity typical of businessmen in the Jacobean plays. We first see him in a flurry of activity, giving orders to several servants and making oblique references to projects and large sums of money which are intended to impress the unwary Fitzdottrel and prime him for the swindle. After telling the gentleman, "I haue a proiect to make you a *Duke*, now" (2.1.26),[58] Meercraft turns to his accomplice Ingine and describes the venture:

> *Meercraft.* I'll driue his pattent for him.
>   We'll take in Cittizens, *Commoners,* and *Aldermen,*
>   To beare the charge, and blow 'hem off againe,
>   Like so many dead flyes, when 'tis carryed.
>   The thing is for recouery of drown'd land,
>   Whereof the *Crowne's* to haue his moiety,
>   If it be owner; Else, the *Crowne* and Owners
>   To share that moyety: and the recouerers
>   T'enjoy the tother moyety, for their charge.
> *Ingine.* Thorowout *England?*
> *Meercraft.*   Yes, which will arise
>   To eyghteene *millions,* seuen the first yeere:
>   I haue computed all, and made my suruay
>   Unto an acre. I'll beginne at the Pan,
>   Not, at the skirts: as some ha' done, and lost,
>   All that they wrought, their timber-worke, their trench,
>   Their bankes all borne away, or else fill'd vp
>   By the next winter. Tut, they neuer went
>   The way: I'll haue it all.
> *Ingine.*   A gallant tract
>   Of land it is!
> *Meercraft.*   'Twill yeeld a pound an acre.
>   Wee must let cheape, euer, at first.
>   (2.1.41–60)

Ever the cunning manipulator, Meercraft subsequently unleashes a barrage of other projects—bottling ale, wine bottles from dog-skins, wine from raisins—but Fitzdottrel has already swallowed the bait and interrupts him: "Saue you the trouble, I'll not look, nor hear / Of any, but your first, there, the drown'd land" (2.1.113–14). Throughout the scene, we can see the competing ideologies in Meercraft's characterization. From the perspective of degree, his greed leads him to violate the class hierarchy not only by preying on a member of the gentry, but by stimulating social mobility: he encourages Fitzdottrel's social aspirations with the promise of a peerage and plans to cheat wealthy "Cittizens, *Commoners,* and *Aldermen*" (although the latter are clearly subterfuges for Fitzdottrel's benefit). The sheer brilliance of Meercraft's performance, however, persuasive in its thoroughness and its careful anticipation of any costly problems the project may encounter, shows him to be a resourceful, if dishonest, entrepreneur whose manipulation of the obtuse Fitzdottrel is admirably inventive and shared with the audience—who is thus positioned in possessive individualism.

It is this ideological contradiction that is absent from Shirley's representation of the projectors. Meercraft's project to reclaim land through drainage alludes to an actual practice in early Stuart England, so it will be illuminating to compare it with one of the nautical inventions in Shirley's antimasque which also alludes to a real project: in November of 1630, one David Ramsey, a prolific Caroline inventor, received a patent for a device "to make boats and ships go against strong wind and tide."[59] In this case, the projector is dressed "like a Seaman, a ship upon his head and holding a line and plummet in his hand" (p. 259), and when he enters, Fancy provides the commentary:

> This is a kind of sea gull too, that will
> Compose a ship to sail against the winds;
> He'll undertake to build a most strong castle
> On Goodwin sands, to melt huge rocks to jelly,
> And cut 'em out like sweetmeats with his keel;
> And thus he sails. [*The sixth Projector dances.*]
>   (Pp. 270–71)

The pun on "gull" is indicative of the way Shirley's antimasque has transformed the conventional businessman from early city comedy: it suggests that the seaman's projects represent not a means to satisfy his greed by duping others, but a self-delusion. He obviously lacks both Meercraft's evil and cunning. In contrast to Meercraft's convincingly detailed use of an actual project for drainage, furthermore, Fancy's remarks combine the invention for which Ramsey received a patent with the fantastic description of the "castle," effectively destroying the seaman as a position of identification for the viewer. Thus, the fortune-hunting and cleverness that eviscerated the traditional class hierarchy in early city comedy are here transformed into an inconsequential foolishness, and the ideological contradiction that had formerly proved to be irreconcilable in the plays is now "resolved" in the antimasque with a representation that removes any threat to social order.

Jonson's *The Devil is an Ass* is especially useful in eludicating Shirley's conservative transformation of city comedy conventions because both play and masque allude to monopolies while drawing on royal speeches and proclamations which prohibit the gentry's residence in London. As Leah Marcus has shown, Jonson's play is quite subversive in its treatment of James's speech before Star Chamber in 1616: it "subtly points to the ways in which James's tolerance for monopolies undermines his most cherished policies," including his effort to control urban growth.[60] When Meercraft adds that "the *Crowne's* to haue his moiety, / If it be owner; Else, the *Crowne* and Owners / To share that moyety," the royal government is implicated in the very commercial activities that lure gentry like Fitzdottrel to the city and away from what would better serve the king's political interests, country housekeeping. Although Fitzdottrel is unsuspecting enough to be prey to confidence artists, he falls for an allusion to an actual project, land drainage, a plausible venture to make money and improve his social status which turns him into a bourgeois threat to the class hierarchy. Shirley's more conservative representation of the projectors not only represses any explicit reference to the king, but disarms the gentry. Opinion first reveals his ignorance of what a projector is and then his utter lack of judgment by praising the ridiculous devices and their inventors with remarks like "A most scholastic project!" and "He will deserve a monument" (p. 270). This enthusiastic approval, like the self-destructive stupidity of the "country fellow" who sold his land to invest in an absurd industrial venture, again raises doubts about whether Charles should rely on the provincial MPs for advice when he frames his economic policies, and thus its effect is to confirm the king's personal rule.

The final sequence of dances in Shirley's antimasque continues to discredit the offending gentry in a way that reflects the king's ideology. These too are pantomimes, and in keeping with the elaborateness that has so far distinguished the antimasque, they are rather indirect in their criticism:

A Landscape, *The scene; and enter three* Dotterels, *and three* Dotterel-Catchers. . . . *After the* Dotterels *are caught by several imitations, enter a* Windmill, *a fantastic* Knight *and his* Squire *armed. The fantastic adventurer with his lance makes many attempts upon the windmill, which his squire imitates; to them enter a* Country-Gentleman *and his* Servant. *These are assaulted by the* Knight *and his* Squire, *but are sent off lame for their folly. Then enter four* Bowlers, *who shew much variety of sport in their game and postures, and conclude the Antimasque.* (Pp. 272–73)

These dances may be taken as references to diversions enjoyed by the gentry: bird-catching, reading chivalric romances like *Don Quixote*,[61] and bowling.[62] At the same time, however, each dance seems to satirize members of this class who are socially ambitious, who seek to elevate their status by imitating preoccupations associated with the nobility. This satire is first signified by the dotterels, a species of plover which, it was believed, allowed itself to be caught by mimicking the fowler's actions; accordingly, the term "dotterel" came to be used as a synonym for "silly person" (*OED*). The allusion to one of the more farcical episodes in Cervantes' work portrays the pretentious gentry as dotterels by showing two gentlemen in ridiculous imitations: a "fantastic" or irrational knight emulates the noble ideal of chivalry by jousting with a windmill, and his squire blindly follows him. These characters are so deluded by their imitations that they assault another country gentleman, perhaps the owner of the windmill who arrives to defend his property. Evidently the point of these dances is that certain gentry are similar to dotterels because they foolishly aspire to nobility but in the end are "caught" in adverse circumstances in which they endanger themselves and other members of their class (the "dotterels," then, seem to convey meanings applicable to the social aspirations of Fitzdottrel in *The Devil is an Ass* and therefore may signal a specific literary allusion, establishing a more direct intertextual relationship between Shirley's antimasque and Jonson's play than a generic affinity). This point would also explain the apparently unrelated entrance of the bowlers. Bowling was a sport on which noblemen gambled away large sums in early seventeenth-century England.[63] Bishop John Earle lamented that a bowling alley "is the place where there are three things throwne away besides Bowls, to wit, time, and money and curses."[64] The gentry also indulged in this sort of amusement when they came to London. A few months after the performance of *The Triumph of Peace*, Charles was responding to another consequence of their visits when he ordered that the bowling green in Spring Garden, a royal park attached to White-hall, be closed to the public because it had become "common" and disorderly.[65] Since the bowlers in Shirley's antimasque follow dances whose theme is social climbing through imitation, "*their game and postures*" can also be read as criticism of the gentry who live above their station by participating in the leisure activities of the nobility and consuming their wealth in gambling. The bowlers are thus another illustration of those "vain Delights and Expences" which Charles cited in his proclamation against the gentry's residence in London.

The extreme discontinuity of these dances seems to resist a coherent reading, especially since the text does not provide a very detailed description of the dancers' performances. Yet as Marcus has demonstrated with Jonson, if "we steep ourselves in the immediate political and social milieu of the masques, . . . incoherent passages will become recognizable as adroit commentary on events."[66] What needs to be emphasized about *The Triumph of Peace* is that the "adroit commentary on events" drawn from a reading of the topical allusions is determined by the royal proclamation; the discontinuous dances can become coherent when the viewer is positioned in the king's ideology. In the context of the entire antimasque, the concluding dances attribute the gentry's London visits to their social pretensions and so reveal the operation of the ideology of degree which informed Charles's political practice. The fact that Charles was guided by this feudal ideology is clear not just in his proclamation to keep the landowning classes in the country, but also in his efforts to strengthen the traditional class hierarchy by stopping the sale of titles and maintaining an overwhelming majority of peers on the Privy Council, among other things.[67] In view of such developments, the quixotic gentlemen and the bowlers who conclude Shirley's antimasque must be regarded as an ideological representation: in their suggestion of pretense and gambling losses, they express a concern that the gentry's pleasure trips to the city may ultimately blur class distinctions and cause undue social mobility.

V

There is, finally, another genre that plays its part in determining the ideology of *The Triumph of Peace*: the masque. We can define the ideological significance of this genre by rewriting Northrop Frye's description of its formal properties from a Marxist perspective. Frye recognizes that the masque "is usually a compliment to the audience, or an important member of it, and leads up to an idealization of the society represented by that audience." As a result of this "main theme," the genre "involves gods, fairies, and personifications of virtues; the figures of the antimasque thus tend to become demonic, and dramatic characterization begins to split into an antithesis of virtue and vice, god and devil, fairy and monster."[68] Recalling Nietzsche's genealogical argument that the binary opposition between good and evil constitutes a basic ideological category of power and domination, we can see the moral distinction between the antimasque and main masque as a means to justify the hegemony of those representatives of the dominant classes who are idealized by the entertainment. The opposition between good and evil achieves this legitimization by representing the dominated classes as the "demonic" forces in the antimasque and making it seem natural that they should be subordinated and superseded by the deity who is presented in the main masque. The transition between the two sections of the masque in spectacular transformation scenes functions as an imaginary solution to real social conflicts, a symbolic (or ritualistic) means to reorder or contain the forces that threaten the dominant class. Yet Jennifer Chibnall notes a change in the ideological functioning of the masque during the prerevolutionary period: "Where Jonson sought to reconcile the elements, to reorder the discorder and vitality of the antimasque, the Caroline masque attempts only to contain it. Spectacle more readily encompasses the flux of creative revel and transcends it. To attempt a resolution is to risk failure."[69] This formal change is evident in the discontinuous textual work of *The Triumph of Peace*, which does not permit a successful ideological resolution.

Shirley's main masque aims to fulfill generic expectations by completing the ideological operation we have been examining in our consideration of topical allusions. When the personifications of peace, law, and justice (Irene, Eunomia, and Diche, respectively) descend from heaven "to wait upon that earth" where Charles and Henrietta Maria will reign, the "profane" antimasquers "go off fearfully" (pp. 277, 273–74), and the social problems for which they shared responsibility are magically solved. The heavenly emissaries refer to the monarchs as the gods "Jove and Themis" who are "the parents of us three" (p. 277), and their descent constitutes a move to the earthly part of Charles's kingdom: "The triumph of Jove's upper part abated, / And all the deities translated" (p. 276). This image of the king and queen expresses the ideology of divine right monarchy not only by deifying them, but also by characterizing their power as absolute: they are the sources of the law that "do[th] beautify increase, / And chain security with peace," and it is their justice that "giv[eth] perfection" to the orderly peacefulness which England is said to enjoy under them (pp. 275–76). Thus, Charles's autocratic rule is legitimized as divine will, and the actual grievances of the gentry and the business community are eclipsed.

The ideological functioning of the main masque, however, is really not so smooth. The allegory seems to point to the limitations of royal power: Jove's descent is shown to reorder the "profane" English citizens in the antimasque, but only because their disorder had "abated" the self-admiring "triumph of Jove's upper part," questioning the nature of this "triumph," perhaps alluding to the Caroline court's politically imprudent isolation from English society. It is important to keep in mind that like the antimasque of projectors, the allegory of the main masque may have elicited different readings from the royal couple and the lawyers who produced the entertainment. At one point, Irene and Eunomia sing, "The world shall give prerogative to neither; / We cannot flourish but together" (p. 275), and this can easily be construed as a message from the legal profession to the king asserting that he must cooperate with them. As Stephen Orgel and Roy Strong put it,

> Legally, British law is made by the king acting through Parliament, by Parliament acting with the assent of the king. But since Charles's dissolution of the Parliament of 1629, Irene, Peace, was the king's: peace had been maintained by the royal prerogative alone, and laws enacted without the consent of Parliament. Peace and Law sing explicitly of their joint prerogatives because the subject of the masque is prerogative rule; and they make the general point of which Bulstrode Whitelocke says the antimasque of projectors was a particular instance: there can be no peace without law.[70]

It is thus possible to see Eunomia, the personification of law, as a symbol of Parliament and read the song as an assertion that the king's peace (Irene) should not have prerogative over the MPs' contribution to the legislative process (Eunomia). Charles would no doubt have been enraged by this presumption, especially if it were boldly trumpeted in a court masque; given his enthusiasm for *The Triumph of Peace,* we are justified in assuming that his attention was focused on another, more flattering detail in the text: Eunomia's status as the divine offspring of Jove. Seen in this light, she symbolizes not Parliament's legislative function, but an aspect of Charles's absolute power, his paternalistic control of political and legal practice in English society. Since the king is the divine "father" of peace, law, and justice, he can freely exercise the royal prerogative without submitting his policies for parliamentary approval.

This is another example of the peculiar indeterminacy of Shirley's text. There are passages whose unstable meaning is determined by the viewer's politics. Whitelocke's commentary shows that he and his colleagues considered the masque to make an important political statement: it would enable them both to profess their allegiance to Charles and to advise him to curb the illegalities of his personal rule. Yet this intention is foiled because of the discontinuous textual work: the allusions and allegory can occasionally support opposed readings. The ideological force of this slippage of meaning becomes clear when we realize that the criticism intended for the royal government is repeatedly deflected onto other social groups, primarily the gentry. Apparently, the merest suggestion that the text criticized the king was enough to give the lawyers the optimistic idea that their position would be heard, even though the dissolution of Parliament had left them without a political institution to represent their interests as well as those of the gentry and the business community. The possibility of opposed readings, however, means that the masque could also function as an ideological apparatus of Charles's absolutist experiment by presenting the conflicts in Caroline society and resolving them in a way that reinforces the king's domination. As Orgel and Strong conclude, Shirley's masque "reveals how exceedingly clumsy as a mode of political statement the form was; for the meaning of *The Triumph of Peace* largely eluded its royal spectator. . . . Everyone, ironically, was vindicated" (pp. 64, 66).

It would seem that the political statement was derailed by generic constraints, raising the issue of whether a progressive social criticism is doomed to ineffectual contradiction if it is articulated in a reactionary genre. But the indeterminacy of Shirley's text is too radical to leave the dominant cultural discourse coherent and uninterrogated: *The Triumph of Peace* rather shows that the genre was undergoing some significant formal changes in the Caroline period as government policies were increasingly under attack. The Caroline masque alters the two-part structure of the masque text by proliferating antimasques, as Shirley's does, each assigned the task of managing social conflicts, often with the specificity of topical allusions. The Caroline masque differs from its Elizabethan and Jacobean predecessors because it is less the self-congratulatory ritual by which an exclusive court group entertained itself; as Joanne Altieri has pointed out, the genre "loses its ritual character during the Caroline years when nonparticipatory theater, vicarious entertainment, encroaches on the masque through comedy and antimasque proliferation as well as mechanical elaboration, emptying the form of its earlier participatory function."[71] The antimasque proliferation and increasing reliance on Inigo Jones's stage spectacle coincide with a curtailment of the "revels"—the dance during the main masque when the court audience merged with its theatrical idealization—but the problem-solving structure of the genre also breaks down because the utopian visions of the main masque are challenged by a succession of social problems. Thus, Altieri's genre history can suggest how the Caroline masques "record a full awareness of the irrelevance of the court's vocabulary to the world outside Whitehall"; and we can see that "their effort to neutralize that other by defeating it in representation is . . . thoughtless and blind" if we analyze what exceeds the masque writers' conscious control—i.e., the discontinuous textual work, or, more specifically, the fragmentation of the genre through antimasque proliferation and the indeterminacy of political statement. The masque may be "an exceedingly clumsy . . . mode of political statement" because it is a court entertainment whose function is to celebrate royal power and assert aristocratic community. Yet Caroline masques like Shirley's demonstrate through symptomatic formal changes that even the culture of the most insular court cannot totally mask the contradictory conditions of its hegemony.

The indeterminacy of Shirley's text is most powerful in its recurrent self-reflexivity. During the main masque, some laborers who worked on the stage and costumes for the production suddenly enter accompanied by the wives of some of their colleagues and pursued by two palace guards. This noisy outburst interrupts the idealization of Charles and Henrietta Maria and seems to be a clear contradiction of the song in which their royal "powers" have just been extolled: "The Island doth rejoice, / And all her waves are echo to our voice, / Which, in no ages past, hath known / Such treasures of her own" (p. 279). The working-class characters show no desire to "rejoice" in Charles's reign because they enjoy no "treasures" under it: they are in fact disturbed that they are not permitted to see the masque. Their comments are full of discontent with the traditional social order that reserves such court entertainments for the aristocracy and wealthy citizens and excludes the lower classes, even those laborers who had a hand in the preparations. Thus, a painter is willing to risk his job, telling the others, "come, be resolute; we know the worst, and let us challenge a privilege; those stairs were of my painting" (p. 281). And an embroiderer's wife chafes at aristocratic privilege: "what though we be no ladies, we are christians in these clothes, and the king's subjects, god bless us" (p. 281). The very appearance of these characters suddenly shifts discursive levels from political allegory to realistic comedy, whereby the royal ideology is interrogated: the laborers represent the unequal class relations mystified by the main masque and expose the royal "powers" as so much costume and stage machinery. As soon as the text becomes self-conscious, expressing a self-reflexive knowledge of its status as fiction, it undermines the idealization of the main masque.

But the scene ends with another self-reflexive gesture in which it constitutes itself as yet one more *antimasque,* and the social conflicts represented by the laborers are contained by the problem-solving structure of the genre. A tailor in the group has a sudden change of heart when he realizes that the court audience is laughing at them:

> *Tailor.* Nay, now I am in, I will see a dance, though my shop
>   windows be shut up for't. Tell us?—hum? d'ye hear?
>   do not they laugh at us? what were we best to do? The
>   Masquers will do no feats as long as we are here: be
>   ruled by me, hark every one; 'tis our best course to
>   dance a figary ourselves, and then they'll think it a
>   piece of the plot, and we may go off again with the
>   credit; we may else kiss the porter's lodge for't;
>   let's put a trick upon'em in revenge, 'twill seem a
>   new device too.
> *Omnes.* Content.
> *Tailor.* And the musicians knew but our mind now!
>   [*The violins play.*]
>   Hark, they are at it; now for a lively frisk.
>   [*They dance.*]
>   Now, let us go off cleanly, and somebody will think this
>   was meant for an antimasque.
>   (P. 281)

This dazzling example of Caroline antimasque proliferation, with its multiple registers of self-reflexivity, generates conflicting meanings with different ideological implications. On the one hand, the tailor's "revenge" is an attempt to "trick" his social superiors which winds up playing into their hands: the dance reduces the subversive working-class characters to antimasquers whose diabolic actions deserve to be put down by the royal deities; when the court audience hears the generic clue "antimasque," they can comfortably allegorize the characters as the irrational "many-headed monster," the conventional feudal representation of laborers and other marginal groups which justifies their subordinate position in the class hierarchy.[72] As a result, a realistic scene which had contradicted the idealization of Charles's reign by presenting a social formation in disarray is resolved in the main masque, when the laborers "being gone, the Masquers are encouraged by a song, to their revels with the ladies" (p. 281). On the other hand, however, the sudden appearance of realistic characters explicitly taking up roles in an antimasque takes an ideological "revenge" on the dominant cultural discourse by indicating its fictional status, treating it as an interested representation to be manipulated in order to avoid being punished by a social superior or to enjoy aristocratic pleasures, like seeing a masque or wearing fashionable clothing ("somebody promised me a fall too, if I came to court," says a feathermaker's wife [p. 281]). The self-reflexive gestures shift between two kinds of dramatic discourse, comic realism and political allegory, destabilizing the ideological determinations of the masque, permitting opposed readings by the king and the lawyers.[73]

In Charles's eyes, for instance, when the sixteen Inns of Court masquers danced the revels with ladies from the audience, removing the distinction between court and lawyers, conflicts between the royal government and law courts could be symbolically resolved: the Inns were positioned in the dominant cultural discourse as his allegorical grandchildren, "the sons of Peace, Law and Justice":

> The children of your reign, not blood;
> Of age, when they are understood,
> Not seen by faction or owl's sight,
> Whose trouble is the clearest light,
> But treasures to their eye, and ear,
> That love good for itself, not fear.
> (Pp. 279–80)

And the king could only be glad to see an apologetic masque which stated that the Inns' "good" intentions toward him had been misrepresented by "faction" (Prynne's attack on theater?) and were not truly

"understood" at court. Members of the planning committee like Whitelocke, however, would be more responsive to the subversive interruption of the revels with the antimasque of the laborers, a shrewd way to
redefine the status of the revels as an interested fiction and thus qualify
the lawyers' subjection to the royal ideology. What may have seemed
like, in Frye's suggestive description, "a final gesture of surrender" to
the king's autocracy "when the actors unmask and join the audience in
a dance"[74] is interrupted by self-reflexive textuality that interrogates the
ideological operation of the genre. Similarly, the lawyers on the planning committee may have intended an ironic effect in this antimasque
by having a property man's wife use a legal principle—"in *forma pap-
eris*" (p. 280)—to argue for her admission to the court masque, establishing a witty analogue to their own use of the Statute of Monopolies
to restrict the patents issued under the royal prerogative. But the text
also limits the irony through the laborer's Bottom-like language: it gives
a misspelling of the phrase—*in forma pauperis*—to indicate not just a
mispronunciation, but the character's misunderstanding of the legal
principle which gave the poor access to the law courts without paying
costs; so that what the lawyers may have seen as a job-related joke with
a political edge can also turn into a dismissal of working-class ignorance under the "many-headed monster" motif of the feudal ideology.

It is remarkable that *The Triumph of Peace* begins with an instance
of self-reflexivity that dislocates the meaning of the entire text. After
the characters all appear on stage and introduce themselves to each
other, Opinion informs Fancy that there are no antimasques to the
court masque they have come to see. Fancy's response is to recommend
that they themselves perform the first dance: "the first antimasque," he
announces, "We will present in our own persons," and the stage direction describes the dance as "*expressing the natures of the presenters*" (pp.
266–67). This gesture of textual self-consciousness has two conflicting
consequences: it relegates everything Opinion and Fancy will subsequently say or do—including their social criticism—to the demonic
antimasque realm of falsehood and evil and sets up the problem-
solving structure of the masque; but simultaneously it insists on their
fictional status as characters in the ideological cultural discourse of a
court entertainment, implicitly questioning the textual operations by
which topical allusion and allegory transform any criticism of the royal
government into figments of the imagination. Hence, the attack on the
gentry can be seen, at least for a moment, as the interested representation of the dominant cultural discourse.

VI

The allusions to the gentry in *The Triumph of Peace* inevitably raise the question of how they responded to it or, more specifically, whether it produced any concrete social effects. We know that the masque was a bestseller: even before it was performed, several thousand copies had been printed, and it went through several editions.[75] This popularity with the book-buying public, however, may have been due not so much to any intrinsic qualities of the published text as to the spectacular procession that traveled through the streets of London before the performance. The complex nature of the masque, furthermore, makes it seem unlikely that the gentry as a whole would have sufficiently grasped the satire on them to be irritated by it; no doubt the subtle allusions and intricate allegory were appreciated most fully, even if very differently, by the king and the learned lawyers who created the entertainment, and perhaps by those members of the nobility, gentry, and manufacturing and mercantile groups who were close enough to the planning committee to know and share its political intentions. The narrowness of the audience who understood the allegories and allusions is suggested by the response of Sir Humphrey Mildmay, an Essex landowner who seems to have violated the proclamation by his frequent visits to London and who witnessed the first performance at Whitehall, but felt it was little more than "stately."[76]

A more plausible hypothesis regarding the social reverberations of Shirley's masque is that like other royal entertainments during Charles's reign, it widened the gap between the insular culture of the court and the provincial opposition to the central government. The elaborate costumes and stage machinery probably nourished the growing suspicions of the court's frivolity and Popish decadence.[77] For Charles, the masque reproduced a social representation that had already been legislated through proclamations and was winning in the courts, so that his sheer pleasure in viewing this theatrical reproduction could easily have encouraged the mistaken idea that his autocracy was more successful than it actually was.[78] Perhaps the most dangerous illusion fostered by the masque had to do with the loyalty of the legal profession. By attacking a group like the gentry who were already grumbling about the royal government, the Inns of Court may have allayed his doubts about their political sympathies. If so, they also prevented him from seeing that lawyers like Bulstrode Whitelocke would figure prominently among the MPs who reversed his policies in the Long Parliament.

Chapter Five

Cavalier Love Poetry and Caroline Court Culture

Rules are empty in themselves, violent and unfinalized; they are impersonal and can be bent to any purpose. The successes of history belong to those who are capable of seizing these rules, to replace those who had used them, to disguise themselves so as to pervert them, invert their meaning, and redirect them against those who had initially imposed them; controlling this complex mechanism, they will make it function so as to overcome the rulers through their own rules.

Michel Foucault, "Nietzsche, Genealogy, History"

CAVALIER LOVE POETRY has suffered the fate of many other Caroline texts: marginalization by individualistic critical discourses. If we judge from the dearth of commentary on poets like Thomas Carew, Sir John Suckling, and Richard Lovelace, their writing seems increasingly less read and researched in contemporary academic institutions, in effect devalued in the canon of English Renaissance literature from the minor status they held since the Restoration, banished now to the apocryphal fringes of the anthology selection and the mixed comparison with major seventeenth-century authors. Modern critical discourse from Eliot to *Scrutiny* and the New Criticism made Cavalier poetry a derivative of the formal innovations in the Renaissance lyric— particularly the "metaphysical" conceit and neoclassicism—situating isolated texts in the "Line of Wit" or the "School of Donne" or the "Tribe of Ben," characterizing the poets as inferior individual talents rescued from oblivion because they were in touch with the Tradition of the organic community and the unified sensibility.[1] Today, many years after the post–World War II wave of humanist historical scholarship redirected the formalist enthusiasms of modern criticism, Cavalier poetry continues to be marginalized by individualistic assumptions which are couched in two different but complementary responses, one more appreciative than the other, both occasionally appearing in the same critic. In the positive response, the texts express the "triumph" of the transcendental subject, an "emancipation of the human will from the vulgar demands of environment," through the "conscious poise" and "harmonious subtlety" of their appropriation of earlier poetry, including the work of their "major" predecessors, Donne and Jonson.[2] In the negative response, the texts express the defeat of human subjectivity by history, with the poet's imagination so chained to his social circumstances that he becomes a decadent "mannerist" who "depends on the supreme accomplishment of his predecessors, unable to say more than they," lacking any "sense of a specifically literary mission and identity."[3]

These two responses are permutations of the same underlying ideological system. Together they produce a strikingly individualistic reading that has strong resemblances to romantic and modern criticism, but that even when based on historical research, whether literary or social, fails to treat the social determinants of the texts except as obstacles to be transcended: today, Cavalier poetry is the story of how the individual talent is regrettably limited by its social situation. We will question this dominant reading by examining its formulation in several recent studies, mostly from the seventies and eighties. Then, we will challenge it with a materialist reading which seeks to think less fearfully about the social conditions of human action: by situating Cavalier poetry in the contradictions of Caroline court culture, it can suggest that the individual talent is an overdetermined social identity, never fully fixed, dispersed across different ideological positions, capable of interrogating them and changing.

I

The key assumptions which underlie the dominant reading also govern much contemporary commentary on poetry: they are, as Antony Easthope has indicated, that "poetry expresses experience; experience gives access to personality, and so poetry leads us to personality."[4] In descriptions of Cavalier poetry, these assumptions become visible in a routine reliance on psychological terms which elide the distinction between author and text. Thus, Joseph Summers' *Heirs of Donne and Jonson* describes the Cavalier "ideal" as "that of a gentleman in moral as well as stylistic *déshabille,* but more nearly in control."[5] Because poetry is assumed to be an act of self-expression, it suffers a psychological reduction in which value is assigned to those texts that appear most "vivid" or "evocative," that produce the strongest effect of authorial presence. This valorization of personality leads directly to the marginalization of Cavalier poetry, for as Herbert Grierson long ago noted, "it is very rarely that one can detect a deep personal note in the delightful love-songs with which the whole period abounds from Carew to Dryden. The collected work of none of them would give such an impression of a real history behind it, a history of many experiences and moods, as Donne's Songs and Sonnets and the Elegies, and, as one must still believe, the sonnets of Shakespeare record."[6] Grierson goes on to qualify this general disparagement of Caroline poetry, but without departing from the privileged assumption of authorial presence: he singles out Carew's texts for praise only because "this careless liver was a careful artist with a deeper vein of thought and feeling in his temperament than a first reading suggests" (p. xxxvi).

This psychological reduction has marginalized Cavalier poetry by processing the text as a transparent representation, evaporating the material determinations—linguistic and cultural, on the one hand; ideological, political, and economic, on the other—that must always be figured into its relationship to the real. The results of this reduction include the now common understanding of the term "Cavalier" as "a thoughtless and faintly debauched way of life," but also the humanist operation of inferring from the text moral themes which are said to "reflect a distinctive understanding of our nature,"[7] and which also inevitably ghettoize Cavalier poetry for its immorality. Thus, Summers is troubled by its "gentlemanly unpleasantness" (p. 49), and Earl Miner asserts somewhat defensively that "despite some circumstantial evidence, Cavalier love poetry is not truly guilty of 'wanton love,'" noting all the same that "the problem we have to face comes down to this: what ages did the Cavalier poets fancy their male wooers and their ladies to be?"[8]

It is not that most versions of the dominant reading ignore the determinate nature of representation in the texts so much as that the valorization of authorial personality and presence returns in insidious biographical narratives which limit and finally forestall any rigorous development of transindividual determinations. Miner's chapter "Love" in *The Cavalier Mode from Jonson to Cotton* is full of research into literary and intellectual history, specifying "certain conventional topics and motifs" which this poetry is shown to assimilate. Yet his reading is so controlled by his assumption of transparency that these intertextual connections are finally cut away in his contradictory conclusion: "Cavalier love poetry provides true versions of true experience in true art," writes Miner, without considering whether this use of "true" is logically consistent with his other assertion that the poetry "combines real experience and numerous conventions for transforming the real into art" (p. 249). If the "conventions" are "transforming the real," in what sense can the text which assimilates them be "true"? Is the text "true" to the real ("truth" as knowledge adequate to its object), or to its own transformation of reality (a "truth" autonomous from its object, an effect of mere textual self-consistency)? Far from mirroring the Cavalier poets' real experience, their poetry can only be taken as an image of that reality refracted by other, earlier uses of the conventions, different cultural moves in different social formations. Richard Helgerson similarly observes that "imitation is, in fact, a leading characteristic of Cavalier verse in all genres," recognizing that "again and again, a title, a turn of phrase, a choice of word or image, a pattern of thought will recall Donne, Jonson, or some other Elizabethan or Jacobean poet." Yet without admitting that this intertextuality may compromise the notion of transparent representation and require the formulation of a different criterion of poetic discourse, Helgerson's argument degrades Cavalier poetry because its effect of authorial presence is too weak: in a statement that seems akin to Grierson's view, many texts are said to "echo the abrupt and conceited manner of Donne but lack the fiercely egocentric obsession of his matter."[9] Cavalier poetry has been marginalized because it is too conventional, because it lacks strong personalities.

With Helgerson, however, the psychological reduction takes a more sophisticated new historicist turn, wherein cultural and social determinations are summoned to explain the intertextual work of imitation only to give way to an ahistorical individualism. Developing Louis Martz's remarks on Carew, Helgerson describes the "stylish refinement" of Cavalier texts as a "mannerist" imitation "at once more obviously skilled than their predecessors and less committed," linking it to a "decline in literary autonomy" in which the poets suffer an imaginative debilitation: "not even in their verse did they stand apart from society. Rather they were an integral part of it" (pp. 194–95, 201). The paradox here, that the court aesthetic of Cavalier poetry is less "committed" in its use of conventions because the poets were socially committed to the Caroline court where those conventions were in fashion, points to Helgerson's assumption of a romantic, individualistic concept of the author as a free, unified consciousness that transcends the contradictory de-

terminations of history. In effect, Helgerson faults Cavalier poetry because the poets were not transcendental subjects, but socially determinate ones with a "collective literary identity," because "they suggested
. . . rather a grace of manner shared with the stylish court than any
differentiating characteristic peculiar to them as poets" (pp. 201, 200).
The canonical "laureate" poets whom Helgerson values most—Spenser,
Jonson, Milton—made individualistic gestures of self-presentation to
give authority and social prestige to their writing, adopting "a role that
set them off from the world," developing an "intense self-consciousness"
(p. 186), deliberately choosing to write in certain genres while refusing
others; the Cavaliers were court amateurs who "gratefully accepted the
literary tradition bequeathed them and were relatively successful and
secure members of the ruling establishment" (p. 200). Helgerson argues that their current apocryphal status, "their failure to impose themselves and their work, as Spenser and Jonson succeeded in doing, on
the imagination of posterity," derives from their integration into a social
group and hence their loss of "a specifically literary mission and identity" (p. 188). In Helgerson's canon of English Renaissance literature,
the major writer is a rugged individualist, struggling against the cultural "establishment," whereas the minor or subminor writer is a "com-
placent" member of it. This is a rationalization of the Renaissance
canon that avoids the modern notion of the literary tradition as the
remains of the organic community and bases itself on romantic genius
theory.

The argument of *Self-Crowned Laureates* articulates a fundamentally
materialist project: it seeks to reconstruct the social and cultural constraints on textual production by elaborating a semiotic system of literary self-presentation. Helgerson criticizes "the argument from individual temperament" because this argument "attributes to the author
the character of his works so that their character can then be derived
from his—a tightly circular argument, irrefutable but tautological" (p.
104). Yet Helgerson also believes that "by looking outside Jonson to the
literary world of which he was a part, we can significantly enlarge the
circle of explanation, though perhaps not eliminate its circularity":
such an explanation would be circular only if it plans to return to the
author by reducing cultural determinations to authorial intentionality,
or "individual temperament." *Self-Crowned Laureates* claims "not to
posit a transcendental self" (p. 19). Yet it is an idealist concept of human subjectivity, the transcendental consciousness of romantic individualism, that emerges to canonize the three "laureate" authors and mar-

ginalize the texts of the Cavalier poets. What this means, however, is that Cavalier poetry demands to be understood through its material determinations—not just through authorial acts of self-presentation, but through the social and cultural conditions of its production, through its discontinuous textuality—and therefore it resists any processing by an individualistic critical discourse which valorizes literary and social autonomy, which attempts to link culture and society by reserving a free undeterminate space for the individual cultural producer, which looks only for authorial presence in the transparency of the text.

Helgerson's notion of the "author" as an "irreducible and active self," "the single intending self," is the core of individualism that derails his materialist project: "the utterances of authorial self-presentation," he observes,

> have authors, though authors who are themselves authorized by the systems that make those acts possible. Neither the author nor the system can be discarded. Each deconstructs the other, but each also constructs the other. If we are to understand literary utterances . . . we must know, whether implicitly or explicitly, the literary system. But we must also know Spenser, Jonson, and Milton. They, after all, make our knowledge of the system worth having. (P. 20)

This "system," however, never "deconstructs" Spenser, Jonson, and Milton; rather, it is repeatedly shown to give way before the individuals who triumph over it with a new "laureate" self-presentation. In Helgerson's view, to remain within the literary system is to accept its role prescriptions and be relegated to court amateur or professional writer, dependent on aristocratic patronage, or the publishing industry, or the public playhouse. The laureate, in contrast, invents new rules of signification on the basis of the system, which he uses in a purely instrumental way, standing outside or above it:

> "I am a laureate" is the statement each of our poets wanted to make. The problem that faced them was whether that statement could be convincingly made in the language of their own particular generation. An appreciation of that problem can only make their accomplishment more humanly important, more relevant to the struggle of men and women in any age to achieve a position of individual authority and preeminence. (P. 15)

Helgerson's individualistic discourse detaches the "laureate" from its historical moment with an essentialist concept of human nature ("humanly important . . . relevant in any age") and then turns it into a utopian vision of upward social mobility. The "struggle" Helgerson imagines is professional competition between atomized individuals, not social conflict between members of different classes and groups; on the contrary, this "struggle" is designed to leave behind the social conditions of the "authority and preeminence" achieved by the "individual."

Insofar as Helgerson's essentialism generalizes the "laureate" by removing it from the specific social practice of cultural production, his rationalization of the literary canon invites comparison to the entrepreneurial image of late capitalism often used to rationalize the conservative social policies of Ronald Reagan's administrations during the 1980s: this is a nineteenth-century image of rugged individualism rooted in classical economics, so inappropriate to the current phase of capitalism where, as the economist Robert Lekachman has pointed out, "advanced economies are dominated by large institutions that prefer merger and collusion to competition. The people who decide their investment policies are members of committees disinclined to . . . 'take the initiative amid radical perils and uncertainties.'"[10] The multinational corporation represses aggressive innovation by standardizing the work process, by demanding conformity to policy aimed to ensure profit margins, and by setting up a bureaucratic administration, all of which simultaneously enable and constrict the possibilities for professional and economic advancement. The cultural consequences of these developments include a compensatory redefinition of "success" as a satisfaction of psychological rather than material needs, which assumes economic stability but gives priority to emotional fulfillment over profit accumulation by emphasizing the construction of a self that is less aggressive, more inhibited. The new definition of success can be seen most clearly in bestselling "how-to" handbooks for "self-help" that range from Dale Carnegie's *How to Win Friends and Influence People* (1936) ("Nine ways to change people without giving offense or arousing resentment") to *Women Men Love, Women Men Leave* (1987) by two clinical psychologists ("Aggressive seduction techniques can backfire").[11] These privatized versions of success, another symptom of the contemporary crisis of subjectivity, show that Helgerson's individualistic rationalization of the literary canon must be taken as an extremely conservative response. When Helgerson asserts the laureate as an eternal human verity, the predicament of the postmodern subject, required by the corporate system to follow its rules in order to realize material benefits without personal satisfaction, is solved by the autonomous individual struggling against the system and attaining self-fulfillment by developing his own rules.

This bourgeois individualism is a weak weapon against the social conditions of the postmodern subject because it masks them. Helgerson's individualistic critical discourse remains unable to think the unacknowledged conditions of human agency: it stops at the agent's monitoring of his behavior, those reflexive acts of consciousness in which intention is measured against social rules, and cultural production against contemporary transformations of cultural resources.[12] Hence, Helgerson's use of terms like "literary system," or "the language of his generation," and the reliance on texts that can stand as a record of intention—prefaces, proems, letters—or portions of texts where the author can be assumed to speak in his own voice. This focus on the agent's self-monitoring represses the unacknowledged conditions of his actions, the inconsistencies among the varied resources organized in cultural production, for example, or the tensions between the social roles prescribed for the cultural producer, or the unconscious motives, sedimented with ideologies, that operate beyond his self-understanding. The "system" can be said to "construct" and "deconstruct" the author only when it is understood as including the unacknowledged conditions of cultural practices, like the power relations of a specific social formation, which can give the text such unintended consequences as social reproduction or change. A materialist reading of Cavalier poetry seeks to combat the postmodern crisis of the subject by developing a historical narrative in which these conditions and consequences can be seen as decentering and fragmenting cultural production, enabling the text to reproduce the hegemony of the Caroline court while raising alternative social possibilities that ultimately threatened that hegemony.

We shall foreground the material determinations which get waylaid in the dominant reading, beginning with the intertextuality of Cavalier poetry, particularly its place in the discursive formation of the Caroline court. These love lyrics, along with such other court forms as masques and plays, biographies and letters, participate in a Platonic love cult that draws on conventional ideas and motifs from Renaissance Neoplatonism for speculation about love and politics as well as salon conversation. In the masques, the Neoplatonic conventions construct an absolutist ideology that combines political allegory informed by the divine right theory of kingship with a personal mythology for Charles and Henrietta Maria. In the love lyrics, however, the conventions undergo a rather different transformation, which implicitly questions the ideological representations produced in the masques and amounts to a subversion of the Caroline ideology.

II

The masques politicize Neoplatonism by using it to represent royal power. In Jonson's first entertainment for the Caroline court, *Love's Triumph through Callipolis* (1631), an antimasque of "certain sectaries, or depraved lovers," who have caused "perturbations" in "the suburbs or skirts" of the "city of beauty or goodness" is reformed in the main masque by the "triumph" of "love in perfection," personified as fifteen masquers led by Charles in the role of "heroic love" (ll. 19–20, 69–72, 100ff.).[13] This Platonic reformation of the "sensual school / Of lust" is also political action that maintains the king's hegemony: "Love presents a world of chaste desires, / Which may produce a harmony of parts," a "harmony" that is both public and private, that characterizes both the social order of Caroline England and the moral balance of the Platonic lover who has rejected lust in favor of the contemplative enjoyment of beauty (ll. 86–87, 47–48). Charles's "power and virtue to remove / Such monsters from the labyrinth of love" enable him to reign over the international political scene (the "depraved lovers" appear "in the scenical persons and habits of the four prime European nations" [ll. 28–29]), but they also operate on a micropolitical level by constituting social agents as royal subjects who are virtuous and loving. To become a Platonic lover is to submit individual desire to royal authority.

Henrietta Maria is given an important role in this ideological discourse through extravagant Platonic compliments on her beauty. The ideas and motifs in her descriptions assume arguments made in Marsilio Ficino's *Commentary on Plato's Symposium,* particularly his Platonization of beauty as "goodness": "goodness," asserts Ficino, is "the outstanding characteristic of God," and "beauty is a kind of force or light shining from Him through everything."[14] The light of the beautiful soul is what attracts the Platonic lover to make his contemplative ascent to God—"splendor in a harmony of knowledge and morals," "that glow of divinity shining in beautiful bodies"—and so he remains "content with mental perceptions alone" (pp. 141, 146–47). In the masques, the divine effulgence of the queen's beauty, following Ficino, "compels lovers to awe, trembling, and reverence" (p. 146), yet this is no longer merely "the passion of a lover," but an ideological operation that subjects social agents to her in a series of analogous hierarchies, metaphysical, political, and moral. As Indamora in Sir William Davenant's *The Temple of Love* (1635), the queen emits a divine light which governs her subjects by turning them into Platonic lovers, correcting their conduct, putting them under moral surveillance:

> As cheerful as the morning's light,
>   Comes Indamora from above,
> To guide those lovers that want sight,
>   To see and know what they should love.
>
> Her beams into each breast will steal,
>   And search what ev'ry heart doth mean,
> The sadly wounded she will heal,
>   And make the foully tainted clean.[15]

Indamora's sunlike "beams" fuse the light of divine beauty with the absolutist ideology of *le roi soleil,* eroticizing James I's description of monarchs as "bright lampes of godlinesse and vertue" who, "going in and out before their people, giue light to all their steps."[16] The masque revises Platonic love with the theory of divine right kingship: because this theory deifies Henrietta Maria, she displaces God as "the ultimate object of the Platonic ascent," as Orgel and Strong note.[17] The queen is represented as omniscient and omnipotent in her moral control over her subjects, and Platonic love is redefined as a process of subjection to her divine authority. In Davenant's *Salmacida Spolia* (1640), "lovers are chaste, because they know / It is her will they should be so" (2:324).

The personal mythology which the masques develop for Charles and Henrietta Maria entails other ideologically inflected revisions of Neoplatonism. The concept of Platonic love is stretched to include conjugal sexuality. Ficino praises "mutual love," but this is a mystical "exchange" of "identities"; he repeatedly insists that "the lust to touch the body is not a part of love . . . we comprehend that light (and beauty) of the soul with the mind alone" (pp. 146–47).[18] Jonson's *Love's Triumph* sets out from these ideas:

> Love is the right affection of the mind,
>   The noble appetite of what is best,

> Desire of union with the thing designed,
> But in fruition of it cannot rest.
>   (Ll. 49–53)

And yet the love praised in this masque is ultimately sexual "fruition," although made licit by marriage. This inconsistency emerges at the end, when Venus appears at the urging of "all the powers that govern marriage" to take a "vow . . . / On earth for perfect love and beauty's sake" and bless the royal couple (ll. 160, 177–78). For Ficino, there are two Venuses, Venus Coelestis and Venus Vulgaris, who personify two cosmic "powers," "intelligence" and "generation," and two corresponding kinds of love, "the first, by innate love is stimulated to know the beauty of God; the second, by its love, to procreate the same beauty in bodies" (p. 142).[19] Jonson's masque, however, conflates these contradictory meanings of Venus to develop what we may call the Venus Nuptialis of reciprocal affection and conjugal sexuality. The "world of chaste desires" presented by "love in perfection" is not sexual abstinence, but marital fidelity. Hence, Henrietta Maria is praised as the "pure object of heroic love alone" (l. 117), and the "perfect lovers" are required by Amphitrite, the wife of Oceanus, to "pay / First fruits; and on these altars lay / (The ladies' breasts) your ample vows . . . Love must have answering love to look upon" (ll. 109–11, 114).

This domestication of Platonic love provides the allegory for Aurelian Townshend's *Albions Triumph* (1632).[20] First, the king's "triumph" over assorted nations and social threats is Platonized and personalized as his moral self-control: "he dayly Conquers a world of Vices . . . All his passions, are his true Subjects" (pp. 80–81). Then he is "hit" by two "bow-bearing Gods," Cupid and "Chast Diana," who signify love "growne wise" and prepare the "yet unconquer'd Conqueror" to be "subdu'd" by the queen's "eyes," made "Loves Sacrifice" (pp. 81, 83–85). The masque narrates Charles's Platonic enamorment of his wife in an ideological style that is at once imperial and personal, transcendental and conjugal. The "valediction" represents them as co-partners of Hymen's deity—"whose mindes within / And Bodyes make but Hymens Twin"—god and goddess of marriage, the new objects of the Platonic ascent (p. 89). In Davenant's *Salmacida Spolia*, their harmonious relationship is a moral exemplar with concrete social effects:

> So musical as to all ears
> Doth seem the music of the spheres,

Are you unto each other still;
Tuning your thoughts to eithers' will.

All that are harsh, all that are rude,
Are by your harmony subdu'd;
Yet so into obedience wrought,
As if not forc'd to it, but taught.
(2:326)

This represents royal power as persuasion, not coercion, as moral instruction that is also ideological subjection. In Davenant's *The Temple
of Love,* similarly, Charles and "the darling of his breast . . . rule b'example as by power" (1:304). Platonizing the royal marriage as the "pattern" of "Chaste Love" makes possible more absolutist micropolitics,
paternalistic interventions into subjects' love lives: Indamora and the
"beauties of her train" indoctrinate the court in Neoplatonism in order
to liberate the Temple of Chaste Love from corrupt magicians "intending to use it to intemperate ends":

They raise strange doctrines, and new sects of Love:
Which must not woo or court the person, but
The mind; and practice generation not
Of bodies but of souls.
(1:292–93)

This Platonic indoctrination implements James's equally Platonic image
of the king's "Court and companie" as "a patterne of godliness and all
honest vertues, to all the rest of the people."[21] Court ladies extend the
dominion of Indamora's "sect of Love" by developing Platonic relationships in which they assume the dominant position in the erotic hierarchy, their divine "beauties" redirecting the "false desire" of "stranger
knights" to the "virtues of the mind," here transformed into a "lawful"
and "loving" marriage:

Let then your soft, and nimble feet
Lead and in various figures meet
    Those stranger knights, who though they came
Seduc'd at first by false desire,
You'll kindle in their breasts a fire
    Shall keep love warm, yet not inflame.

At first they wear your beauties' prize,
Now offer willing sacrifice

> Unto the virtues of the mind,
> And each shall wear, when they depart,
> A lawful though a loving heart,
> And wish you still both strict and kind.
> (1:301–2)

The valediction of Davenant's *Britannia Triumphans* (1638) is the most domesticated version of Platonic love in the masques, portraying the royal couple as divine beauty and love who have a remarkable ideological control over their subjects' sexuality:

> To bed, to bed! may every lady dream
> From that chief beauty she hath stolen a beam,
> Which will amaze her lover's curious eyes!
> Each lawful lover, to advance his youth,
> Dream he hath stolen his vigour, love, and truth;
> Then all will haste to bed but none to rise!
> (2:290)

In this revision of Platonic love to include conjugal sexuality, the Caroline ideology can colonize the unconscious depths of subjectivity by determining wishful erotic dreams based on identification with the Platonic roles created for Charles and Henrietta Maria.

The Neoplatonism in the masques performs several ideological functions at the Caroline court. The personal mythology it develops for the king and the queen is an element in an absolutist ideology which mystifies the years of prerogative or "personal" rule when, without any consultation with Parliament, the royal government instituted a series of controversial measures, particularly fiscal expedients and religious innovations. The use of Platonic love to represent the monarch-subject hierarchy permits a personalization of the political relationship in which the king becomes the "monarch of men's hearts": subjection is figured as love. Thus, the image of a personal relationship between king and subject can solve the increasing social withdrawal of the court during the 1630s, reconciling the cultural and ideological differences that alienated segments of the city and country.

These differences are repeatedly represented in Caroline antimasques as a source of dissent to be reordered by the main masque. In Davenant's *The Temple of Love,* one of the antimasques of spirits conjured up by the corrupt magicians is a satirical royalist ideologeme of a Puritan, described as "a modern devil, a sworn enemy of poesy, music, and all ingenious arts, but a great friend to murmuring, libelling, and all seeds of discord, attended by his factious followers" (1:296). The antimasques of Townshend's *Albions Triumph* include a Platonic dialogue which acknowledges that the ideological representation of Charles's reign in the main masque is too esoteric for his subjects to understand and appreciate, although with this acknowledgment the problem-solving structure of the genre itself comes into question. The interlocutors are two citizens, the patrician Platonicus and the plebeian Publius, who differ in their interpretation of the king's "triumph" because Publius is not familiar with the dominant mode of representation in court culture: allegory. Publius relies on sensory observation, representing the "triumph" as concrete social effects: "Before Caesar march't Captive Kings, with their hands bound. And Ladies, with their Armes acrosse, furious Wild Beasts, great Giants, and little Dwarfes with Lictors, and Pictors, and a number of Priests that were as you would have them, in their shirts" (pp. 80–81). Platonicus, in contrast, is adept at allegorical thinking: he opposes Publius' empiricism with the assertion that "under every Fable, nay (almost) under every thing, lyes a Morall" and formulates Charles's "triumph" into a moral theme: "no Vyce is so small, to scape him, nor so great, but he overcomes it" (pp. 81, 82). The cultural difference between Publius and Platonicus is also ideological, a difference in ways of representing royal power: the former sees only coercion, the latter only moral self-control. The dialogue fails to resolve these cultural and ideological differences because Publius never learns his Platonic lesson and in fact resists it: he still prefers sense to reason, physical entertainments like "Gladiators, Saltators, and sights to please the People" to the more intellectual masque, admitting that he "should sleep" if he were to stay to "see Caesar present himselfe to this fayre Goddesse, seeking sweete rest, after all his labors" (p. 81). In these moments of textual self-consciousness, the Platonic thinking that personalizes Charles's hegemony is shown to be the fiction of an elite court culture which excludes other classes and has little control over public opinion.

The personalized representation of royal power can only increase the court's cultural insularity because it inevitably leads to an idealization of Charles and Henrietta Maria's marriage which also relies on abstruse Neoplatonism. By domesticating Platonic love, the personal mythology reflects the contradictory meanings of the family during this period: it shows the absolutist family combining the dynastic with the affective, creating a "private realm of warmth and virtue" which is said to have a moral influence on the public realm.[22] Moreover, the metaphysical and erotic hierarchies set up in Platonic love—divine beauty contemplated by the earthbound soul—are equalized in the marriage of the royal deities: Charles and Henrietta Maria are depicted as the model of consent and harmony. This representation of their relationship, however, remains patriarchal in its assignment of sexual roles. The idealization of female beauty reduces woman to a passive ornament which serves man's active reason, and in many masques, Charles's "triumphs" are allegories of military, political, and religious domination, whereas Henrietta Maria's are usually psychological and moral reformations of her subjects' sexual morality accomplished by the mere sight of her.[23]

The Neoplatonism also develops an idealized representation of the Caroline court which may have been intended to reform sexual behavior there, but which functions as an interested mystification of it. As Orgel notes of the masque, "Philosophically, it is both Platonic and Machiavellian; Platonic because it presents images of the good to which the participants aspire and may ascend; Machiavellian because its idealizations are designed to justify the power they celebrate."[24] The Platonic philosophy of the genre makes the Caroline masques contradictory, didactic but also utopian, intended as moral instruction for the courtier yet simultaneously praising his moral perfection, treating it as already achieved. This contradiction is symptomatic of the Machiavellian philosophy in the Caroline masques, the ideological operation by which an idealization of the courtier resolves the sexual immorality at court in order to establish its moral authority and legitimize its hegemony.

Davenant's *The Temple of Love* alludes to the discrepancy between court sexuality and Platonic love by having a group of courtiers act as a "company of noble Persian youths, borderers on India," who are "enflamed" with a glimpse of the Temple of Chaste Love given to them by "Divine Poesy" (1:286). They are said to have adopted a "somewhat hard doctrine to most young men" because they are "spirits of the highest rank," a phrase that makes their high social position an emblem of their innate moral worth, splicing the feudal class hierarchy with the Platonic ladder, mixing degree with Neoplatonism. The page who announces their entrance, however, sceptically suggests that this "doctrine" has in fact brought about a sudden and extreme change in their sexual behavior:

> My Master is the chief that doth protect,
> Or, as some say, miss-lead this precise sect:

> One heretofore that wisely could confute
> A lady at her window with his lute,
> Devoutly there in a cold morning stand
> Two hours, praising the snow of her white hand;
> So long, till's words were frozen 'tween his lips,
> And lute-strings learnt their quav'ring from his hips.
>
> (1:297)

The page's speech questions the ideological representation of court sexuality in this masque not only by satirizing the courtiers who play the Platonic lovers, but by impugning the morality of the ladies in the audience:

> To think, forsooth, they are so fond to take
> So long a journey for your beauty's sake!
> For know, th'are come! but sure, ere they return,
> Will give your femaleships some cause to mourn!
> For I must tell you, that about them all
> There's not one grain, but what's Platonical!

Indamora's "miracle," her Platonic reformation of love "in a dull northern isle, they call Britaine," is "more increas'd," says one of the corrupt magicians, "in that / It first takes birth and nourishment in the Court" (1:293). Davenant's masque repeatedly records an attitude of incredulity toward any idealization of court morality. The use of India may be its most subversive gesture, however, if we construe this setting as an ironic allusion to Townshend's *Tempe Restor'd* (1632), where Circe's sensual reign is figured in "all the Antimasques, consisting of Indians and Barbarians, who naturally are bestiall, and others which are voluntaries, and but halfe transformed into beastes" (p. 97). In *The Temple of Love,* produced three years later, not only do the courtiers play Persian youths who are described as "borderers on India," but Henrietta Maria plays the Indian queen Indamora. Orgel points to the ideological function of Davenant's Eastern motifs, "allying Caroline reforms with the world of regenerative mysteries and epiphanies,"[25] but as soon as we recognize the intertextual connection, a racist stereotype in the ideological discourse of the Caroline court comes back to ironize the mystification of court sexuality in Davenant's masque.

The role of moral exemplar assigned to Charles and Henrietta Maria in the masques seems to have shaped their behavior in many ways. The early years of their marriage were plagued by religious differences and Buckingham's interference—his enormous influence over

Charles, his efforts to make the women in his family the queen's attendants, his grandiose military plans to liberate the French Protestants on
the Isle of Rhé. Yet after the duke's assassination in 1628 the king and
queen's relationship apparently improved, and, untroubled by ill health
or infidelity, they enjoyed a happy marriage which produced nine children.[26] Sir William Sanderson, a royalist biographer who spent much
of his life at court, observes that Charles had "a most strict temperature
in the natural disposition of flesh and blood, and by the effects of
Divine grace, [was] the most exact observer of Conjugal Rites, and
therein for his continency was much admired."[27]

Not only did Charles live out the moral ideal figured in the Caroline
ideology, but he also sought to impose it on his courtiers' behavior by
controlling their sexuality, sometimes through repressive legal action.
Clarendon notes that "he was so great an Example of Conjugal affection, that they who did not imitate him in that particular, durst not
brag of their Liberty," since he directed the ecclesiastical courts to prosecute "those scandalous Vices . . . against Persons of eminence, and
near Relations to his Service."[28] Sexual crimes, like incest, rape, or sod-
omy, especially when they violated familial relationships, provoked the
king's personal intervention in court cases. When the Court of High
Commission fined Sir Giles Alington in 1631 for marrying his niece,
he avoided payment by successfully appealing the decision before a
common-pleas court. Charles, however, berated the common-pleas
judges for what he felt was imprudence and an affront to his law court
and ultimately had the case returned to High Commission for a different disposition. Sanderson reports that Alington was fined £12,000
and enjoined "not to cohabit or be in private with" his niece; the incestuous couple was also ordered to perform "penance at St. *Pauls Crosse
London,* and great St. *Maries* in *Cambridge.*"[29]

On at least one occasion, Charles tried to influence court sexuality
by reconciling an estranged noble couple, James Marquis Hamilton and
Lady Mary Fielding, Buckingham's niece. This rocky marriage was engineered by the duke to ensure his niece's economic security; in return,
the marquis was appointed Master of the Horse. The king intervened
during the couple's visit to court in 1628, when, wrote one observer,
Hamilton "lay with his lady that same night. For the king would have
it so, notwithstanding the marquis pretended his long journey of the
same day, and his want of clean linen. Whereupon his majesty commanded his own barber to attend him with a shirt, waistcoat, and
nightcap of his majesty's, and would not be satisfied till he had seen

them both in bed together."[30] When Hamilton danced in *Love's Triumph through Callipolis* as one of the "perfect lovers," however, the social conditions of his difficult marriage, the casualty of the aristocratic pursuit of self-interest at court, were resolved by the Platonic idealization of the conjugal affection among Charles's courtiers.

Charles's micropolitics of desire, whether expressed in the royal government's prosecution of sexual offenders or in his personal intervention into aristocratic marriages, was used selectively against courtiers. Several of the women who served Henrietta Maria as confidants and maids of honor were engaged in illicit affairs which were well known at court, but did not result in embarrassing public disclosures or legal action, unlike the other sexual crimes of Charles's reign. Appointed to the queen's bedchamber in 1626, Lucy Hay, Countess of Carlisle, was reported to have had several adulterous relationships, including one with Buckingham which offers a glimpse of the Machiavellian sexual politics at court. In 1628, a letter writer situated the affair in a web of self-serving political intrigues which involved the queen, the countess's husband, the Earl of Carlisle, and Buckingham's mother, wife, and sister: "if we say true [of the Earl's plans to travel abroad] he is sent away only to be put out of the way, and to be ruined for doing the Duke ill offices when he was at Rhe. For putting him off for the better access to his lady, it needed not, for he was quiet enough with all [that] was done by her. To content them both the better, she hath lately [had] given [to] her a 2,000*l.* pension, which perhaps will never be paid her, for, in the writer's opinion, he will not be half his journey before she be turned out of the Court, for the Duke's mother, wife and sister hate her, not only for the Duke's intimacy with her, but also that she has the Queen's heart above them. She has already brought her to paint, and in time will lead her into more debaucheries."[31] Of course, neither the duke nor the countess was summoned before the Court of High Commission or lost their financially rewarding influence at court, and neither she nor her husband was found too scandalous to participate in the idealizing masques. In 1633, similarly, Henrietta Maria's Vice Chamberlain Henry Jermyn impregnated Eleanor Villiers, one of the queen's maids of honor, but he refused to marry her because, he asserted, she had already been the mistress of himself, Lord Newport, and Lord Fielding. Although Jermyn was briefly imprisoned and banished from the court by the king, he returned to the queen's service within four years.[32]

The discreet tolerance shown these leading court figures also characterized the treatment of Frances Harrison, another of the queen's maids of honor. She seems to have been quite sought after by courtiers, and once, when she was being wooed by three gentlemen at the same time, she precipitated a duel. She later consented to marry one of the duelists, Roger Boyle, Baron Broghill, but grew reluctant because her future brother-in-law, wrote a contemporary, had "not kept his wedding night yet, by reason he is still under medical treatment. This has put Mrs. Harrison a little out of countenance, for fear the like may be her case with the other brother, yet I believe that business is so far advanced, though she will not acknowledge it, that she must adventure herself with him. It is said they are both very debauched, and though perhaps the latter may use more discretion in fixing the wedding day, yet it is feared they will be equally ill husbands. Having no matters of consequence to advertise you of, I adventure to acquaint you with these light passages to serve you for recreation, which I am sure you want rather than business. I commit them to your discretion to be spoken of as matters that concern persons of honor, though light in themselves, they are commonly known here, yet none speak them aloud."[33] The courtiers' sexual behavior should be viewed as inconsequential, "light passages," but hushed up to prevent them from acquiring reputations for immorality, repressed to avoid any public interrogation of the connections between the court's social prestige, its ideological representations in the masques, and its contradictory sexuality.

This attitude toward the courtier's sexuality, what we shall call Caroline discretion, is morally negligent, but it includes an awareness that the negligence carries implications for class domination and personal gain. In adopting this discretion, the Caroline courtier can be seen as cultivating, but clearly transforming, Castiglione's concept of "grace" or *sprezzatura*:

> I, imagynyng with my self oftentymes how this grace commeth, leaving a part such as have it from above, fynd one rule that is most general whych in thys part (me thynk) taketh place in al thynges belongyng to a man in worde or deede above all other. And that is to eschew as much as a man may, and as a sharp and daungerous rock, Affectation or curiosity and (to speak a new word) to use in every thyng a certaine Reckelesness [*sprezzatura*] to cover art withall, and seeme whatsoever he doth and sayeth to do it wythout pain, and (as it were) not myndyng it.[34]

Sprezzatura is a form of socially symbolic action that solves the loss of class power and autonomy facing the feudal aristocracy with the emergence of the absolutist state: the courtier's effortless grace, spontaneity, nonchalance constitute a knowing concealment or dissimulation of the material conditions of his actions, not only his education or training, his "art," but also his dependence on the prince's patronage.[35] Caroline discretion is also a form of socially symbolic action, but the conditions which this variation on the courtier's *sprezzatura* is designed to solve have changed somewhat. Nonchalance toward court sexuality reflects continued aristocratic dependence on royal patronage because such an attitude can be useful in winning preferment: if the Earl of Carlisle, for example, had chosen not to be "quiet enough with all [that] was done by" his wife, if he had created a public scandal by accusing her of adultery and seeking a formal separation, he risked the loss of the royal pension she had been awarded and, more generally, their influential positions in the favor of a king and queen who thought of themselves as guardians of the marital bond. Caroline discretion, like Castiglione's *sprezzatura,* is a means for the courtier to conceal the contradictory conditions of his behavior and make himself attractive to the prince, thereby serving the aristocratic pursuit of self-interest at court.[36] Yet this attitude also does the work of the Caroline ideology of absolutism because it mystifies court sexuality, quite like the masques, by maintaining the politically useful appearance that Charles's courtiers are "persons of honor," affirming the equation between impeccable morality and high social rank which legitimizes the class hierarchy. Here the conditions which the courtier's nonchalance solves include the court's increasingly precarious position in English society, the strained relations between the court aristocracy and other classes which have been exacerbated by cultural and ideological differences and by reports of sexual immorality.[37]

The Platonic love cult at court can be considered another manifestation of Caroline discretion. This cult was modeled not on the Platonic symposia held in Ficino's Florentine Academy, but rather on French aristocratic salons, like Madame de Rambouillet's *chambre bleue,* where witty conversation, poetry, and amateur theatricals were often inspired by the Neoplatonism in Honoré d'Urfé's pastoral romance *L'Astrée* (published in successive volumes from 1607 to 1627).[38] Henrietta Maria was acquainted with these salons in her youth, and shortly after her arrival in England, she initiated a vogue for Platonic love by encouraging the production of, and occasionally performing in, a series of plays and masques which made use of the same cultural materials as d'Urfé's romance—Racan's *Artenice* (1626), Walter Montagu's *The*

Shepherd's Paradise (1634), the anonymous *Florimène* (1635). The result
was that Neoplatonism influenced the courtiers' behavior most decisively not by effecting a moral reformation of it, as the masques asserted, but by providing a set of stylish ideas and motifs which were
used by members of an exclusive court coterie in conversation, letters,
and biographies.

Since participation in this erotic discourse signified membership in
the coterie, the vogue for Platonic love was able to reinforce the exclusivity and prestige of the most elite social group in English society. Yet
it also contributed to the Caroline ideology of absolutism by functioning as yet another mystification of court sexuality. Sir Kenelm Digby,
who was appointed Gentleman of the Privy Chamber at Charles's
accession, relies on Neoplatonism in his autobiographical romance
Loose Fantasies (1628) to idealize his marriage to Venetia Stanley and
redeem her reputation for lasciviousness. His narrative of their courtship makes Platonic pronouncements like "the love of a virtuous soul,
dwelling in a fair and perfect body, is the noblest and worthiest action
that a man is master of."[39] At one point, however, Digby's pseudony-
mous hero Theagenes gains entrance to his lady Stelliana's bedroom
while she is still asleep and offers a much less spiritual appreciation of
her beauty, the Platonic idealization giving way to pornographic fantasy: "Her belly was covered with her smock, which it raised up with a
gentle swelling, and expressed the perfect figure of it through the folds
of that discourteous veil, which yet was too weak a let for [his] exalted
fantasy, who, not satisfied with the external appearing beauties, did by
profound contemplation dive into and represent unto himself the fairer
hidden parts" (p. 115). In 1637, James Howell, a clerk of the Privy
Council whose letters often refer to the Platonic love cult, offered a
more subtle allusion to the Caroline courtier's sexuality: he wrote to a
friend at the Inns of Court that "F. C. soars higher and higher every day
in pursuance of his platonic love, but T. Man is out with his, you know
whom."[40] Howell's facetious tone suggests that the relationships in
question lack the philosophical profundity and moral earnestness
which Ficino assigns to Platonic love. The omission of the ladies'
names, furthermore, indicates not only that the recipient of the letter
belonged to the coterie and already knew them quite well, but also
perhaps that Howell is fashionably adhering to the doctrine of secrecy
in love maintained by d'Urfé's characters, and, in view of the sexual
promiscuity at court, that he is being discreet in case the letter should
fall into the wrong hands, "wrong" defined here as lacking membership
in the court group.

In the end, however, all such gestures of Caroline discretion failed miserably in shielding Charles's courtiers from the moral indignation of other social groups, Puritan or otherwise. Instead of improving the court's public image, the vogue for Platonic love actually damaged it by provoking a spate of books and pamphlets which pointed to the discrepancy between the courtiers' sexuality and the Neoplatonism they were fond of using in their speech and writing. In *The Lover: Or, Nvptiall Love* (1638), for example, one Robert Crofts attacked precisely the sort of Platonic courtship practiced by Howell's friends when he addressed "you courtiers and others, who thinke it a trimme peece of glory to get a Mistresse, and a Ladyes favour forsooth, you who esteeme and call your Minnions, Goddesses and divine creatures . . . and think your selves most happy when you can tempt the Pudicity of these female creatures and overcome them to your Lusts."[41] The Platonic love cult is a discursive formation that backfired politically: although it drew on the same idealistic conventions as the propagandistic masques, it used them in ways which ultimately weakened their ideological function. While the cult maintained the exclusivity and cohesiveness of the Caroline court, providing a set of shared cultural forms and specific social uses for them, it also created an opposition of other social groups which eroded the court's hegemony.

III

Much Cavalier love poetry participates in Caroline court culture by exacerbating its ideological contradictions, by developing subversive strategies of appropriating the same cultural materials. Like the masques, it puts to work the Renaissance tradition of erotic idealism, extending from the *dolce stil novisti,* through Dante and Petrarch, to the Florentine Neoplatonists, the Pléiade, and such English poets as Spenser, Sidney, and Donne.[42] Yet the distinctive Cavalier transformation departs most strikingly from the masques by seeking to undermine the idealism of this tradition. Cavalier love poetry uses the conventional ideas and motifs self-consciously, insisting on their conventionality, on their status as rather artificial linguistic forms, often exposing them as ideological representations which transform real sexual relations to serve different interests, male or female, sexual and social, in a struggle for dominance.

In the conventional poetic discourse, the relationship between lady and lover is given a hierarchical representation by the poetizing lover: the lady, deified for her perfect beauty and morality, her divine chastity,

dominates the all too human lover, showing disdain for his moral imperfections, his tendency to be alternately worshipful and lustful of her
beauty, to be both chastened and aroused by her exemplary morality.
In Carew's poem "To a Lady that desired I would love her," however,
this representation is democratized, reduced to an instrument of self-
aggrandizement, with the lover using it to gain sexual gratification, and
the lady to produce a public image for her social advancement. Carew's
"poetic strategy," as Bruce King notes, "depends upon the power of a
poet in a small courtly society where, like newspaper gossip, verses
make and unmake reputations."[43] The idealism of the conventional poetic discourse thus becomes the casualty of the sexual politics at court,
and the motifs which idealize the lady are made counters in a conflict
where each agent seeks to control the other's sexuality. What the lady
"desired" from the lover is social preeminence; what he shows her is
that her reputation conceals an oppression that is simultaneously sexual and social—a repression of his and her own sexual desire, and an
exploitation of his socially powerful poetry:

> Now you have freely given me leave to love,
>   What will you doe?
> Shall I your mirth, or passion move
>   When I begin to wooe;
> Will you torment, or scorne, or love me too?
>
> Each pettie beautie can disdaine, and I
>   Spite of your hate
> Without your leave can see, and dye;
>   Dispence a nobler Fate.
> 'Tis easie to destroy, you may create.
>
> Then give me leave to love, and love me too,
>   Not with designe
> To rayse, as Loves curst Rebells doe,
>   When puling Poets whine,
> Fame to their beautie, from their blubbr'd eyne.
>
> Griefe is a puddle, and reflects not cleare
>   Your beauties rayes,
> Joyes are pure streames, your eyes appeare
>   Sullen in sadder layes,
> In chearfull numbers they shine bright with prayse;
>
> Which shall not mention to expresse you fayre,
>   Wounds, flames, and darts,
> Stormes in your brow, nets in your haire,

> Suborning all your parts,
> Or to betray, or torture captive hearts.

> I'le make your eyes like morning Suns appeare,
>   As milde, and faire;
>   Your brow as Crystall smooth, and cleare,
>   And your dishevell'd hayre
> Shall flow like a calm Region of the Ayre.

> Rich Natures store, (which is the Poets Treasure)
>   I'le spend, to dresse
>   Your beauties, if your mine of Pleasure
>   In equall thankfulnesse
> You but unlocke, so we each other blesse.[44]

Carew's lover revises the Neoplatonic description of the lady's chaste beauty to include sexuality, arguing that her celestial "rayes" are most "cleare" in poetry which reflects the "joyes" of sex, not the "griefe" of repressive Platonic love; what makes her more than a "pettie beautie," what makes her a goddess who can "dispence a nobler Fate," is not her moral example, but her sexual submission to him. The lover wants not to abandon totally the conventional idealism, with its hierarchical representation of their relationship, but rather to use it with an awareness of its falsehood to mystify the individualistic contract that determines their sexual relations, the exchange of his poetry for her sex. The lover commodifies both through economic metaphors—"the Poets Treasure," the lady's "mine of Pleasure"—asserting that he will idealize the lady with the conventional nature imagery, but simultaneously emptying the convention of idealism by turning it into double entendre. This devaluing commodification enables the contract which equalizes lover and lady and explodes the conventional erotic hierarchy: "in equall thankfulnesse" each will "blesse" the other, and they will be consecrated in his poetic idealization of their sexual exchange. The poem is a seduction by a proponent of economic liberalism who imagines "Love" as a bourgeois nation-state, where it is a crime to construct hierarchical sexual relations except in poetry ("Suborning all your parts, / Or to betray, or torture captive hearts") and where the "curst Rebells" are those who violate the law of exchange, who refuse to submit to the equalizing effects of a labor contract.

Carew's transformation of the conventional poetic discourse involves an individualistic subversion of its idealism in which its hierarchical representations of social life are nonetheless valued because they

conceal atomized individuals seeking their self-interest. The lover in
Lovelace's "The Scrutinie" similarly aims to stand outside the ideological mechanism of sexual subjection figured in the conventional "vow"
of fidelity to the lady, escaping the inferior position he is typically assigned by the erotic hierarchy, preferring to maintain a sexual equality
which frees her too from the idealistic conventions by giving her control over her own sexuality. She, however, implicitly construes his plans
as a loss of her power. The lover is a libertine: his vow functions as an
instrument of seduction, a purely tactical move to gratify a momentary
access of desire, binding only until orgasm:

> Why should you sweare I am forsworn,
>   Since thine I vow'd to be?
> Lady it is already Morn,
>   And 'twas last night I swore to thee
> That fond impossibility.
>
> Have I not lov'd thee much and long,
>   A tedious twelve houres space?
> I must all other Beauties wrong,
>   And rob thee of a new imbrace;
> Could I still dote upon thy Face.
>
> Not, but all joy in thy browne haire,
>   By others may be found;
> But I must search the black and faire
>   Like skilfull Minerallist's that sound
> For Treasure in un-plow'd-up ground.
>
> Then, if when I have lov'd my round,
>   Thou prov'st the pleasant she;
> With spoyles of meaner Beauties crown'd,
>   I laden will returne to thee,
> Ev'n sated with Varietie.[45]

The lover's refusal of his conventionally submissive role is made analogous to mining, one of several industrial ventures in which the royal
government could intervene to raise money or reward favorites by issuing patents and licenses.[46] A test case in 1568 gave the crown ownership of all mines of precious metals; Elizabeth created the Mines
Royal Company to extend the royal monopoly to lead, and by 1638
Charles was trying to monopolize copper mining as well. Lovelace's
reference to "Mineralist's" equates the lover's chest-thumping sexual
potency with the bourgeois enterprise at court.

Yet this erotic liberalism never quite represents the lady as a sexual equal. "Varietie" is what the conventional ideas and motifs exclude from female sexuality: the lady is the chaste, passive object of the lover's attention. The lover's libertine revisionism offers the lady sexual freedom, but it continues to represent her as an object who gives the "joy" of sex to "others," passive, but also partial, suffering a metonymic reduction: the conventional motifs for female beauty—blond or "faire" hair, starlike eyes, rosy cheeks, and so on—get reduced to the lover's fetish for different shades of pubic hair. The mining metaphor quickly turns this sexual fetish into commodity fetishism: defloracing virgins is likened to the industrial exploitation of "un-plow'd-up ground," and the suggestion that the lover is seeking to rape land which could be plowed, that there will be enclosures and displacement of farming, shows that the lover's erotic liberalism really mystifies exploitative sexual/social relations. The conventional erotic hierarchy is not actually equalized in Lovelace's poem, but inverted: the lady is now among the dominated, while the lover dominates. In the last stanza, words like "spoyles" and "crowned" figure male sexual aggression and domination as an imperial triumph, indicating that this lover has finally abandoned his initial individualism and is now adopting the ideological style of Caroline absolutism. Lovelace's strategy is to replace the Platonization of conjugal sexuality in the masques with a commodification of sexual promiscuity which serves an absolutist patriarchy.

Suckling's "Sonnet II" cultivates a libertine individualism grounded in a sceptical critique of the conventional motifs for the lady's beauty, but also does not let go of hierarchical social representations:

> Of thee (kind boy) I ask no red and white
> to make up my delight,
> no odd becomming graces,
> Black eyes, or little know-not-whats, in faces;
> Make me but mad enough, give me good store
> Of Love, for her I Court,
> I ask no more,
> 'Tis love in love that makes the sport.
>
> There's no such thing as that we beauty call,
> it is meer cousenage all;
> for though some long ago
> Like't certain colours mingled so and so,
> That doth not tie me now from chusing new;
> If I a fancy take

> To black and blue,
> That fancy doth it beauty make.
>
> 'Tis not the meat, but 'tis the appetite
>   makes eating a delight,
>   and if I like one dish
> More then another, that a Pheasant is;
> What in our watches, that in us is found,
> So to the height and nick
>   We up be wound,
> No matter by what hand or trick.[47]

This starts off as an address to Cupid by a hedonistic lover for whom beauty is not a divine effulgence, but a cultural stereotype, a form of sexual fantasy that can arouse desire, or grow boring. The lover is suffering a kind of cultural exhaustion, where reigning concepts of female beauty have come to seem conventional: the Petrarchan "red and white" is an overly familiar poetic gesture, no more attractive than anti-Petrarchan "black eyes." The fact that even "odd becomming graces" and "little know-not-whats, in faces" have been conventionalized shows that the lover has lost interest in the latest fashions of the Caroline court: the fad for wearing facial patches of velvet or silk cut into hearts or diamonds.[48] These phrases show that the lover's boredom has ideological implications as well, because they also suggest his rejection of the dominant court aesthetic during the Renaissance, the concept of grace, where beauty is defined as an inexpressible naturalness, a chance or divinely created effect, Castiglione's *sprezzatura,* the *je ne sais quoi* of French neoclassicism, Pope's "a grace beyond the reach of art, / Which, without passing through the judgment, gains / The heart" (*Essay on Criticism,* 1.155–57).[49] In Suckling's first stanza, the court aesthetic implicit in phrases like "becomming graces" and "little know-not-whats" is degraded to a noticeable affectation ("odd"), or a tired cosmetic fad that originated at court: what was at first an attractive chance effect that exceeded the conventions of fashion has become mere fashion, and a concept of beauty as unknowable ("know-not-what") is now known as trendy. The lover's failure of desire issues from an overwhelming sense that dominant social representations have lost their emotive power, their truth value, their transparency.

In the second stanza, this becomes an epistemological crisis, in which the stereotypes of female beauty in court culture, defined as what was "like't" by "some long ago," are exposed as "meer cousenage," and the lover cuts his "tie" to the aristocratic tradition with a self-validating idealist epistemology, a solipsism, where private "fancy" creates "beauty," and personal taste imagines a world to compensate for his disillusionment with the court. This imaginary world is ultra-individualistic, but not at all democratic: it does not bring sexual equality between lover and lady; on the contrary, it is associated with physical abuse of her ("black and blue") and leads, in the final stanza, to her further, metaphoric reduction when love is redefined as a bodily function, a sexual "appetite" for female "meat." Like Lovelace's "The Scrutinie," this is another Cavalier inversion of the conventional erotic hierarchy, the lover displacing the lady in the dominant position. The lover's hierarchical thinking is clear in his aristocratic penchant for "Pheasant" and "watches," which ironically show that he is hardly "chusing new," suggesting that his desire can't escape the cultural forms of the aristocracy, that when freed from these forms, it is difficult to imagine new ones. The lover's awareness that he is not a free, unified subject but determinate and contradictory can be glimpsed in the clock metaphor: the body is characterized as a sexual mechanism, not so much self-operated as dependent on external stimulation, any "hand or trick," masturbation, or imaginary representations, like his "fancy" about the "Pheasant" or the stereotypes of female beauty he had rejected at the outset. The poem began with the aristocratic lover so jaded that he found the latest court fashions too passé and had turned away from Platonic salon conversation for "mad" physical "sport": he seemed to be following the plebeian Publius in Townshend's masque *Albions Triumph* by preferring more material "sights to please the People" over rarefied court culture. But at the end the lover's defection from the court aristocracy proves to be only momentary, since it appears unlikely that he will give up his class-coded "fancy."

The Cavalier transformation of the conventional poetic discourse is ideologically inconsistent: the love poems by Carew, Lovelace, and Suckling present individualistic subversions of the conventional erotic idealism which wind up recuperating its hierarchical thinking, occasionally going so far as to maintain a contradictory nostalgia for it. Suckling's "Against Fruition [II]" argues that the idealistic conventions, while undoubtedly mystifications, can nonetheless help the lady to control her lover's affection:

> Love's a *Camelion,* that lives on meer ayre,
> And surfets when it comes to grosser fare:

> 'Tis petty Jealousies, and little fears,
> Hopes joyn'd with doubts, and joyes with *April* tears,
> That crowns our Love with pleasures: these are gone
> When once we come to full *Fruition;*
> Like waking in a morning, when all night
> Our fancy hath been fed with true delight.
>
>   (Ll. 5–12)

Here is Suckling's solipsistic epistemology of "fancy" once again, but this time it is used not to encourage promiscuity, as a stimulant of flagging desire, but to warn against it: since personal desire constitutes its own concept of beauty as the real, even the "delight" of dreaming can be described as "true," provided action is informed by aristocratic cultural codes like the conventional erotic idealism "That crowns our Love with pleasures." The lover's view is that real sex is to be avoided because it is the great leveler, that when "hearts . . . burn with mutual fire," each suffers a loss of power over the other, the "two minds that breath but one desire" are equalized (ll. 1–2), and the conventional erotic hierarchy is flattened out, much to the lady's cost: the airy idealism of the conventions which nourishes the "*Camelion*" love also creates "that monster Expectation [who] feeds too high / For any Woman e're to satisfie" (ll. 15–16), and so a sexual encounter means disappointment and perhaps her abandonment. The lover's advice to the enterprising lady is cautionary and preventive: reassert your dominance by adopting the conventional chastity purely as a tactical move:

> Shee's but an honest whore that yeelds, although
> She be as cold as ice, as pure as snow:
> He that enjoys her hath no more to say
> But keep us Fasting if you'l have us pray.
> Then fairest Mistresse, hold the power you have,
> By still denying what we still do crave:
> In keeping us in hopes strange things to see
> That never were, nor are, nor e're shall be.
>
>   (Ll. 19–26)

Suckling's "Against Fruition" poems subvert the conventional idealism by not taking it seriously, by using it for contradictory purposes. The subversive strategy of Lovelace's "Sonnet" is to take it too seriously. The conventionality of the idealistic motifs is established by the lover's Petrarchan fanaticism: he is devoted not so much to the lady as to the ideas and motifs with which he had canonized her youthful beauty:

When I by thy faire shape did sweare,
And mingled with each Vowe a teare,
  I lov'd, I lov'd thee best,
  I swore as I profest;
For all the while you lasted warme and pure,
  My Oathes too did endure;
But once turn'd faithlesse to thy selfe, and Old,
They then with thee incessantly grew Cold.

I swore my selfe thy Sacrifice
By th'Ebon Bowes that guard thine eyes,
  Which now are alter'd White,
  And by the glorious Light
Of both those Stars, of which (their Spheres bereft)
  Only the Gellie's left:
Then changed thus, no more I'm bound to you
Then swearing to a Saint that proves untrue.

The lover measures the lady against the idealized representation she is given in the conventional poetic discourse, and she doesn't live up to it, she's aged, her eyes no longer approximate the "glorious Light" of her divine beauty, now "only the Gellie's left," the rather repulsive earthly residue of her fallen "Stars" (*OED*). The discrepancy that opens up between lady and idealization shakes the lover's faith not in the idealization, but in the lady, and he exploits it to discard her. Lovelace's poem undermines the dominant stereotype of female beauty in court culture by using it simultaneously to idealize and victimize the lady.

These poems by Carew, Suckling, and Lovelace will suggest some of the textual strategies by which Cavalier love poetry assimilates the conventional poetic discourse, subverting it with individualistic themes and images, then recuperating it in much altered forms. They demonstrate that Cavalier love poetry can be seen as the site of a conflict over cultural materials which it shares with court theater, a conflict in which the poems challenge the ideological uses to which Neoplatonism is put in the masques. Whereas the masques offer an idealistic representation of court morality in which the king and queen's exemplary love has led their courtiers to become chaste Platonic lovers worshipful of their ladies' divine beauty, Cavalier love poems frequently represent the courtiers as individualists who aim to satisfy material needs, sexual, social, economic. Because the conventional discourse carries an ideological burden in the masques, more is at stake in the Cavalier transformation than just sexual morality: Cavalier poetry puts into question the Caroline ideology of absolutism. It eroticizes the conventional ideas and motifs in opposition to the Neoplatonic political allegories in the masques which implicitly represent sex outside of marriage as rebellion against Charles and Henrietta Maria's Platonic government. Cavalier love poetry represents lovers who evade the absolutist micropolitics of desire assigned to the king and queen in the masques. The erotic triumph of Lovelace's imperial lover in "The Scrutinie" is a parodic inversion of the military and political triumphs Platonized as Charles's moral self-control in Jonson's *Love's Triumph through Callipolis* or Townshend's *Albions Triumph*.

More generally, Cavalier love poetry interrogates the use of Neoplatonism at court, in the masques, in memoirs and characters, in conversation, by showing that the conventional erotic idealism, with its hierarchical representation of sexual relations, mystifies the individualistic struggle for sexual gratification and social advancement among Charles's courtiers. Some poems go further to demystify this individualism as well, to show that it only masks new hierarchies, sexual and social, or to long for the old ones again, aristocratic if not absolutist. In all its interrogative strategies for treating sexual behavior in social terms, Cavalier love poetry points to the basic ideological contradiction of the absolutist state which the textual operations of the masques aim to solve: the hierarchy, metaphysical and moral, that legitimizes the feudal class structure and absolute monarchy conceals the bourgeois individualism encouraged by the royal government's fiscal policies, by the court competition for royal patents, pensions, and the like, where courtiers like Buckingham and the Countess of Carlisle exploited sex and marriage in their aggressive pursuit of political power and economic gain.[50]

Cavalier love poetry sometimes shows an awareness of its ideological subversions by deploying specifically political imagery. The conventional "red and white works now no more on" the jaded lover of Suckling's "Sonnet I," so he concludes that "Sure beauty's empires, like to greater states, / Have certain periods set, and hidden fates" (ll. 6, 20–21). This metaphoric couplet revises a proverbial expression, "States have their conversions and periods as well as natural bodies," by adding a phrase—"beauty's empires"—which implicitly refers to the masques' Platonic equations of royal power with divine beauty. The problem raised by the metaphor is both erotic and political: the royal government, legitimized by the conventional erotic idealism, may eventually change, losing its power over the subject, just as "the fate of faces" made attractive by the conventional motifs is to grow conventionalized, no longer capable of commanding the lover's "vow" (ll. 1–2, 5).[51] Suckling's "Loving and Beloved" bluntly asserts at the beginning that "Kings and Lovers are alike in this / That their chief art in reigne dissembling is" (ll. 4–5) and then proceeds to treat the idealistic conventions as mystifications of real sexual and social relations: "Oh! 'tis torture all, and cozenage; / And which the harder is I cannot tell, / To hide true love, or make false love look well" (ll. 16–18). The poem ends with the lover making a remark that is dangerously close to sedition: he alludes to the title of Jonson's first masque for Charles's court, *Love's Triumph through Callipolis,* subtly identifying the corrupt "State" as Caroline England:

> Since it is thus, God of desire,
>   Give me my honesty again,
>   And take thy brands back, and thy fire;
>   I'me weary of the State I'me in:
> Since (if the very best should now befal)
> Loves Triumph, must be Honours Funeral.
>   (Ll. 19–24)

Puritan pamphleteers like William Prynne were also criticizing the threats to "honesty" in court theater and poetry. But the book for which Prynne was convicted of treason—*Histrio-Mastix, or the Scourge of Players* (1633)—does not follow Suckling's poem in suggesting that the conventional erotic idealism is an illusory device to further a lover's seduction or a king's domination. The passage from *Histrio-Mastix* which the attorney general construed as an offense to the queen— "Women-Actors, notorious whores"—is an elliptical moral pronouncement which appears in the index. The conditions of Prynne's conviction have less to do with his attack on theater—by the 1630s a familiar move in Puritan pamphlets—than with his criticism of Archbishop Laud's innovations in church ceremony and government and his social position as a barrister at Lincoln's Inn, politically threatening to the royal government because close to gentry who were radically conservative in morality and religion.[52] Among these conditions must be included the generic difference of Prynne's book: his social criticism is a seditious transformation of the Puritan attack on theater into a vitriolic jeremiad, roughly a thousand pages long, articulated in what Butler calls "scandalously extravagant and inflammatory language against virtually the entire social order." *Histrio-Mastix* most indubitably lacks the discreet tones and polite Platonic discourse of court genres like the love lyric. This is not to say, however, that the social representations in court genres are necessarily royalist. On the contrary, the ideological subversions in Cavalier love poetry take the form of subtle new wrinkles on shared cultural conventions which are most perceptible to members of the exclusive court group: Suckling's poem eviscerates the Caroline ideology of absolutism, even if it possesses the formal elegance and refinement which were valued in court culture.

Carew's "A Rapture" hurls a more formally ambitious challenge at the masques' use of Neoplatonism: it is a pastiche of Renaissance erotic literature. Written in a genre, the pastoral erotic fantasy, which typically presents libertine parodies of the idealistic conventional motifs, the Golden Age myth, and Genesis, Carew's poem specifically imitates passages from other, related texts, like Tasso's pastoral tragicomedy *Aminta* (1573), Donne's Ovidian elegies (1590s), even the Catullan seduction of Celia in Jonson's *Volpone* (1605), and adds the Caroline masque to the formal mix.[53] In Carew's own masque *Coelum Britannicum* (1635), the king and queen's micropolitics of desire extended its dominion throughout the cosmos. Mercury declares to Charles and Henrietta Maria that the premise of the masque is their ideological representation, setting it up as the position from which the performance will become intelligible for the king and queen as well as the audience:

> Your exemplar life
> Hath not alone transfus'd a zealous heat
> Of imitation through your vertuous Court,
> By whose bright blaze your Pallace is become
> The envy'd patterne of this underworld,
> But the aspiring flame hath kindled heaven;
> Th'immortall bosomes burne with emulous fires,
> *Jove* rivalls your great vertues, Royall Sir,
> And *Iuno,* Madam, your attractive graces;
> He his wild lusts, her raging jealousies
> She layes aside, and through th'Olympic hall,
> As yours doth here, their great Example spreads.
> (Ll. 62–73)

Whereas Mercury's speech confirms the personalized political mythology developed for Charles and Henrietta Maria in previous Caroline masques by Jonson, Townshend, and Shirley, the lover in "A Rapture" attempts a libertine inversion. The poem, masquelike in its succession of elaborately visualized scenes, begins with a reference to the masque which exposes the genre as an ideological cultural apparatus, a fictive moral allegory designed to control "baser subjects," while the "nobler" court aristocracy indulge their sexual desire. The lover's ideological critique suggests that the idealistic representations in masques like *Coelum Britannicum* only conceal the political and economic interests served by the royal government:

> I will enjoy thee now my *Celia,* come
> And flye with me to Loves Elizium:
> The Gyant, Honour, that keepes cowards out,
> Is but a Masquer, and the servile rout
> Of baser subjects onely, bend in vaine
> To the vast Idoll, whilst the nobler traine
> Of valiant Lovers, daily sayle betweene
> The huge Collosses legs, and passe unseene
> Vnto the blissfull shore; be bold, and wise,
> And we shall enter, the grim Swisse denies
> Only tame fooles a passage, that not know
> He is but forme, and onely frights in show
> The duller eyes that looke from farre; draw neere,
> We shall see how the stalking Pageant goes
> With borrowed legs, a heavie load to those
> That made, and beare him; not as we once thought
> The seed of Gods, but a weake modell wrought
> By greedy men, that seeke to enclose the common,
> And within private armes empale free woman.
>
> (Ll. 1–20)

It is curious that no king is mentioned, but "Honour" must be a royal "Masquer," who performs in a monarchy, because social agents are described as "subjects." Following the Platonic allegorization of the Caroline masques, we might conceive of this "Gyant" called "Honour" as the "seed" or offspring of "Gods" because his name signifies a virtue, chastity, and as Ficino asserts, "goodness is said to be the outstanding characteristic of God" (p. 140). This "seed" may also refer to the deification of the royal marriage in the masques: "Honour" as the offspring of the marriage between the queen's Divine Beauty and the king's Heroic Virtue, the "Honour" of marital fidelity. The strange absence of a king to preside over this "Masquer" points to the ideological contradictions of Caroline absolutism: the divinely appointed monarch, the "seed of

Gods," has become no more than an actor in a royal entertainment, "with borrowed legs," financed by a group of patriarchal individualists who seek to dominate women by turning them into "private" property. The lover is trying to seduce Celia with a vision of sexual freedom in a new monarchy, a libertine utopia. The conventional erotic idealism of the masques is metamorphosed into a pornographic rhetoric: the Petrarchan motif of the lover's soul as a ship, for instance, tossed on a sea of conflicting emotions, under the uncertain control of Love, the "lord who steereth with cruelness" (Wyatt's version of Petrarch's sonnet 189)—this gets eroticized, with the lady's "bold hand" becoming the "tryde, / And skilful Pilot, [who] shalt steere, and guide / My Bark into Loves channell, where it shall / Dance, as the bounding waves doe rise or fall" (ll. 87–90). This pornotopia, however, remains patriarchal: the poetizing lover produces the lady as a highly fantasized object of desire who departs from the passivity of the conventional idealization mainly by serving as a sexual tool.[54] What the name "Celia" signifies in the text is a series of pornographic inversions of conventional ideas and motifs, so that the lady becomes just as imaginary as "Loves Elizium."

Carew's self-conscious text treats the libertine utopia as fantasy by means of indicators like the extensive use of the future tense throughout the conventionalized representations of sexual organs and acts as well as the opening lines: "I will enjoy thee now," asserts the lover, but he never does in the here and now. As Paula Johnson has noted, "the general meaning . . . of *there* and *shall* is that of any-time-but-now-any-place-but-here, the realm of fantasy, untrammeled by problems or probabilities, by repression or restraints, a land freer than even our dreams."[55] The future tense indicates that Carew's poem, like Suckling's solipsistic epistemology of "fancy," is aware of itself as a wish-fulfilling "rapture," as an imaginary compensation for real dissatisfactions: "since the poem is an imaginative construction," Johnson points out, "this use of the non-present produces a fantasy within a fantasy, at a safe distance from the self that ordinary life demands we maintain" (p. 148).

At the end it becomes clear that this fantasy-within-a-fantasy performs an ideological function, that the contradictions of "ordinary life" which must be solved through libertinism are created by the Caroline ideology of absolutism. The tense shifts to the present, the poem returns to reality from that fantastic future place, and we learn that it was "Honour," the "Masquer," who was the king after all, that the king is no more than an allegorical image, a royal actor, a "proud *Vsurper*" who is a "false Impostor":

Come then my *Celia,* wee'le no more forbear
To taste our joyes, struck with a Pannique feare,
But will depose from his imperious sway
This proud *Vsurper* and walke free, as they
With necks unyoak'd; nor is it just that Hee
Should fetter your soft sex with Chastitie,
Which Nature made unapt for abstinence;
When yet this false Impostor can dispence
With humane Justice, and with sacred right,
And maugre both their lawes command me fight
With Rivals, or with emulous Loves, that dare
Equall with thine, their Mistresse eyes, or haire:
If thou complaine of wrong, and call my sword
To carve out thy revenge, upon that word
He bids me fight and kill, or else he brands
With marks of infamie my coward hands,
And yet religion bids from blood-shed flye,
And damns me for that Act. Then tell me why
This Goblin Honour which the world adores,
Should make men Atheists, and not women Whores.
                                        (Ll. 147–66)

The lover's libertinism, his seduction of Celia, becomes an effort to "depose from his imperious sway" the conventional erotic idealism personified by "Honour" because, he argues, its commitment to social prestige leads him to criminal and antireligious behavior: to avoid "marks of infamie," "Honour" forces the lover to break the "lawes" of "humane Justice" and "sacred right" by engaging in duels with rivals and defamers of his lady's beauty. It isn't "just," he tells Celia, that "Honour" makes him an atheistic murderer and her a prisoner of sex. Carew's "A Rapture" ends with the lover suggesting that the erotic idealism which informs the Caroline ideology is tantamount to atheism. Yet in the lover's final question, in his use of "Whores," he slips back into the conventional idealistic language. "Whores" shows that he has failed to realize his libertine fantasy about a language devoid of sexual and moral meaning: he imagined the "Elizian ground" as the place where "the hated name / Of husband, wife, lust, modest, chaste, or shame, / Are vaine and empty words" (ll. 107–10). "Whores" finally demonstrates that all this is no more than a fantasy, that the lover's erotic inversion of the conventional "words" can never be complete or seamless, that however much he eroticizes the idealistic language, he cannot transform words which stigmatize extramarital female sexuality. The lover's seductive fantasy is defeated by a cultural convention, but not before he exposes its contradictory conditions: "Honour" conceals the collusion between the absolute monarch and the patriarchal individualists and the double bind imposed by class and religion, social prestige and murder. Although the lover cannot himself escape the conventional erotic idealism, he can nonetheless interrogate it through pornotopian fantasies which imagine other sexual and social possibilities, however limited by the cultural forms in which they are imagined.

"A Rapture" casts these interrogative fantasies in the pastoral, another indication that genre is an arena of ideological conflict in Caroline court culture. Carew's poem "To the Queene" praises Henrïetta Maria with a pastoral version of the conventional Platonic motifs: "the Awe / Of [her] chaste beames, doest give the Law" to nature, to the sexual morality of both humans and animals; even "the wilde / Satyr [is] already reconciled" to "the path / Of Modestie, and constant faith" (ll. 3–4, 13–14, 19–20). Here, as in the masques, the queen commands a moral reformation of Love's "Kingdome," which before her reign knew "no rule but this, / *What ever pleaseth lawfull is*" (ll. 11–12). In "A Rapture," however, Henrietta Maria is displaced by the Venus Vulgaris, "the Queene of Love, and Innocence, / Beautie and Nature," who will "banish all offence / From our close Ivy twines," and nature is eroticized: "Th'enamoured chirping Wood-quire shall adore / In varied tunes the Deitie of Love," who has made "all things . . . lawfull there, that may delight / Nature, or unrestrained Appetite" (ll. 25–27, 111–12). Both "To the Queene" and "A Rapture" cultivate the pastoral, but the first does so to express the political Neoplatonism of the Caroline ideology, while the second presents a subversive eroticism.

Orgel describes the ideological significance of pastoral in the masques: "The Caroline productions . . . tend to resolve all action through pastoral transformations. . . . Jones's pastoral visions become most elaborate during the 1630s, the decade of prerogative rule. Monarchs like Charles and his queen are doubtless attracted to the visions of themselves as pastoral deities because the metaphor expresses only the most benign aspects of absolute monarchy. If we can really see the king as the tamer of nature, the queen as the goddess of flowers, there will be no problems about Puritans or Ireland or Ship Money."[56] This ideological use of the pastoral, however, is derailed by the multiple codes—erotic, political, economic—in a Cavalier love poem like Lovelace's "To Chloe, Courting her for his Friend." This is a pastoral seduction which transforms the Platonic concept of love as a mutual exchange of identities into the basis for a ménage à trois:

Chloe behold! againe I bowe,
Againe possest, againe I woe;
From my heat hath taken fire,
    Damas, noble youth, and fries:
    Gazing with one of mine eyes
  Damas, halfe of me expires:
Chloe behold! Our Fate's the same,
Or make me Cinders too, or quench his Flame.

I'd not be King, unlesse there sate
Lesse Lords that shar'd with me in State;
    Who by their cheaper Coronets know
    What glories from my Diadem flow:
    It's use and rate values the Gem,
    Pearles in their shells have no esteem;
And I being the Sun within thy Sphere,
'Tis my chiefe beauty thinner lights shine there.

The Us'rer heaps unto his store,
By seeing others praise it more;
    Who not for gaine, or want doth covet,
    But 'cause another loves, doth love it:
    Thus gluttons cloy'd afresh invite
    Their Gusts, from some new appetite;
And after cloth remov'd, and meate,
Fall too againe by seeing others eate.

The names "Chloe" and "Damas" are the first signal of the pastoral genre, while the epithet "noble youth" further suggests the pastoral motif of aristocrats posing as shepherds in romances like Sidney's *Arcadia* or d'Urfé's *L'Astrée*. Celadon, for example, the shepherd who enjoys "a mutuall affection" with the shepherdess Astrea, "is of one of the principall Families of this Countrey" (i.e. fifth-century Gaul).[57] Also relevant to Lovelace's poem is the fact that Celadon's love is Platonic: just as Ficino states that "whenever two people are brought together in mutual affection, one lives in the other and the other in him" (p. 144), we learn that Celadon is so "overtaken . . . with the perfections of *Astrea,* that the hatred that was betweene their parents, could not hinder him from losing himselfe wholy in her" (p. 2). Because Lovelace's lover is involved in two relationships, however, his love for Chloe and his friendship with Damas, he undergoes a double exchange of identities which so complicates his psychological state that he seeks to merge the relationships into a sexual triangle. Chloe has already "possest" the lover, physically as well as spiritually it seems, and since Damas is "halfe" of him, Damas "from [the lover's] heat hath taken fire." The lover's argument in effect parodies Platonic accounts of enamorment like those in Ficino and d'Urfé: whereas Ficino asserts that in love "two so become one, that each of the two, instead of one alone, becomes two" (p. 145), the lover's friendship gives him a threefold identity, leading to the libertine conclusion that Chloe's sexual gratification of Damas will simultaneously gratify the lover.

Given the Platonic exchange of identities assumed in this parodic argument, the reverse conclusion would also be possible, that Chloe's gratification of the lover will simultaneously gratify Damas. The omission of this logical possibility is symptomatic of the libertine agenda of the poem—to overturn the conventional erotic idealism by making the lady promiscuous instead of chaste and by exploding the hierarchical representation of their relationship. Chloe is reduced to a passive sexual object who is desired not for her perfect beauty and morality, not because she exemplifies the Ficinian "glow of divinity shining in beautiful bodies" (p. 141), but because she has aroused the lust of the lover's friend. The lover adopts the conventionally submissive role by continuing to "bowe" before and "woe" Chloe not because he is a soul inserted in a metaphysical hierarchy, awed by the lady's divinity, but because his subjectivity is determined by his friendship with Damas. The lover, Chloe, and Damas are not spiritual essences who, according to the idealistic tenets of Neoplatonism, long to return to their original state, transcending the contingencies of earthly existence with their contemplative love; they are rather determinate subjects, constituted by their relationships with others, their love contingent on the satisfaction of physical needs like sexual desire. By enabling the lover's libertine revisionism, this concept of determinate subjectivity opposes the transcendental subject underlying the Platonized ideology of absolutism in the masques and subversively transforms their use of the pastoral: the triangle in Lovelace's poem deviates from the moral reformation in Townshend's *Tempe Restor'd,* for instance, wherein the "vale of Tempe" is purged by Henrietta Maria as "divine Beauty" (pp. 97, 99).

The second stanza strikes at the heart of the Caroline ideology by examining the social determinations of kingship. The lover is revealed to be not just an aristocratic shepherd, but the "King," yet what determines his political identity is not Providence, as in the divine right theory of kingship, but the hierarchical social relations in which he is situated: the lover would not be king if his power, wealth, and social prestige were not "shar'd" by, and thus distinguished from, the class

beneath him, the "lesse Lords"; Damas' inferior class rank is the difference that defines the lover's dominance—the king dependent on the
aristocracy. Chloe, construed as one of the "glories" which "flow" from
her lover's "Diadem," becomes a royal gift to aristocratic favorites; the
lover is king only because such an emblem of his royal magnificence as
Chloe can be given to Damas. Jewel imagery is conventionally used to
idealize the lady's beauty, but since "Gem" and "Pearles" can refer am-
biguously to both Chloe and her royal lover, they continue the lover's
displacement of her in the erotic hierarchy and argue that beauty and
kingship are not intrinsic, transcendental qualities, but socially determinate: their value is an effect of "use and rate," of social conditions
like custom and the market, the aristocratic competition for royal preferment, Damas' sexual desire. The solar metaphor transforms another
conventional motif for praising the lady's beauty into a reference to *le
roi soleil* absolutism which, however, confirms the king's dependence
on the aristocracy. It is the lover who is the "chiefe beauty" in his relationship with Chloe, but only insofar as his "Sun" shows a higher degree of brightness than the "thinner lights," like Damas, who "shine" in
her "Sphere," an analogy in which idealization is simultaneously double
entendre. By presenting the social conditions of the lover's libertinism,
the second stanza interrogates the ideological representation of the Caroline court in the masques, pointing to the courtiers' use of sexuality
to compete for social advancement.

The third stanza pushes this interrogation of the Caroline ideology
to an extreme by implicitly comparing the royal shepherd to a "us'rer"
and then to "gluttons." Here bourgeois individualism becomes another
ideological casualty of the determinate subject: the profit motive is said
to originate not in self-interest or poverty, but in dominant social representations ("praise") which colonize the agent's desire with their valorization of wealth. The analogies with usury and gluttony thoroughly
trash the idealistic conventions and divine right theory: Chloe is first
turned into capital, an interest-accruing loan to Damas, then gro-
tesquely objectified as "meate," while her royal lover is driven to accumulate and consume by prevailing values or someone else's appetite,
the king ruled by the sexual desire of his aristocratic friend. The usury
analogy shows that the absolute monarch is dependent not on Providence, but on bourgeois economic practice, the values of other, lower
classes, and thereby glances at the fiscal expedients of the Caroline
government (they included not only customs concessions and patents
or licenses, industrial and commercial, but also forced loans), the bour-

geois enterprise supporting the king's political hegemony in the absence of Parliament. Lovelace's libertine pastoral debases the cultural forms used to mystify government policies in the masques and represents court extravagance and sexuality in an unsavory way.

The discontinuous textual work of this poem is what makes it most subversive, most interrogative of the ideological cultural materials it assimilates. The lover's argument unwinds through a rapid succession of disparate images, moving abruptly from pastoral lovers, to kings and lords, to usurers and gluttons, parodying the pastoral and Neoplatonism, discrediting divine right theory and possessive individualism. This disruptive movement is aided by the utter ambiguity of the jewel analogies, and by the images of usury and gluttony in the last stanza, shocking in their contradiction of the rhetorical situation announced in the title, "To Chloe, Courting her for his Friend": they are obviously designed to make the sexual triangle seem not merely uninviting, but scandalous and repulsive. Cavalier love poetry is filled with similar instances of textual discontinuity; their effect is to weaken the coherence of the subject-positions set up for the reader and hence to skew the ideological positioning. The lover in Lovelace's "The Scrutinie" metamorphoses from bourgeois "Minerallist" to imperial monarch; the lover in Suckling's "Sonnet II" defects from aristocratic culture to plebeian "sport" in the beginning, but winds up returning to patrician "Pheasant" at the end; in Carew's "A Rapture," the lover himself contradicts his libertine fantasy by using the language of erotic idealism ("Whores"). And consider the abrupt transformation which the lover undergoes between the second and third stanzas of Carew's "Disdaine returned":

> Hee that loves a Rosie cheeke,
>   Or a corrall lip admires,
> Or from star-like eyes doth seeke
>   Fuell to maintaine his fires;
> As old *Time* makes these decay,
> So his flames must waste away.
>
> But a smooth, and stedfast mind,
>   Gentle thoughts, and calme desires,
> Hearts, with equall love combind,
>   Kindle never dying fires,
> Where these are not, I despise
> Lovely cheekes, or lips, or eyes.

No teares, *Celia,* now shall win,
　　My resolv'd heart, to returne;
I have searcht thy soule within,
　　And find nought, but pride, and scorne;
I have learn'd thy arts, and now
　　Can disdaine as much as thou.
Some power, in my revenge convay
That love to her, I cast away.

The first two stanzas present a Platonic lover who attaches a moral significance to the conventional motifs for the lady, valuing spirit over matter with a *contemptus mundi* attitude, equating beauty with goodness and love with mutual affection and fidelity. He seems a conventional enough lover, consistent with the king and queen's Platonic reformation of love in Jonson's *Love's Triumph through Callipolis* or Davenant's *The Temple of Love*—at least until the last stanza, where the lover's rejection of Celia is a striking departure from the erotic idealism of the masques. The lady's "pride, and scorne" refer to the conventional hierarchical representation, the lady's perfect morality leading her to "disdaine" the lover's moral imperfections; yet here the lover's Neoplatonism makes him the moral superior, whereas Celia has turned the convention into "arts" intended to maintain her control of their relationship by refusing "equall love." The last stanza shows the lover abandoning "gentle thoughts, and calme desires," imagining a "revenge" against Celia in which the power relations in their relationship are reversed, in which he adopts the lady's conventional "arts" to dominate her by rejecting her love for him. In the first two stanzas, the lover established as the position of intelligibility a Neoplatonism with ascetic and then conjugal overtones, but his final shift to an aggressive and rather detached exploitation of the conventions dislodges the reader from their erotic idealism and hence from the ideological position of the masques. Carew's contemporaries evidently perceived this incoherence in the lover's characerization and found it distancing enough to require revision: anthologies like Walter Porter's *Madrigales and Ayres* (1632) often omit the last stanza from the poem.[58]

Cavalier love poetry of course presents itself as possessing formal unity, so its discontinuous textual work competes with, and is often elided by, its illusionistic effect of a speaking voice.[59] Cavalier versification usually includes enough metrical variants to have a conversational quality, its pronomial indicators are consistent, and it aims to

maintain semantic coherence by continuing syntactical structures over
lines, making the rhyme scheme less pronounced, the sound more
natural:

> Know *Celia*, (since thou art so proud,)
>   'Twas I that gave thee thy renowne:
> Thou hadst, in the forgotten crowd
>   Of common beauties, liv'd unknowne,
> Had not my verse exhal'd thy name,
> And with it, ympt the wings of fame.
>   (Carew, "Ingratefull beauty threatned," ll. 1–6)

> I cannot tell who loves the Skeleton
> Of a poor Marmoset, nought but boan, boan.
> Give me a nakednesse with her cloath's on.
>   (Lovelace, "La Bella Bona Roba," ll. 1–3)

> I pray thee spare me, gentle Boy,
> Presse me no more for that slight toy,
> That foolish trifle of an heart;
> I swear it will not do its part,
> Though thou dost thine, employ'st thy power and art.
>   (Suckling, "[Loves Feast]," ll. 1–5)

The transparency of Cavalier verse, its strong sense of authorial pres-
ence, is what elicits Millamant's appreciative phrase "natural, easy
Suckling," driving her to anthropomorphize the lines she recites in
Congreve's *The Way of the World* (1700) just as it invites the psychological and biographical reductions of modern and contemporary critics.
Suckling's admiration for Lord Dudley North's essay "Concerning petty
Poetry" is an indication that the Cavalier metric is a calculated effect of
illusionism, grounded in the court aesthetic of *sprezzatura*: "In Verses,"
writes North, "there is to bee exprest a naturall spirit and moving ayre
(or accent) more alluring and charming the affection, then others of a
farre more rich, faire and curious composition."[60] What we shall stress
is that the "naturall spirit and moving ayre (or accent)" fix libertinism,
the libertine transformation of the conventional erotic idealism, as the
standpoint from which many Cavalier love poems are intelligible, positioning the reader in a subversion of the ideological representations
produced by the masques.

Yet Cavalier verse is not *completely* transparent: sometimes the rhymes are slightly too pronounced and the meter is too regular, there are refrains or syntactical peculiarities that create a too studied natural-ness, like Lovelace's "I lov'd, I lov'd thee best" in "Sonnet," or the lover's voice is too mannered, as in the stilted opening of Lovelace's "To Chloe, Courting her for his Friend," or he is finally dislocated by the logic of his own argument. At these points, Cavalier verse loses its "natural, easy" illusionism, it becomes opaque language instead of an individual speaking, and the position of intelligibility becomes incoherent, so that the ideological subversion is itself transformed, and the lover's libertine individualism may slide into a declaration of new hierarchies, sexual and social, or a nostalgia for old ones. "Ingratefull beauty threatned," for example, is one of Carew's most vivid performances, an abrasive seduction that tries to browbeat the "proud" lady into sexual submis-sion by reminding her of the conventionity of the idealistic motifs, of her dependence on the lover's poetry for her "fame," and by suggesting the existence of an individualistic contract between them (her "bor-rowed sphere"). As in other Cavalier love poems, however, this liber-tine individualism leads to an inversion, rather than abandonment, of the conventional erotic hierarchy and therefore loses its ideological coherence:

> That killing power is none of thine,
> I gave it to thy voyce, and eyes:
> Thy sweets, thy graces, all are mine;
> Thou art my starre, shin'st in my skies;
> Then dart not from thy borrowed sphere
> Lightning on him, that fixt thee there.
>
> Tempt me with such affrights no more,
> Lest what I made, I uncreate;
> Let fooles thy mystique formes adore,
> I'le know thee in thy mortall state:
> Wise Poets that wrap't Truth in tales,
> Knew her themselves, through all her vailes.
> (Ll. 7–18)

The lover overthrows the lady by reducing her idealization to a poetic fiction and by idealizing himself through the analogy between poet and divine creator which recurs in Renaissance court literature: he takes such statements as Sidney's "With the force of a divine breath, [the poet] bringeth things foorth far surpassing [nature's] doings" to expose

his idealization of Celia as mere mystification, a fantastic "second nature," and while the "real" Celia is portrayed as more "brasen" than
"golden," the lover glorifies his own "erected wit" in a libertine parody
of the divine analogy.[61] The last stanza contains a similar move to elevate the lover: it assumes an idealistic defense of poetry like Boccaccio's, where it is asserted that poetry "veils truth in a fair and fitting
garment of fiction,"[62] although the lover's libertine transformation lit-
eralizes the clothing metaphor in order to legitimize his carnal knowledge of Celia. Carew's poem, it turns out, can undermine his conventional idealization of the lady only by relying on a conventional
idealization of the poet-lover, i.e., on the divine analogy or the defense
of poetry as truth. This discontinuity in the logic of the lover's argument recuperates the metaphysical hierarchy that underlies Neoplatonism, the Platonized politics of the masques, the divine right theory of
kingship, the ideology of degree—but not without demystifying any
such idealizing representations as tools of sexual gratification and social
advancement. The transparency of the verse, the consistency of the
aggressive tone, distract attention from the logical slip to position the
reader in the lover's ideological subversion. This effect of transparency
is designed to bring off libertine gestures effortlessly, with considerable
sprezzatura, as if "not myndying it," making Cavalier love poetry another manifestation of that moral negligence we have labeled Caroline
discretion, yet one that is much more interrogative than such other
forms of the Platonic love cult as the masques, biographies, and letters.
Caroline discretion, an attitude of discriminating rationality that conceals the contradictory social conditions of court culture, is reflected
yet perverted in verse that aims to treat the most scandalous sexual
transgression lightly, that opposes the Caroline ideology of absolutism
by nonchalantly revealing the contradictions at court, and that in its
metric minimizes the textual discontinuities which constrain its ideological subversions and show that it finally cannot leave behind the
hierarchical thinking it challenges.

IV

The ideological subversiveness that distinguishes the Cavalier
transformation of the conventional poetic discourse can be characterized more precisely in a comparison with similar reworkings of the
idealistic conventions in aristocratic coterie poetry from the Elizabethan and Jacobean periods. Cavalier love poetry continues the strain of

libertinism in Donne's Ovidian elegies and *Songs and Sonnets*, often echoing images and ideas, rephrasing specific lines.[63] "The Indifferent," who "can love both faire and browne" (l. 1), for instance, is quite like the hair fetishist in Lovelace's "The Scrutinie." Donne's lover is also an individualist who chafes at the conventional motif of fidelity in political terms: "Must I, who came to travaile thorow you / Grow your fixt subject, because you are true?" (ll. 17–19). Arthur Marotti points out that the libertine transformation of Renaissance erotic idealism in Donne's early poems and other Inns of Court writing is an imaginary compensation for the court amateur's social dependence: since "from Queen Elizabeth on down to wealthy women of the middle class, the game of petrarchan mistress and lover was played with men whose social and economic dependence found expression in the language of courtly amorous verse," the "socially, economically, and politically vulnerable Inns gentlemen . . . found it pleasant to turn the tables imaginatively by composing, circulating, and collecting love poetry of another sort, literature that celebrated male social, economic, and sexual power."[64] When Donne's scandalous marriage ruined his progress through the patronage system during James's reign, Marotti argues, his love poetry again turned compensatory: "He treated mutuality of affection as the space within which he could find an analogous private world of value and satisfaction apart from the public world of selfish competition, but he found the one world constantly intruding upon the other" (pp. 136–37).

What is particularly remarkable here is that Donne's revision of the conventional erotic idealism, his idealization of mutual love and conjugal sexuality, becomes the personal mythology developed for the king and queen in the Caroline masques. In poems like "The Sun Rising," "The Good Morrow," and "The Canonization," Donne's lovers withdraw from social action, from court competition and financial gain, in order to create a private realm where they are deified and return to society, remaking it, installed in their own absolute monarchy. The lovers "to whom love was peace, that now is rage" in "The Canonization" are petitioned for "a patterne of [their] love" (ll. 39, 45), just as later Charles and Henrietta Maria's marriage will be Platonized in the masques as a moral exemplar which governs their subjects. By the 1630s, Donne's love poems must have no longer seemed "rebellious and atheistical in their manipulation of the *arcana imperii*" from the masques,[65] because the Cavalier transformation of the idealistic conventions goes further in its politicization of love by showing how all personal relations are always already politically divisive, how the atomized sexual and social relations at court have made impossible the Platonized mutual love of Donne's poems or the masques. In Carew's "A deposition from Love," the lover is both crowned and canonized by his sexual relationship with the lady, yet she nonetheless rebels to reassert her power, with "her breach of faith" replacing "her scorne" as the instrument of her domination (ll. 19–20). Carew's lover concludes with a reversal of the politicized Neoplatonism in Donne's poems and the masques: "he that is cast downe / From enjoy'd beautie, feeles a woe, / Onely deposed Kings can know" (ll. 29–30).

What changes in aristocratic culture brought forth the Cavaliers' more subversive transformation of their predecessors' love poetry? By the 1630s, the literary system in which Donne presented himself had changed: the Cavalier poets did not experience the same social uncertainty and vulnerability, or have the same career expectations, as the court amateur who sought patronage under Elizabeth and James. They were members of the court coterie for which they wrote because they were Charles's courtiers, some holding such official appointments as Gentleman of the Privy Chamber and Sewer-in-Ordinary; and while some of them were engaged in producing the royal ideology by writing masques and by idealizing their aristocratic patrons in occasional poems, it cannot be denied that the primary, if not the sole, intention of their love poetry was to entertain a select court audience. As Richard Helgerson points out, "the system of differences in terms of which both the amateurs and the laureates of previous generations had presented themselves . . . retained little structural integrity" in the Caroline period: "The poet merged with the gentleman, poetry with the gentlemanly activities of [the] court."[66] The Cavalier poets remained court amateurs throughout their careers because, unlike their Elizabethan and Jacobean predecessors, they no longer viewed poetry as a means to recommend themselves for a position in the royal government that would give them greater social authority than authoring amusing poems.

Helgerson goes on to assert that the Cavaliers "presented themselves as men in society, men whose pursuit of business or pleasure and whose activity as courtiers . . . was continuous with their literary engagement" (p. 201), but our analyses of their love poetry require this assertion to be qualified. Although the Cavaliers were closely integrated into the court coterie and even the royal household, and although their literary entertainments served king and court just as much as their work as royal attendants, their love poems can be considered ideologically inconsistent with their activity as courtiers: they subvert the Caroline ideology of absolutism and thereby question the court's hegemony. The crucial question posed by Cavalier love poetry, therefore, is not whether the poet's "decline in autonomy" was aesthetically damaging, as Helgerson's individualistic rationalization of the literary canon leads him to argue, but rather how this poetry can enact ideological subversions potentially destructive of a privileged social group and yet be extremely popular with, and in fact patronized by, this group.

The collapse of the literary system under Charles means that the libertine poems of the Caroline court amateur offered pleasures which compensated not for the poet's own uncertain and vulnerable social position, but for the precariousness of the court aristocracy in English society as a whole. These poems are not subversive in the sense that in their challenge to the royal ideology they are somehow revolutionary texts which can be aligned with specific social groups against the king. Their ideological subversions are very much part of ruling class culture, a parlor game which is enjoyed by an exclusive social elite and helps to maintain its cohesiveness: circulating in manuscript and set to music for court performance, poems by Carew, Suckling, and Lovelace were accessible to an extremely small audience during the 1630s. We should rather take the ideological subversiveness as an inversion of dominant cultural values that is "carnivalesque" in Bakhtin's sense: Cavalier love poetry carnivalizes the Caroline masques by degrading the conventional poetic discourse, often through parody, bodily imagery, and billingsgate genres like curses, but only during definite periods which are stipulated as entertainment, festivity, celebration, and hence finally dissociated from any revolutionary thought and action.[67] The libertinism of Cavalier love poetry didn't overthrow, but was sanctioned by, the social calendar at court. The Cavaliers gave their aristocratic readers and listeners the cheap thrill of flirting with class anxiety by developing an irreverent attitude toward the royal ideology which legitimized their class domination. The witty insouciance with which the libertine poems treat the personal and political mythology of Caroline absolutism was a cultural practice, like the courtiers' discretion, which managed the contradictory social conditions of the court, not only the sexual promiscuity and self-aggrandizing intrigue, but the political and economic conflicts that proliferated as the royal government implemented various fiscal and religious policies.

Since Cavalier love poetry participated in the Platonic love cult, it contributed to the insularity of the aristocratic fraction at court, exacerbating the division which opened up between the court and other segments of English society during the years of Charles's personal rule. The Cavaliers' libertine transformation of the conventional poetic discourse provided a kind of pleasure which even as it increased the exclusivity and cohesiveness of the court incensed critics of the royal government, drawing virulent attacks in Puritan pamphlets and sermons. Cavalier love poetry exploited the same cultural materials as the Caroline ideology in order to invert their meaning, but Carew, Suckling, and Lovelace hardly saw themselves as making a revolutionary cultural intervention "to overcome the rulers through their own rules." All the same, their libertine poems had the unanticipated consequence of urging other social groups to do so.

Conclusion

Political Criticism

But quaint Emblems and devices begg'd from the old Pageantry of some Twelf-nights entertainment at *Whitehall,* will doe but ill to make a Saint or Martyr . . .

John Milton, *Eikonoklastes*

IT REMAINS to reflect on the model of political criticism which has shaped the present study, to probe the political limits and potentialities of a materialist critical project amid the current cultural malaise, the crisis of subjectivity and historicity under consumer capitalism. A political hermeneutic, argues Jameson, "provides the means for maintaining contact with the very sources of revolutionary energy during a stagnant time, of preserving the concept of freedom itself, underground, during geological ages of repression."[1] Because the symptomatic reading, like every critical method, is an ideological cultural practice, it assumes a concept of subjectivity which defines the possibilities for human action, "our sense of the mutability of our being-in-the-world," and which, therefore, also implies a concept of freedom.[2] In a political hermeneutic, a concept of freedom issues from a dissatisfied rejection of the present, a negation of the critic's own social situation, and it functions as both an interpretive device and an instrument of political action, representing its dissatisfaction and stimulating thinking about social change through the interpretation of culture, past and present. Thus, we can ask what concept of freedom is projected in the foregoing symptomatic readings of Renaissance culture, and how this concept answers to the social situation in which these readings have been produced. Why this reading of Caroline literature now? What sources of revolutionary energy does this reading tap in prerevolutionary texts?

The symptomatic reading is determined by the social situation which it seeks to oppose. This reading rests on the poststructuralist theory of textuality, admits its antihumanist critique of representation and the centered subject, and thus, in terms specific to critical discourse, reflects the fragmentation and decentering of subjectivity in postmodern cultural phenomena like media simulation. The post–World War II metamorphosis of representation into simulacra linked to the economic cycle, into a continuum of heavily coded images in which the codes are commodified and naturalized, rendered transparent by advanced communications technology, has made humanistic concepts of textual production and reception outmoded and politically ineffective. Humanism has come to seem no more than a compensatory repression of its cultural predicament, a withdrawal into a transcendental realm of Literature and Human Values where individualistic aesthetic categories like authorial intentionality, organic unity, and the illusionistic effect of transparency can keep alive the centered subject. The political cost of this compensatory critical discourse is that it encourages the culturally induced habit of naturalizing the commodified codes in the media. To struggle against the crisis of subjectivity, the symptomatic reading first accepts the critique of representation which that crisis has precipitated and transforms the text into a heavily mediated object, fragmented by the materials it puts to work and decentered from the author's intention. Yet this reading refuses to naturalize the mediations, refuses to be positioned in the obviousnesses imposed by the text. In the symptomatic reading, the simulacral text loses its hypnotic illusionism because its mechanisms of ideological interpellation are exposed and the material conditions of its representation are examined. Hence, the symptomatic reading of Caroline texts focuses on their constitutive materials, on their sedimented forms, the strata of genre and convention they contain, but these materials are demystified as ideological, seen as implicated in ideological forms of social domination current during the Renaissance—feudal, absolutist, bourgeois, patriarchal—all of which the texts submit to varying degrees of interrogation. The symptomatic reading opens up difference within the text, between its announced project and its implementation of that project, yet this reading also differs from the text by evading and making clear its ideological positioning.

In its assumption of poststructuralist textuality, this reading might well seem to perpetuate the postmodern fragmentation and decentering of subjectivity, the breakdown of temporal experience, and the primacy of privatized moments of intensity. Yet because ideological determinations are collective in their significance and functioning, specific to social classes and groups, ideological critique can rather serve as the first historicizing gesture of the symptomatic reading, its first move to overcome the crisis of historicity. This move, although historicizing, is simultaneously a representation of the past in present terms. The symptomatic reading shares the tendency of recent posthumanist Renaissance studies to represent the period, in Jean Howard's account, "as *neither* modern nor medieval, but as a boundary or liminal space between two or more monolithic periods where one can see acted out a clash of paradigms and ideologies, a playfulness with signifying systems, a self-reflexivity, and a self-consciousness about the tenuous solidity of human identity which resonate with some of the dominant elements of postmodern culture."[3] What distinguishes the symptomatic reading from other postmodern representations of the Renaissance, however, is that it aims to go beyond an identity between two very different historical periods in order to suggest the differences that make the reading historical, that bring back the past as the past rather than as merely the image of the present. In the symptomatic reading, difference and discontinuity characterize not only its historical narratives, but also its relationship to the historical materials it processes.

To facilitate the ideological critique of Caroline texts, therefore, the previous chapters focus on genres and topical allusions, but they sketch no teleology in the development of cultural forms which corresponds to the development of social conflicts in Caroline England. The relationship between culture and its social ground is not homologous, but differential. While England changed from a conjuncture in which conflicts were displaced over different levels of social practice—economic, political, ideological—to a conjuncture in which they reached the explosive state of condensation that propelled the country to revolution during the 1640s, Caroline cultural forms underwent their own, relatively autonomous development, uneven in their relationship to social changes, reflecting the latter in discontinuous ways. The accumulating social conflicts do not necessarily make a genre like city comedy more critical of royal policy and more receptive to bourgeois values on the eve of the Long Parliament. On the contrary, the feudal nostalgia that gradually emerges in this genre during the prerevolutionary period constitutes a conservative reaction to shifting class alignments which presents a limited criticism of the court. Similarly, the masque reflects social developments through its extreme topicality, but also indirectly, through such formal changes as the proliferation of antimasques to figure social conflicts. The result of this indirection is not that the genre becomes more subversive or more affirmative of absolutist ideology during the years of personal rule, but rather that it becomes so discontinuous that its ideology can be determined only by the ideological standpoint of its different audiences. The audience of Cavalier love lyrics likewise defines their political significance. These poems can be seen as ideologically subversive only because they transform the idealistic poetic conventions prevalent in court culture by advocating libertinism and by alluding to the accumulation of wealth fostered by royal policy. Yet the class-specific nature of these conventional poetic materials means that the interrogation of absolutist ideology in Cavalier poetry is contained within the aristocratic coterie.

By assuming a materialist historicism that privileges social contradiction and transformation, the symptomatic reading resists not only the bourgeois teleology of Whig historiography, especially its treatment of early Stuart culture as increasingly decadent and escapist, but also the conservatism of recent revisionist history of the seventeenth century. During the seventies and early eighties, revisionist historians like Conrad Russell, Kevin Sharpe, and Anthony Fletcher decisively challenged the stereotypical oppositions of Whig historiography by developing a more complex representation of the early Stuart period—of the royal government, Parliament, the county community, of political allegiances and ideological standpoints. Unfortunately, this increase in complexity often occurred at the cost of discouraging any thinking about social contradictions as the basis of historical change. "So anxious have some of the revisionists been to emphasize consensus politics," Barry Coward notes, "that they have diverted attention away from the constitutional conflicts that did take place in the later parliaments of Elizabeth I's reign, in the parliaments of James I's and Charles I's reigns and in 1640, all occasions when there were long debates about the royal prerogative and constitutional issues."[4] Thus, Russell prefers to take at face value John Pym's use of the "ancient constitution" to criticize the Caroline government, reading it as an expression of parliamentary conservatism in the face of the radical innovations introduced by royal policy.[5]

The early Stuart governments were indeed innovative in many ways—financial, administrative, constitutional, among others—because they embodied the contradictions of the absolutist state, joining feudal privilege to bourgeois interests, legitimizing profit accumulation with the royal prerogative. Yet Parliament was equally innovative: the historiographical concept of the ancient constitution shows parliamentary leaders paradoxically using a feudal social representation to serve bourgeois interests, to legitimize parliamentary privilege and question the king's hegemony. It is important for a materialist critical project to develop historical narratives which emphasize such economic, political, and ideological contradictions because, unlike revisionist history, it aims to imagine the conditions of social change. Hence, the symptomatic reading embeds Caroline texts in the contradictory social determinations which led to political revolution, reading the civil war not, in Fletcher's words, as "that most surprising and unintended catastrophe,"[6] but as radical political practice which was rationalized by social agents, even if it also included conditions and consequences that were not entirely under their conscious control.

The historicity of the symptomatic reading is indicated, moreover, by its effort to preserve the historical difference of its objects, by the capacity of this difference to deliver a judgment on the present. The interrogation of ideologies in Renaissance texts must also be seen as the interrogation of ideologies which prevail today. If the feudal nostalgia of late city comedy is reactionary in the seventeenth century, it can nonetheless be seen as having a progressive dimension in the twentieth because it implies a collective social model that contradicts and judges the atomization of social life under late capitalism. This was in fact the sort of ideological opposition which L. C. Knights wanted to articulate with his reading of city comedy. Implementing the *Scrutiny* cultural project of preserving the precapitalist values of the organic community against monopoly capitalism, Knights canonizes Jonson's plays for their "anti-acquisitive attitude," their "vivified" evocation of the "tradition." Yet it is in late city comedy, read symptomatically, that this attitude receives its clearest valorization and feudal values are more insistently advocated, in texts like Brome's *The Antipodes* or Shirley's *The Lady of Pleasure,* rather than in Jonson's *The Alchemist* or *Bartholomew Fair.* Knights's bourgeois critical categories read the Caroline plays as the products of a "decadence" whose ultimate origins are social, their too close alignment to aristocratic groups under Charles: "Fashionable society, or the imitation of fashionable society, provides their themes. . . . Shirley has perhaps an even narrower range [than Brome]. His comedy is the comedy of polite society, and when wider issues are mentioned they seem to have a literary ancestry rather than to be the result of direct observation."[7]

The notion of textuality implied in this opposition between "liter-

ary ancestry" and "direct observation" betrays Knights's individualistic
assumptions and brings into question the historicity and the oppositional stance of his reading. The statement expresses his preference for
the illusionistic effect of transparency by describing the text in epistemological terms, as the product of a transcendental subject whose cognition is free of cultural determinations ("a literary ancestry"). But
transparency is an illusion: it is an effect of the subject-positioning by
which the action becomes intelligible in a text or dramatic production.
Late city comedy also has its illusionistic moments when a deferential
audience can be positioned in specific ideologies. Yet since these are
moments of ideological subjection, they can lose their illusionism for a
different audience, one that is differential because determined by conflicting ideologies which resist the positioning. Because the ideology of
Caroline "polite society" consists of a collective model of social life, the
feudal class hierarchy which legitimized aristocratic hegemony,
Knights's marginalization of the Caroline plays where this ideology is
most valorized can be seen, in effect, as an abandonment of the medieval organic community for bourgeois individualism, a rejection of a
historically specific "tradition" for the individual initiative displayed in
early city comedy in the form of commercial activity. For the scenes
which have the strongest illusionism in the Jacobean plays are those
which are so structured as to position the audience in the businessmen
and confidence artists and make us complicit with their fraudulent
economic practices. What is perhaps most revealing of the ideological
significance of Knights's reading, however, is the fact that it rests on
Whig historiography: by calling a cultural form decadent because it is
aligned with the court and aristocracy in the prerevolutionary period,
Knights is implicitly subscribing to the Whig assumption of the "vitality" of bourgeois culture.

Avoiding Knights's individualistic critical categories in a symptomatic reading will permit a more effective intervention against the crisis
of historicity in postmodern culture. The symptomatic reading preserves the historical difference of city comedy by situating a diachronic
generic construct in the prerevolutionary conjuncture, processing it as
the contradictory site of an emergent individualism and various feudal
and absolutist ideologies, some residual, others hegemonic. Historicizing the texts simultaneously judges the postmodern present by showing how its dominant ideologies are interrogated in a past when they
are still emergent, unmasking the contradictory conditions of individualism and patriarchy, juxtaposing individualism and the collective so-

cial models in feudal and absolutist ideologies, making visible the ultimate lack of any concept of social responsibility in individualism, exposing its inadequacy to promote democratic social formations. This historicization shatters any illusion of "direct observation" in city comedy and escapes any ideological effect of positioning in the texts. Yet Renaissance collectivist ideologies, despite their hierarchical social representations, stand out in their irreducible difference from the present. The feudal collectives restored at the end of so many late city comedies, the absolutist order which resolves social problems in the masques, the aristocratic group of poets and readers which is implied in the ideological subversions of Cavalier love lyrics—these are the signs of the texts' historicity, of what makes them different from contemporary culture, because collective social representations are marginalized or broken down in the atomized present, in the extreme specialization of the divison of labor, in the privatization of subjectivity, in the serial simulacra which privilege individualistic cultural codes.

The nature of the political intervention conducted by the symptomatic reading can be made more precise in a contrast with the model of political criticism offered in Milton's *Eikonoklastes.* The differences between Milton's demystification of royal culture and the ideological critiques presented here not only issue from two conflicting critical methods, but also throw into relief two different historical moments: a revolutionary conjuncture in the seventeenth century, which witnessed the proliferation of concepts of freedom grounded in possessive individualism, in Christian and secular humanisms,[8] and the contemporary social situation, where the images of freedom that circulate in postmodern culture tend to defer rather than promote social transformation, calling forth the competing images of a materialist critical project. Milton's social situation will inevitably indicate the social and political limitations of the symptomatic reading, the extent to which it is mired in a stagnant time, remote from revolutionary social change. Yet the concepts of subjectivity and political action in Milton's text can also show what very different assumptions are required to think about social change today.

Writing in the service of the parliamentary Council of State set up after the fall of the royal government, Milton aims to defend the regicides by answering the *Eikon Basilike: The Pourtraicture of His Sacred Majestie in his Solitudes and Sufferings* (1649), an absolutist hagiography of Charles I which was popularly believed to have been authored by the king himself. In the preface to *Eikonoklastes,* published later that same year, Milton observes that this canonization of the king is less a defense of royal policies than the strategic cultural intervention of royalist adherents, the ideological prelude to political action, "the promoting of thir own future designes."[9] Milton sees his project as a political struggle against the "enemies" of the parliamentary government, but he is also aware that it is a struggle which must be conducted in the discursive terms presented by an opposing text, that critical references to the king are not enough to justify his execution. "The proper scope of this work in hand," Milton writes, is "not to ripp up and relate the misdoings of his whole life, but to answer only, and refute the missayings of his book" (p. 342). Thus, *Eikonoklastes* carries out its project in specific textual strategies: it abandons the genre of its object, biography, in order to perform a systematic ideological critique of absolutist discourse, a point-by-point refutation of the royal version of the events leading to civil war, often relying on parliamentary documents like the Grand Remonstrance of 1641.

The refutation Milton promises is actually a strongly transformative reading of its object, one which self-consciously processes the text on the basis of the political agenda he is defending. In the preface, he gives a glimpse of how he transforms *Eikon Basilike* by presenting a brief reading of its Latin "Motto." Milton argues that the political interest served by the publication of this text, the counterrevolutionary "intent" of "stirring up the people to bring [the king] that honour, that affection, and by consequence, that revenge to his dead Corps, which hee himself living could never gain to his Person," is revealed in a discontinuity in the frontispiece between the engraving of the king in prayer and the Latin, "*Vota dabunt quae bella negarunt;* intimating, That what hee could not compass by Warr, he should atchieve by his Meditations" (p. 342). In Milton's reading, "though the Picture sett in Front would Martyr him and Saint him to befool the people, yet the Latin Motto in the end, which they understand not, leaves him, as it were a politic contriver to bring about that interest by faire and plausible words, which the force of Armes deny'd him" (p. 343). Milton locates a slippage of meaning in the frontispiece and reads it as a symptom of the absolutist ideology at work in the *Eikon Basilike,* wherein the divine right theory of kingship is developed into a martyrology to mystify the political "intent" of those royal adherents who published the text. At one point, moreover, Milton shows his awareness that his own operations on the text produce an equally interested representation of the king: "in words which admitt of various sense," he asserts, "the libertie is ours to choose that interpretation which may best minde us of what our restless enemies endeavor, and what wee are timely to prevent" (p. 342). Milton's assumption is that the reader's ideological standpoint fixes meaning in the text, that reading is an ideological cultural practice which answers to the most pressing social problems of the reader's historical moment. Milton's observations on the politics of reading thus edge toward a materialist concept of "libertie," one in which human action is simultaneously enabled and constrained by social conflict.

Most of the preface, however, refuses this materialism. Milton sees his own discourse not as an ideological representation, but as a transparent medium of timeless, universal values like "truth" and "libertie." Thus, the *Eikon Basilike* is characterized as a false image of the king— it "washes over with a Court-fucus the worst and foulest of his actions" (p. 347)—whereas *Eikonoklastes,* it is implied, gives the reader immediate access to reality, presents the king's actual "deeds," not the mystifying "words" of royal adherents or "of one man in his own cause":

> allegations, not reasons are the main contents of this Book; and need no more then other contrary allegations to lay the question before all men in an eev'n ballance; though it were suppos'd that the testimony of one man in his own cause affirming, could be of any moment to bring in doubt the autority of a Parlament denying. But if these his fair spok'n words shall be heer fairly confronted and laid parallel to his own farr differing deeds, manifest and visible to the whole Nation, then surely we may look on them who notwithstanding shall persist to give to bare words more credit than to op'n deeds, as men whose judgement was not rationally evinc'd and perswaded, but fatally stupifi'd and bewitch'd, into such a blinde and obstinate beleef. (P. 347)

The shifts in the logic of this passage are remarkable. The first sentence begins by likening Milton's arguments against the royal government to the absolutist representations of the *Eikon Basilike:* they are both no more than "allegations," although Milton's are "contrary" ones which are somehow of such persuasive force as to provoke "doubt" or a suspension of judgment ("an eev'n ballance") even in the royal adherent who "suppos'd" the king's hegemony over Parliament. Milton's phrasing in this sentence shows that he regards his allegations as persuasive not because they have been substantiated, but because they are associated with the "autority" of a political group in power ("a Parlament") as opposed to the mere "testimony" of one deceased political figure. In Milton's construction, it is sheer political power that turns allegations into truths, that gives the ruling party a monopoly on truth. At this point, another sentence is begun, and all references to the political interests served by Milton's own text vanish, indeed, the very linguistic materiality of his text evaporates, and the king's "deeds" require no means of representation to prove his criminality: they are "op'n." This reference to the king's "deeds" not only assumes the objectivity of Milton's representation, but contradicts his previously announced intention "not to ripp up and relate the misdoings of his whole life, but to answer only, and refute the missayings of his book." And it is now "the whole Nation," not just "a Parlament," which recognizes the truth of what was initially described as "contrary allegations." The passage begins by linking Milton's text to a specific political group opposing the king, but then represses this social situation by concluding with democratic pronouncements.

The shifty logic in Milton's preface is due to his assumption of transcendental concepts of language and subjectivity. It is ultimately divine Providence which has "dignify'd" Parliament "with the defence of truth and public libertie" (p. 348). Parliament has become God's agent on earth, displacing the king, and the parliamentary author of *Eikonoklastes* has the benefit of divine omniscience, free of the contradictory social conditions which put into question his assertions of transcendence. For when Milton notes that "they who adhere to wisdom and to truth, are not . . . to be blam'd, for beeing so few as to seem a sect or faction" (p. 348), he makes clear that Parliament does not speak for "all men," that the criminality of the king's "deeds" is not "op'n," and that the hegemony of the revolutionary government depends not on the providential order of history, but on the development of a consensus among competing political factions. Milton needs transcendental concepts of language and subjectivity not just to legitimize Parliament by masking these contradictory conditions of its power, but also to challenge the different but nonetheless transcendental concepts assumed in absolutist ideology. Because the royal prerogative is legitimized by a Christian metaphysics, the divine right theory of kingship, Milton's struggle against Caroline absolutism must enlist a concept of "libertie" that is likewise metaphysical, grounded in Christian humanism, in the notion of subjectivity as a spiritual essence positioned in a metaphysical hierarchy.

Postmodern culture, however, has dissipated the revolutionary energy of Milton's humanism, of any metaphysics, making it seem no longer a viable strategy for political criticism and drawing attention instead to the glimpses of a materialist critical project in *Eikonoklastes*. These glimpses—the references to Milton's revolutionary situation, to the parliamentary faction, to his own ideologically programmed reading of *Eikon Basilike*—interrogate any contemporary version of the essentialist subject that brings with it a concept of transcendental freedom, and rather encourage the adoption of a materialist concept of freedom defined by the historically specific determinations in which political action is performed and rationalized. The model of oppositional criticism exemplified by the symptomatic reading, therefore, must recognize that it is simultaneously facilitated and limited by its social situation, particularly by the fact that it is housed primarily in cultural institutions like the university.

As an ideological cultural intervention against consumer capitalism, the symptomatic reading is restricted to the specific materials and methods of this academic culture and disseminated through academic publications, curricula, lectures. Even as I write, books and journals tumble from university presses, journal pages are filled with advertisements and reviews (genres which often get blurred in the writing), and theoretically based, politically inflected studies have led to the founding of new journals and the development and implementation of new curricula, achieving new levels of academic authority and social power. The commodification of scholarly criticism goes on apace, absorbing even those cultural activities that seek to interrogate and change the very economic process of commodification, forcing them to develop modes of opposition that must enter the continuum of simulacra in order to avoid the ultimate strategy of withdrawal, i.e., silence and capitulation. Textual production in contemporary culture is so highly specialized that an oppositional criticism is confined to the transformation of specific cultural practices on their own ground, figuring opposition in their terms, in this instance by questioning the canonization and marginalization of texts, revising critical judgments and curricula, constructing new objects-for-criticism which answer to the most pressing social problems in the present.

Academic specialization obviously limits the political power of institutionalized criticism and effectively undermines any suggestion that intellectuals today can or should form a cultural elite to function somehow as a vanguard political party. Yet the authority of academic cultural criticism, although it does not equal that of a political institution like Milton's Parliament and has been eroded today by the extensive dissemination, heterogeneity, and technology of popular culture, does in fact go beyond the boundaries of academic disciplines, university departments and presses, not only because scholarship may be brought into the service of government agencies and private foundations, but also because educational institutions are ideological apparatuses involved in the subjection and qualification of agents for social roles. Marxist cultural criticism housed in academic institutions is engaged in the production of subjects and the articulation/disarticulation of ideological discourses, and hence it can make a crucial intervention by interrogating and transforming the processes of ideological interpellation which currently dominate those institutions, particularly individualistic and humanistic notions of culture which refuse to examine their social situation. Marxist cultural criticism can also extend its social reach through an engagement with popular culture, investigating the possibilities for contest and change in the forms of media simulation themselves, juxtaposing past and present cultural objects to create that critical confrontation between two historical moments which judges the present. For although the politics of contemporary popular culture has been questioned by the present study, cultural forms in television, film, and music put to work prevalent ideologies and sometimes do transform them in ways that can be called progressive from a materialist standpoint.[10] Whatever cultural object is processed by the symptomatic reading, however, the political value of this critical method lies precisely in the fact that it is a discursive practice, "a rhetorical gesture," although one functioning at a time when rhetoric is increasingly seen as always already political.

Notes

Index

Notes

BEYOND THE debts recorded in the text and in the notes below, I would like to express my gratitude to a number of people who aided me in bringing out this book. I could not have done without the advice, encouragement, and patience of Barbara Hanrahan, my editor at the University of Wisconsin Press. I am very grateful to the Press's two readers, Leah Marcus and an anonymous British critic, for their detailed comments which, although extremely different, were nonetheless of great help in improving the manuscript. Thanks also to those who read some of this material over the past several years and made useful suggestions: Richard Burt, Timothy Corrigan, Gabriele Bernhard Jackson, Peggy Knapp, Daniel O'Hara, Wayne Rebhorn, Alan Singer, Philip E. Smith, Susan Stewart, Edward Tayler, and Susan Wells. Grateful acknowledgment is made to *Boundary 2, Assays: Critical Approaches to Medieval and Renaissance Texts,* and *English Literary Renaissance,* where earlier versions of Chapters 1, 3, and 4 appeared. Part of the research and writing was supported by Summer Research Fellowships from Temple University. The lines in the dedication conclude John Ashbery's poem "Robin Hood's Barn" from *Self-Portrait in a Convex Mirror* (New York: Viking, 1975).

INTRODUCTION: *The Symptomatic Reading*

1. This follows Fredric Jameson's distinction between "ideology" and "utopia" in *The Political Unconscious: Narrative as a Socially Symbolic Act* (Ithaca: Cornell Univ. Press, 1981), p. 291: "Any Marxist analysis of culture . . . can no longer be content with its demystifying vocation to unmask and to demonstrate the ways in which a cultural artifact fulfills a specific ideological mission, in legitimating a given power structure, in perpetuating and reproducing the latter, and in generating specific forms of false consciousness (or ideology in the narrower sense). It must not cease to practice this essentially negative hermeneutic function . . . but must also seek, through and beyond this demonstration of the instrumental function of a given cultural object, to project

its simultaneously Utopian power as the symbolic affirmation of a specific historical and class form of collective unity."

2. See Louis Althusser and Etienne Balibar, *Reading* Capital, trans. Ben Brewster (London: New Left Books, 1970), p. 28. Further elaborations and illustrations of the symptomatic reading can be found in Althusser, "A Letter on Art in Reply to André Daspre," *Lenin and Philosophy and Other Essays,* trans. Ben Brewster (London and New York: Monthly Review Press, 1971), pp. 221–27; Pierre Macherey, *A Theory of Literary Production,* trans. Geoffrey Wall (London: Routledge and Kegan Paul, 1978); Terry Eagleton, *Criticism and Ideology* (London: New Left Books, 1976); Thomas E. Lewis, "Notes toward a Theory of the Referent," *PMLA* 94 (1979): 459–75; and Jameson, *Political Unconscious,* chap. 1.

3. *The Marx-Engels Reader,* ed. Robert C. Tucker, 2d ed. (New York: W. W. Norton, 1978), p. 4. See also the statement of this concept in *Theses on Feuerbach* VI (ibid., p. 145): "The human essence is no abstraction inherent in each single individual. In its reality it is the ensemble of the social relations."

4. Althusser, *Reading* Capital, p. 180. Cf. Fredric Jameson, *Fables of Aggression: Wyndham Lewis, the Modernist as Fascist* (Berkeley and Los Angeles: Univ. of California Press, 1979), pp. 111–12: "The determination of the individual subject is an objective and historical process which must be approached on three distinct levels: (1) the linguistic, in which the individual subject is determined by language structures, as the subject of enunciation, or the shifter, and on the narrative level, as the effect of categories like the literary character, or point of view, or the more purely operational procedures of the reader of the schizophrenic 'text'; (2) the psychoanalytic, in which the 'existential experience' of consciousness is decentered and deconstructed as the constituted 'effect' of a structure whose dynamics are comprehensible only in terms of the hypothesis of an Unconscious; (3) the legal or juridical, in which the 'autonomy' of the bourgeois subject is generated by the 'equality'—or rather, the sheer equivalence—of the market system and by the 'freedom' to sell your own labor-power." Althusser's theory of the social formation is argued in "On the Materialist Dialectic," *For Marx,* trans. Ben Brewster (London: New Left Books, 1977), pp. 161–218.

5. Louis Althusser, "Ideology and Ideological State Apparatuses," *Lenin and Philosophy,* pp. 127–86. In this essay Althusser develops his earlier treatment of ideology in "Marxism and Humanism," *For Marx,* pp. 219–47. For a critical exposition of Althusser's formulations and revisions, see Ted Benton, *The Rise and Fall of Structural Marxism: Althusser and His Influence* (Basingstoke and London: Macmillan, 1984), esp. chap. 5.

6. Althusser, "Ideology and Ideological State Apparatuses," pp. 162, 169. For a clarification of the distinction between "cognitive" and "materialist" conceptions of ideology, see Jonathan Dollimore, *Radical Tragedy: Religion, Ideology, and Power in the Drama of Shakespeare and His Contemporaries* (Brighton: Harvester, 1984), pp. 9–11.

7. Tony Bennett, *Formalism and Marxism* (London and New York: Methuen, 1979), p. 138. Benton also offers an incisive critique of Althusser's science-ideology dichotomy in *Rise and Fall of Structural Marxism,* pp. 45–51, 83–96. Althusser's epistemological arguments are presented in "On the Materialist Dialectic," *For Marx,* pp. 161–218, and "From *Capital* to Marx's Philosophy," *Reading* Capital, pp. 11–69. Althusser attempted, unsuccessfully, to revise some of these arguments in his *Essays in Self-Criticism,* trans. Grahame Locke (London: New Left Books, 1976).

8. Benton, *Rise and Fall of Structural Marxism,* p. 105.

9. Anthony Giddens, *Central Problems in Social Theory: Action, Structure, and Contradiction in Social Analysis* (Berkeley and Los Angeles: Univ. of California Press, 1979), chap. 2, "Agency, Structure."

10. Catherine Belsey, *Critical Practice* (London and New York: Methuen, 1980), esp. chap. 3.

11. This follows Göran Therborn's description of the "three fundamental modes of ideological interpellation" in *The Ideology of Power and the Power of Ideology* (London: Verso, 1980), p. 18.

12. I am here indebted to the theory of discourse presented in Ernesto Laclau and Chantal Mouffe, *Hegemony and Socialist Strategy: Toward a Radical Democratic Politics,* trans. Winston Moore and Paul Cammack (London: Verso, 1985), pp. 105–14. In order to develop Althusser's theories of the social formation and ideology, Laclau and Mouffe appropriate poststructuralist theories of textuality and subjectivity put forth by Jacques Derrida and Michel Foucault. Some of Laclau and Mouffe's developments are incisive and useful (e.g., their arguments against the priority Althusser assigns to economic determinations—"in the last instance"—in any social formation), but their appropriation of poststructuralism leads to the extreme of reducing the social formation to discourse and unnecessarily abandoning the distinction between discursive and nondiscursive social practices. This distinction recognizes the specificity and relative autonomy of social practices and is therefore important not only for materialist cultural history, with its project of reconstructing the contradictory social determinations of cultural practices, but also for any political project of social transformation, which must be based on such a reconstruction.

13. Frederic Jameson, *Marxism and Form: Twentieth-Century Dialectical Theories of Literature* (Princeton: Princeton Univ. Press, 1971), pp. 84–85. See also Cornel West's helpful treatment of Jameson's work, "Ethics and Action in Fredric Jameson's Marxist Hermeneutics," in *Postmodernism and Politics,* ed. Jonathan Arac (Minneapolis: Univ. of Minnesota Press, 1986), pp. 123–44.

14. See Fredric Jameson, "Postmodernism, or the Cultural Logic of Late Capitalism," *New Left Review* 146 (July–August 1984): 53–92.

15. Clodovis Boff and Leonardo Boff, *Liberation Theology: From Dialogue to Confrontation,* trans. Robert R. Barr (San Francisco: Harper and Row, 1986), pp. 13–14.

16. Ernesto Laclau, *Politics and Ideology in Marxist Theory* (London: New Left Books, 1977), p. 110. Chantal Mouffe derives this nonreductionist conception of ideology from Gramsci: see her "Hegemony and Ideology in Gramsci," in *Gramsci and Marxist Theory,* ed. Chantal Mouffe (London: Routledge and Kegan Paul, 1979), pp. 168–204.

17. A survey of some of the main ideological positions in early Stuart historiography is offered by Lawrence Stone in his review essay "The Century of Revolution," *New York Review of Books* 34:3 (February 26, 1987): 38–43. See also R. C. Richardson, *The Debate on the English Revolution* (New York: St. Martin's, 1977).

18. Martin Butler criticizes this traditional view in *Theater and Crisis, 1632–1642* (Cambridge: Cambridge Univ. Press, 1980).

19. In "The Halcyon Moment of Stillness in Royalist Poetry," *Huntington Library Quarterly* 44 (1981): 205–21, Dolores Palomo discusses the recurrence of the word "halcyon" in Caroline texts as an allusion to the Ovidian myth of Ceyx and Alcyone (*Metamorphoses* XI), arguing that "before the [civil] war, the use of the halcyon myth suggests the awareness of conflict looming on the horizon" (p. 206).

CHAPTER ONE: *The Ideology of the Individual in Anglo-American Criticism*

1. Fredric Jameson and Tony Bennett have made important contributions in this area. See Jameson, "Marxism and Historicism," *New Literary History* 11 (1979): 41–73, and *The Political Unconscious: Narrative as a Socially Symbolic Act* (Ithaca: Cornell Univ. Press, 1981), esp. chaps. 1 and 2; and Bennett, *Formalism and Marxism* (London and New York: Methuen, 1979), esp. pt. 2, and "Text and History," in *Re-reading English,* ed. Peter Widdowson (London and New York: Methuen, 1982), pp. 223–36. For a related perspective that seeks to read recent critical trends in the context of contemporary American social developments, see Edward Said, "Opponents, Audiences, Constituencies, and Community," *Critical Inquiry* 9 (1982): 1–26.

2. Frank Kermode, "Institutional Control of Interpretation," *Salmagundi* 43 (1979): 72–86.

3. Stephen Lukes offers a convenient survey of the concept in *Individualism* (Oxford: Basil Blackwell, 1973). Among literary critics, Lillian Furst discusses "individualism" as a defining characteristic of the romantic movement in *Romanticism in Perspective* (New York: St. Martin's, 1969), pp. 55–115.

4. For the work of rehabilitation, see, for example, M. H. Abrams, *The Mirror and the Lamp: Romantic Theory and the Critical Tradition* (Oxford: Oxford Univ. Press, 1953), pp. 222–25, and Richard Harter Fogle, *The Idea of Coleridge's Criticism* (Berkeley and Los Angeles: Univ. of California Press, 1962), pp. 66–67. René Wellek finds fault with Coleridge's contradictions in

A History of Modern Criticism, 1750–1950 (New Haven: Yale Univ. Press, 1955), 2: 185–87.

5. In *The Statesman's Manual*, in *Lay Sermons*, ed. R. J. White (Princeton: Princeton Univ. Press, 1972), p. 29, Coleridge defines the imagination as "that reconciling and mediatory power, which incorporating the Reason in Images of the Sense, and organizing (as it were) the flux of the Senses by the permanence and self-circulating energies of the Reason, gives birth to a system of symbols, harmonious in themselves, and consubstantial with the truths of which they are the *conductors*."

Unless otherwise noted, citations of Coleridge's criticism will be drawn from the following editions: *Biographia Literaria*, ed. J. Shawcross (Oxford: Oxford Univ. Press, 1907), 2 vols., hereafter designated as *BL* in the text; *Shakespearean Criticism*, ed. T. M. Raysor (London: J. M. Dent, 1960), 2 vols., hereafter designated as *SC* in the text.

6. Abrams, *Mirror and the Lamp*, p. 225. Jonathan Culler has also called attention to the contradictory nature of romantic "organicism" in "The Mirror Stage," in *High Romantic Argument: Essays for M. H. Abrams*, ed. Lawrence Lipking (Ithaca: Cornell Univ. Press, 1981), pp. 149–63. Cf. Kant's principle for the "will" in *The Moral Law* (1785; trans. H. J. Paton, 1956): "All maxims are repudiated which cannot accord with the will's own enactment of universal law. The will is therefore not merely subject to the law, but is so subject that it must be considered as also *making the law* for itself and precisely on this account as first of all subject to the law (of which it can regard itself as the author)." Quoted in Lukes, *Individualism*, pp. 54–55.

7. I borrow the term "grades of relevance" from Catherine Lord, "Organic Unity Reconsidered," *Journal of Aesthetics and Art Criticism* 22 (1964): 263–68. William K. Wimsatt also offers a skeptical "reconsidered" view of organic unity in "Organic Form: Some Questions about a Metaphor," in *Organic Form: The Life of an Idea*, ed. G. S. Rousseau (London and Boston: Routledge and Kegan Paul, 1972), pp. 61–81.

8. Thomas McFarland, *Romanticism and the Forms of Ruin: Wordsworth, Coleridge, and Modalities of Fragmentation* (Princeton: Princeton Univ. Press, 1981), p. 21. For the succession of phases in Coleridge's criticism, see Timothy Corrigan, *Coleridge, Language, and Criticism* (Athens: Univ. of Georgia Press, 1982). In *Coleridge's Poetics* (Oxford: Basil Blackwell, 1983), Paul Hamilton offers a much more detailed development of the gaps and inconsistencies in the *Biographia Literaria* than I can give here, specifically calling attention to Coleridge's "repression" of a materialist and collective notion of language, his "theory of desynonymy," a "radical notion that philosophical discovery springs from the discriminating use of a shared language" (p. 97).

9. Jerome McGann, *The Romantic Ideology: A Critical Investigation* (Chicago: Univ. of Chicago Press, 1983), p. 91.

10. For the historical view, the seminal works are Arnold Hauser, *The Social History of Art*, trans. Stanely Godman (New York: Vintage, 1958), 3:177–79,

208; Raymond Williams, *Culture and Society, 1780–1950* (New York: Harper and Row, 1958), chap. 2, "The Romantic Artist"; and Allan Rodway, *The Romantic Conflict* (London: Chatto and Windus, 1963). It is only in recent years that this view of romanticism has had renewed interest for critics. In addition to Jerome McGann's work cited above, see also David Aers, Jonathan Cook, and David Punter, *Romanticism and Ideology* (London: Routledge and Kegan Paul, 1981).

11. Jameson, *Political Unconscious,* p. 81.

12. See Marilyn Katz, "Early Dissent between Wordsworth and Coleridge: Preface Deletion of October, 1800," *Wordsworth Circle* 9 (1979): 50–56. In a letter to Robert Southey in 1802 Coleridge stated that "Wordsworth's Preface is half a child of my own Brain / & so arose out of Conversations so frequent, that with few exceptions we could scarcely either of us perhaps positively say, which first started any particular Thought" (*Collected Letters of Samuel Taylor Coleridge,* ed. Earl Leslie Griggs [Oxford: Oxford Univ. Press, 1956], 2:830). All quotations of the preface to the 1800 edition of *Lyrical Ballads* follow the text in *The Prose Works of William Wordsworth,* ed. W. J. B. Owen and Jane Worthington Smyser (Oxford: Oxford Univ. Press, 1974), 1:118–58.

13. In this fragmentary lecture note, Coleridge makes several autobiographical references which apparently date it to 1812, although the date remains doubtful. T. M. Raysor points out that "the watermark is 1805" (*SC,* 1:186n).

14. Williams, *Culture and Society,* p. 40.

15. Cf. David Morse, *Perspectives on Romanticism* (London: Macmillan, 1981), p. 36: "The discourse of romanticism postulates two selves within the individual: a deep, authentic self and a social self. The contradiction between these two selves produces insincerity and inauthenticity, but this has to be overcome by a psychic movement that will bring them once more into alignment. . . . Initially the social sphere—which is to say the performed, ready-made identity of social existence—overlays the deeper self, simultaneously producing within the individual a sense of hypocrisy and a sense of powerlessness."

16. This repression can also be seen in romantic poetry. In "Wordsworth's Model of Man in 'The Prelude'" (in Aers, Cook, and Punter, *Romanticism and Ideology,* pp. 64–81), David Aers argues that Wordsworth "manifests a consistent tendency to delete social activities and relationships which are essential to human identity, to strip man of all specific determinants as a historical being, erecting a cult of abstract individualism quite as thoroughgoing as any he attacked (cf. 'Prelude,' XII.69–87 and such typical claims as that at IV. 222–5)."

17. Louis Althusser, "Marxism and Humanism," *For Marx,* trans. Ben Brewster (London: New Left Books, 1977), pp. 219–47 (233–34).

18. Williams, *Culture and Society,* p. 43.

19. Nicos Poulantzas, *Political Power and Social Classes,* trans. Timothy O'Hagan (London: Verso, 1975), p. 219.

20. Karl Marx, *Grundrisse,* trans. Martin Nicolaus (New York: Vintage, 1973), p. 83; Poulantzas, *Political Power and Social Classes,* p. 215.

21. Louis Althusser, "A Letter on Art in Reply to André Daspre," *Lenin and Philosophy,* trans. Ben Brewster (London and New York: Monthly Review Press, 1971), p. 221–28 (223).

22. See M. H. Abrams, "English Romanticism: The Spirit of the Age" (1963), rpt. in *Romanticism and Consciousness,* ed. Harold Bloom (New York: W. W. Norton, 1970), pp. 91–119; E. P. Thompson, "Disenchantment or Default? A Lay Sermon," in *Power and Consciousness,* ed. Conor Cruise O'Brien and William Dean Vanech (New York: New York Univ. Press, 1969), pp. 149–82; and Stuart Peterfreund, "Coleridge and the Politics of Critical Vision," *Studies in English Literature, 1500–1900* 21 (1981): 585–604.

23. See Murray Krieger, *The New Apologists for Poetry* (Minneapolis: Univ. of Minnesota Press, 1956); Frank Kermode, *Romantic Image* (London: Routledge and Kegan Paul, 1957); George Bornstein, *Transformations of Romanticism in Yeats, Eliot, and Stevens* (Chicago: Univ. of Chicago Press, 1976); and Edward Lobb, *T. S. Eliot and the Romantic Critical Tradition* (London: Routledge and Kegan Paul, 1981). Krieger argues that the antiromantic theories of T. E. Hulme are also indebted to the Coleridgean imagination: see pp. 46–56.

24. T. S. Eliot, *Selected Essays* (New York: Harcourt, Brace, and World, 1950), pp. 7–8. Unless otherwise noted, all quotations from Eliot's criticism follow this edition of his essays; page references will be given in the text.

25. Quoted by F. O. Matthiessen, *The Achievement of T. S. Eliot: An Essay on the Nature of Poetry,* 2d ed. (London: Oxford Univ. Press, 1947), p. 90. Cf. Coleridge's remark that the "great poet" has "the power of so carrying on the eye of the reader as to make him almost lose the consciousness of words—to make him *see* everything—and this without exciting any painful and laborious attention" (*SC,* 1:189).

26. See Antony Easthope, *Poetry as Discourse* (London and New York: Methuen, 1983), pp. 8–9, 135–37.

27. Lobb finds, however, that "the inconsistency is only apparent" and attempts a distinctively romantic (and equally contradictory) rehabilitation of Eliot's discourse by characterizing the artist as a transcendental subject: "We cannot hope to escape from our personalities: we necessarily see the world from a point of view and write from our own, at least partly private, sense of the world. The artist therefore need not eliminate what is distinctive and personal in his view of things, but he must be careful to prevent its seeming *merely* personal, an addition to the facts" (*T. S. Eliot and the Romantic Critical Tradition,* p. 50). But cf. Eliot in "John Ford" (1932): "A man might, hypothetically, compose any number of fine passages or even of whole poems which would each give satisfaction, and yet not be a great poet, unless we felt them

to be united by one significant, consistent, and developing personality. Shakespeare is the one, among all his contemporaries, who fulfills these conditions" (p. 179).

28. T. S. Eliot, "London Letter," *The Dial* 70 (1921): 448–53; hereafter designated in the text as *D 70*.

29. T. S. Eliot, "London Letter," *The Dial* 72 (1922): 510–13; hereafter designated in the text as *D 72*.

30. Terry Eagleton, *Literary Theory: An Introduction* (Minneapolis: Univ. of Minnesota Press, 1983), p. 39. Eagleton offers a sketch of Eliot's revision of the literary tradition: "The Metaphysical poets and Jacobean dramatists were suddenly upgraded; Milton and the Romantics were rudely toppled; selected European products, including the French Symbolists, were imported" (p. 38).

31. In *To Criticize the Critic* (New York: Farrar, Straus, and Giroux, 1965), Eliot confessed that when he wrote his early critical essays, "both in my general affirmations about poetry and in writing about authors who had influenced me, I was implicitly defending the sort of poetry that I and my friends wrote" (p. 16).

32. My observations on the class anxiety in Eliot's discourse are indebted to Fredric Jameson's discussion of the crisis of the subject during the 1920s in *Fables of Aggression: Wyndham Lewis, the Modernist as Fascist* (Berkeley and Los Angeles: Univ. of California Press, 1979), pp. 110–14. Regarding the similarity between Lewis and Eliot, Jameson notes that "both the defense of individualism and the strong personality against the inroads of the masses, and the abdication of the personality to the security of spiritual and temporal authority remain locked into the categories of the individual subject, and, mere ideological permutations of the same underlying [ideological] system, stand as complementary responses to the same fundamental experience of *anomie*" (p. 116).

33. Poulantzas, *Political Power and Social Classes*, p. 219. In "Deconstruction and Social Theory: The Case of Liberalism," included in *Displacement: Derrida and After*, ed. Mark Krupnick (Bloomington: Indiana Univ. Press, 1983), pp. 154–68, Michael Ryan similarly notes that "the institution of political sovereignty mediates between natural right or equality and the actual social inequality caused by the disproportion in property ownership that liberal theory is designed to legitimate. Liberal theory accomplishes this legitimation by recourse either to the concept of a contractual exchange of rights for security (Hobbes, *Leviathan*) or to the concept of a scientific ratio or proportion in civil society between between unequal parts (Rousseau, *The Social Contract*)" (p. 157). For the antinomies of liberal political theory, see also Andrew Levine, *Liberal Democracy: A Critique of Its Theory* (New York: Columbia Univ. Press, 1981).

34. Robert Weimann, *Structure and Society in Literary History*, rev. ed. (Baltimore: Johns Hopkins Univ. Press, 1984), pp. 77–78.

35. For Eliot's relation to the New Criticism and the *Scrutiny* group, see

John Guillory, "The Ideology of Canon-Formation: T. S. Eliot and Cleanth Brooks," *Critical Inquiry* 10 (1983): 173–98; Frank Lentricchia, *After the New Criticism* (Chicago: Univ. of Chicago Press, 1980), pp. 109–10; and Weimann, *Structure and Society in Literary History,* pp. 59–60.

36. Ernest Mandel, *Late Capitalism,* trans. Joris De Bres (London: New Left Books, 1975), pp. 190–91; the italics in this passage are Mandel's.

37. *The Popular Culture Reader,* ed. Christopher D. Geist and Jack Nachbar, 3d ed. (Bowling Green: Bowling Green Univ. Popular Press, 1983), contains several interesting ideological critiques of popular stereotypes, myths, and heroes: see especially Madonna Marsden, "The American Myth of Success: Visions and Revisions," pp. 67–80; Bruce Lohof, "The Higher Meaning of Marlboro Cigarettes," pp. 111–21; and Eric Patterson, "The Critique of Authority in Clint Eastwood's Police Movies," pp. 246–61.

38. Jean Baudrillard, "The Implosion of Meaning in the Media," in *In the Shadow of the Silent Majorities . . . Or the End of the Social,* trans. Paul Foss, Paul Patton, and John Johnston (New York: Semiotext[e], 1983), pp. 95–110 (102).

39. Jean Baudrillard, *Simulations,* trans. Paul Foss, Paul Patton, and Philip Beitchman (New York: Semiotext[e], 1983), pp. 117, 130; hereafter designated as *S* in the text.

40. Max Horkheimer and Theodor Adorno, "The Culture Industry: Enlightenment as Mass Deception," *Dialectic of Enlightenment,* trans. John Cumming (New York: Continuum, 1972), pp. 120–67 (137, 140); hereafter designated as *CI* in the text.

41. Fredric Jameson, "Postmodernism, or the Cultural Logic of Late Capitalism," *New Left Review* 146 (July–August 1984): 53–92 (71).

42. Chantal Mouffe, "Hegemony and Ideology in Gramsci," in *Gramsci and Marxist Theory,* ed. Mouffe (London: Routledge and Kegan Paul, 1979), pp. 168–204 (170).

43. Roland Barthes, "The Death of the Author," in *Image-Music-Text,* ed. and trans. Stephen Heath (New York: Hill and Wang, 1977), pp. 142–48 (146).

44. Weimann, *Structure and Society in Literary History,* p. 275–76. Michel Foucault's brand of poststructuralist historicism would seem to be an exception to this trend, although Weimann is careful to observe that "even when a good many poststructuralist critics, especially those following Michel Foucault, would grant the validity of such involvement of the text in the world of nondiscursive history, they still tend to ignore or minimize the implication of their own writing in historical acts of social practice and political power" (p. 275).

45. Jacques Derrida, "Structure, Sign, and Play in the Discourse of the Human Sciences," in *The Structuralist Controversy: The Languages of Criticism and the Sciences of Man,* ed. Richard Macksey and Eugenio Donato (Baltimore: Johns Hopkins Univ. Press, 1970), pp. 247–65 (280); Roland Barthes, *The*

Pleasure of the Text, trans. Richard Miller (New York: Hill and Wang, 1975), p. 14; Gilles Deleuze and Félix Guattari, *Anti-Oedipus: Capitalism and Schizophrenia,* trans. Robert Hurley, Mark Seem, and Helen R. Lane (Minneapolis: Univ. of Minnesota Press, 1983), p. 370.

46. Lentricchia, *After the New Criticism,* pp. 181–82; see also p. 186: "American poststructuralist literary criticism tends to be an activity of textual privatization, the critic's doomed attempt to retreat from a social landscape of fragmentation and alienation. Criticism becomes, in this perspective, something like an ultimate mode of interior decoration whose chief value lies in its power to trigger our pleasures and whose chief measure of success lies in its capacity to keep pleasure going in a potentially infinite variety of ways."

47. Jameson, *Political Unconscious,* p. 125.

48. Jameson, "Postmodernism," pp. 73, 66.

CHAPTER TWO: *The Marginalization of Philip Massinger's Plays*

1. *The Plays and Poems of Philip Massinger,* ed. Philip Edwards and Colin Gibson (Oxford: Oxford Univ. Press, 1976), p. lxvi. Edwards and Gibson mention two critics who omit Massinger from their historical surveys: Una Ellis-Fermor, *Jacobean Drama* (London: Chatto and Windus, 1936), and Robert Ornstein, *The Moral Vision of Jacobean Tragedy* (Madison: Univ. of Wisconsin Press, 1959). Massinger is also missing from Brian Gibbons, *Jacobean City Comedy,* 2d ed. (London and New York: Methuen, 1980).

2. John Webster's plays might also seem to occupy a similarly marginal position in the canon. In the introduction to their edition of *The Selected Plays of John Webster* (Cambridge: Cambridge Univ. Press, 1983), Jonathan Dollimore and Alan Sinfield rightly note that the conflicting opinions Webster has provoked from a number of influential critics make him "one of the most controversial of English playwrights" (p. xi). Yet the fact remains that unlike Massinger, Webster has not encountered the consensus of dismissive judgments and subsequent neglect which define the status of marginal or even minor playwrights; on the contrary, as his editors point out, "his work has attracted a vast amount of critical attention as can be seen from the various collections of, and bibliographical guides to it" (p. xi).

3. Tony Bennett, "Text and History," in *Re-reading English,* ed. Peter Widdowson (London and New York: Methuen, 1982), p. 235.

4. *Coleridge's Miscellaneous Criticism,* ed. T. M. Raysor (1936; rpt. Folcroft, Pa.: Folcroft Press, 1969), p. 93. Unless otherwise noted, quotations from Coleridge's criticism of Massinger will follow this edition, hereafter designated as *MC* in the text.

5. See also *Specimens of the Table Talk of the Late Samuel Taylor Coleridge,* ed. H. N. Coleridge (London: John Murray, 1835), 2:135–36: "Massinger often deals in exaggerated passion. Malefort senior, in *The Unnatural Combat,*

however he may have had the moral will to be so wicked, could never have actually done all that he is represented as guilty of, without losing his senses. He would have been, in fact, mad."

6. The phrase "envy demonstrated" is the reading of Coleridge's manuscript accepted by R. F. Brinkley, the editor of the compilation *Coleridge on the Seventeenth Century* (1955; rpt. New York: Greenwood Press, 1968), p. 674, hereafter designated as *CS* in the text. In a note Brinkley adds that Raysor (*Coleridge's Miscellaneous Criticism,* p. 95) reads "'democratic' with a question, but the word is clear."

7. The lecture notes were first published in *The Literary Remains of Samuel Taylor Coleridge,* ed. H. N. Coleridge (London: William Pickering, 1836), 1:108–13; additional comments appeared in *Specimens of the Table Talk of the Late Samuel Taylor Coleridge,* ed. H. N. Coleridge.

8. Terry Eagleton, *The Function of Criticism: From The Spectator to Post-Structuralism* (London: Verso, 1984), p. 57.

9. All quotations of this essay follow the text reprinted in Stephen's collection *Hours in a Library* (New York: G. P. Putnam's Sons, n.d.), pp. 334–81. Edwards and Gibson note the influence of Stephen's essay on Arthur Symons and Swinburne in *Plays and Poems of Philip Massinger,* p. lxiv. My discussion of the marginalization of Massinger's plays is indebted to Edwards and Gibson's "miniature history of taste" in their introduction (pp. xlv–lxvii).

10. In *Specimens of the English Dramatic Poets* (1808; rpt. London: George Bell and Sons, 1890), pp. 356–82, Charles Lamb presents selected excerpts from Massinger's plays with such remarks as that the playwright is ineffective in "many of those scenes in which [he] has attempted a deeper passion and more tragical interest. . . . He never shakes or disturbs the mind with grief" (pp. 364–65). A. W. Ward included Massinger in *A History of English Dramatic Literature* (1875, rev. ed. 1899; rpt. New York: Octagon, 1966), 3:1–47. Ward reiterates "the absence of high poetic genius" in Massinger, singling out his "defectiveness in characterization" for special blame: "The truth simply is that Massinger fell short of conspicuous success in exhibiting the successive stages of a moral conflict, and in thus securing personal sympathy to his representation of its progress, by means of the development of character in action. Thus he fails to satisfy the highest test of dramatic power" (p. 43).

11. See R. H. Ball, *The Amazing Career of Sir Giles Overreach* (1939; rpt. New York: Octagon, 1968), chaps. 3–5. Edwards and Gibson point out that measured by the number of editions of Massinger's works, the number of theatrical revivals and their success, and the number and prestige of the writers who read and commented on him, "the period between the publication of the Monck Mason edition in 1779 and the publication of Harness's edition in 1830, 'Adapted for family reading, and the use of young persons, by the omission of objectionable passages,' is Massinger's great half-century" (p. lv).

12. S. R. Gardiner, "The Political Element in Massinger," *Contemporary Review* 28 (1876): 495–507.

13. For an account of Whig historiography of the seventeenth century, see R. C. Richardson, *The Debate on the English Revolution* (New York: St. Martin's, 1977), chap. 4.

14. Eagleton, *Function of Criticism*, p. 49.

15. Eagleton, *Function of Criticism*, pp. 65–67; Fredric Jameson, *Fables of Aggression: Wyndham Lewis, the Modernist as Fascist* (Berkeley and Los Angeles: Univ. of California Press, 1979), p. 116.

16. Edmund Gosse, *The Jacobean Poets* (London: John Murray, 1899), pp. 208, 212.

17. A. H. Cruickshank, *Philip Massinger* (Oxford: Oxford Univ. Press, 1920), p. 19.

18. "Philip Massinger (1583–1640)," *Times Literary Supplement,* March 16, 1940, p. 134.

19. T. A. Dunn, *Philip Massinger: The Man and the Playwright* (London: Thomas Nelson and Sons, 1957). The quotations appear on pp. 54 and v, respectively.

20. Robert A. Fothergill, "The Dramatic Experience of Massinger's *The City Madam* and *A New Way to Pay Old Debts,*" *Univ. of Toronto Quarterly* 43 (1973): 68–86.

21. Michael Riffaterre, "Criteria for Style Analysis," *Word* 15 (1959): 154–74 (162).

22. All quotations of Massinger's play follow *The Plays and Poems of Philip Massinger,* ed. Edwards and Gibson.

23. Antony Easthope, *Poetry as Discourse* (London and New York: Methuen, 1983), chaps. 1–4.

24. Louis Althusser, "Ideology and Ideological State Apparatuses," *Lenin and Philosophy and Other Essays,* trans. Ben Brewster (London and New York: Monthly Review Press, 1971), pp. 127–86 (172).

25. Jonathan Powis offers some trenchant comments on the association of nobility with military distinction in *Aristocracy* (Oxford and New York: Basil Blackwell, 1984), chap. 1. The classic work is Marc Bloch, *Feudal Society,* trans. L. A. Manyon (Chicago: Univ. of Chicago Press, 1961), pp. 289–92. My understanding of feudal ideology is particularly indebted to Georges Duby's masterful treatment, which revises Bloch: see *The Three Orders: Feudal Society Imagined,* trans. Arthur Goldhammer (Chicago: Univ. of Chicago Press, 1980).

26. For the persistence and development of feudal social representations in England during the sixteenth and seventeenth centuries, see Lawrence Stone, *The Crisis of the Aristocracy* (Oxford: Oxford Univ. Press, 1965), chap. II, and Keith Wrightson, *English Society, 1580–1680* (London: Hutchinson, 1982), chap. 1. David Cressy presents a convenient survey of class hierarchies formulated by Renaissance writers in "Describing the Social Order of Elizabethan and Stuart England," *Literature and History* 3 (1976): 29–44.

27. Perry Anderson discusses the impact of absolutism on the feudal aristocracy in *Lineages of the Absolutist State* (London: New Left Books, 1974),

esp. chaps. 1 and 2. In particular, Anderson notes that "absolutism was essentially just this: *a redeployed and recharged apparatus of feudal domination*, designed to clamp the peasant masses back into their traditional social position—despite and against the gains they had won by the widespread commutation of dues. . . . it was the political carapace of a threatened nobility. . . . The new form of noble power was in its turn determined by the spread of commodity production and exchange, in the transitional social formations of the early modern epoch" (p. 18).

28. *The Political Works of James I,* ed. C. H. McIlwain (Cambridge: Harvard Univ. Press, 1918), pp. 22–24.

29. Gordon Schochet discusses the use of patriarchal arguments in defense of absolutism in *Patriarchalism in Political Thought* (Oxford: Basil Blackwell, 1975), esp. chap. 5.

30. Catherine Belsey, *Critical Practice* (London and New York: Methuen, 1980), p. 92. My approach here is also indebted to Jonathan Dollimore's *Radical Tragedy: Religion, Ideology, and Power in the Drama of Shakespeare and His Contemporaries* (Brighton: Harvester, 1984): "Jacobean tragedy discloses ideology as misrepresentation, it interrogates ideology from within, seizing on and exposing its contradictions and inconsistencies and offering alternative ways of understanding social and political process" (p. 8). My approach differs from Dollimore's by investigating the *social* determinants of this textual interrogation of ideology, whereas his study concentrates on intellectual currents, like the decay of belief in the providential order and the rediscovery of Greek scepticism, reading them as an ideological configuration in transition.

31. Dollimore, *Radical Tragedy,* chap. 10.

32. Belsey, *Critical Practice,* p. 86.

33. Eugene Waith, *The Pattern of Tragicomedy in Beaumont and Fletcher* (New Haven: Yale Univ. Press, 1952), pp. 38–39. Madeleine Doran's description of the genre also suggests the importance of "protean" characters: "As a conventional form, we usually mean by English Renaissance tragicomedy the Beaumont-and-Fletcher sort of thing, typically represented by either *Philaster* or *A King and No King*, the former more pathetic, the latter more melodramatic, but alike in the high rank of the principal characters, in a certain solemnity of sentiment, and in the clever management of plot so that *a surprise recognition or change of heart* brings about a dramatic reversal from extreme peril to good fortune" (*Endeavors of Art: A Study of Form in Elizabethan Drama* [Madison: Univ. of Wisconsin Press, 1954], pp. 186–87, my emphasis).

34. See Fredric Jameson, *The Political Unconscious: Narrative as a Socially Symbolic Act* (Ithaca: Cornell Univ. Press, 1981), chap. 2, esp. pp. 140–41: "In its emergent, strong form a genre is essentially a socio-symbolic message, or in other terms, that form is immanently and intrinsically an ideology in its own right. When such forms are reappropriated and refashioned in quite different social and cultural contexts, this message persists and must be functionally reckoned into the new form. . . . The ideology of the form itself, thus

sedimented, persists into the later, more complex structure as a generic message which coexists—either as a contradiction or, on the other hand, as a mediatory or harmonizing mechanism—with elements from later stages."

35. All quotations of *A King and No King* follow the text edited by Robert K. Turner, Jr. (Lincoln: Univ. of Nebraska Press, 1963).

36. Arthur Mizener, "The High Design of *A King and No King*," *Modern Philology* 38 (1940–41): 133–54 (144). John Danby has noted a similar feature in the erratic speeches of the title character in *Philaster* (1609): "It is a law of the Beaumont world that absolute committal removes the need for moral deliberation, and supervenes on conflict by suppression of one of the warring terms" ("Beaumont and Fletcher: Jacobean Absolutists," *Poets on Fortune's Hill* [1952; rpt. Port Washington, N.Y.: Kennikat Press, 1966], p. 167).

37. Nicos Poulantzas, *Political Power and Social Classes,* trans. Timothy O'Hagan (London: Verso, 1975), p. 207.

38. The locus classicus for the correspondences between body politic and microcosm is of course E. M. W. Tillyard, *The Elizabethan World Picture* (New York: Vintage, n.d.), pp. 94–99. W. H. Greenleaf discusses the equation of reason with princes and passion with subjects in *Order, Empiricism, and Politics: Two Traditions of English Political Thought, 1500–1700* (London: Oxford Univ. Press, 1964), pp. 30–31, where he quotes a relevant passage from Edward Forset's *A Comparative Discovrse Of The bodies Natvral And Politique* (London, 1606):

> The affections, so long as they be obedient vnto reason, standeth the soule in great steede; but if they become violent and vnrulie, then (of their disordering, and disturbing of the minds tranquillitie) they be rightly tearmed perturbations. Such is the Soueraignes case: If the people be tractable, and truely seruiceable, with all dutious subiection, in the nature of right alleagiance, then as louing subjects, by their forwardnesse in cooperating with him, they giue strength and stay vnto his gouernment: but if they turne mutinous and tumultuous, troubling the gouernour and State with seditious disorders, then be they as Rebels by the Iustice of the law to be suppressed, euen as the perturbations of the mind must be subdued by reason.

39. Cf. Dunn, *Philip Massinger*, p. 163: "In his political thought Massinger has two main concerns. The first of these is liberty, and the second, which is indissolubly linked with the first, is wise and just government. Inevitably, Massinger sees these, except perhaps in *The Bondman,* in a monarchical field of reference. But there is in him a Whiggism before the Whigs and a foreshadowing of that academic republicanism which crops up in eighteenth-century Whiggism as a sentiment rather than as practical politics and which at last became a doctrine with Tom Paine, Godwin, and Horne Tooke."

In "Shakespeare and the Stoicism of Seneca" (1927), Eliot noted the individualistic aspect of the Renaissance revival of Roman Stoicism: "Elizabethan England . . . was a period of dissolution and chaos; and in such a period any emotional attitude which seems to give a man something firm, even if it be only the attitude of 'I am myself alone,' is eagerly taken up. . . . the Senecan attitude of Pride, the Montaigne attitude of Scepticism, and the Machiavelli attitude of Cynicism, arrived at a kind of fusion in the Elizabethan individualism" (p. 112). More closely related to Massinger's play is J. W. Lever's view that "Renaissance Stoicism was not so much an academic theory as a practical discipline for men involved in the world of action, caught, whether they wished it or not, in the meshes of 'state'" (*The Tragedy of State* [London: Methuen, 1971], p. 10).

40. Stone, *Crisis of the Aristocracy*, chap. 8.

41. Anderson, *Lineages of the Absolutist State*, p. 128. Stone examines the political and financial situations of the conspirators in Essex's revolt (1600) and the Main and Bye plot (1603) in *Crisis of the Aristocracy*, pp. 481–88.

42. Stone, *Crisis of the Aristocracy*, p. 466. The factional struggles at court during the early part of James's reign are discussed by Menna Prestwich, *Cranfield: Politics and Profits under the Early Stuarts* (Oxford: Oxford Univ. Press, 1966), chap. 1.

43. Danby, "Beaumont and Fletcher," p. 157.

44. Poulantzas, *Political Power and Social Classes*, p. 203. My critique of Danby's reading has profited from Alan Sinfield, "Power and Ideology: An Outline Theory and Sidney's *Arcadia*," *ELH* 52 (1985): 259–77. It is noteworthy that the demystification of absolutist ideology which occurs in the tragicomedies of Beaumont and Fletcher and Massinger is also a feature of Jacobean tragedy: see Dollimore, *Radical Tragedy*, and Franco Moretti, *Signs Taken for Wonders: Essays in the Sociology of Literary Forms*, trans. Susan Fischer, David Forgacs, and David Miller (London: Verso, 1983), chap. 2.

45. The term "privileged" refers to Ann Jennalie Cook's study of Renaissance theater audiences, *The Privileged Playgoers of Shakespeare's London, 1576–1642* (Princeton: Princeton Univ. Press, 1981). Martin Butler offers some helpful criticisms of Cook's thesis and presents a considerable amount of evidence for the diverse political attitudes of the audiences in *Theater and Crisis, 1632–1642* (Cambridge: Cambridge Univ. Press, 1984), chap. 6 and appendix 2. See also Margot Heinemann, *Puritanism and Theater: Thomas Middleton and Opposition Drama under the Early Stuarts* (Cambridge: Cambridge Univ. Press, 1980), pp. 22–26.

46. Edwards and Gibson indicate that "there is no firm evidence for the dating of *The Maid of Honour* except for its publication in 1632," and on the basis of Massinger's relations with the acting companies at the Phoenix, they argue for a date of 1621–22 (*Poems and Plays of Philip Massinger*, pp. 105–6). Yet the evidence does point to the popularity of the play throughout Charles

I's reign: in addition to its publication, the fact that the text was protected by the Lord Chamberlain in 1639 suggests that it remained in the repertory during the 1630s and was frequently revived (Edwards and Gibson, p. 113).

47. Roger Lockyer, *Buckingham* (London and New York: Longman, 1981), chaps. 2–4.

48. Anderson, *Lineages of the Absolutist State*, p. 54.

49. Most recently, Heinemann has developed Gardiner's identification of Massinger's topical allusions in *Puritanism and Theater*, pp. 213–21.

50. Philip Edwards, *Threshold of a Nation* (Cambridge: Cambridge Univ. Press, 1979), p. 254n. Cf. the introduction to *The Maid of Honour* in *The Poems and Plays of Philip Massinger*, ed. Edwards and Gibson, 1:105–6: "The impartiality with which Massinger handles the motives and responses of the personalities, the expediency of the proposals, and the principles involved, make the idea that he was conducting political propaganda an absurdity." For similar criticisms of Gardiner's approach, see Alan Gross, "Contemporary Politics in Massinger," *Studies in English Literature, 1500–1900* 6 (1966): 279–90.

51. Butler, *Theater and Crisis*, p. 198. See also Anne Barton's insightful treatment of Elizabethanism in *Ben Jonson, Dramatist* (Cambridge: Cambridge Univ. Press, 1984), chap. 14.

52. Hayden White, "Historicism, History, and the Figurative Imagination," *Tropics of Discourse: Essays in Cultural Criticism* (Baltimore: Johns Hopkins Univ. Press, 1978), pp. 101–20 (117).

53. Fredric Jameson, "Marxism and Historicism," *New Literary History* 11 (1979): 41–73 (67).

54. Karl Marx, *Capital*, trans. Ben Fowkes (New York: Vintage, 1977), 1:170; Poulantzas, *Political Power and Social Classes*, pp. 211, 214–15.

55. Jameson, *Political Unconscious*, p. 95. Jameson is here following Poulantzas' development of the concept of mode of production in *Political Power and Social Classes*, pp. 15–16.

56. Jameson, "Marxism and Historicism," p. 70.

57. See Richard A. Burt, "'Licensed by Authority': Ben Jonson and the Politics of Early Stuart Theater," *ELH* 34 (1987): 529–60, and "'Tis Writ by Me': Massinger's *The Roman Actor* and the Politics of Reception in the English Renaissance Theater," *Theater Journal* 40 (1988): 332–46.

58. *Theater and Crisis*, p. 100.

59. *Coleridge on the Seventeenth Century*, pp. 655, 656.

60. Jameson, "Marxism and Historicism," p. 70.

CHAPTER THREE: *Transformations of City Comedy*

1. Knights's sociological approach is the point of departure for both the genre-oriented readings of Brian Gibbons, *Jacobean City Comedy*, 2d ed. (London and New York: Methuen, 1980), and the historical emphasis on patronage

and topical allusion of Margot Heinemann, *Puritanism and Theater: Thomas Middleton and Opposition Drama under the Early Stuarts* (Cambridge: Cambridge Univ. Press, 1980); and while both critics admit social determinants in textual production, like Knights they are limited by their inability to give equal attention to the text and its historical ground. The point is made by Susan Wells in *The Dialectics of Representation* (Baltimore: Johns Hopkins Univ. Press, 1985), pp. 104–5. Knights's influence on the reception of city comedy can also be seen in D. J. Enright, "Elizabethan and Jacobean Comedy," in *The Age of Shakespeare,* vol. 2 of *The Pelican Guide to English Literature,* ed. Boris Ford (Harmondsworth: Penguin, 1955), pp. 416–28; Patricia Thomson, "The Old Way and the New Way in Dekker and Massinger," *Modern Language Review* 51 (1956): 168–78; and C. L. Barber's introduction to his edition of Middleton's *A Trick to Catch the Old One* (Berkeley and Los Angeles: Univ. of California Press, 1968), pp. 1–7.

2. The seminal work is Francis Mulhern, *The Moment of "Scrutiny"* (London: New Left Books, 1979). My discussion of *Scrutiny* is also indebted to the more specialized studies of Derek Longhurst, "'Not for all time, but for an Age': An Approach to Shakespeare Studies," in *Re-reading English,* ed. Peter Widdowson (London and New York: Methuen, 1982), pp. 150–63, and Don E. Wayne, "Drama and Society in the Age of Jonson: An Alternative View," *Renaissance Drama* 13 (1982): 103–30.

3. F. R. Leavis and Denys Thompson, *Culture and Environment* (1933; rpt. London: Chatto and Windus, 1960), pp. 3, 48. Further page references will be given parenthetically in the text.

4. Mulhern distinguishes between the concepts of "tradition" developed by Eliot and *Scrutiny* (*Moment of "Scrutiny,"* pp. 116, 130), although something like the "organic community" can be glimpsed in Eliot's comments on "Elizabethan morality" in his essay on Massinger: "The Elizabethan morality was an important convention; important because it was not consciously of one class alone, because it provided a framework for emotions to which all classes could respond, and it hindered no feeling. It was not hypocritical, and it did not suppress" (*Selected Essays,* p. 189). Knights will later perform this same mystifying valorization of feudal ideology in his historical reconstruction of the organic community.

5. L. C. Knights, *Drama and Society in the Age of Jonson* (1937; rpt. New York: W. W. Norton, 1968), p. 17. Further page references will be given parenthetically in the text.

6. Mulhern, *Moment of "Scrutiny,"* p. 311.

7. Fredric Jameson, *The Political Unconscious: Narrative as a Socially Symbolic Act* (Ithaca: Cornell Univ. Press, 1981), p. 105. The quoted passages in my next two sentences, also from Jameson's discussion of genre, appear on pp. 106–7, 145. Wells has stressed the ad hoc quality of the generic concept "city comedy" in *The Dialectics of Representation,* p. 104.

8. For the concept of a transitional mode of production during the Ren-

aissance, see the theoretical arguments of Barry Hindess and Paul Q. Hirst, *Pre-Capitalist Modes of Production* (London: Routledge and Kegan Paul, 1975), chap. 6. Hindess and Hirst push the early Althusser's notion of a Marxist science to extremes of theoreticism, as Ted Benton notes: "an effective collapse of the order of the real into the order of theoretical discourse." See Benton's critique, *The Rise and Fall of Structural Marxism: Althusser and His Influence* (Basingstoke and London: Macmillan, 1984), pp. 181–97. For a more historically detailed presentation, see the classic debate in *The Transition from Feudalism to Capitalism,* ed. Rodney Hilton (London: Verso, 1978), esp. Hilton's contributions. The decisive rise of capitalism during the seventeenth century is argued by Christopher Hill, "A Bourgeois Revolution?" in *Three British Revolutions: 1641, 1688, 1776,* ed. J. G. A. Pocock (Princeton: Princeton Univ. Press, 1980), pp. 109–39.

9. Christopher Hill, *The Century of Revolution, 1603–1714* (New York: W. W. Norton, 1961), chap. 3; Lawrence Stone, *The Causes of the English Revolution, 1529–1642* (New York: Harper and Row, 1972), pp.72–76.

10. Lawrence Stone, *The Crisis of the Aristocracy, 1558–1641* (Oxford: Oxford Univ. Press, 1965), chaps. 6–7, and pp. 628–32.

11. Perry Anderson, *Lineages of the Absolutist State* (London: New Left Books, 1974), pp. 40–42.

12. Stone, *Crisis of the Aristocracy,* chap. 10 and pp. 184–88, 335–36, 381–84.

13. R. H. Tawney, *Religion and the Rise of Capitalism* (1926; rpt. Gloucester, Mass.: Peter Smith, 1962); Christopher Hill, "Covenant Theology and the Concept of 'A Public Person,'" in *Powers, Possessions, and Freedom,* ed. Alkis Kontos (Toronto: Univ. of Toronto Press, 1979), pp. 3–22; C. B. Macpherson, *The Political Theory of Possessive Individualism: Hobbes to Locke* (Oxford: Oxford Univ. Press, 1962).

14. Christopher Hill, *Society and Puritanism in Pre-Revolutionary England* (New York: Schocken, 1967), p. 494.

15. Robert Weimann, *Structure and Society in Literary History,* rev. ed. (Baltimore: Johns Hopkins Univ. Press, 1984), pp. 288–89.

16. All quotations of Jonson's plays follow the text in *Ben Jonson,* ed. C. H. Herford, Percy Simpson, and Evelyn Simpson, 11 vols. (Oxford: Oxford Univ. Press, 1925–52).

17. Stone, *Crisis of the Aristocracy,* p. 41.

18. Macpherson, *Political Theory of Possessive Individualism,* p. 3.

19. Gibbons' list of the cultural materials assimilated by city comedy includes the morality play, Roman comedy, the commedia dell'arte, Elizabethan nondramatic satire, and cony-catching pamphlets: see *Jacobean City Comedy,* chap. 1. Wells's generic construct for city comedy productively draws on Bakhtin's notion of the "carnivalesque" and includes various folk genres, pageants, satire, billingsgate: see *The Dialectics of Representation,* chap. 3.

20. The Plautine source for *The Alchemist* was noted by Herford, Simpson, and Simpson in *Ben Jonson,* 2:94–98.

21. I quote Plautus' *Mostellaria* from E. F. Watling's inventive translation, *The Ghost,* included in *The Rope and Other Plays* (Harmondsworth: Penguin, 1964). This passage appears on pp. 26–27; further page references will be given in the text. Quotations of Plautus' Latin follow *T. Macci Plauti Comoediae,* ed. W. M. Lindsay (Oxford: Oxford Univ. Press, 1905), vol. 2.

22. Donald Earl, *The Moral and Political Tradition of Rome* (London: Thames and Hudson, 1967), chap. 1. Michael Crawford describes the class hierarchy in *The Roman Republic* (Brighton: Harvester, 1978), chap. 3.

23. For the sumptuary legislation, see Crawford, *Roman Republic,* pp. 79–80, 88.

24. The definition for *erus* is taken from the *Oxford Latin Dictionary.* In *Ancient Slavery and Modern Ideology* (London: Chatto and Windus, 1980), p. 73, M. I. Finley notes the preference for *erus* in the comedies of Plautus and Terence. For the legal status of Roman slaves, see Finley, chap. 2, esp. pp. 73–77, and Erich Segal, *Roman Laughter: The Comedy of Plautus* (Cambridge: Harvard Univ. Press, 1968), pp. 102–3.

25. George Duckworth, *The Nature of Roman Comedy* (Princeton: Princeton Univ. Press, 1952), p. 251.

26. David Konstan, *Roman Comedy* (Ithaca: Cornell Univ. Press, 1983), p. 25. Konstan presents ideological critiques of several plays by Plautus, although unfortunately he does not include the *Mostellaria.* Regarding the position of the slave in the Roman ideology, Konstan writes that "he was a member of the household or *familia,* under the absolute dominion of the master, of course, but in this little different, at least in Rome, from the freeborn sons and daughters of the family, who were equally dependent on the sole authority of the paterfamilias" (p. 62). For an incisive treatment of social changes in Republican Rome, see Keith Hopkins, "Economic Growth and Towns in Classical Antiquity," in *Towns in Societies: Essays in Economic History and Historical Sociology,* ed. Philip Abrams and E. A. Wrigley (Cambridge: Cambridge Univ. Press, 1978), pp. 35–77; Hopkins discusses the economic expansion and mass slavery which followed Roman conquest on pp. 59–68.

27. Segal, *Roman Laughter,* pp. 9, 13.

28. W. Beare, *The Roman Stage,* 3d ed. (London: Methuen, 1964), pp. 162–63.

29. F. H. Sandbach, *The Comic Theater of Greece and Rome* (New York: W. W. Norton, 1977), p. 107.

30. See, for example, Alexander Leggatt, *Citizen Comedy in the Age of Shakespeare* (Toronto: Univ. of Toronto Press, 1973), p. 74: "We find ourselves taking sides. The confidence tricks are jokes shared with the audience."

31. Robert Greene, *A Notable Discovery of Cozenage,* in *Cony-Catchers and Bawdy Baskets,* ed. Gamini Salgado (Harmondsworth: Penguin, 1972), p. 171.

All quotations of Greene's pamphlets follow this edition; page numbers will be given parenthetically in the text. The allusion to Greene's pamphlet in *The Alchemist* is noted by Herford, Simpson, and Simpson, *Ben Jonson,* 10:57.

32. Walter Davis, *Idea and Act in Elizabethan Fiction* (Princeton: Princeton Univ. Press, 1969), pp. 184–85.

33. A. L. Beier, "Vagrants and the Social Order in Elizabethan England," *Past and Present* 64 (1974): 3–29; the quoted passage appears on pp. 10–11. See also Beier's study *Masterless Men: The Vagrancy Problem in England, 1560–1640* (London: Methuen, 1985), esp. chap. 1, where he traces the development and legislation of the theory that unemployment was a crime, noting that "the rogue literature . . . more than confirmed the learned theory of vagrancy; it elaborated and propagated it" (p. 8).

34. Surley's commodity swindle seems to allude to *The Defence of Cony-Catching* (1592), a pamphlet published under the pseudonym "Cuthbert Cony-Catcher" but long attributed to Greene; F. H. Mares annotates Mammon's lines by citing this pamphlet in his Revels edition of the play (Cambridge: Harvard Univ. Press, 1967), pp. 44–45.

35. Thomas Middleton, *A Chaste Maid in Cheapside,* ed. Alan Brissenden (London: Ernest Benn, 1968). My quotations are from this edition.

36. Thomas Dekker, *The Shoemaker's Holiday,* ed. D. J. Palmer (London: Ernest Benn, 1975). All quotations of the play are from this edition. Palmer discusses Eyre's suspect dealings in his introduction (pp. xv–xvi). See also Joel H. Kaplan, "Virtue's Holiday: Thomas Dekker and Simon Eyre," *Renaissance Drama* 2 (1969): 103–22.

37. Thomas Middleton, *Michaelmas Term,* ed. Richard Levin (Lincoln: Univ. of Nebraska Press, 1966).

38. Philip Massinger, *A New Way to Pay Old Debts,* ed. T. W. Craik (London: Ernest Benn, 1964). All quotations of the play are from this edition.

39. Friedrich Nietzsche, *On the Genealogy of Morals,* trans. Walter Kaufmann (New York: Vintage, 1969), pp. 20, 31. My use of Nietzsche is indebted to Jameson's problematization of Northrop Frye's concept of romance: see *The Political Unconscious,* pp. 113–19.

40. *Michaelmas Term,* ed. Levin, pp. xi–xiii. Massinger's Overreach has often been seen as an allusion to the notorious Sir Giles Mompesson: see Knights, *Drama and Society,* pp. 274–75.

41. I borrow the term "ideologeme" from P. N. Medvedev and M. M. Bakhtin, *The Formal Method of Literary Scholarship: A Critical Introduction to Sociological Poetics,* trans. Albert J. Wehrle (Baltimore: Johns Hopkins Univ. Press, 1978), pp. 21–23.

42. Gibbons, *Jacobean City Comedy,* pp. 129–30. See also pp. 118–19, where Gibbons states that "in the plays the growth of emphasis on the capitalist and lawyer in the city is accompanied by an increasing ambivalence of attitude towards their method and appetites."

43. Leggatt has pointed out the similar characterization of William Small-shanks, the prodigal gentleman in David, Lord Barry's comedy *Ram Alley* (c. 1608): "Our sympathy is enlisted for a hero who, instead of battling the vices of society, uses those vices for his own ends" (*Citizen Comedy,* p. 65).

44. *Michaelmas Term,* ed. Levin, pp. xviii–xix. See also Leggatt, *Citizen Comedy,* pp. 73–74: "At the last moment Middleton's anxiety to make a moral point throws the intrigue comedy off balance."

45. R. B. Parker, "Middleton's Experiments with Comedy and Judgment," in *Jacobean Theater,* ed. John Russell Brown and Bernard Harris (London: Edward Arnold, 1960), pp. 179–99.

46. Leggatt also cites the anonymous comedy *The Puritan* (1606): "The young scholar Pye-board intrigues against the family of a lately deceased usurer; he and one of his compatriots are about to seal their success by marrying the widow and her daughter when a noble reveals their deception and arranges safe, respectable marriages for the women instead. Throughout the play everything has been done to rouse our sympathies in favor of the young scoundrels and against the usurer's family, and their final defeat is simply disappointing" (*Citizen Comedy,* p. 74n). Jonson's *Bartholomew Fair* goes much farther than other city comedies in valorizing individualism, as Don Wayne has shown in "*Drama and Society in the Age of Jonson:* An Alternative View," pp. 120–27: "The Saturnalian conclusion of *Bartholomew Fair* compensates for the felt loss of a coherent moral code based on traditional, feudal conceptions of hierarchy, status, and *noblesse oblige* by offering a momentary vision that is as close as Jonson ever comes in his satires to an image of utopia, a vision of society in which mutual respect and tolerance are fundamental to the 'interests' of all members" (p. 124).

47. Unless otherwise noted, all quotations of Brome's plays follow *The Dramatic Works of Richard Brome,* 3 vols. (London: John Pearson, 1873). R. J. Kaufmann mentions the generic transformation represented by Crasy in *Richard Brome, Caroline Playwright* (New York: Columbia Univ. Press, 1961), p. 49.

48. Philip Massinger, *The City Madam,* ed. Cyrus Hoy (Lincoln: Univ. of Nebraska Press, 1964). All quotations of the play are from this edition.

49. This transformation of the conventional plot is also symptomatic of the conservative nature of late city comedy, since earlier plays in the genre, particularly Jonson's *The Alchemist* and *Bartholomew Fair,* subvert the "disguised duke": see Gibbons, *Jacobean City Comedy,* pp. 137–38, 149.

50. Alan Gerald Gross, "Social Change and Philip Massinger," *Studies in English Literature, 1500–1900* 7 (1967): 329–42; Martin Butler, "Massinger's *The City Madam* and the Caroline Audience," *Renaissance Drama* 13 (1982): 157–88.

51. Thomas Nabbes, *Covent Garden* (London, 1638).

52. C. V. Wedgwood similarly compares Overreach to the businessmen in the Caroline plays and finds that "beside him, financiers like Brome's Vermine

and Shirley's Hornet [in *The Constant Maid* (1640)] are mere pygmies." See her article "Comedy in the Reign of Charles I," in *Studies in Social History,* ed. J. H. Plumb (London: Longmans, Green, 1955), p. 119.

53. All quotations of this play follow *The Dramatic Works and Poems of James Shirley,* ed. William Gifford and Alexander Dyce (1833; rpt. New York: Russell and Russell, 1966), vol. 4. Page numbers will be given parenthetically in the text.

54. Martin Butler, *Theater and Crisis, 1632–1642* (Cambridge: Cambridge Univ. Press, 1984), p. 174.

55. Gordon Schochet, *Patriarchalism in Political Thought* (Oxford: Basil Blackwell, 1975), p. 64.

56. Quoted in ibid., p. 79.

57. S. M. Amussen, "Gender, Family, and the Social Order, 1560–1725," in *Order and Disorder in Early Modern England,* ed. Anthony Fletcher and John Stevenson (Cambridge: Cambridge Univ. Press, 1985), pp. 196–217.

58. I follow Catherine Belsey's lucid formulation of this moment in the history of the family in *The Subject of Tragedy: Identity and Difference in Renaissance Drama* (London and New York: Methuen, 1985), pt. 2, and "Disrupting Sexual Difference: Meaning and Gender in the Comedies," in *Alternative Shakespeares,* ed. John Drakakis (London and New York: Methuen, 1985), pp. 166–90, esp. pp. 167–77.

59. Hill, *Society and Puritanism in Pre-Revolutionary England,* p. 464.

60. Richard Levin, *New Readings vs. Old Plays: Recent Trends in the Reinterpretation of English Renaissance Drama* (Chicago: Univ. of Chicago Press, 1979), p. 159. Levin's discussion of this approach occurs on pp. 146–66.

61. Ibid., pp. 152–53.

62. Cf. the "uneasy ambiguity" that Michael Neill finds in Overreach's "patriarchal authority": "Massinger the conservative satirist is forced to argue that even the worst masters deserve to be obeyed, even while Massinger the romancer is vindicating the overthrow of tyrannical fathers. A sincere patriarchalist can hardly have it both ways, since the authority of fathers and masters is one and indivisible. But both ways are the way Massinger likes to have it." See Neill's "Massinger's Patriarchy: The Social Vision of *A New Way to Pay Old Debts,*" *Renaissance Drama* 10 (1979): 185–213, esp. 208ff.

63. See Eli Zaretsky, *Capitalism, the Family, and Personal Life* (New York: Harper and Row, 1976).

64. Wedgwood mentions a similar intrigue in Shirley's *The Gamester* (1633): "An unfaithful husband is reformed by being deceived into a belief that his virtuous wife has been unfaithful too. She herself is a cheerfully consenting party to his deception which goes on for several acts" ("Comedy in the Reign of Charles I," p. 124).

65. Northrop Frye, *Anatomy of Criticism* (Princeton: Princeton Univ. Press, 1957), pp. 163–64, 167.

66. John Fekete discusses the reification in Frye's criticism in *The Critical*

Twilight: Explorations in the Ideology of Anglo-American Literary Theory from Eliot to McLuhan (London: Routledge and Kegan Paul, 1977), chap. 9.

67. All quotations of *The Antipodes* follow the text edited by Ann Haaker (Lincoln: Univ. of Nebraska Press, 1966).

68. Ruth Kelso, *The Doctrine of the English Gentleman in the Sixteenth Century* (Urbana: Univ. of Illinois Press, 1929), pp. 88–91; Marc Bloch, *Feudal Society*, trans. L. A. Manyon (Chicago: Univ. of Chicago Press, 1961), p. 311; Stone, *Crisis of the Aristocracy*, pp. 41–44.

69. Ann Haaker notes that in antipodean London, "Brome . . . not only amasses mannerisms, prejudices, changing attitudes, and fears of London habitués, but employs all that is passing current in the theatrical chronicles of the time" (*Antipodes*, p. xiv). In *The World Upside-Down: Comedy from Jonson to Fielding* (Oxford: Oxford Univ. Press, 1970), pp. 89–90, Ian Donaldson adds that "the absurdities may remind us not only of those popularly depicted in illustrations of 'the world upside down,' but also of many of the classic absurdities of stage comedy." See also Kaufmann, *Richard Brome,* pp. 64–66.

70. Joe Lee Davis, "Richard Brome's Neglected Contribution to Comic Theory," *Studies in Philology* 40 (1943): 520–29; *Antipodes,* pp. xvii–xviii; Donaldson, *World Upside-Down,* pp. 95–96.

71. Donaldson, *World Upside-Down,* p. 97.

72. Robert Ashton, *The City and the Court, 1603–1643* (Cambridge: Cambridge Univ. Press, 1979), p. 108.

73. See also William H. Price, *The English Patents of Monopoly* (Boston: Houghton Mifflin, 1906).

74. Barry Coward, *The Stuart Age: A History of England, 1603–1714* (London: Longman, 1975), pp. 142–45.

75. My distinction between antagonistic and nonantagonistic forms of social contradiction is indebted to Mao Zedong, "On Contradiction," *Selected Works* (Beijing: Foreign Language Press, 1965), 1:311–47, and Louis Althusser, "Contradiction and Overdetermination" and "On the Materialist Dialectic," *For Marx,* trans. Ben Brewster (London: New Left Books, 1977), pp. 87–128, 161–218.

76. "Roger Manwaring: A Sermon Preached before the King at Oatlands, 4 July 1627," in *The Stuart Constitution, 1603–1688: Documents and Commentary,* ed. J. P. Kenyon (Cambridge: Cambridge Univ. Press, 1966), p. 16. Charles's attorney general, William Noy, argued similarly in his posthumously published *Treatise of the Principall Grounds and Maxims of the Laws of England* (Albany, N.Y.: Joel Munsell, 1870): "A Liberty is a Royal Privilege in the hands of a Subject. All Liberties are derived from the Crown" (pp. 60–61).

77. "Pym's Speech at Manwaring's Impeachment, 4 June 1628," in *The Stuart Constitution,* pp. 16–17. My treatment of the ideological ensemble of the parliamentary opposition to the royal government implicitly takes issue with the conservative portrait of Pym in Conrad Russell, "The Parliamentary Career of John Pym, 1621–9," in *The English Commonwealth, 1547–1640: Essays*

Presented to Joel Hurstfeld, ed. Peter Clark, Alan G. R. Smith, and Nicholas Tyacke (New York: Barnes and Noble, 1979), pp. 147–65.

78. Kenyon includes an excerpt from the "Proclamation Enjoining Residence in the Country, 20 June 1632," in *The Stuart Constitution* (pp. 502–3), treating it as part of Charles's "most ambitious scheme for the supervision of local government" (p. 493). I discuss the many social determinants and effects of this proclamation—political, economic, ideological—in the next chapter. On the allusions in Jonson's *The Devil is an Ass,* see Leah S. Marcus, *The Politics of Mirth: Jonson, Herrick, Milton, Marvell, and the Defense of Old Holiday Pastimes* (Chicago: Univ. of Chicago Press, 1986), chap. 3. My argument distinguishing the ideological standpoint of late city comedy from that of Parliament on the eve of the personal rule implicitly takes issue with Butler's view that they are the same: see *Theater and Crisis,* pp. 173–74.

79. Wardship is discussed by Stone, *Crisis of the Aristocracy,* pp. 600–605. For parliamentary opposition to wardship, see Alan G. R. Smith, "Crown, Parliament, and Finance: The Great Contract of 1610," in *English Commonwealth,* pp. 111–27.

80. Christopher Hill, "Sir Edward Coke—Myth-Maker," *Intellectual Origins of the English Revolution* (Oxford: Oxford Univ. Press, 1965), pp. 225–66; the quotations are taken from Hill's summary, pp. 256–57. The statements from Coke in this paragraph are quoted from Hill, p. 246.

81. J. G. A. Pocock, *The Ancient Constitution and the Feudal Law* (1957; rpt. New York: W. W. Norton, 1967), p. 75.

82. *Ben Jonson,* ed. Herford, Simpson, and Simpson, 10:223–26.

83. Butler, *Theater and Crisis,* pp. 134–40.

CHAPTER FOUR: *Topical Allusion and Textuality in the Court Masque*

1. For a suggestive account of these recent critical developments, see Jean E. Howard, "The New Historicism in Renaissance Studies," *English Literary Renaissance* 16 (1986): 13–43. I depart from Howard, however, in distinguishing the cultural materialism of British critics like Catherine Belsey, Antony Easthope, Jonathan Dollimore, and Alan Sinfield from American new historicism. These two developments in contemporary Renaissance studies originate in distinct social and cultural contexts, characterized by theoretical materials with different political meanings and aims. The origins of British cultural materialism lie in *Scrutiny* and New Left cultural historians like E. P. Thompson, Raymond Williams, Perry Anderson; those of American new historicism in the New Criticism and humanist historicism. For a discussion of these differences, see Don E. Wayne, "Power, Politics, and the Shakespearean Text: Recent Criticism in England and the United States," in *Shakespeare Reproduced: The Text in History and Ideology,* ed. Jean E. Howard and Marion F. O'Connor (London and New York: Methuen, 1987), pp. 47–67.

2. Stephen Orgel, *The Jonsonian Masque* (1965; rpt. New York: Columbia Univ. Press, 1981), p. viii. My observations on Orgel's work have profited from two recent studies: Jennifer Chibnall, "'To that secure fix'd state': The Function of the Caroline Masque Form," in *The Court Masque,* ed. David Lindley, The Revels Plays Companion Library (Manchester: Manchester Univ. Press, 1984), pp. 78–93, and Joanne Altieri, *The Theater of Praise: The Panegyric Tradition in Seventeenth-Century English Drama* (London and Toronto: Associated Univ. Presses, 1986), chap. 1.

3. Howard, "New Historicism in Renaissance Studies," p. 15.

4. Fredric Jameson, "Marxism and Historicism," *New Literary History* 11 (1979): 41–73, esp. pp. 50–51. Jameson's term for humanist historicism is "existential historicism." Thomas Greene neatly describes the theoretical lineage of post–World War II American Renaissance criticism in the preface to *The Vulnerable Text: Essays on Renaissance Literature* (New York: Columbia Univ. Press, 1986): "In my critical beginnings I was a child of the (Anglo-Saxon) New Criticism and Continental historicism; later I was exposed to the values of Renaissance Humanism" (p. xi).

5. Erich Auerbach, *Mimesis: The Representation of Reality in Western Literature,* trans. Willard R. Trask (Princeton: Princeton Univ. Press, 1953), p. 557. Auerbach discusses the relationship between his historicist method and modern fiction on pp. 546–53.

6. Stephen Orgel and Roy Strong, *Inigo Jones: The Theater of the Stuart Court* (Berkeley and Los Angeles: Univ. of California Press, 1973), 2 vols.; Orgel, *The Illusion of Power: Political Theater in the English Renaissance* (Berkeley and Los Angeles: Univ. of California Press, 1975). Unless otherwise noted, quotations in the next two paragraphs are drawn from *The Illusion of Power.*

7. Discussing Orgel's opposition to the "democratic imagination," David Norbrook argues that "the new defenders of the masque have sometimes been in danger of replacing one stereotype by another," what he describes as "a simple polarization" between "Puritans" and "Renaissance culture" as represented in court theater, among other forms of royal culture. See his article "The Reformation of the Masque," in *Court Masque,* pp. 94–110.

8. R. Malcolm Smuts, *Court Culture and the Origins of a Royalist Tradition in Early Stuart England* (Philadelphia: Univ. of Pennsylvania Press, 1987), p. 254.

9. Jonathan Goldberg, *James I and the Politics of Literature* (Baltimore: Johns Hopkins Univ. Press, 1983). My observations on Goldberg's study are indebted to the reviews of Jonathan Dollimore (*Criticism* 26 [1984]: 83–86) and Richard Helgerson (*Renaissance Quarterly* 38 [1985]: 180–83) and to Alan Sinfield, "Power and Ideology: An Outline Theory and Sidney's *Arcadia,*" *ELH* 52 (1985): 259–77.

10. Clifford Geertz, *Negara: The Theater State in Nineteenth-Century Bali* (Princeton: Princeton Univ. Press, 1980), pp. 9–10. Geertz describes the emergence of the textual model in the social sciences in "Blurred Genres: The

Refiguration of Social Thought" (1980), rpt. in *Critical Theory since 1965,* ed. Hazard Adams and Leroy Searle (Tallahassee: Florida State Univ. Press, 1986), pp. 514–23.

11. Vincent Crapanzano, "Hermes' Dilemma: The Masking of Subversion in Ethnographic Description," in *Writing Culture: The Poetics and Politics of Ethnography,* ed. James Clifford and George E. Marcus (Berkeley and Los Angeles: Univ. of California Press, 1986), pp. 51–76. Geertz discusses Elizabethan pageantry in "Centers, Kings, and Charisma: Reflections on the Symbolics of Power," in *Culture and Its Creators: Essays in Honor of Edward Shils,* ed. Joseph Ben-David and Terry Clark (Chicago: Univ. of Chicago Press, 1977), pp. 150–71.

12. Fredric Jameson, "The Ideology of the Text," *Salmagundi* 31–32 (1975–76): 204–46. Goldberg links poststructuralist textuality, advanced communications technology, and Renaissance culture in *Voice Terminal Echo: Postmodernism and English Renaissance Texts* (London and New York: Methuen, 1986).

13. That the poststructuralist fetish for indeterminacy can lead criticism to an extreme privatization of language is evident in Goldberg's "Reading (Herbert's 'Vertue') Otherwise," *Mississippi Review* 11:3 (1983): 51–64: "To speak of reading otherwise, to allow the act to take place with someone watching over your shoulder, means to reinscribe the primal scene. . . . What matters is the scene watching the scenario in the head. As in masturbation. So is the text there. So the reader. Such the economy of expenditure. Such the engagement with the text" (p. 52).

14. Sinfield, "Power and Ideology," p. 260.

15. In addition to the seminal studies of the masque by Orgel and Strong, Leah S. Marcus' work has done much to focus attention on topical allusions: see especially *The Politics of Mirth: Jonson, Herrick, Milton, Marvell, and the Defense of Old Holiday Pastimes* (Chicago: Univ. of Chicago Press, 1986). Rhodes Dunlap has identified the many allusions in Carew's *Coelum Britannicum* (1634) in his edition of *The Poems of Thomas Carew* (Oxford: Oxford Univ. Press, 1949), and they have been suggestively analyzed by Joanne Altieri in *The Theater of Praise,* pp. 79–87.

16. Ben Jonson, *The Complete Masques,* ed. Stephen Orgel (New Haven: Yale Univ. Press, 1969), p. 76. Line numbers will be given in the text within parentheses. Arthur Marotti has also warned against relying too heavily on seventeenth-century critical concepts in his review of Richard Peterson's *Imitation and Praise in the Poems of Ben Jonson* (New Haven: Yale Univ. Press, 1981): see *Renaissance Quarterly* 35 (1982): 526–28.

17. Goldberg illuminates the role of *arcana imperii* in absolutist ideology in *James I and the Politics of Literature,* pp. 56–57, 68–69.

18. Orgel identifies the preface's allusion to the Jonson-Daniel rivalry in *The Complete Masques,* pp. 474–75. See also the discussion in *The Jonsonian Masque,* pp. 103–6.

19. Bulstrode Whitelocke, *Memorials of the English Affairs* (London, 1682), p. 18. Further references will be given in the text.

20. James I was also disturbed by this development, and his criticisms of it in a speech delivered in Star Chamber became a source for Jonson's masque *The Vision of Delight* (1617). In *The Politics of Mirth,* pp. 67–76, Marcus finds Jonson's treatment to be conservative: "*The Vision of Delight* follows the king's analysis closely and creates through art the transformation his policies were intended to produce in reality" (p. 70).

21. F. J. Fisher, "The Development of London as a Center of Conspicuous Consumption in the Sixteenth and Seventeenth Centuries," in *Essays in Economic History,* ed. E. M. Carus-Wilson (New York: St. Martin's, 1962), 2:197–207; Lawrence Stone, *The Crisis of the Aristocracy, 1558–1641* (Oxford: Oxford Univ. Press, 1965), pp. 386–87; Philip Lee Ralph, *Sir Humphrey Mildmay: Royalist Gentleman* (New Brunswick, N.J.: Rutgers Univ. Press, 1947), pp. 17, 29, 53–57.

22. Stone, *Crisis of the Aristocracy,* pp. 387–92; Ralph, *Sir Humphrey Mildmay* pp. 25–26, 41, 44, 46–52.

23. Stone, *Crisis of the Aristocracy,* pp. 41–44; Marc Bloch, *Feudal Society,* trans. L. A. Manyon (Chicago: Univ. of Chicago Press, 1961), p. 311; Ruth Kelso, *The Doctrine of the English Gentleman in the Sixteenth Century* (Urbana: Univ. of Illinois Press, 1929), pp. 88–91; L. A. Clarkson, *The Pre-Industrial Economy of England, 1500–1750* (London: Batsford, 1971), pp. 228–32.

24. Stone, *Crisis of the Aristocracy,* pp. 392–93, 397–98; Christopher Hill, *The Century of Revolution, 1603–1714* (New York: W. W. Norton, 1961), pp. 26–28.

25. Sidney Webb and Beatrice Webb, *English Local Government* (London: Longmans, Green, 1906), 1:287, 294; L. M. Hill, "County Government in Caroline England, 1625–40," in *The Origins of the English Civil War,* ed. Conrad Russell (London: Macmillan, 1973), pp. 66–90.

26. L. M. Hill, "County Government in Caroline England," p. 70.

27. "The Book of Orders, 5 January 1631," rpt. in *The Stuart Constitution, 1603–1688: Documents and Commentary,* ed. J. P. Kenyon (Cambridge: Cambridge Univ. Press, 1966), p. 497.

28. Thomas G. Barnes, *Somerset, 1625–1640: A County's Government during the "Personal Rule"* (Cambridge: Harvard Univ. Press, 1961), pp. 196–202; L. M. Hill, "County Government in Caroline England," pp. 77–83; Anthony Fletcher, *A County Community in Peace and War: Sussex, 1600–1660* (London: Longman, 1975), pp. 224–26; Peter Clark, *English Provincial Society from the Reformation to the Revolution: Religion, Politics, and Society in Kent, 1550–1640* (Brighton: Harvester, 1977), pp. 350–53; Barry Coward, *The Stuart Age: A History of England, 1603–1714* (London: Longman, 1980), pp. 145–46.

29. "A Proclamation Commaunding the Gentry to keep their Residence at their Mansions in the Country, and forbidding them to make their Habitations in *London* and places adjoining," rpt. in *Foedera, conventiones, literae et cuiuscunque generis acta publica,* ed. Thomas Rymer and Robert Sanderson (1704–32), 19: 374.

30. Stone, *Crisis of the Aristocracy,* p. 398.

31. Christopher Hill, *Century of Revolution,* pp. 71–72; *Stuart Constitution,* p. 492; Fletcher, *County Community in Peace and War,* p. 224.

32. J. T. Cliffe, *The Yorkshire Gentry from the Reformation to the Civil War* (London: Athlone, 1969), pp. 295–96; Lawrence Stone, *The Causes of the English Revolution, 1529–1642* (New York: Harper and Row, 1972), p. 126; J. S. Morrill, *Cheshire, 1630–1660: County Government and Society during the English Revolution* (Oxford: Oxford Univ. Press, 1974), p. 26.

33. Alan Everitt, *Change in the Provinces: The Seventeenth Century,* Leicester University Department of English Local History Occasional Papers, Second Series, No. 1 (Leicester: Leicester Univ. Press, 1969), pp. 17–18. See also C. W. Chalkin, *Seventeenth-Century Kent* (London: Longman, Green, 1961), p. 203; Barnes, *Somerset,* p. 28; and Everitt, "The County Community," in *The English Revolution, 1600–1660,* ed. E. W. Ives (London: Edward Arnold, 1968), pp. 48–63.

34. Derek Hirst, *Authority and Conflict: England, 1603–1658* (London: Edward Arnold, 1986), p. 7. The "county community" school of local historians has been criticized by Clive Holmes, "The County Community in Stuart Historiography," *Journal of British Studies* 19:2 (1980): 54–73. See also Anthony Fletcher, "National and Local Awareness in the County Communities," in *Before the Civil War: Essays on Early Stuart Politics and Government,* ed. Howard Tomlinson (New York: St. Martin's, 1983), pp. 151–74.

35. In *The German Ideology* Marx observes: "If now in considering the course of history we detach the ideas of the ruling class from the ruling class itself and attribute to them an independent existence, if we confine ourselves to saying that these or those ideas were dominant at a given time, without bothering ourselves about the conditions of production and the producers of these ideas, if we thus ignore the individuals and world conditions which are the source of the ideas, we can say, for instance, that during the time that the aristocracy was dominant, the concepts honor, loyalty, etc., were dominant, during the dominance of the bourgeoisie the concepts freedom, equality, etc. The ruling class itself on the whole imagines this to be so" (*The Marx-Engels Reader,* ed. Robert C. Tucker, 2d ed. [New York: W. W. Norton, 1978], p. 173).

36. Fisher, "Development of London," p. 207; Christopher Hill, *Century of Revolution,* p. 72; Stone, *Causes of the English Revolution,* p. 124; Morrill, *Cheshire,* pp. 26–30; Coward, *Stuart Age,* p. 146. Charles's proclamation may have also been intended to subdue the London merchants and financiers who opposed his fiscal expedients by driving away their most wealthy clients, the nobility and gentry. For the business community's growing opposition to the royal government, see Robert Ashton, *The City and the Court, 1603–1643* (Cambridge: Cambridge Univ. Press, 1979).

37. All quotations of *The Triumph of Peace* follow *The Dramatic Works and Poems of James Shirley,* ed. William Gifford and Alexander Dyce (1833; rpt.

New York: Russell and Russell, 1966), 6:253–85. Page numbers will be given in the text.

38. For the "old fashioned" quality of Opinion's clothing, see C. Willet and Phillis Cunnington, *Handbook of English Costume in the Seventeenth Century* (London: Faber and Faber, 1955), pp. 13–22, 41–54, 65–70.

39. Richard Brathwaite, *The English Gentlewoman* (London, 1631), p. 11. Brathwaite's courtesy book turns into a jeremiad when it describes the morally corrupting effects which awaited women who frequented taverns: "what are our City or Country Ale-Houses, for most part, but the *Devils Boothes*, where all enormities are acted, all impieties hatched, all mischievous practices plotted and contrived? These are those sinkes of sinne, where all pollution and uncleannesse reigneth, where fearfull oathes and prophanation rageth, whence all sensuall libertie ariseth" (pp. 178–79).

40. William Rossky, "The Imagination in the English Renaissance: Psychology and Poetic," *Studies in the Renaissance* 5 (1958): 49–73. Opinion was regarded with the same suspicion. In what became a sourcebook for masque characters, Cesare Ripa's *Iconologia, overe descrittione di diverse imagini cavate dall'antichità, e di propria inventione* (1603; rpt. Hildesheim and New York: Georg Olms, 1970), opinion is defined as follows: "Opinion is perhaps everything in the mind and imagination of man, or at least in the former alone, which is not evident through demonstration" ("Opinione è forse tutto quello che ha luogo nella mente, & nell'imaginazione dell'huomo, o almeno quello solo, che non è per dimostratione apparente" [p. 369]).

41. Frederick C. Dietz, *English Public Finance, 1558–1641* (1932; rpt. London: Frank Cass, 1964), pp. 262–63; Cliffe, *Yorkshire Gentry,* p. 296; Stone, *Causes of the English Revolution,* p. 122.

42. Cliffe, *Yorkshire Gentry,* pp. 299–301, 303. The preparations for *The Triumph of Peace* had begun in October of 1633; see G. E. Bentley, *The Jacobean and Caroline Stage* (Oxford: Oxford Univ. Press, 1956), 5:1154.

43. Barnes, *Somerset,* pp. 168–70. See also W. B. Willcox, *Gloucestershire: A Study in Local Government, 1590–1640* (New Haven: Yale Univ. Press, 1940), pp. 121–22, and Morrill, *Cheshire,* p. 27.

44. "A proclamation for suppressing of false rumours touching parliaments, 27 March 1629," rpt. in *Stuart Constitution,* p. 86.

45. William H. Price, *The English Patents of Monopoly* (Boston and New York: Houghton Mifflin, 1906), pp. 14–17, 31; Christopher Hill, *Century of Revolution,* pp. 31–32; Clarkson, *Pre-Industrial Economy of England,* pp. 112, 160–61.

46. Price, *English Patents of Monopoly,* pp. 35–42.

47. Ibid., pp. 119–22; S. R. Gardiner, *The History of England, 1603–1642* (1883–84; rpt. New York: AMS, 1965), 8:71–72.

48. Christopher Hill, *Century of Revolution,* pp. 33–35; Ashton, *City and the Court,* pp. 141–47.

49. Price, *English Patents of Monopoly,* pp. 43–44, 120; Gardiner, *History of England,* 8:73.

50. Price, *English Patents of Monopoly,* pp. 44–45.

51. "The Winthrop Papers," *Collections of the Massachusetts Historical Society* (Boston: Massachusetts Historical Society, 1863), 4th Series, 6:418.

52. *A Short and Trve Relation Concerning the Soap-busines* (London, 1641), pp. 4–5.

53. *Englands Complaint to Jesus Christ against the Bishops Canons* (London, 1640), quoted in Christopher Hill, *Century of Revolution,* p. 34.

54. T. Brugis, *The Discovery of a Projector. Shewing the beginning, progresse, and end of the Projector and his Projects. Also the Projectors last Will and Testament. With an Epitaph to his Memory* (London, 1641), pp. 4, 12, 27–28.

55. *Historical Collections of Private Passages of State,* ed. John Rushworth (London, 1659–1701), 4:33.

56. Bentley, *Jacobean and Caroline Stage,* 5:1158–59.

57. In *The Improbable Puritan: A Life of Bulstrode Whitelocke, 1605–1675* (London: Faber and Faber, 1975), Ruth Spalding notes that Whitelocke's *Memorials* (1682) was the published version of "his largest single work," *The Annals of his Own Life Dedicated to his Children,* a memoir he had started in 1655 to replace a diary.

58. All quotations of *The Devil is an Ass* follow the text in *Ben Jonson,* ed. C. H. Herford, Percy Simpson, and Evelyn Simpson, vol. 6 (Oxford: Oxford Univ. Press, 1938).

59. *Calendar of State Papers Domestic 1630,* p. 382. Ramsey's patent was enacted in a proclamation at the beginning of 1631; he was required to pay "the yearly rent of *Three Pounds, Six Shillings Eight Pence.*" The proclamation is printed in *Foedera,* 19:239–41. For Meercraft's project, see Clarkson, *Pre-Industrial Economy of England,* pp. 56–57. Among the projectors Brugis exposes is one who "had got a fine device to make Vessels rowe themselves against Wind and Tide" (*Discovery of a Projector,* pp. 21, 27).

60. Marcus, *Politics of Mirth,* p. 101.

61. See Louis B. Wright, *Middle-Class Culture in Elizabethan England* (1935; rpt. Ithaca: Cornell Univ. Press, 1958), pp. 375–94.

62. Cliffe, *Yorkshire Gentry,* pp. 115, 126. See also Carl Bridenbaugh, *Vexed and Troubled Englishmen, 1590–1642* (New York: Oxford Univ. Press, 1968), pp. 154–55.

63. Stone, *Crisis of the Aristocracy,* pp. 567–72.

64. John Earle, "A Bowl-Alley," in *Microcosmographie. Or, a peece of the world discovered; in essayes and characters* (London, 1642), p. 42.

65. Peter Cunningham and Henry B. Wheatley, *London Past and Present* (London: John Murray, 1891), 3:293–95; Fisher, "Development of London," pp. 204–5.

66. Leah Marcus, "'Present Occasions' and the Shaping of Ben Jonson's Masques," *ELH* 45 (1978): 201–25 (202).

67. Stone, *Crisis of the Aristocracy*, pp. 34, 117–19, 397–98, 751; G. E. Aylmer, *The King's Servants: The Civil Service of Charles I, 1625–1642* (New York: Columbia Univ. Press, 1961), pp. 20–21.

68. Northrop Frye, *Anatomy of Criticism* (Princeton: Princeton Univ. Press, 1957), pp. 287, 290.

69. Chibnall, "'To that secure fix'd state,'" p. 81.

70. Orgel and Strong, *Inigo Jones*, 1:65–66.

71. Altieri, *Theater of Praise*, p. 35.

72. Christopher Hill, "The Many-Headed Monster," *Change and Continuity in Seventeenth-Century England* (Cambridge: Harvard Univ. Press, 1975), pp. 181–204.

73. See also Kevin Sharpe's observations on the formal peculiarites of Shirley's masque in *Criticism and Compliment: The Politics of Literature in the England of Charles I* (Cambridge: Cambridge Univ. Press, 1987): "*The Triumph of Peace* . . . makes its argument concerning the king's obligation to guarantee the benefits of law for all his subjects through carnival and intrusions in the masque of artisans who do not belong there. It questions the political values of the masque, that is, primarily by a challenge to its form" (p. 293).

74. Frye, *Anatomy of Criticism*, p. 288.

75. Bentley, *Jacobean and Caroline Stage*, 5:1160–62.

76. Ralph, *Sir Humphrey Mildmay*, pp. 50–51.

77. See P. W. Thomas, "Two Cultures? Court and County under Charles I," in *Origins of the English Civil War*, pp. 168–93, and R. Malcolm Smuts, "The Political Failure of Stuart Cultural Patronage," in *Patronage in the Renaissance*, ed. Guy Fitch Lytle and Stephen Orgel (Princeton: Princeton Univ. Press, 1981), pp. 165–87. Smuts has revised the court-country opposition in Whig historiography and developed a more complicated notion of the cultural insularity of the Caroline court in *Court Culture and the Origins of a Royalist Tradition in Early Stuart England*, esp. pp. 274–76, 286–87.

78. This reading of Caroline court literature was put forth by C. W. Wedgwood in *Poetry and Politics under the Stuarts* (1960; rpt. Ann Arbor: Univ. of Michigan Press, 1964). See also Orgel, *Illusion of Power*, pp. 88–89. In a similar vein, Stone has pointed out that Archbishop Laud's reports on religious dissent in the provinces involved mispresentation: *Causes of the English Revolution*, p. 121.

CHAPTER FIVE: *Cavalier Love Poetry and Caroline Court Culture*

1. See especially T. S. Eliot, "The Metaphysical Poets" (1921), *Selected Essays* (New York: Harcourt, Brace, and World, 1950), pp. 241–50; George Williamson, *The Donne Tradition* (1930; rpt. New York: Noonday, 1958); F. R. Leavis, "The Line of Wit," *Revaluation* (1936; rpt. London: Chatto and Windus, 1959), pp. 10–36; A. Alvarez, *The School of Donne* (London: Chatto and

Windus, 1961); Douglas Bush, *English Literature in the Earlier Seventeenth Century, 1600–1660,* 2d ed. (Oxford: Oxford Univ. Press, 1962).

2. H. M. Richmond, *The School of Love: The Evolution of the Stuart Love Lyric* (Princeton: Princeton Univ. Press, 1964), p. 262. Richmond's reliance on literary history gestures toward a revision of the canon by asserting that "the poets of the period of the Stuarts form a remarkably homogeneous group in audience, tastes, and tone," but as soon as he mentions Shakespeare and Milton, he adds, "In such a larger scale of reference the significant place of the Stuart lyricists might well be questioned," restricting their value to "their influence" on Restoration and later writers (pp. 262–63). A. J. Smith also calls attention to Carew's "self-consistent poetic poise" and to Suckling"s "pose of negligent indifference or bland self-mockery" as "a means of preserving self-respect, one's cool independence of a humiliating enslavement which can pervert social style," while adding that they "seem pathetically small fry as the heirs of the great European masters from Cavalcanti to Tasso." See his "The Failure of Love: Love Lyrics after Donne," in *Metaphysical Poetry,* ed. Malcolm Bradbury and David Palmer (London: Edward Arnold, 1970), pp. 41–72, later reprinted in a slightly revised version in Smith's *The Metaphysics of Love: Studies in Renaissance Love Poetry from Dante to Milton* (Cambridge: Cambridge Univ. Press, 1985), pp. 221–53.

3. Richard Helgerson, *Self-Crowned Laureates: Spenser, Jonson, Milton, and the Literary System* (Berkeley and Los Angeles: Univ. of California Press, 1983), pp. 194, 188. See also G. A. E. Parfitt, "The Poetry of Thomas Carew," in *Seventeenth-Century English Poetry: Modern Essays in Criticism,* ed. William Keast, rev. ed. (Oxford: Oxford Univ. Press, 1971), pp. 279–90, where Parfitt disparages Cavalier poetry for its social determinations: "Cavalier poetry shows a narrowing of range of reference and interest, becoming courtly in a sense which suggests a decisive split between 'court' and 'country' and a consequent concentration upon relatively few areas of emotional experience and, more specifically, upon narrowly circumscribed facets of society. One result is cynical knowingness and surface sophistication; another is that reactions to experience become conventional and simplified" (p. 279). Following Leavis' "line of wit," however, Parfitt distinguishes Carew from other Cavalier poets by arguing that "Carew can react to a wide range of experiential stimuli."

4. Antony Easthope, *Poetry as Discourse* (London and New York: Methuen, 1983), pp. 4–5.

5. Joseph Summers, *The Heirs of Donne and Jonson* (London and New York: Oxford Univ. Press, 1970), p. 42.

6. *Metaphysical Lyrics and Poems of the Seventeenth Century,* ed. Herbert J. C. Grierson (1921; rpt. London and New York: Oxford Univ. Press, 1959), p. xxx.

7. Smith, *Metaphysics of Love,* p. 234.

8. Earl Miner, *The Cavalier Mode from Jonson to Cotton* (Princeton: Princeton Univ. Press, 1971), pp. 210, 207. Parfitt notes the "conventional" under-

standing of "Cavalier" in *English Poetry of the Seventeenth Century* (London: Longman, 1985), p. 30.

9. Helgerson, *Self-Crowned Laureates,* p. 192.

10. Robert Lekachman, *Greed Is Not Enough: Reaganomics* (New York: Pantheon, 1982), p. 55.

11. Madonna Marsden discusses the impact of corporate capitalism on popular culture and offers an analysis of Dale Carnegie's book in "The American Myth of Success: Visions and Revisions," in *The Popular Culture Reader,* ed. Christopher Geist and Jack Nachbar, 3d ed. (Bowling Green: Bowling Green Univ. Popular Press, 1983), pp. 67–80. Drs. Connell Cowan and Melvyn Kinder are the authors of *Women Men Love, Women Men Leave* (New York: Clarkson Potter, 1987).

12. My observations on human agency are indebted to Anthony Giddens, *Central Problems in Social Theory: Action, Structure, and Contradiction in Social Analysis* (Berkeley and Los Angeles: Univ. of California Press, 1979), esp. chap. 2, "Agency, Structure."

13. All quotations of Jonson's masques follow *The Complete Masques,* ed. Stephen Orgel (New Haven: Yale Univ. Press, 1969). Line numbers will be given in the text.

14. Marsilio Ficino, *Commentary on Plato's Symposium,* ed. and trans. Sears Jayne, *University of Missouri Studies* 19 (1944): 140. Page numbers will be given in the text. For Ficino's influence in England, see Jayne, "Ficino and the Platonism of the English Renaissance," *Comparative Literature* 4 (1952): 214–38.

15. *The Dramatic Works of Sir William Davenant,* ed. James Maidment and W. H. Logan (1874; rpt. New York: Russell and Russell, 1964), 1:289. Volume and page numbers will be given in the text.

16. *Basilikon Doron* (1599), in *The Political Works of James I,* ed. Charles H. McIlwain (Cambridge: Harvard Univ. Press, 1918), p. 12. See also p. 42, where James advises his son Henry, Prince of Wales: "preasse then to shine as farre before your people, in all vertue and honestie; as in greatnesse of ranke."

17. Stephen Orgel and Roy Strong, *Inigo Jones: The Theater of the Stuart Court* (Berkeley and Los Angeles: Univ. of California Press, 1973), 1:52.

18. See also James A. Devereux, "The Object of Love in Ficino's Philosophy," *Journal of the History of Ideas* 30 (1969): 161–70. Devereux shows that although Ficino allows for a reciprocal attachment between human lovers, this has divine love as its foundation (pp. 165–67).

19. Erwin Panofsky presents a detailed analysis of Ficino's Venus symbols in *Studies in Iconology: Humanistic Themes in the Art of the Renaissance* (1939; rpt. New York: Harper and Row, 1972), pp. 141–44.

20. *The Poems and Masques of Aurelian Townshend,* ed. Cedric C. Brown (Reading, Eng.: Whiteknights Press, 1983). Page numbers will be given in the text.

21. *Political Works of James I,* pp. 3, 51.

22. The quotation comes from Catherine Belsey, "Disrupting Sexual Difference: Meaning and Gender in the Comedies," in *Alternative Shakespeares*, ed. John Drakakis (London and New York: Methuen, 1985), p. 171. To show the emergence of an affective realm within the absolutist, dynastic family, Belsey analyzes a portrait of the Duke of Buckingham's family, thereby locating the ideological shift in the Caroline aristocracy, among other social groups.

23. These observations have profited from Joan Kelly's discussion of patriarchy and Renaissance Neoplatonism in "Did Women Have a Renaissance?" *Women, History, and Theory* (Chicago: Univ. of Chicago Press, 1984), pp. 19–50.

24. Stephen Orgel, *The Illusion of Power: Political Theater in the English Renaissance* (Berkeley and Los Angeles: Univ. of California Press, 1975), p. 40. E. W. Talbert discusses Jonson's fusion of panegyric with didactic elements in "The Interpretation of Jonson's Courtly Spectacles," *PMLA* 61 (1946): 454–73.

25. Stephen Orgel, "Inigo Jones's Persian Entertainment," *Art and Archaeology Research Papers* 2 (1972): 59–70 (63).

26. Pauline Gregg, *King Charles I* (London: J. M. Dent, 1981), chaps. 13, 19.

27. Sir William Sanderson, *A Compleat History of the Life and Raigne of King Charles from his Cradle to his Grave* (London, 1658), pp. 160–61, 1139. In *A Detection of the Court and State of England during the Four Last Reigns, and the Inter-regnum*, 2d ed. (London, 1696), Roger Coke similarly states that to Charles's "Natural Endowments may be added, A Temperance in Eating and Drinking; and Chastity (tho' his Enemies unjustly traduced him otherways) rarely to be found in Princes" (1:195).

28. Edward Hyde, Earl of Clarendon, *The History of the Rebellion and Civil Wars in England Begun in the Year 1641* (Oxford, 1707), 3:197–98. In *Memoirs of the Life of Colonel Hutchinson*, ed. James Sutherland (London: Oxford Univ. Press, 1973), Lucy Hutchinson, wife of the parliamentary colonel, also observes that "the face of the Court was much chang'd in the change of the King, for King Charles was temperate and chast and serious; so that the fooles and bawds, mimicks and Catamites of the former Court grew out of fashion, and the nobility and courtiers, who did not quite abandon their debosheries, had yet that reverence to the King to retire into corners to practise them" (p. 46).

29. Sanderson, *Compleat History*, pp. 154–61. See also Christopher Hill, *Society and Puritanism in Pre-Revolutionary England*, 2d ed. (New York: Schocken, 1972), p. 349. In *The Reign of King Charles. An History Disposed into Annals. The Second Edition Revised, and Somewhat Enlarged* (London, 1656), the royalist historian Hamon L'Estrange notes that in 1627 "the Lady *Purbeck* was tryed in High Commission for Incontince, or to speak more explicitly, for *Adultery* with Sir *Robert Howard*, and being found guilty, was censured to do Penance in the *Savoy*, to pay the Court five hundred Marks, and to be imprisoned, during the pleasure of the Court" (pp. 69–70).

30. *The Court and Times of Charles I,* ed. Thomas Birch (London: Henry Colburn, 1848), 1:419; Lawrence Stone, *The Crisis of the Aristocracy, 1558–1641* (Oxford: Oxford Univ. Press, 1965), pp. 606–8.

31. *Calendar of State Papers Domestic 1628–1629,* p. 81.

32. *Calendar of State Papers Domestic 1633–1634,* p. 50; Carola Oman, *Henrietta Maria* (London: Hodder and Stoughton, 1936), pp. 98–99.

33. *Calendar of State Papers Domestic 1639–1640,* p. 297. See also Mary Rich, Countess of Warwick, *Some Specialities in the Life of M. Warwicke,* ed. T. Crofton Croker (London: Percy Society, 1848), 22:4–6. Mary Rich was Roger Boyle's sister.

34. Baldassare Castiglione, *The Book of the Courtier,* trans. Sir Thomas Hoby, ed. Walter Raleigh (1900; rpt. New York: AMS, 1967), p. 59. Hoby's odd use of "Reckelesness" to translate *sprezzatura* also has ideological implications specific to Elizabethan culture: see Lawrence Venuti, "The Translator's Invisibility," *Criticism* 28 (1986): 179–212.

35. Kelly suggests this ideological critique of *The Courtier* in "Did Women Have a Renaissance?" p. 42. Daniel Javitch construes *sprezzatura* as dissimulation in *Poetry and Courtliness in Renaissance England* (Princeton: Princeton Univ. Press, 1978).

36. Caroline discretion is an example of what Norbert Elias calls "court rationality," or the "restraint of the affects for the sake of certain vital interests": "The competition of court life," Elias argues, "enforces a curbing of the affects in favor of calculated and finely shaded behavior in dealing with people" (*The Court Society,* trans. Edmund Jephcott [New York: Pantheon, 1983], pp. 110–11).

37. Stone discusses the political damage done by the sexual scandals at court in *The Crisis of the Aristocracy,* pp. 388–98, 667–68.

38. For the French aristocratic salons, see Erica Harth, *Ideology and Culture in Seventeenth-Century France* (Ithaca: Cornell Univ. Press, 1983), pp. 37–38. For the Platonic love cult at the Caroline court, see Jefferson Butler Fletcher, "Precieuses at the Court of Charles I," *The Religion of Beauty in Woman* (New York: Macmillan, 1911), pp. 166–205, and Kathleen M. Lynch, *The Social Mode of Restoration Comedy* (1926; rpt. New York: Biblo and Tannen, 1965), chaps. 3, 4.

39. Sir Kenelm Digby, *Loose Fantasies,* ed. Vittorio Gabrieli (Rome: Edizioni di Storia e Letteratura, 1969), pp. 131–32, 115. In *British Autobiography in the Seventeenth Century* (London: Routledge and Kegan Paul, 1969), Paul Delany observes that "although Digby was ostensibly not writing for publication, he wrote as if for an invisible audience of detractors, with the vehemence and over-emphasis typical of works of controversy" (p. 129).

40. *Epistolae Ho-Elianae, or The Familiar Letters of James Howell,* ed. Agnes Repplier (Boston and New York: Houghton Mifflin, 1908), 2:168.

41. Quoted in George Sensabaugh, "Platonic Love and the Puritan Revolution," *Studies in Philology* 37 (1940): 457–81.

42. There are many humanist treatments of the tradition of erotic idealism in Renaissance literature and its conventional ideas and motifs. See, for example, Leonard Forster, *The Icy Fire: Five Studies in European Petrarchism* (Cambridge: Cambridge Univ. Press, 1969); John Charles Nelson, *Renaissance Theory of Love* (New York: Columbia Univ. Press, 1958); David Kalstone, *Sidney's Poetry: Contexts and Interpretations* (1965; rpt. New York: W. W. Norton, 1970); William Nelson, *The Poetry of Edmund Spenser: A Study* (New York: Columbia Univ. Press, 1963); Donald Guss, *John Donne, Petrarchist: Italianate Conceits and Love Theory in the Songs and Sonnets* (Detroit: Wayne State Univ. Press, 1966); and, most recently, A. J. Smith, *The Metaphysics of Love,* cited above.

43. Bruce King, "The Strategy of Carew's Wit," *Review of English Literature* 5 (1964): 42–51.

44. Carew's poems are quoted from *The Poems of Thomas Carew with his Masque Coelum Britannicum,* ed. Rhodes Dunlap (Oxford: Oxford Univ. Press, 1949).

45. Lovelace's poems are quoted from *The Poems of Richard Lovelace,* ed. C. H. Wilkinson (Oxford: Oxford Univ. Press, 1930).

46. Stone discusses mining investment during this period in *The Crisis of the Aristocracy,* pp. 338–55, 433–35.

47. Suckling's poems are quoted from *The Works of Sir John Suckling: The Non-Dramatic Works,* ed. Thomas Clayton (Oxford: Oxford Univ. Press, 1971).

48. For the popularity of facial patches, see C. Willet and Phillis Cunnington, *Handbook of English Costume in the Seventeenth Century* (London: Faber and Faber, 1955), pp. 119, 128. See also Lovelace's two poems on "A Black patch on Lucasta's Face."

49. Samuel H. Monk traces the tradition of this aesthetic principle in "A Grace Beyond the Reach of Art," *Journal of the History of Ideas* 5 (1944): 131–50. See also M. H. Abrams, *The Mirror and the Lamp: Romantic Theory and the Critical Tradition* (Oxford: Oxford Univ. Press, 1953), pp. 193–95.

50. Raymond Anselment offers a carefully documented discussion of the Countess of Carlisle's "struggle for position" at court in "The Countess of Carlisle and Caroline Praise: Convention and Reality," *Studies in Philology* 82 (1985): 212–33.

51. Thomas Clayton identifies this proverbial expression in *The Works of John Suckling: The Non-Dramatic Works,* p. 250.

52. For discussions of the issues raised by Prynne's book and conviction, see Martin Butler, *Theater and Crisis, 1632–1642* (Cambridge: Cambridge Univ. Press, 1984), chap. 5, esp. pp. 84–85, and Orgel, *Illusion of Power,* pp. 43–44.

53. The range of sources and analogues for Carew's "A Rapture" is suggested by Dunlap, *Poems of Thomas Carew,* pp. 236–39, Frank Kermode, "The Argument of Marvell's 'Garden,'" rpt. in *Seventeenth-Century English Poetry,* ed.

Keast, pp. 333–47, and Paula Johnson, "Carew's 'A Rapture': The Dynamics of Fantasy," *Studies in English Literature, 1500–1900* 16 (1976): 145–55. Johnson's detailed reading of Carew's poem, while not explicitly an ideological critique, is sensitive to textual discontinuities.

54. I borrow the generic concept "pornotopia" from Steven Marcus, *The Other Victorians: A Study of Sexuality and Pornography in Mid-Nineteenth-Century England,* 2d ed. (New York: Basic Books, 1974), chap. 7: "The literary genre that pornographic fantasies—particularly when they appear in the shape of pornographic fiction—tend most to resemble is the utopian fantasy. . . . I call this fantasy pornotopia" (p. 268).

55. Johnson, "Carew's 'A Rapture,'" p. 148.

56. Orgel, *Illusion of Power,* pp. 51–52.

57. Honoré d'Urfé, *The history of Astrea, The first part* (London, 1620), p. 8. No translator's name is given.

58. *Poems of Thomas Carew,* ed. Dunlap, p. 222.

59. The following analysis of Cavalier poetic discourse assumes Easthope, *Poetry as Discourse,* chaps. 1–4.

60. L. A. Beaurline reprints North's essay and his 1638 letter responding to Suckling's request for a copy in "Dudley North's Criticism of Metaphysical Poetry," *Huntington Library Quarterly* 25 (1962): 299–313. Beaurline dates the essay "as early as 1610–1612."

61. For the divine analogy, see Robert Durling, *The Figure of the Poet in Renaissance Epic* (Cambridge: Harvard Univ. Press, 1965), pp. 123–32, and S. K. Heninger, *Touches of Sweet Harmony: Pythagorean Cosmology and Renaissance Poetics* (San Marino, Calif.: Huntington Library, 1974), pt. 3, chaps. 1 and 3. Quotations from Sidney's *Defense of Poesie* (1595) follow *The Prose Works of Sir Philip Sidney,* ed. Albert Feuillerat (1912; rpt. Cambridge: Cambridge Univ. Press, 1962), vol. 3.

62. *Boccaccio on Poetry,* ed. and trans. Charles Osgood (New York: Liberal Arts, 1956), p. 39.

63. See F. O. Henderson, "Traditions of *Precieux* and *Libertin* in Suckling's Poetry," *ELH* 4 (1937): 274–98, and King, "Strategy of Carew's Wit," esp. pp. 44–47. Donne's poems are quoted from *The Elegies and Songs and Sonnets of John Donne,* ed. Helen Gardner (Oxford: Oxford Univ. Press, 1965).

64. Arthur Marotti, *John Donne, Coterie Poet* (Madison: Univ. of Wisconsin Press, 1986), p. 73.

65. In *James I and the Politics of Literature* (Baltimore: Johns Hopkins Univ. Press, 1983), Jonathan Goldberg recognizes "the common rhetoric shared by James's arcana, representations of the patriarchal family, and the driving, domineering, urgent voice that sounds throughout Donne's love poems. The mystification of love, the disguise of sexuality in platonized spirituality, the parade of learning to cover ribaldry, these are characteristics of the *Songs and Sonnets,* rebellious and atheistical in their manipulation of the *arcana imperii.* Long

before he considered his own rebellious body silently murmuring the secrets of state, Donne had appropriated royal absolutism for his own private sphere" (p. 107).

66. Helgerson, *Self-Crowned Laureates*, p. 203.

67. See Mikhail Bakhtin, *Rabelais and His World*, trans. Helene Iswolsky (1968; rpt. Bloomington: Indiana Univ. Press, 1984), especially the introduction.

CONCLUSION: *Political Criticism*

1. Fredric Jameson, *Marxism and Form: Twentieth-Century Dialectical Theories of Literature* (Princeton: Princeton Univ. Press, 1971), pp. 84–85.

2. Göran Therborn, *The Ideology of Power and the Power of Ideology* (London: Verso, 1980), p. 18.

3. Jean E. Howard, "The New Historicism in Renaissance Studies," *English Literary Renaissance* 16 (1986): 13–43 (16–17).

4. Barry Coward, "Was There an English Revolution in the Middle of the Seventeenth Century?" in *Politics and People in Revolutionary England: Essays in Honor of Ivan Root,* ed. Colin Jones, Malyn Newitt, and Stephen Roberts (Oxford: Basil Blackwell, 1986), pp. 9–40 (17). Lawrence Stone notes that the "aim" of the revisionist historians is "a conservative rewriting of history" in his review essay, "The Century of Revolution," *New York Review of Books* 34:3 (February 26, 1987): 38–43.

Kevin Sharpe has moved away from the revisionist position in his later work; as Stone points out, "He rejects any concept of 'opposition,' except one emerging from within the court itself" (p. 39). This change is further developed in Sharpe's *Criticism and Compliment: The Politics of Literature in the England of Charles I* (Cambridge: Cambridge Univ. Press, 1987), where he attacks Whig historiographical concepts like the court-country opposition and instead locates "evidence" of "debates and tensions, anxieties, doubts and criticisms articulated within the culture of the court, indeed opinions akin to those often identified only with the ideology of the 'country'" (p. x). Sharpe's study of Caroline literature is an important corrective to the Whig view of court culture as decadent, and it contains critical observations on the texts which are consistent with some of those argued in the present study (e.g., the treatment of the formal innovations in Shirley's *The Triumph of Peace*). Yet it is also important to note that Sharpe explicitly avoids any theoretical reflection and wants so much to banish "*a priori* assumptions" from criticism that he pays no attention to his own humanistic assumptions: his tendency to read texts in moral terms, for example, is particularly unable to deal with the libertinism of Cavalier love lyrics.

5. Conrad Russell, "The Parliamentary Career of John Pym, 1621–9," in *The English Commonwealth, 1547–1640: Essays Presented to Joel Hurstfeld,* ed.

Peter Clark, Alan G. R. Smith, and Nicholas Tyacke (New York: Barnes and Noble, 1979), pp. 147–65. Christopher Hill argues against taking seventeenth-century political statements at face value in "Political Discourse in Early Seventeenth-Century England," in *Politics and People in Revolutionary England*, pp. 41–64.

6. Anthony Fletcher, "National and Local Awareness in the County Communities," in *Before the Civil War: Essays on Early Stuart Politics and Government*, ed. Howard Tomlinson (New York: St. Martin's, 1983), pp. 151–74 (174).

7. L. C. Knights, *Drama and Society in the Age of Jonson* (1937; rpt. New York: W. W. Norton, 1968), pp. 297–98.

8. For some treatments of these concepts, see C. B. Macpherson, *The Political Theory of Possessive Individualism: Hobbes to Locke* (Oxford: Oxford Univ. Press, 1962); Christopher Hill, *The World Turned Upside Down: Radical Ideas during the English Revolution* (London: Temple Smith, 1972); Maurice Goldsmith, "Levelling by Sword, Spade, and Word: Radical Egalitarianism in the English Revolution," in *Politics and People in Revolutionary England*, pp. 65–80; and *Freedom and the English Revolution: Essays in History and Literature*, ed. R. C. Richardson and G. M. Ridden (Manchester: Manchester Univ. Press, 1986). For the view that liberal humanism emerged in the seventeenth century, see Catherine Belsey, *The Subject of Tragedy: Identity and Difference in Renaissance Drama* (London: Methuen, 1985). Jonathan Dollimore argues for the different view that during this period the essentialist concept of subjectivity was in transition "between its Christian/metaphysical formulations and the later secular/Enlightenment mutations of these": see his *Radical Tragedy: Religion, Ideology, and Power in the Drama of Shakespeare and His Contemporaries* (Brighton: Harvester, 1984), chap. 10, esp. 155–56.

9. All quotations from *Eikonoklastes* follow the third volume of *The Complete Prose of John Milton*, ed. Merritt Y. Hughes (New Haven: Yale Univ. Press, 1962). Page numbers will be given parenthetically in the text.

10. See, for example, Dick Hebdige, *Subculture: The Meaning of Style* (London and New York: Methuen, 1979).

Index

Abrams, M. H., 19–20

Absolutism: ideology of, 73, 75, 78; and patriarchalism, 75, 146–47; Jacobean, 85–86, 88; Elizabethan, 86, 126; contradictions of, 95, 111, 158–61, 242, 264; Caroline, 158, 184–86, 206, 270

Adorno, Theodor, and Max Horkheimer, 49

Alington, Sir Giles, 228

Althusser, Louis, 3–7, 28, 46, 71, 277n12

Altieri, Joanne, 206–7

Amussen, S. D., 147

Ancient constitution, 162–63, 264

Anderson, Perry, 86, 89, 111, 298n1

Anglican Church, 111–12

Aristocracy: Caroline, 13, 228–33, 258–60; feudal, 72–73; and the absolutist state, 73, 95; Jacobean, 79, 85–88, 91, 113; Elizabethan, 86; in the Roman Republic, 118, 120–21

Arnold, Matthew, 30

Ashbery, John, 109

Ashton, Robert, 158

Auerbach, Erich, 168; *Mimesis,* 169–71

Bagehot, Walter, 60

Bakhtin, Mikhail, 259

Barber, C. L., 291n1

Barry, Lord David, *Ram Alley,* 295n43

Barthes, Roland, 51–52, 173

Baudrillard, Jean, 48–49

Beaumont, Sir Francis, and John Fletcher, 80; *A King and No King,* 80–87; *Philaster,* 87

Beckett, Samuel, 109

Beier, A. L., 126

Belsey, Catherine, 3, 8, 77, 79, 298n1, 313n8

Bennett, Tony, 5–6, 57

Benton, Ted, 6, 292n8

Boccaccio, Giovanni, 256

Boff, Clodovis, 11–12

Book of Orders, 183–84

Brathwaite, Richard, *The English Gentlewoman,* 188

Broghill, Roger Boyle, Baron, 230

Brome, Richard, 56; *The Antipodes,* 152–57, 163, 164, 265; *The City Wit,* 136–37; *The Damoiselle,* 139, 149–50; *The Sparagus Garden,* 141–42, 151

Brugis, T., *The Discovery of a Projector,* 195

Buckingham, George Villiers, Duke of, 88, 89, 90, 227–28, 229, 242

Burt, Richard, 95

Butler, Martin, 90–91, 96, 145, 164

Capitalist mode of production: consumer phase, 3, 11, 12, 47–49, 170, 177, 265; market phase, 11, 17, 29; monopoly phase, 11, 17, 41, 169, 265; and industrialization, 25, 47–48, 60–61; and specialization, 29, 44, 46, 64, 176; and mass communications, 47–49; nascent phase, 110–11; and the